THE Prevention AND Intervention OF Genocide

THE Prevention AND Intervention OF Genocide

GENOCIDE:
A CRITICAL BIBLIOGRAPHIC REVIEW
VOLUME 6

EDITED BY
SAMUEL TOTTEN

Routledge
Taylor & Francis Group
LONDON AND NEW YORK

The Prevention and Intervention of Genocide
Volume 6 in the Series

First published 2008 by Transaction Publishers

2 Park Square, Milton Park, Abingdon, Oxfordshire OX14 4RN
711 Third Avenue, New York, NY 10017

Routledge is an imprint of the Taylor & Francis Group, an informa business

First issued in paperback 2017

Copyright © 2008 by Institute on the Holocaust and Genocide.

All rights reserved. No part of this book may be reprinted or reproduced or utilised in any form or by any electronic, mechanical, or other means, now known or hereafter invented, including photocopying and recording, or in any information storage or retrieval system, without permission in writing from the publishers.

Notice:
Product or corporate names may be trademarks or registered trademarks, and are used only for identification and explanation without intent to infringe.

Library of Congress Catalog Number: 2004059881

Library of Congress Cataloging-in-Publication Data

Genocide at the millennium : a critical bibliographical review / Samual Totten, editor; with a foreword by Israel W. Charny ; Marc I. Sherman, bibliographic editor.
    p. cm.—(Genocide ; v. 5)
Includes index.
ISBN 0-7658-0263-5
  1. Genocide. 2. Genocide—Bibliography. I. Totten, Samuel. II. Sherman, Marc I. III. Series.

Z7164.G45 G45 1988 vol. 5
[HV6322.7]
016.3046'63s—dc22
[304.6'63]   2004059881

ISBN 13: 978-0-7658-0384-9 (hbk)
ISBN 13: 978-1-138-51675-5 (pbk)

Contents

Introduction   1
   Samuel Totten

1. The Prevention and Intervention of Genocide   7
   During the Cold War Years
      Alex Alvarez

2. Prevention and Intervention of Genocide   31
   in the 1990s and early 2000s
      Samuel Totten and Paul R. Bartrop

3. Development and Implementation of Genocide   63
   Early Warning Systems: Conceptual and Practical Issues
      Barbara Harff

4. The Prevention of Genocide: Missed Opportunities,   83
   Complexities, and Possibilities
      Samuel Totten

5. Sanctions as Counter-Genocide Instruments   131
      George A. Lopez and Kathryn Stuhldreher

6. The Tension between Sovereignty and Intervention   145
   in the Prevention of Genocide
      Bruce Cronin

7. The Intervention of Genocide   161
      Samuel Totten

8. Peace Operations and their Ramifications vis-à-vis the   213
    Prevention and Intervention of Genocide
       Lawrence Woocher

9. After the Killing Stops: Postgenocide Societies   231
    and Issues Relating to Prevention and Intervention
       Paul R. Bartrop

10. Punishing Genocidaires: A Deterrent Effect or Not?   255
       Martin Mennecke

11. Building an Anti-Genocide Regime   281
       Gregory H. Stanton

About the Editor and Contributors   303

Index   307

Introduction

Samuel Totten

In 1988, Dr. Israel W. Charny, director of the Institute on the Holocaust and Genocide (Jerusalem), published the first volume in his now noted *Genocide: A Critical Bibliographic Series*. In that volume, Charny contributed a chapters entitled "Intervention and Prevention of Genocide, and opened the chapters with these words: "The title of this chapter clearly spells out a hope rather than an existing reality in the history of humankind, but the fact that the idea of doing something about genocide—intervening in an ongoing eruption of mass killing and seeking to prevention potential genocide--has become the subject of serious study is to be celebrated" (Charny, 1988, p. 20). And he closed the chapter with these words: " Today we know enough to identify most societies at risk for genocide. It remains to be determined if we can develop sufficient human will to act to prevent these terrible occurrences of mass death" (Charny, 1988, p. 30).

Reading his words now, almost twenty years later, is bound to leave one with radically mixed feelings. The field of genocide studies has grown exponentially, and even Charny, a wonderfully optimistic and forward-looking human being, must be somewhat taken aback by its growth, development, and sophistication. Indeed, it is something to celebrate, if for no other reason than the fact that serious minds are looking for effective ways to stanch genocide. At one and the same time, though, it is also true that since 1988 the world has witnessed four major genocides (Iraq, 1988; Rwanda, 1994; Srebrenica, 1995; and Darfur, 2003-present) in which approximately one and a half million people have met untimely and horrific deaths. Tellingly, Charny's (1988) aforementioned statement, which was made nearly twenty years ago, is as true, unfortunately, today as it was when he first wrote it: "it remains to be determined if we can develop sufficient human will to act to prevent these terrible occurrences of mass death" (p. 20).

Genocide has become so prevalent in our world today that many seemingly neglect to stop and *really* ponder the types of horror individual human beings suffer because are were deemed to be "others" by the perpetrators. To truly contemplate the fear that the victims felt as they were hunted down and attacked, and the pain and horror they experienced as they were gassed (Iraq), butchered with machetes (Rwanda), beaten to death with the butts of rifles and lined up and shot (Srebrenica), and bombed, shot, and/or left to starve to death (Darfur) is a gruesome but necessary task if we, humanity, truly wish to confront and tackle the problems that lead to genocide and prevent the international community from stanching genocide.

Granted, in certain and significant ways, the international community has made some solid progress in its battle against genocide. The establishment of the two ad hoc international criminal tribunals (the International Criminal Tribunal for the Former Yugoslavia and the International Criminal Tribunal for Rwanda) and the establishment of the International Criminal Court are sure signs of progress. At the very least, perpetrators know that they may end up in court to face charges of crimes against humanity and/or genocide. Furthermore, the two interventions in 1999, those in Kosovo and East Timor, despite the heated, and legitimate, controversy over the first and the fact that both came late in the killing process, did signal that pending certain circumstances (which were, of course, political in nature), the international community could step up and act to halt a potential genocide in the making when it mustered the political will to do so. Also hopeful was the study undertaken by the International Commission on Intervention and State Sovereignty—at the urging of UN Secretary General Kofi Annan—for the express purpose of trying "to find, once and for all, a new consensus on how to approach" the thorny issue of "when, if ever, it is appropriate for states to take coercive—and in particular military action, against another state for the purpose of protecting people at risk in that other state" (p. vii). That study, *The Responsibility to Protect*, resulted in the assertion that sovereign states do, in fact, have a responsibility to protect their citizens from manmade disasters such as mass murder (massacres, crimes against humanity and genocide), mass rape, and planned starvation, and when they are either unwilling or unable to do so, then "measures by other members of the community of states may be required" (p. 29). But to paraphrase Charny, whether the international community will actually act on the principles delineated in the study "remains to be determined." One can, of course, say, "time will tell," and that is true. But those are the last words the mothers, fathers, children, and babies who are being attacked because they are members of a particular targeted group, want, or should have, to hear. Those who are being brutalized, raped, and killed--as they are in Darfur today as these very words are being written--don't have time on their side.

That said, the focus of this book, Volume Six of *Genocide: A Critical Bibliography Review*, is the prevention and intervention of genocide. At this point in time, it seems, there is a critical need to assess where the international community is at in its efforts to prevent genocide and to intervene (once a genocide is under way) in an effective and timely manner. The contributors to the volume are all noted scholars, some of whom specialize in the study of genocide, others who specialize in such areas early warning, peacekeeping, and sanctions. While numerous scholars (Paul Bartrop Barbara Harff, Martin Mennecke, Samuel Totten) have contributed essays to previous volumes in this series, a number of scholars (Alex Alvarez, George Lopez, Elisabeth Moltke, Greg Stanton, Lawrence Woocher) are contributing for the first time.

The book is comprised of twelve chapters that provide an overview of a host of issues germane to the prevention and intervention of genocide. In Chapter One, Dr. Alex Alvarez, professor of criminal justice at Northern Arizona University, and the author of *Governments, Citizens, and Genocide: A Comparative and Interdisciplinary Approach*, presents a succinct but cogent discussion of the issues of prevention and intervention during the Cold War years.

In chapter 2, "The Intervention and Prevention in the 1990s and early 2000s," Samuel Totten and Paul Bartrop, instructor of history, Deakin University, Victoria, Australia, discuss the abject failures and moderate (though, in some cases, highly controversial) successes vis-a-vis prevention and intervention carried out in the 1990s and early 2000s. Totten's insights herein are based, in part, on his work with the U.S. State Department's Atrocities Documentation Project in Chad, whose data, in part, resulted in the U.S. determination that genocide was being perpetrated in Darfur, Sudan.

In chapter 3, "Development and Implementation of Genocide Early Warning Systems: Conceptual and Practical Issues," Barbara Harff, professor emerita of political science at the U.S. Naval Academy (Annapolis), provides a succinct but cogent discussion vis-à-vis the latest efforts to develop a workable, effective and efficient genocide early warning system. Harff has dedicated a good part of her professional career to the development and implementation of a genocide early warning system, and thus her insights are particularly valuable.

In chapter 4, "The Prevention of Genocide," Totten discusses the complexity of and barriers to prevention, and examines many of the latest ideas/efforts/"advancements" in the area of genocide prevention.

In chapter 5, "Sanctions and Genocide," George Lopez, a specialist on the development and implementation of sanctions who is based at The Joan B. Kroc Institute for International Peace Studies at the University of Notre Dame, presents a discussion of the complexity of developing, applying, evaluating and enforcing sanctions and a sanctions regime. In doing so, he examines the pros and cons and strengths and weaknesses of different types of sanctions as they relate to applying pressure on perpetrators of genocide.

In chapter 6, "The Issue of Sovereignty and the Intervention of Genocide," Bruce Cronin, professor of political science at the City University of New York, examines the history of and latest thinking vis-à-vis the issue of state sovereignty and the intervention of genocide. In doing so, Cronin explores how the international community tries to protect those populations threatened with genocide without threatening the principle of state sovereignty. Among some of the many issues he discusses are: some of the perceived problems with intervention, the concept of the "right" to intervention, and how those nations and bodies that have the ability to intervene in the case of genocide have not, for the most part, done so and why.

In chapter 7, "The Intervention of Genocide," Totten examines the issue of intervention and why and how it has met with only limited success. He also examines major factors that lead to successful interventions versus those that fail miserably and result in outright disasters for the victim population.

In chapter 8, "Peace Operations and Their Ramifications Vis-à-Vis the Prevention and Intervention of Genocide," Lawrence Woocher discusses various peace operations employed in various nations where genocide had broken out (including but not limited to Rwanda in 1994 and the former Yugoslavia in 1995) and what led, in the latter two cases, abject failure, and, in other cases, moderate success.

In chapter 9, "The Post-Conflict Period and Genocide," Bartrop discusses key issues related to post-genocidal periods and that which needs to be addressed in order to establish stability in a wounded land and populace as well as to prevent future genocides erupting from the ashes of the last one.

In chapter 10, "Bringing Perpetrators to Justice: Its Impact Vis-à-Vis Breaking Impunity, Deterrence, Truth Finding, and Reconciliation," Martin Mennecke (Senior Research Associate Danish Institute for Holocaust and Genocide Studies) and Elisabeth Moltke (graduate student, Danish Institute for Holocaust and Genocide Studies) discuss whether, in fact, bringing perpetrators to justice has any impact in breaking impunity, ensuring deterrence and/or bringing about reconciliation.

Finally in chapter 11, "Toward the Development of an International Anti-Genocide Regime: New Initiatives and Proposals for the Intervention and Prevention of Genocide," Gregory Stanton, director, International Prevention of Genocide, provides a fascinating discussion of the concept of an anti-genocide regime. In doing so, he discusses the progress that has been made in developing such a regime as well as how far the international community still must go in order to implement a fully functioning and effective regime.

My ardent hope is that in the very near future the international community will put as much urgency, creativity, energy and funding into the development and implementation of a sophisticated and highly effective anti-genocide regime as certain states and scholars in the past put into the Manhattan Project and the race to place a man on the moon. Again, whether such a hope comes to fruition remains to be seen.

In closing, I wish to sincerely thank all of the contributors to this volume for their hard work in their respective fields, and their fine contributions to this volume. I also wish to commend them for their dedication to the prevention and intervention of genocide.

References

Charny, Israel W. (1988). Intervention and Prevention of Genocide," pp. 20-38. In Israel W. Charny (ed.) *Genocide: A Critical Bibliographic Review*. New York: Facts on File.

International Commission on Intervention and State Sovereignty (2001). *The Responsibility to Protect*. Ottawa, Ontario: International Development Research Centre.

1

The Prevention and Intervention of Genocide During the Cold War Years

Alex Alvarez

The Cold War, which began in 1945 and ended in 1991, was an era that witnessed genocidally inclined states acting, largely, with impunity. Intervention, when it occurred, was selective, haphazard, and often impotent. Other times, genocidal crimes were aided and abetted by states interested in strengthening alliances or thwarting Cold War enemies. Influenced by the political realities of a world polarized into two camps, national security interests invariably trumped humanitarian concerns. As the world's two superpowers, the Soviet Union and the United States were able to exert tremendous influence on countries around the world and both relied upon a mixture of intimidation and threats, as well as rewards and incentives, to develop alliances, define enemies, and bring nations into their respective circles of influence.

The Cold War emerged after the end of the Second World War as the United States and the Soviet Union increasingly pursued divergent policies in Europe and defined their own national interests in opposition to each other. The former World War II allies disagreed over the occupation and reconstruction of a number of eastern European countries. Indeed, the United States and Great Britain were alarmed over the blatant ways in which Josef Stalin brutally suppressed democratic influences in various eastern European countries and installed communist governments. Many in the west saw Stalin as little better or even worse than Hitler and feared the spread of communist influences in Europe and the rest of the world. Increasingly, therefore, the U.S. worked to contain the threat of communist expansionism. The Soviet Union, meanwhile, perceived such actions to be high-handed interference in the Soviet sphere of influence. The increasingly confrontational relationship was only exacerbated by the creation of the North Atlantic Treaty Organization (NATO) in 1949, which was countered soon after by the rival Warsaw Pact in 1955. Comprised of the United States, Great Britain, Canada, France, the Netherlands, Belgium, Luxembourg, Italy, Portugal, Norway, Denmark, and Iceland, NATO was ultimately aimed at constraining the growth and influence of the Warsaw Pact nations of the Soviet Union, Albania, Bulgaria, Czechoslovakia, East Germany, Hungary, Poland, and Romania.

The Cold War was not a war in the classic sense of the word. Rather it was a time of ongoing tension and hostility that characterized the relationship between the United States, the Soviet Union and their respective allies (Walker, 1993). The specific nature of the conflict was dictated by the nuclear capabilities of the two superpowers. The United States had developed nuclear weapons in the last stages of the Second World while the Soviet Union became a nuclear power in 1949 (Vinen, 2000). The destructive power of nuclear armaments meant that each side avoided direct confrontation and fighting as much as possible because of the potential escalation to a nuclear exchange. Given the aptly named policy of mutual assured destruction (MAD), this was no idle fear and confrontations over the Berlin blockade (1948-49), the Korean War (1950-1953), and the Cuban missile crisis of October 1962 served only to reinforce this well-founded hesitancy. As the Soviet premier Nikita Khrushchev articulated in 1959, "Our country and the United States are the two most mighty powers in the world. If other countries fight among themselves, they can be separated. But if war breaks out between America and our country, no one will be able to stop it. It will be a catastrophe on a global scale" (quoted in Walker, 1993, p. 127). This kind of recognition had the practical effect of inhibiting the United States and the Soviet Union from engaging in direct military conflict and encouraged a sort of gamesmanship as each side worked surreptitiously to garner strategic advantage or deny advantage to the other. Often fought through proxies, not only in Europe, but in Africa, Asia, and South America as well, this conflict eventually spread throughout the globe and was the dominant political reality of the second half of the twentieth century. It was as much an ideological and economic struggle as a political one and came to be seen the west as a fight between the forces of freedom, democracy, and capitalism on the one side and repressive communist tyranny on the other.

Ironically, the Cold War was waged at the same time that a new regime of human rights was developing out of the ashes of the Holocaust. The military collapse of the Third Reich resulted in the liberation of a great number of concentration camps and death camps and awakened the world to the horrors of the Nazi regime. While information about the Holocaust had been known to a number of political and military leaders among the allies, widespread knowledge as to the nature and extent of the Holocaust was largely lacking until the end of the war. One person who was aware of what the Nazis had been perpetrating was an expatriate Polish attorney named Raphael Lemkin who, in his 1944 book *Axis Rule in Occupied Europe*, coined the term "genocide" in order to describe the Nazi-perpetrated atrocities against the Jews. He felt that traditional terms such as mass murder or massacre did not capture the essence of an attempt to destroy an entire population and he accordingly came up with the word genocide to describe this phenomenon.

Once World War II was over, the desire to hold the perpetrators accountable for their crimes was reinforced by the widespread outrage and condemnation engendered by the genocidal crimes and military excesses of the Nazis. Accordingly, the victorious allied powers created the International Military Tribunal that indicted and put on trial a number of high-ranking Nazi officials in the German city of Nuremberg (Taylor, 1992). Ultimately, nineteen Nazis leaders were found guilty and twelve were executed by hanging. They had been charged with crimes against peace, war crimes, and crimes against humanity, but importantly, they were not tried for genocide as the latter crime had not yet been enacted into law. After the end of the war and the subsequent trials, Raphael Lemkin campaigned to create an international treaty prohibiting genocide and, in large part due to his advocacy, the United Nations began working on a resolution in 1946 intended to define genocide as a crime under international law. This initiative resulted in the eventual adoption of the UN Convention on the Prevention and Punishment of the Crime of Genocide (UNCG) on December 9, 1948 (Beigbeder, 1999), which at its core affirms, under article II, that:

> Genocide means any of the following acts committed with intent to destroy, in whole or in part, a national, ethnical, racial, or religious group, such as killing members of the group; causing serious bodily harm to members of the groups; deliberately inflicting on the group conditions of life calculated to bring about its physical destruction in whole or in part; imposing measures to prevent births within the group; forcibly transferring children of the group to another group.

Article 1 of the UNCG also asserts that, "The Contracting Parties confirm that genocide, whether committed in time of peace or in time of war, is a crime under international law which they undertake to prevent and punish." This is significant in that it mandated that signatories act to prevent this crime and to punish those responsible.

The UNCG was followed by a host of other human rights initiatives that were also designed to facilitate states intervening in human rights violations (Ishay, 2004). These legal developments helped move human rights issues further into the international arena. Historically, human rights were perceived primarily if not exclusively as internal political issues subject solely to the dictates of sovereign states. International human rights law such as the UNCG, however, made the protection of human rights an international legal and political issue with the international community having not only the right to act, but the obligation to do so (Beigbeder, 1999).

It wasn't long, however, before the optimism that accompanied these developments faded as the political exigencies of the Cold War effectively ended the ability or willingness of governments to act against genocide and gross human rights violations and, in fact, encouraged states to turn a blind eye to the excesses of allies and client states. This apparent inability and unwillingness to act also impacted the United Nations itself (even as dedicated as it ostensibly was to preventing and intervening in genocide and other human rights situations), and that is because the permanent members of the Security Council (China, France, Russia, the United Kingdom, and the United States) were enmeshed in their superpower rivalries (Fasulo, 2004; Gold, 2004).

These contradictory impulses toward humanitarian altruism on the one hand and amoral national security calculations on the other were motivated by a number of factors. The new humanitarian developments that were so philosophically appealing often foundered on the shoals of *realpolitik*. Most states, in fact, relied on traditional political arrangements and traditions; ones which placed humanitarian concerns on the margins of diplomacy and international relations. Traditional diplomacy was largely concerned with preserving sovereign integrity from internal and external pressures and human rights issues were not seen as central to national security (Finnemore, 2003; Moomaw, 1997). Additionally, the notion that sovereign states had sole legitimate authority over populations within national borders was slow to erode even though the philosophical and legal climate began to change in the post-World War II years. And thus, sovereignty continued to reign supreme because of pragmatic self interest and national security concerns exacerbated by Cold War fears and ideologies.

Accordingly, the new legal developments either failed to be implemented or were blatantly and cynically manipulated by politicians intent on furthering less altruistic goals and agendas, and thus the second half of the twentieth century was marked by numerous examples of genocide and egregious human rights violations that included the Chinese invasion and occupation of Tibet, the Indonesian massacres, the invasion of East Timor, and the Cambodian genocide. As noted earlier, in most instances, the international community failed to act to prevent these crimes and sometimes even helped facilitate the genocidal violence. This is not to say that humanitarian intervention never took place. Sometimes, local or regional motivations outweighed the Cold War. For example, in 1971 India intervened militarily in Bangladesh (then East Pakistan) after the military of West Pakistan (now Pakistan) perpetrated widespread atrocities and abuses in their attempts to suppress the East Pakistan independence movement (Brown, 1972). In this case, India's national security concerns, combined with a long standing antipathy towards Pakistan, moved India into action. Similarly, Cambodia was invaded in 1978 by Vietnam which brought an end to the genocide there. The invasion, however, was not launched with that particular goal in mind, instead it was instigated in response to cross border raids launched by the Cambodian Khmer Rouge against Vietnamese border communities. These kinds of examples, however, were more the exception than the rule and, as noted, were not exclusively nor even primarily motivated by humanitarian concerns.

In short, most governments simply gave lip service to the high-minded ideals articulated by documents such as the UNCG and failed to couple their rhetoric to concrete plans of action and implementation. The language of human rights was often applied selectively, depending upon the affiliations of the perpetrators and the victims.

Time and again, during the Cold War, the United States, for example, chose not to intervene in genocidal crimes because of the potential implications of that intervention. Worse yet, in its efforts to combat communism, the U.S. and its client states often subverted democratic principles and practices. Fearful of the spread of communist influence, U.S. political leaders knowingly supported and assisted repressive regimes engaged in widespread human rights abuses and genocide at the same time that the United States was advocating for and supporting various human rights initiatives. With the support and aid of the United States, many regional military dictatorships in countries such as Argentina, Chile, the Dominican Republic, Guatemala, El Salvador, and Uruguay resorted to widespread human rights abuses and, in certain cases, even genocide to defend the status quo of their often repressive regimes (Blum, 1995; Gareau, 2004; Menchu, 1987; Valentino, 2004). A United Nations (1999) report, for example, asserts that between 1981 and 1983 government forces in Guatemala perpetrated genocide against several Mayan groups in the course of their (the government forces) counterinsurgency operations (Blum, 1995; Manz, 2002). The support, training, financing, and military advisors provided by the U.S. was often instrumental in allowing these regimes to brutally suppress segments of their population. Importantly, any movement or initiative which challenged the status quo was defined as a communist inspired threat. Speaking of this period, Gill (2004) asserts that

> From Chile to East Timor, Congo, Guatemala, El Salvador, Colombia, and many other cold war battlegrounds, ordinary people who desired land reform, better wages, improved health care, education, and the basic right of self-determination were labeled communists by U.S.-backed regimes and murdered, tortured, and disappeared by shadowy paramilitary death squads and state security forces trained by the United States (p. 2).

In fact, many of the worst perpetrators of human rights abuses in Central and South America were graduates of the notorious School of the Americas (Gill, 2004). Originally based in Panama but later moved to Fort Benning, Georgia, this school was intended to help prevent the spread of communism in the Americas by training Latin American security forces in counterinsurgency techniques. Unfortunately, the efforts of the graduates of this school to eliminate internal subversion usually translated into torture, murder, massacres and genocide. In a number of cases, U.S. intelligence agencies actually worked to overthrow democratically elected politicians in various countries who were seen as being too sympathetic to leftist ideologies and movements (Blum, 1995). In 1954, for example, the CIA organized an invasion force that overthrew the democratically elected government of Jacobo Arbenz in Guatemala who was depicted as a communist because of his policies of land reform and because of his support for unions and the poor. Similarly, in 1973 the United States helped encourage and support a military coup that overthrew the democratically elected Chilean government of Salvador

Allende and installed the military dictatorship of General Augusto Pinochet (Blum, 1995; Dinges, 2004; Gareau, 2004).

These cases illustrate the selective nature of Cold War intervention and the ways in which countries such as the United States sometimes aided and abetted genocidal crimes, but they are by no means the only such examples. Many other instances from the Cold War exist and illustrate further the ways in which humanitarian concerns were subverted by Cold War politics. One of the best examples involves the invasion of Tibet by Communist China. More specifically, on October 7, 1950, the Chinese People's Liberation Army invaded Tibet with a large army of battle hardened troops. The stated rationale was to "liberate" Tibet from feudalism and western imperialism (Craig, 1999). Since the Tibetan army was a tenth the size of the invasion force and since its generals had no military training, they were soon overwhelmed by the much larger and more experienced Chinese military. After attempting to solicit the help of Nepal, Great Britain, India, and the United States but to no avail, the Tibetan government appealed to the United Nations for assistance in protecting their national sovereignty. The Chinese military stopped their advance in order to ascertain what the international reaction would be (Craig, 1999). They needn't have been concerned. Most nations did not know anything about Tibet nor did they care. Tibet did not have official ties with any nation save India and was not a member state of the United Nations. Tibet's appeal also fell on deaf ears because of fears of antagonizing China. A few months earlier, on June 4, 1950, North Korea had invaded South Korea and had quickly routed the South Korean and U.S. army forces (LaFeber, 1991). The military and political leadership of North Korea had ties with both the Soviet Union and Communist China and there were fears that confronting China over the situation in Tibet could potentially escalate the Korean War. Only El Salvador sponsored a resolution condemning the Chinese invasion. Preoccupied with the new war in Korea, the U.N., however, acceding to the recommendations by India, Great Britain, and the United States, chose not to debate the resolution and did not even include it in the U.N.'s general assembly agenda (Shakya, 1999). China then completed its military takeover and some estimates suggest that over a million Tibetans died in the next twenty years through starvation, execution, torture, and in the course of armed resistance (Craig, 1999). The only assistance from the United States came when the Central Intelligence Agency (CIA) covertly provided limited training and weapons for the Tibetan resistance in the late 1950s. Clearly, Cold War fears and tensions kept intervention from occurring more positively or overtly in the case of Tibet.

Another example involves Indonesia in the mid 1960s. The immediate trigger to the violence occurred in 1965 when six generals were kidnapped and then murdered. While ultimate responsibility for the attacks remains unclear, it appeared that elements of the Indonesian Communist Party (PKI) were at least partially involved. Evidently, the kidnappers had wanted to thwart a rumored coup d'état by the army, but botched the job and decided to kill the men they had abducted (Cribb, 1997; Cribb, 2001). In response to the murder of the generals and acting out of a deep seated antipathy to communism, the military under General Suharto took power from President Sukarno and organized a series of massacres that lasted until March of 1966. During that period it is estimated that approximately a half million people were killed, most of whom were members of the PKI (Dwyer and Santikarma, 2003; Robert, 2001). While this example would not be considered genocide using a strict reading of the UNCG definition since political groups are excluded, in every other sense of the word this case was clearly genocidal and the world barely noticed. Even though news outlets reported on the killings soon after they began, no international action or censure was forthcoming (Cribb, 1997). The role of the U.S. in facilitating this violence reveals much about the nature of *realpolitik* strategies during the Cold War. The Communist Party of Indonesia was the world's largest behind only the Soviet bloc nations and China and was therefore seen as a threat to U.S. interests in the region. It didn't help that President Sukarno was seen as being to sympathetic or soft toward the PKI. Some evidence suggests that the CIA helped orchestrate the military coup that ousted Sukarno (Gareau, 2004) and that the U.S. military establishment had long forged close ties with the Indonesian military (Blum, 1995). Regardless of whether or not the takeover was assisted by the CIA, evidence shows that U.S. diplomats compiled lists of communist "agents" which they turned over to the Indonesian military so that those identified could be killed. Over 5,000 names were provided by these diplomats (Blum, 1995). Intervention in this case was intended not to prevent abuses, but to facilitate them.

The Indonesian military was at it again when it invaded East Timor in 1975 and was allowed to proceed unhindered. East Timor was in the process of decolonization and moving forward on a path that would likely have ended with self-determination. A Portuguese colony, East Timor's national aspirations clashed with the Indonesian government's intent to control as many of the former island colonies as possible; in fact, the territory of West Timor was already under their authority (Dunn, 1997; Jardine, 1995). On November 28, 1975, East Timor declared independence and nine days later was invaded by the Indonesian military. The fighting, massacres, and executions were so intense that between 1975 and 1991, the population decreased by around 12 percent. By 1979 some sources suggested that up to 120,000 East Timorese had been killed (Kiernan, 2003). Tragically, this violence did not erupt on an unsuspecting world; rather the signs had been there for a while.

While publicly the Australian government condemned the invasion and supported a U.N. resolution to the same effect, beneath the public facade the story was a bit different. The Australian government had been aware of the Indonesian military's plans for invasion, but had chosen to accede to the takeover because of economic interests and because of pressure from the U.S. government. Within several years, the Australian government would be the first to officially sanction Indonesia's claim over East Timor.

Several days before the invasion, U.S. President Ford and U.S. Secretary of State Henry Kissinger met with President Suharto in Jakarta and essentially gave him the go ahead for the invasion (Jardine, 1995). As Kissinger expressed afterwards, "the U.S. understands Indonesia's position on the question," while President Ford asserted that if it came to a choice between East Timor and Indonesia, the U.S. would back Indonesia (Jardine, 1995, p. 38). This meeting was only a short time after Cambodia and Vietnam fell to communism and it was correctly believed that the Indonesian military was strongly anti-communist. Over the subsequent years, advocates of the East Timorese cause lobbied the United Nations to apply the Genocide Convention to the situation, but were unsuccessful as the United Nations and various states carefully and continuously avoided use of the word genocide (Dunn, 1997). The latter recognized, of course, that applying the term genocide to the situation in East Timor would have increased the pressure to intervene because of Article 1 of the UNCG.

And there is the case of Cambodia. On April 17, 1975, the communist Khmer Rouge took power when they entered the capitol city Phnom Penh after five years of fighting. The U.S. had unintentionally aided the Khmer Rouge when American aircraft began bombing Vietnamese bases in Cambodia in 1969 and sent in troops in 1970 (Kiernan, 1996).

The bombing only ended in 1973. Additionally, the U.S. government helped support a military coup in the country that ousted the popular Prince Norodom Sihanouk and substituted the corrupt, repressive, and ultimately incompetent Lon Nol. These moves had the effect of destabilizing the country and creating support for the Khmer Rouge. The Khmer Rouge were led by Saloth Sar who went by the revolutionary name of Pol Pot, and upon taking over the country he immediately set about his genocidal plan of reshaping the country into a utopian agrarian society based on Stalinist/Maoist principles (Weitz, 2003). The Khmer Rouge began by sealing the country and evacuating the cities, starting with the capital of Phnom Penh. During the next five years, out of a population of approximately 8 million, the regime killed around 1.7 million people through starvation, disease, torture, and murder comprising just under one fourth of the population (Kiernan, 2003; Kiernan, 1999). The killing was only brought to an end when Vietnam invaded in late December of 1978.

The fact that the Khmer Rouge ran a very secretive and insular society and because refugee reports of widespread killing and brutality were largely unconfirmed and often challenged by skeptics meant that the situation in Kampuchea (as the Khmer Rouge renamed Cambodia) was largely ignored during the perpetration of the genocide. Having just ended an unsuccessful war in neighboring Vietnam, the U.S., in particular, was loath to get entangled again in that part of the world.

Over time, as the evidence mounted, it became clear that the Khmer Rouge were in fact perpetrating genocide in Cambodia. Yet in spite of the growing horror and awareness and sporadic calls for intervention from journalists, a few state department officials, and a number of politicians, the U.S. and the international community did little to nothing (Power, 2002). Ironically, after the Vietnamese invasion in late 1978 and early 1979, which brought an end to the genocide and sent the Khmer Rouge leadership into the jungles, the U.S. sided with the ousted Khmer Rouge regime. Motivated in part by the demands of sovereignty because Vietnam had invaded the sovereign state of Cambodia, the U.S. was also influenced by the Cold War rationale of limiting the spread of Soviet influence through their Vietnamese client. Furthermore, the Khmer Rouge was supported by China which the U.S. was interested in developing a better relationship with (Power, 2002). In fact, the United States went so far as to sponsor and protect the Khmer Rouge's status in the United Nations.

The examples discussed above are a selective representation of numerous genocide and human rights abuses that were perpetrated unhindered during the Cold War period. As shown, during the Cold War most states, including the U.S., marginalized the humanitarian aims of preventing and intervening in genocide in order to prioritize national security agendas. More damning, genocide and other abuses were actually assisted and enabled by many states, including the United States. Genocide was perpetrated time and again during the second half of the twentieth century with remarkable impunity because of Cold War politics.

The intervening sixteen years since the end of the Cold War have seen increasing attempts to intervene in human rights violations and punish those responsible for such crimes. Flawed and often too little too late, they still represent more positive action than was typically present during the Cold War. Prevention, however, remains as problematic as ever. That said, the future of genocide intervention and prevention is ultimately dependent upon the ability of states and international organizations to define humanitarian concerns as being central to national self interest and security.

References

Beigbeder, Yves (1999). *Judging War Criminals: The Politics of International Justice.* New York: St. Martin's Press.

Blum, William (1995). *Killing Hope: U.S. Military and CIA Interventions Since World War II.* Monroe, ME: Common Courage Press.

Brown, W. Norman (1972). *The United States and India, Pakistan, Bangladesh.* Cambridge, MA: Harvard University Press.

Craig, Mary (1999). *Tears of Blood: A Cry for Tibet.* Washington, DC: Counterpoint Press.

Cribb, Robert (1997). "The Indonesian Massacres," pp. 236-263. In Samuel Totten, William S. Parsons, and Israel W. Charny (eds.) *Century of Genocide: Eyewitness Accounts and Critical Views.* New York: Garland Publishing.

Cribb, Robert (2001). "Genocide in Indonesia, 1965-1966." *Journal of Genocide Research*, 3(2): 219-239.

Dinges, John (2004). *The Condor Years: How Pinochet and his Allies Brought Terrorism to Three Continents.* New York: The New Press.

Dunn, James (1997). "Genocide in East Timor," pp. 264-290. In Samuel Totten, William S. Parsons, and Israel W. Charny (eds.)*Century of Genocide: Eyewitness Accounts and Critical Views.* New York: Garland Publishing.

Dwyer, Leslie, and Santikarma, Degung (2003). "When the World Turned to Chaos: 1965 and Its Aftermath in Bali, Indonesia," pp. 289-306. In Robert Gellately, Robert and Kiernan, Ben (eds.) *The Specter of Genocide: Mass Murder in Historical Perspective.* New York: Cambridge University Press.

Fasulo, Linda (2004). *An Insider's Guide to the U.N.* New Haven, CT: Yale University Press.

Finnemore, Martha (2003). *The Purpose of Intervention: Changing Beliefs About the Use of Force.* Ithaca, NY: Cornell University Press.

Gareau, Frederick H. (2004). *State Terrorism and the United States: From Counterinsurgency to the War on Terrorism.* Atlanta, GA: Clarity Press.

Gill, Lesley (2004). *The School of the Americas: Military Training and Political Violence in the Americas.* Durham, NC: Duke University Press.

Gold, Dore (2004). *Tower of Babble: How the United Nations Has Fueled Global Chaos.* New York: Crown Forum.

Ishay, Micheline R. (2004). *The History of Human Rights: From Ancient Times to the Globalization Era.* Berkeley and Los Angeles: University of California Press.

Jardine, Matthew (1995). *East Timor: Genocide in Paradise.* Tucson, AZ: Odion Press.

Kiernan, Ben. (1999). "The Cambodian Genocide and Its Leaders," pp. 129-132. In Israel W. Charny (Ed.) *Encyclopedia of Genocide, Volume 1, A-H.* Santa Barbara, CA: ABC-CLIO.

Kiernan, Ben (2003). "The Demography of Genocide in Southeast Asia: The Death Tolls in Cambodia, 1975-79, and East Timor, 1975-80." *Critical Asian Studies*, 35(4):585-597.

Kiernan, Ben (1996). *The Pol Pot Regime: Race, Power, and Genocide in Cambodia Under the Khmer Rouge, 1975-1979.* New Haven, CT: Yale University Press.

LaFeber, Walter (1991). *America, Russia, and the Cold War 1945-1990.* New York: McGraw Hill.

Manz, Beatriz (2002). "Terror, Grief, and Recovery: Genocidal Trauma in a Mayan Village in Guatemala," pp. 292-309. In Alexander Laban Hinton (ed.) *Annihilating Difference: The Anthropology of Genocide.* Berkeley and Los Angeles, CA: University of California Press.

Menchu, Rigoberta (1987). *I, Rigoberta Menchu: An Indian Woman in Guatemala.* London: Verso Books.

Moomaw, William R. (1997). "International Environmental Policy and the Softening of Sovereignty." *The Fletcher Forum of World Affairs.* Summer/Fall, 21(2):7-15.

Power, Samantha (2002). *"A Problem from Hell": America and the Age of Genocide.* New York: Basic Books.

Reisman, W. Michael, and Antoniou, Chris T. (eds.) (1994). *The Laws of War: A Comprehensive Collection of Primary Documents on International Laws Governing Armed Conflict.* New York: Vintage Books.

Shakya, Tsering (1999). *The Dragon in the Land of Snows: A History of Modern Tibet Since 1947.* New York: Columbia University Press.

Steiner, Henry J., and Philip Alston (eds.) (2000). *International Human Rights in Context: Law, Politics, Morals* Oxford: Oxford University Press.

Taylor, Telford (1992). *The Anatomy of the Nuremberg Trials.* Boston, MA: Back Bay Books.

Valentino, Benjamin A. (2004). *Final Solutions: Mass Killing and Genocide in the 20th Century.* Ithaca, NY: Cornell University Press.

Vinen, Richard (2000). *A History of Fragments: Europe in the Twentieth Century.* Cambridge, MA: Da Capo Press.

Walker, Martin (1993). *The Cold War: A History.* New York: Henry Holt.

Weitz, Eric D. (2003). *A Century of Genocide: Utopias of Race and Nation.* Princeton, NJ: Princeton University Press.

Annotated Bibliography

Ball, Howard (1999). *Prosecuting War Crimes and Genocide.* Lawrence: University Press of Kansas. 288 pp.

This book provides an analysis of attempts to punish the perpetrators of genocide throughout the entire twentieth century. Focusing primarily on legal developments in international law that involve the prosecution of war criminals and perpetrators of genocide, the author also provides a discussion of several examples of genocide including that of Cambodia. Important segments of the book also deal with the hesitancy of the U.S. to ratify the United Nations Convention on the Prevention and Punishment of the Crime of Genocide (UNCG) as well the ways in which issues of national sovereignty have been affected by changes in international human rights law.

Becker, Elizabeth (1998). *When the War Was Over: Cambodia and the Khmer Rouge Revolution.* New York: Public Affairs. 606 pp.

A journalist with much first-hand experience with Cambodia and the Khmer Rouge, Elizabeth Becker's work is a comprehensive and thorough examination of the Khmer Rouge-perpetrated genocide. She is particularly good at describing the international dimension of the events leading up to the Khmer Rouge takeover in 1975, as well as the reaction to the Vietnamese invasion in 1979 which brought down the regime.

Beigbeder, Yves (1999). *Judging War Criminals: The Politics of International Justice.* New York: St. Martin's Press. 230 pp.

Focusing primarily on international humanitarian and criminal law, this volume provides a discussion about the legal initiatives that have developed out of the desire to punish the perpetrators of massacres and genocides. A prime focus concerns the way in which modern legal developments arose out of World War II and the resulting trials in Europe and the Far East. Also included is a discussion of various alternatives to punishment, including truth and reconciliation commissions. Of particular interest is the section titled "Problems and Prospects" which discusses how *realpolitik* policies ought to be balanced with the need to punish perpetrators.

Blum, William (1995). *Killing Hope: U.S. Military and CIA Interventions Since World War II.* Monroe, ME: Common Courage Press. 457 pp.

While not about genocide per se, this book chronicles the ways in which the United States intervened in the affairs of nations around the world. A number of the cases discussed concern examples of genocide such as Cambodia, Guatemala, and Indonesia. Scathing in its criticism, this book illustrates the ways in which Cold War attitudes enabled U.S. political leaders to condone torture, murder, and the suppression of human rights in the name of fighting communism. Blum provides an object lesson in the shortcomings of U.S. policy toward genocide and human rights violations when it felt that national security interests were at stake.

Callahan, David (1997). *Unwinnable Wars: American Power and Ethnic Conflict.* New York: Hill and Wang. 273 pp.

With a focus on ethnic conflict rather than on genocide, David Callahan provides a history of American intervention in ethnic conflicts during the Cold War and after. He offers an insightful assessment of the ways in which the United States has responded to various ethnic conflicts and offers concrete suggestions for more consistent and effective prevention and intervention strategies in order to reduce the frequency and severity of ethnic conflict. He provides one of the most thorough and comprehensive discussions about the various options states have available to them for intervention.

Chanda, Nayan (1986). *Brother Enemy: The War After the War.* New York: Collier Books. 479 pp.

This is one of the few works that places the Cambodian genocide within the larger framework of the Indochinese politics and conflicts. This is an excellent volume for examining the Cold War politics around Vietnam, Cambodia, the United States, China, and the Soviet Union during the 1970s. Written in an accessible style, this book allows the reader to see the big picture of events as they affected the region.

Chigas, George (2000). "The Politics of Defining Justice After the Cambodian Genocide." *Journal of Genocide Research*, 2(2):245-265.

This journal article examines the international attempts to bring to justice the perpetrators of the Cambodian genocide. Beginning in 1979, after the Vietnamese invasion ended Khmer Rouge rule, the article examines the political and legal developments that have prevented legal accountability up through and including the present day.

Cribb, Robert (2001). "Genocide in Indonesia, 1965-1966." *Journal of Genocide Research*, 3(2):219-239.

Cribb provides a competent review of the events leading up to the massacres of the Indonesian Communist Party members as well as the violence itself. He illustrates in detail the historical rise of nationalist and ethnic identity and ideology in the region as well as the pernicious influence of colonization, and the impact these elements had on the violence of the 1960s.

Dugger, Ronnie (1996). "To Prevent or To Stop Mass Murder." In Strozier, Charles B., and Michael Flynn, (eds.) *Genocide, War, and Human Survival*. Lanham, MD.: Rowman & Littlefield, pp. 59-73.

This short chapter provides a fine overview of some of the issues in regards to international politics, the United Nations, and intervention to prevent genocide. While most of the writing focuses on what needs to happen instead of what has happened, this piece still provides some insight into the nature of politics, especially during the Cold War, as it affects what states say and do about genocide.

Falk, Richard (1998). "A Half Century of Human Rights." *Australian Journal of International Affairs*, 52(3):255-272.

This article provides a fairly comprehensive review of human rights in the post-World War II era. Much of the discussion concerns the hypocrisy and double standards that were so evident in U.S. policy during the Cold War years. Falk is especially good at pointing out the ways in which human rights issues and norms were opportunistically exploited in order to score points and claim a moral high ground against Cold War adversaries.

Fein, Helen (ed.) (1992). *Genocide Watch*. New Haven, CT: Yale University Press. 204 pp.

This excellent edited volume is divided into three primary parts, the third of which is dedicated to approaches to preventing and punishing genocide. With articles by Leo Kuper, Ervin Staub, and others, these articles provide a succinct review of some of the major issues surrounding the prevention of genocide. Additionally, several articles that address Cold War era genocides (e.g., in Burundi, Cambodia, Iraq) provide specific examples.

Finnemore, Martha (2003). *The Purpose of Intervention: Changing Beliefs About the Use of Force*. Ithaca, NY: Cornell University Press. 173 pp.

Martha Finnemore provides a solid discussion about how and why nations use military intervention around the world. Her discussion does not directly address the problem of genocide intervention, rather she more broadly discusses the evolving nature of intervention. Specifically, Finnemore asserts that while the ways in which states intervene has not changed dramatically, the reasons given for intervention have in fact altered. She points out that intervention in the present day is much different from interventions during the Cold War since states now intervene primarily for humanitarian concerns, rather than purely for the pragmatic self-interest of *realpolitik*.

Gareau, Frederick (2004). *State Terrorism and the United States: From Counterinsurgency to the War on Terrorism*. Atlanta, GA.: Clarity Press. 254 pp.

This small volume offers the reader a better understanding about the ways in which Cold War politics helped shape the United States relationship with Central and South American military regimes. Based in large part on the documentation provided by national truth commissions from a number of states, this sobering book helps illustrate some of the dynamics that influenced the U.S.'s response to human rights violations and genocide during the Cold War.

Gomez, Mayra (2001). "The Role of International Intervention in Facilitating Violence and Peace in El Salvador, 1977-1998." *Human Rights Review*, April-June, 2(2):76-92.

The prime thrust of this article concerns the relationship between human rights abuses in El Salvador and how they were affected by international attention and pressure. Relatively little attention is paid, however, to examining the role of other countries, most notably the U.S. in helping to facilitate the violence in the first place.

Hirsch, Herbert (2002). *Anti-Genocide: Building an American Movement to Prevent Genocide*. Westport, CT: Praeger Books. 213 pp.

While this book is not principally about the intervention and prevention of genocide during the Cold War and while Hirsch relies primarily on post-Cold War references and examples, this book has a well written section on the politics and history of genocide intervention and prevention which provides a good introduction to this particular topic.

Jardine, Matthew (1995). *East Timor: Genocide in Paradise*. Tucson, AZ: Odonion Press. 95 pp.

This slim volume presents an account of the violence in East Timor caused by the invasion of the Indonesian military. The author pays particular attention to the roles that the U.S. and Australian governments played in facilitating the takeover and subsequent killing. Also of note, Jardine briefly reviews the response of the world community to the events that took place in East Timor.

Kiernan, Ben (2002). "Cover-up and Denial of Genocide: Australia, the USA, East Timor, and the Aborigines." *Critical Asian Studies*, 34(2):163-192.

This article provides a review of the ways in which genocide was covered up and denied by the Australian government and, to a lesser extent, the United States. This article is particularly useful for situating the genocide in East Timor within the context of the Cold War and how that struggle helped shape how the genocide was perpetrated, defined, and perceived.

Kiernan, Ben (1996). *The Pol Pot Regime: Race, Power, and Genocide in Cambodia under the Khmer Rouge, 1975-1979*. New Haven, CT: Yale University Press. 477 pp.

Perhaps the best and most comprehensive book about the Cambodian genocide, this is not primarily a book about intervention, but instead focuses more on the specific processes whereby the Khmer Rouge regime perpetrated genocide. Nevertheless, it remains an important source for information about this Cold War era genocide.

Knaus, John Kenneth (1999). *Orphans of the Cold War: America and the Tibetan Struggle for Survival.* New York: Public Affairs. 398 pp.

This volume examines the Chinese invasion of Tibet and the role international community and the United Nations in allowing this military takeover. The author examines in detail the behind the scenes machinations and decisions that allowed Tibet to become a casualty of cold war politics as the United States made the strategic decision not to officially challenge the invasion and takeover.

Kuper, Leo (1981). *Genocide: Its Political Use in the Twentieth Century.* New Haven, CT: Yale University Press. 255 pp.

Sadly, this classic and pioneering work on genocide is nowadays all too often ignored, yet the analysis and insights are still timely and relevant. For purposes of the focus of this chapter and bibliography, Kuper's work is valuable in that he contextualizes some Cold War era genocides within the political and structural framework of colonization and decolonization. Additionally, his discussion of the nature of sovereignty as it relates to genocide is highly useful.

LeBlanc, Lawrence J. (1991). *The United States and the Genocide Convention.* Durham, NC: Duke University Press. 291 pp.

This book has as its focus the political debates surrounding the U.S. decision to ratify the United Nations Convention on the Prevention and Punishment of the Crime of Genocide which lasted almost forty years. LeBlanc's detailed review of the issues and positions reveals quite clearly the United States' schizophrenic attitudes toward preventing and intervening in cases of genocide.

Lemarchand, Rene (1994). *Burundi: Ethnic Conflict and Genocide.* Washington, DC: Woodrow Wilson Center Press. 206 pp.

While this book is largely about the causes and consequences of the 1972 genocide in Burundi, throughout the text Lemarchand weaves in information about the complicity and silence of various countries. This provides the reader with an understanding of the ways in which intervention was avoided by the international community in this Cold War-era genocide. This book is also valuable for helping the reader understand the violence in the neighboring state of Rwanda that resulted in the genocide during 1994.

Marchak, Patricia (2003). *Reigns of Terror*. Montreal: McGill-Queens University Press. 224 pp.

Marchak's book provides a discussion of states that have perpetrated genocide and gross human rights violations and asserts that states with high levels of inequality and rigid institutions resistant to social change are more likely to engage in crimes against their citizens. This theoretical work on the nature of genocidal governments is a well reasoned and argued addition to the literature. The author also provides a discussion about how and why interventions occur in these kinds of cases and provides a number of case studies that include Cold War-era examples such as Burundi, Rwanda, and in the 1970s.

Mendlovitz, Saul, and John Fousek (1996). "The Prevention and Punishment of the Crime of Genocide." In Strozier, Charles B., and Michael Flynn (eds.) *Genocide, War, and Human Survival*. Lanham, MD.: Rowman & Littlefield, pp. 137-151.

This article provides a brief and somewhat superficial overview and history about some of the main issues that concern preventing and intervening in genocide. The main argument put forward by the authors is that a standing Genocide Police Force needs to be organized if prevention and intervention is to be effectively initiated.

Midlarsky, Manus I. (2001). "*Raison d'état, Raison d'église*: Realpolitik and the Onset of Genocide." Unpublished paper presented at the Fourth International Biennial Conference of the Association of Genocide Scholars, Minneapolis, Minnesota, June 9-12. 22 pp.

Realpolitik was a type of political calculus that was very much in evidence during the Cold War and Manus Midlarsky, a political scientist, does an excellent job of examining this type of foreign policy calculation and its relationship to and responsibility for genocides. While his examples are not classic Cold War ones, this paper is quite useful for better understanding the nature of the pragmatic choices of Cold War politics.

Power, Samantha (2002). *A Problem From Hell: America and the Age of Genocide*. New York: Basic Books. 610 pp.

This Pulitzer Prize-winning book offers an in depth discussion about the debates and decisions that affected the ways in which U.S. politicians consistently avoided action whenever genocide reared its head in the post-Holocaust world. On a case-by-case basis, Power examines specific examples of genocides and dissects not only the nature of genocide, but the political issues and actors that helped shape American policy in regards to this crime. Powerfully written with a tremendous ability to humanize the people involved, Samantha Powers's book is perhaps the best single volume needed to help understand the political dynamics of genocide prevention and intervention.

Robertson, Geoffrey (2002). *Crimes Against Humanity: The Struggle for Global Justice, 2nd edition*. New York: Penguin Books. 658 pp.

Powerful, witty, and impassioned is perhaps the best way to describe Robertson's book about crimes against humanity. His analysis of events since the Nuremberg trials is knowledgeable and thorough and he offers an excellent discussion of the ways in which sovereignty has dissuaded governments from intervening and holding accountable political leaders for the wars, genocide, and human rights violations that they have unleashed.

Ronayne, Peter (2001). *Never Again: The United States and the Prevention and Punishment of Genocide Since the Holocaust*. Lanham, MD: Rowman & Littlefield. 223 pp.

Very similar in some ways to Samantha Power's book, Peter Ronayne's *Never Again* provides a concise and scholarly review of the ways in which the United States dealt with genocide during the second half of the twentieth century. The central theme of this volume concerns the contradiction between the United States' professed abhorrence of genocide and its unwillingness to prevent or intervene in them when they occur.

Shakya, Tsering (1999). *The Dragon in the Land of Snows: A History of Modern Tibet Since 1947.* New York: Columbia University Press. 608 pp.

This book is an excellent volume for understanding the situation in Tibet. Skillfully blending the global geopolitics of the Cold War with more regional concerns, Shakya has written an extremely readable and compelling account of the Chinese invasion of Tibet that never ignores the human actors involved in making policy, negotiating, and influencing events.

Silove, Derrick (2000). "Conflict in East Timor: Genocide or Expansionist Occupation?" *Human Rights Review*, April-June, 1(3):80-92.

This article examines the Indonesian takeover of East Timor and the applicability of the term "genocide" to describe the events. Of particular note is his discussion of the responsibility of various world powers in helping engineer the military invasion. This article provides a solid primer in understanding the main elements of the violence in East Timor.

Taylor, John G. (2003). "Encirclement and Annihilation: The Indonesian Occupation of East Timor." In Robert Gellately and Ben Kiernan (eds.) *The Specter of Genocide: Mass Murder in Historical Perspective.* New York: Cambridge University Press, pp.163-185.

This book chapter provides an excellent summary and overview of the events leading up to the invasion of East Timor by the Indonesian military in 1975 as well as the aftermath of the genocidal assault. Particular attention is paid to the role of the international community in facilitating and then ignoring the violence that it helped unleash.

Totten, Samuel, William S. Parsons, and Israel W. Charny (eds.) (2004). *Century of Genocide: Critical Essays and Eyewitness Accounts*. New York: Routledge. 507 pp.

This edited collection provides chapters on a number of Cold War era cases of genocide including the killing in Indonesia and East Timor, Bangladesh, Burundi, and Cambodia. A particular strength of this book is that each chapter is organized along the same lines and includes eyewitness accounts as well. While not directly about genocide intervention and prevention, these chapters all provide excellent overviews of specific examples of genocide. A concluding chapter, though, by Samuel Totten is entitled "The Intervention and Prevention of Genocide: Where There *Is* the Political Will, There Is a Way."

Walzer, Michael (2000). *Just and Unjust Wars*. 3rd edition. New York: Basic Books. 361 pp.

This book provides important insight into the philosophy and legal issues surrounding interventions. Even though its focus is on wars rather than on genocides, it still offers excellent background information about the ideas, legal history, and constraints that guide international interventions during times of war. Much of the material, however, is relevant to the study of genocide given that genocide often accompanies wars and the intervention for genocide often involves military forces.

2

Prevention and Intervention of Genocide in the 1990s and Early 2000s

Samuel Totten and Paul R. Bartrop

Introduction

The record of the international community vis-à-vis the prevention of genocide in the 1990s and early 2000s was abysmal. Its record for halting genocide once it had begun was, with one major exception (East Timor in 1999), equally abysmal. Oddly, and ironically, this is true despite the fact that the UN and other members of the international community engaged in more humanitarian interventions throughout the 1990s and early 2000s than ever before. That said, it is important to note that the conflicts the international community confronted in the 1990s and early 2000s essentially moved away from those it had been accustomed to addressing (e.g., conflict and warfare between sovereign nations) to those with which it was largely unfamiliar (e.g., intrastate violence, often set off by religious, ethnic and political triggers). That, of course, is no excuse; rather, it is a recognition that the world had become a radically different, if not somewhat more complex, place in the aftermath of the Cold War.

At one and the same time, it is also important to note that the relatively new concept of "the responsibility to protect" grew out of the ever-increasing concern over the seemingly constant perpetration of crimes against humanity and genocide across the globe in the 1990s. While the concept has been hotly debated, it has grown in visibility and stature; still, only time will tell whether or not it results in something positive--meaning the imposition of early and effective actions to prevent (and when necessary, halt) the perpetration of crimes against humanity and genocide.

The Early Years of the Post-Cold War Period

When the Cold War came to an end in 1989 there was a great surge of optimism and hope that the world would be a more peaceful place. Unfortunately, such optimism was short-lived.

With the collapse of Communism, internal tensions broke out in violent conflict (or, in certain cases, continued apace) in numerous places across the globe, including the Middle East (e.g., Iraq), Europe (e.g., the former Yugoslavia) and Africa (e.g., Somalia and Rwanda). Some of the situations resulted in crimes against humanity, while still others degenerated into genocide. No longer prevented by the USSR and the USA from intervening in such matters, the international community made one attempt after another, depending upon the circumstances, to keep the peace, enforce the peace, or make the peace.

The earliest—and one of the most successful--post-Cold War interventions took place in Iraq in April 1991, when the United States and its allies conducted Operation Provide Comfort. This involved creating a "safe haven" for Kurds threatened by Saddam Hussein's troops in northern Iraq. While allied troops established relief camps and safe havens in northern Iraq, NATO planes established a no-fly zone over the area. As Samantha Power (2002) noted in her Pulitzer Prize-winning *"A Problem from Hell: America and the Age of Genocide*, "Operation Provide Comfort was perhaps the most promising indicator of what the post-Cold War world might bring in the way of genocide prevention.... This marked an unprecedented intervention in the internal affairs of a state for humanitarian reasons. Thanks to the allied effort, the Iraqi Kurds were able to return home and, with the protection of NATO jets overhead, govern themselves" (p. 241).

In the aftermath of the success in Iraq and with an eruption of strife in post-Communist Yugoslavia, various parts of Africa and Asia, and elsewhere, UN Secretary General Boutros Boutros-Ghali issued *An Agenda for Peace* (1992) in which he delineated an optimistic and grand plan with regard to UN peace operations. While his plan for implementing such operations in a more effective manner in the hope that it would result in a more peaceful world was well-meant, it was also sorely naive. That was true due to the complex machinations of the UN Security Council; the issue of *realpolitik* practiced by states (including those on the UN Security Council); the lack of political will that prevented many states from contributing to key peace operations; the complexity of the intrastate violence that was to be confronted by various peace operations; and, last, but certainly not least, the UN's own Byzantine, slow moving, and often inept way of handling major peace operations in locales where a combination of complex politics, heated ethnic differences and/or major religious divisions made for a toxic stew that was volatile and lethal. Put another way, Boutros-Ghali's ideas regarding the implementation of preventive diplomacy, peacekeeping, peace enforcement and peace making, all of which were highlighted and discussed in *Agenda for Peace*, were, more often than not, no match for the complicated and wrenching facts on the ground. The disasters that were already under way (e.g., in the former Yugoslavia), as well as those that would be within a year or two (e.g., in Somalia and Rwanda), provided ample proof of the latter.

The Former Yugoslavia

In 1991, following the fall of the former Soviet Union and the end of the Cold War, the former Yugoslavia began to disintegrate and degenerate into internecine conflict between and amongst the three major groups-- Serbs, Muslims, and Croats--that had lived in peace in Tito's Yugoslavia. More specifically, in the wake of extreme nationalist sentiments espoused by Serbian president Slobodan Milosevic, first Slovenia seceded, then Croatia and not long afterwards Bosnia. Upon each secession, Serb forces attacked the break-away states. For the next eight years, horrific atrocities, including crimes against humanity and genocide, were committed. The U.S. Central Intelligence Agency (CIA) reported that "90 percent" of the atrocities perpetrated between June 1991 and January 1995 were committed by Serb military and paramilitary forces (Power, 2002, p. 310).

The international community was well aware of Milosevic's words and threats, and the fear they instilled in the Muslim and Croat populations. It was also well aware of the ever-increasing and brutal actions committed by the Serb troops against their former neighbors and newly declared enemies. Based on her analysis of declassified documents, Power (2002) asserts that "no other atrocity campaign in the twentieth century was better monitored and understood by the U.S. government. U.S. analysts fed their higher-ups detailed and devastating reports on Serbian aims and tactics" (p. 264). And yet, the world basically stood by and watched the horrific events unfold. More specifically, "despite unprecedented public outcry about foreign brutality, for the next three and a half years the United States, Europe, and the United Nations stood by whole some 200,000 Bosnians were killed, more than 2 million were displaced, and the territory of a multiethnic European republic was sliced into three ethnically pure statelets" (Power, 2002, p. 251).

The reasons for the lack of action on the behalf of the victims varied from nation to nation. In the United States, alone, it varied from such attitudes as "we don't have a dog in this fight" (the words of then Secretary of State James Baker), to the Vietnam analogy (e.g., the military's fear of getting bogged down in a quagmire that the public did not support and which might lead to a large loss of military personnel), to the so-called "Somalia factor" (an intervention likely to go awry and result in the deaths of U.S. troops). And those were only three of what were numerous reasons.[11]

This is not to say that the international community did nothing. In fact, it became deeply involved in attempting to quell the violence in the former Yugoslavia, broker cease-fires, and establish peace agreements. But the attempts at intervention were, more often that not, either too little, too late, or totally ineffective. Ineffective mandates, diplomatic efforts, and even threats seemed to result in little to nothing and/or fall on deaf ears; and when weak attempts, or none at all, were used to carry out the threats, the perpetrators of the violence seemed to become even more emboldened to have their way. Indeed, the Western powers, led by the UN, the European Union and the North Atlantic Treaty Organization (NATO) (and pre-eminently, the United States and Britain), failed consistently both to resolve the conflict and to stop the killing.

In regard to the UN's efforts, Thomas Weiss (1993), a political scientist and specialist in the field of intervention, argued that

> Incremental measures under United Nations auspices paradoxically fostered Serbia's genocidal war aims. Given their traditional constraints and operating procedures, UN soldiers were not strong enough to deter the Serbs. But they deterred the international community from more assertive intervention because the troops, along with aid workers, were vulnerable targets. While assistance to refugees saved lives, it also helped foster ethnic cleansing by stimulating movement of unwanted populations. Air-drops of food made it seem as if people counted; while massive and unspeakable human rights abuses and war crimes continued unabated.
>
> Inadequate military and humanitarian action, combined with half-hearted sanctions and a negotiating charade, thus constituted a powerful diversion. They collectively impeded more vigorous Western diplomatic and military pressure or lifting the arms embargo for Muslims to help level the killing fields (p. 7).

Rwanda

Tensions between the ruling Hutu and the Tutsi people were nothing new in the 1990s. Indeed, beginning in 1959, the Tutsis had been subjected to discrimination and had been the victims of periodic outbreaks of mass killing.

Tensions, though, increased dramatically in 1990, following an invasion by the Rwandan Patriotic Front (RPF) (which was primarily comprised of exiled Tutsi). As the RPF made headway in its battle against the Hutu-run government, Tanzania, with the assistance of major Western powers, brought the warring parties together in order to bring about a cease-fire. Ultimately, both sides signed the Arusha Peace Accords in 1993, which provided for shared governance of Rwanda by both the Hutus and the Tutsis.

Alarmed at the potential impact of the Arusha accords, not only did Hutu extremists set out to totally undermine the talks and the peace accords, but did all in their power to terrorize the Tutsis and moderate Hutus who supported the accords. Ultimately, the Hutu extremists made preliminary plans for doing away with their perceived enemies. The terrorist tactics of the Hutu extremists were evident to all who were residing in Rwanda, and scholar-activist Alison Des Forges (a noted human rights researcher with Human Rights Watch, and Co-Chair of the International Commission on Human Rights Abuses in Rwanda 1992-1993) asserts that the donor states and international organizations working in Rwanda "could and should have anticipated" the 1994 genocide in Rwanda (quoted in Fein, 1994, p. 21).

As a result of the Arusha Accords, the UN inserted a peace mission (the UN Assistance Mission for Rwanda) for the express purpose of overseeing the cease-fire, helping with the demobilization and demilitarization of the area, and working to establish a modicum of safety as the Tutsis in exile returned to Rwanda. The ensuing turmoil, though, took place despite the signing of the Arusha accords; and, in fact, the increased tensions and ultimate genocide were largely a result of the Hutu extremists' fear that the RPF was going to take over Rwanda as well as their the extremists' disdain for the conditions set by the Arusha accords. As time went on, the Hutu extremists grew bolder in their attacks on the Tutsis, while also building up huge caches of weapons, establishing and training militias, and issuing broadcasts decrying the very existence of any and all Tutsi in Rwanda. As Alison Des Forges has correctly asserted, ultimately, "the international community was not resolute in holding the Rwandan government and the RPF to the peace accords signed on August 4, 1993" (quoted in Fein, 1994, p. 21), and that, as the world now knows, was a grave error.

Within a relatively short period, it was obvious to the UN force commander, Lt. General Romeo Dallaire, that a Chapter VI peace mission was an inadequate mandate, but his call for a more robust mandate fell on deaf ears at the UN (and, in particular, within the UN Security Council), not to mention the capitals of the most powerful nations across the globe. That was due to a host of reasons and, in reality, a commixture of them: the international community feeling overburdened by the ongoing war in the former Yugoslavia; a tentativeness by the international community about becoming immersed in another African ethnic conflict; and the continuing bitter aftertaste of the recent disaster in Somalia. Some even asserted that it was due to the fact that those in danger in Rwanda, unlike those in the former Yugoslavia, were black and that the Western powers cared less about their fate than they did that of white victims.

What it was not due to, though, was a dearth of information. In fact, throughout the early 1990s, the United Nations, the United States, and various European nations (including France and Belgium) were well aware about what was transpiring there (Barnett, 2002; Des Forges, 1999; Melvern, 2000; Power, 2002).

To add insult to injury, as the killing was underway, the United Nations Security Council scaled back the size and scope of the peacekeeping forces already present on the ground, and worked hard to ensure that no aid of a practical nature was sent to Rwanda (Barnett, 2002). Belgium, the former mandatory power in Rwanda, withdrew from Rwanda altogether, along with most other Western countries. France, after the worst of the killing had taken place, established a so-called "safe zone" in the south, but its ultimate effect was to protect the tens of thousands of Hutu killers who had poured into the area escaping the advancing Tutsi rebel army (Melvern, 2000, pp. 210-226).

Ultimately, the result was the so-called "machete genocide" in which at least 500,000 Tutsi men, women and children, along with moderate Hutus (e.g., non-extremist Hutus and/or those who attempted to defend the Tutsis from slaughter), were slain in a three month period.

In the introduction to its report entitled "International Panel of Eminent Personalities (IPEP): Report on the 1994 Genocide in Rwanda and Surrounding Events," the Organization of African Unity (2001) asserted that "the U.N.'s Rwandan failure was systemic and due to a lack of political will.... Just about every mistake that could be made was made" (p. 140). The Panel also declared that the U.N. had compromised its integrity by maintaining "insistent and utterly wrong-headed neutrality regarding the genocidaires" (Organization of African Unity, 2001, p. 140). Finally, the Panel found clear evidence that "a small number of major actors," including Belgium, France, and the United States, could have directly "prevented, halted, or reduced the slaughter" (Organization of African Unity, 2001, p. 140).

The Establishment of the ICTY and the ICTR

In 1993 and 1994 two ad-hoc international courts were established by the United Nations Security Council for the express purpose of trying those indicted for genocide, crimes against humanity, and war crimes, as they pertained to the former Yugoslavia and Rwanda. The International Criminal Tribunal for the former Yugoslavia (ICTY) and the International Criminal Tribunal for Rwanda (ICTR) have both been moderately successful (if excruciatingly slow) in bringing prosecutions, and in September 1998 the ICTR made history when it found Jean-Paul Akayesu, the former mayor of the Rwandan town of Taba, guilty of the crime of genocide. This was the first time any international court had issued such a verdict for this specific crime. Other prosecutions have followed, and case-law precedents in the law of genocide prosecutions are now growing.

It is noteworthy that during the trial of Jean-Paul Akayesu, Pierre Richard Prosper, a U.S. citizen serving as a prosecutor at the ICTR, argued passionately "to convince the court that sexual violence against women could be carried out with an intent that amounted to genocide" (Power, 2002, p. 485). As Power (2002) notes, Prosper argued that "a group could physically exist, or escape extermination, but be left so marginalized or so irrelevant to society that it was, in effect, destroyed" (p. 486). Ultimately, the ICTR found that the "systematic rape of Tutsi women in Rwanda's Taba commune was found to constitute the act of "causing serious bodily or mental harm to members of the group," and, as a result, Akayesu was found guilty of genocide.

International Criminal Court (ICC)

As if to demonstrate the firmness of the international community's resolve to do something about genocide--and to prove that impunity is no longer an option for those who commit it--the Rome Statute of the International Criminal Court (ICC) was adopted on 17 July 1998. The Court was established by the United Nations under the aegis of the UN Security Council. The Statute gives the Court jurisdiction for the crime of genocide, crimes against humanity, and war crimes. It is both an extension of the ICTY and the ICTR, and the fulfillment of the promises first articulated in the aftermath of 1945 (Schabas, 2001, pp. 1-21).

After considerable debate, the ICC decided to absorb the UN Convention on Genocide, including its definition, directly into its Charter. The Court became operative on 1 July 2002, after a minimum of sixty UN countries had ratified it. Notable among those refusing to ratify was the United States. Cognizant of the United States' intransigence, most European countries had earlier decided that the leadership of the United States would not be required for the purpose of establishing what was seen as a highly moral body, the purpose of which would be to assist in safeguarding the peace of the world and the lives of its citizens. Controversially, the United States promptly sought, and received, an agreement within the UN that would place U.S. citizens serving in foreign postings outside the Court's jurisdiction.

Srebrenica

Even when the international community attempted to be proactive, it did so in a haphazard manner with inadequate UN mandates and missions that were, more often than not, sorely under-manned, under-resourced and poorly supported. In fact, its half-hearted approach resulted in, and in some cases, even abetted (though inadvertently) the crimes against humanity and genocide that were perpetrated. The classic case was the tragedy that befell the so-called "safe area" of Srebrenica, in Bosnia, in July 1995.

The UN, NATO, and individual nations, such as the United States Great Britain had knowledge about and the wherewithal to prevent this genocide but basically chose not to do so. (For a detailed discussion of the factors that led the international community to allow Srebrenica to fall, see David Rhode's *End Game: The Betrayal and Fall of Srebrenica: Europe's Worst Massacre Since World War II*. New York: Farrar, Straus and Giroux, 1997.)

In 1993, Serb attacks on Bosnian Muslims increased in eastern Bosnia, and the latter fled from their homes and villages to seek protection in the nearby town of Srebrenica (and a thirty-square-mile area surrounding it), which had been designated a UN-sponsored "safe area." The "safe area" had been developed as a result of Security Council Resolution 819 on April 16, 1993. In part, the wording of the resolution read as follows: "...the Government of the Federal Republic of Yugoslavia (Serbia and Montenegro) should immediately, in pursuance of its undertaking in the Convention on the Prevention and Punishment of Genocide of 9 December 1948, take all measures within its power to prevent the commission of the crime of Genocide" (UN Security Council, 1993, p. 1). Subsequently, the UN forged an agreement in which the Muslim troops in the enclave of Srebrenica would disarm, the Serbs would halt their attacks on the Srebrenica enclave, and the UN would oversee and enforce the cease-fire.

While it is common knowledge that both the Serbs and Muslims periodically violated the agreement, the Serb forces were the ones who, over the years, applied ever-increasing pressure on the Muslims in Srebrenica--as well as on the Dutch peacekeepers (code-named Dutchbat) charged with protecting the safe area--by periodically shelling them, and preventing humanitarian assistance from entering the enclave.

As the attacks increased in number and ferocity, NATO authorities discussed the possibility of air strikes against Serb-held areas. However, the United Nations itself, along with many of the European nations that had contributed troops to the UNPROFOR peacekeeping mission, argued against the air strikes, asserting that such attacks would endanger their troops--both those on the ground and those who were being held hostage by the Serbs. As a result, the air-strikes were not carried out.

Though one debate after another was held by the Security Council regarding the safe area policy, the Council refused to provide, for example, the Dutchbat troops with an adequate mandate that would have helped to save innocent and imperiled people. And while the council made frequent promises to help the UN contingents protecting the safe areas, such promises were often not forthcoming.

The culmination of the constant harassment and attacks by the Serbs was the all-out attack and subsequent take over of Srebrenica on July 11, 1995. The attack was led by Ratko Mladic (the Bosnian Serb Army commander), Radislav Kristic (the commander of the Drina Corps), and others. Dutchbat was out-manned, under-resourced, on a highly restrictive Chapter VII mandate (which, in fact, constituted more of a Chapter VI or peacekeeping versus a peace enforcement mandate) and under-supported, even though it had been promised air support. Ultimately, the way in which the so-called safe area was established and "protected" was tantamount to making the Muslim people easy targets at the mercy of the heavily armed and well-trained Serb militia and troops.

Acting on the Serbs' orders, Dutchbat even expelled 5,000 people from the Dutchbat headquarters in Potocari, where the Muslims had gathered seeking protection. Ultimately, between 7,000 and 8,000 Muslim boys and men were captured by the Serbs, bussed to the woods murdered. Understandably, some have asserted that Srebrenica was "not so much a safe area as a besieged area" (War Crimes Watch, 1996, p. 2). Ultimately, the genocide in Srebrenica became the largest single act of genocide in Europe in since the Nazi Holocaust.

A Revision of *An Agenda for Peace*

In 1995, Bostros-Ghali issued his *Supplement to An Agenda for Peace,* which called for a rethinking of his earlier statement and a dramatic overhaul of UN peace operations. It was obvious to anyone who followed international matters that there had been and continued to be a major and catastrophic disconnect between what the UN had promised in its agendas and new programs, and the facts on the ground.

Among the major flaws Boutros-Ghali now addressed were the UN's dismal failure to differentiate between peacekeeping and peace enforcement mandates, the severe problems posed by missions that were under-manned and under-resourced, and the weaknesses and problems inherent in previous peace operation command structures. Again, there was hope among some that changes would be made by the U. and that by doing so peace operations would be more effective than they had been in the recent past.

Kosovo

In 1999, almost as an acknowledgment of a guilty conscience concerning their failure to act in Bosnia, the combined air forces of the United States, the United Kingdom, France, Germany, Italy, and the Netherlands, operating together as part of NATO, attacked Serbia with the intention of forcing the Serbs to stop their persecution of the ethnic Albanian population living in the Serbian province of Kosovo (Weymouth and Henig, 2001). It was the first occasion in which a war was fought for the express purpose of stopping a genocide before its worst horrors took place. Under international law, however, the attack was illegal; it was neither called for nor approved by the United Nations. Nonetheless, after a lengthy and intensive bombing campaign lasting three months, the Serbian regime of Slobodan Milosevic pulled its troops out of Kosovo. UN peacekeepers moved into the province, allowing the one million persecuted Kosovars, who had been expelled from the country in a huge outbreak of so-called "ethnic cleansing," to return home.

The NATO intervention in Kosovo is an example of how a potential genocide can be addressed early on if the international will to do so is present. Still, some were highly critical of the intervention due to the West's delayed reaction. Joyce P. Kaufman (1999) is one such critic:

> Despite the lessons of Bosnia, despite the clear indications that crisis was imminent, in the case of Kosovo, NATO still waited until armed conflict erupted before getting involved, and as was true with Bosnia, then reacted to the circumstances. Alliance leaders once again sought diplomatic and negotiated settlements before authorizing the use of force, holding out the threat of NATO military strikes should negotiations fail. But, as in the past, diplomatic initiatives continued long after it became apparent that they would come to naught, especially in the case of a leader like Slobodan Milosevic (p. 33).

The Kosovo intervention was even more severely criticized by those who viewed the intervention as illegal. Not only was there the issue of acting without the imprimatur of the UN, but the fact that many innocent people were killed as a direct result of NATO air sorties. Critics also asserted that the use of ground troops would have likely avoided a good number of the innocent deaths that resulted from the bombings. The controversy was so great that threats were made by various parties to bring the United States and NATO up on charges of genocide.

East Timor—An Anomaly?

For many years, the international response to what was happening in East Timor was one of indifference. Indonesia's neighbor, Australia, was especially keen not to antagonize the populous nation to its north, and was the first (and for a long time, only) country to recognize the *de jure* incorporation of East Timor into the body of Indonesia after the latter's invasion of the tiny ex-Portuguese territory in 1975 (Aubrey, 1998). United Nations resolutions calling on Indonesia to withdraw were ignored, and the United States, anxious lest a hard-line approach toward the annexation be seen by the Indonesians as a reason to look elsewhere for support--for example, to non-aligned nations--trod softly on the whole issue (Gunn, 1997). Only in 1999, after a long period of Indonesian oppression and the threat of another outbreak of genocidal violence (this time committed by Indonesian-backed militias and units of the Indonesian army), was East Timor freed. In 2002, the first parliament, elected by universal suffrage and guaranteed by the United Nations, allowed East Timor to take its place among the community of nations.

But the freedom did not come about without a great deal of violence, followed by international intervention. In 1999, in a U.N.-sponsored referendum, the people of East Timor voted overwhelmingly for independence. Immediately following the election, the Indonesian military and pro-Indonesian militia gangs went on a rampage that resulted in an estimated 1,500 people being killed and massive destruction throughout the territory (e.g., about 70 percent of East Timor's buildings were destroyed, telephone exchanges were wrecked, electrical lines ripped out, and farms burned to the ground). An estimated 800,000 people were forced into military-operated camps in Indonesian-controlled West Timor. Ultimately, the terror and killing drew international attention, and pressure was placed on the United Nations to act by various foreign ministries and human rights organizations. The killing and destruction only came to an end once international peacekeepers (who were authorized by the U.N. Security Council to use "all necessary measures" against violent militias) intervened to halt the violence and place East Timor under United Nations rule on September 20, 1999, some three weeks after the election. Ultimately, and notably, Indonesia voluntarily relinquished its claim to the territory. This came as a relief to the countries taking part in the intervention, for although the declared mission was to rescue civilians, "the unspoken premise was potentially explosive: the international community was effectively coming to the aid of a separatist movement in a sovereign nation" (King, 1999, p. A9). Had the international community not intervened when it did, many more innocent victims would almost certainly have been slaughtered--possibly in the tens of thousands or more.

Some claim that the intervention in East Timor bodes well for the future with regard to outside nations being proactive when crimes against humanity and/or potential genocide is on the horizon. Indeed, some assert that the actions undertaken by Australia constitute a precedent that could have profound implications for the future. Others are not so sanguine. For example, James Cotton argues that the 1999 intervention in East Timor was an anomaly, and for that reason the intervention is not an indication of a change of principle regarding the "sanctity" of non-interference in the region. More specifically, he states that

> The principle of non-interference is an integral part of the "Asian Way." Countries of the region have doggedly opposed any suggestion that state sovereignty should be softened by a new doctrine of "humanitarian intervention." The participation of some countries in the 1999 intervention in East Timor–an action sanctioned by the United Nations for specifically humanitarian purposes–was thus out of character. But this departure, far from reflecting a re-evaluation of doctrine, was a consequence of specific historical and political factors, most important of these was the fact that the UN had never accepted the Indonesian incorporation of the territory as legitimate. Once the United States adopted a more critical attitude, after Australia pressured Indonesia to test local opinion on East Timor's future, the internationalization of the issue became inevitable. In the aftermath of the post-ballot militia violence, Indonesia's uncertain transitional leadership could not resist calls for an intervention by peacekeepers. There are certainly lessons in the East Timor case for coalition operations and other interventions. But the actions of the Australia-led coalition do not indicate a wider regional acceptance of the norm of humanitarian intervention (Cotton, 2001, p. 127).

The "Brahimi Panel"

On 7 March 2000, Secretary General Kofi Annan convened the Panel on United Nations Peace Operations "to undertake a thorough review of the United Nations peace and security activities, and to present a clear set of specific, concrete and practical recommendations to assist the United Nations in conducting such activities better in the future" (p. I).[2]

In the Introduction to the *Report*, the authors commented as follows:

> Over the last decade, the United Nations has repeatedly failed to meet the challenge [of addressing complex peace operations], and it can do no better today. Without renewed commitment on the part of Member States, significant institutional change and increased financial support, the United Nations will not be capable of executing the critical peacekeeping and peace- building tasks that the Member States assign it in coming months and years.... [W]hen the United Nations send[s] its forces to uphold the peace, they must be prepared to confront the lingering forces of war and violence, with the ability and determination to defeat them.... For preventive initiatives to suceed in reducing tension and averting conflict, the Secretary-General needs clear, strong and sustained political support from Member States. Furthermore, as the United Nations has bitterly and repeatedly discovered over the last decade, no amount of good intentions can substitute for the fundamental ability to project credible force if complex peace-keeping, in particular, is to succeed.... Moreover, the changes that the Panel recommends will have no lasting impact unless Member States summon the political will to support the United Nations politically, financially and operationally (UN, 2000, p. i).

"The Responsibility to Protect: Report of the International Commission on Intervention and State Sovereignty" (ICISS)

In light of the international community's abysmal record vis-a-vis halting crimes against humanity and genocide prior to the deaths of tens of thousands, if not millions, of people, various individuals and parties began exploring "the question of when, if ever, it is appropriate for states to take coercive–and in particular military—action against another state for the purpose of protecting people at risk in that other state" (International Commission on Intervention and State Sovereignty, 2001, p. 1). The International Commission on Intervention and State Sovereignty (ICISS) was asked by UN Secretary General Kofi Annan to address a wide range of questions (legal, moral, operational and political) in regard to the issue of "the right of humanitarian intervention." The upshot of the Commission's study, discussions and debates was that "the idea that sovereign states have a responsibility to protect their own citizens from avoidable catastrophe, but that when they are unwilling or unable to do so, that responsibility must be borne by the broader community of states" (p. 1).

As to what this forward-looking document (and the recommendations therein) will result in over the long haul, only time will tell. However, based on the current fiasco in Darfur, Sudan (a weak mandate with an under-manned, under-trained, and under-resourced mission), the recommendations of the report appears to have largely fallen on deaf ears.

Darfur

The Arab and the "black Africans" of the Sudanese province Darfur, all of whom are Muslim, traditionally lived in relative peace. Though much of Darfur is comprised of stark and forbidding desert, some areas have been cultivated. While these areas were primarily occupied by sedentary farmers and cattle owners who tended to be black Africans, at various times during each year the grazing areas were used by semi-nomadic Arabs for grazing their cattle and camels. The livestock, in turn, fertilized and renewed the soil for subsequent growing seasons. While local disputes between the two groups were not uncommon, they were generally resolved in a peaceful manner.

This relationship, however, began to fray in the 1970s, and in successive decades it disintegrated altogether as drought and desertification vastly increased competition for fewer and fewer natural resources. Over time, as weapons seeped and then flooded into Darfur from battles raging in the region (both in Chad and southern Sudan) the traditional methods of resolving disputes were generally overtaken by heavily armed self-defense groups and militias.

At one and the same time, many black Africans grew increasingly irritated that while their needs were largely ignored by the Sudanese government, Arab groups were being accorded the very rights, resources and assistance that they (the black Africans) sought. Ultimately, out of sheer frustration, black African rebel groups began attacking Government of Sudan (GOS) facilities. In February 2003, the ever-increasing tension exploded into a heated and prolonged conflict when the GOS began to carry out a violent campaign purportedly against two rebel groups (the Sudan Liberation Army or SLA and the Justice and Equality Movement or JEM) as a result of the latter's attacks on government facilities. More specifically, in retaliation against the rebel groups, the GOS and the *Janjaweed* (Arab militia) not only engaged in battles with the rebel groups, but carried out a scorched earth policy against civilians (primarily members of the Massalit, Fur, and Zaghawa tribal groups) that share the same ethnicity as the rebel groups. In so doing, the GOS and the *Janjaweed* burned down hundreds of villages, carried out ethnic cleansing (in which over two million people have been driven from their homes), and committed mass rapes, mass killings, and, according to the United States government and many scholars and human rights activists, genocide. Estimates of those who have been killed and/or died from injuries, illnesses, and/or malnutrition range from 250,000 to over 400,000. Based on a careful examination of mortality rates in Darfur, various scholars and human rights organizations believe the larger number is the more accurate of the two.

Beginning in December 2003, various national and international bodies began focusing attention on the situation in Darfur and calling on the international community to step in to halt the ongoing killing and mass rape of the black African civilians.

Following a U.S. State Department-sponsored investigation (the Darfur Atrocities Documentation Team--ADT) in Chad in July and August 2004, U.S. Secretary of State Colin Powell declared, on September 9, 2004, that genocide had been (and possibly continued to be) perpetrated in Darfur. At the same time, Powell called on the international community to act to stanch the killing.

Subsequently, December 2004 and January 2005 the United Nations conducted its own investigation, the Commission of Inquiry (COI), and upon the conclusion of its field-based study, it declared that crimes against humanity were definitely being committed, but asserted that it could not, at the time, declare that genocide had been perpetrated.

In the months following the ADT's and COI's findings, the international community and individual nations supported a Chapter VI intervention in Darfur by the African Union (AU). The trouble, however, is that the AU's mandate was an inadequate one of peacekeeping rather than peace enforcement, meaning that AU troops would not be permitted to engage GOS troops and *Janjaweed* in battle if they caught the latter attacking civilians in their villages or in internally displaced persons' camps. And while the UN, NATO, and numerous individual nations (e.g., including Canada, the United States, and Great Britain) provided transport and key supplies for AU troops (and hundreds of millions of dollars for humanitarian support of the victim population), not a single nation outside of Africa volunteered to send troops to help halt the killing and mass rape.

Throughout 2005, the violence in Darfur flowed and ebbed, but then exploded again in October of that year. As of December 2005, various sources estimate that several thousand people a month continue to die in Darfur as a result of outright murder or unattended injuries, sickness and/or starvation or dehydration.

Conclusion

Following the end of the Cold War, it appeared that a sea change could be taking place in international relations regarding the willingness of nations to intervene in the prevention of genocide. Yet, as Geoffrey Robertson (2000) notes in his book, *Crimes Against Humanity: The Struggle for Global Justice*:

> It was not until 1993, after the Cold War was over and as the spectre of "ethnic cleansing" returned to Europe, that there was sufficient superpower resolve to apply the *proviso* to Article 2(7) [of the United Nations Charter, which reads, in part, "Nothing contained in the present Charter shall authorize the United Nations to intervene in matters which are essentially within the domestic jurisdiction of any State..."], namely that it could be overridden by Chapter VII. This is the chapter of the Charter which permits the Security Council to order armed intervention against any state once it has determined that such a response is necessary to restore international peace and security. Since Article 55 expressly makes the observance of human rights a condition necessary for peaceful relations, the appalling crimes against humanity [and genocide] which occurred after 1945 could have been forcibly combated by the UN under its Chapter VII power, but until the Balkan atrocities in the 1990s, the Security Council never sought or even thought to invoke military action upon human rights grounds (p. 25).

That is true, but, in fact, did a sea change occur? In actuality, the verdict is still out.

Certainly, the issue of "sovereignty" in the post-Cold War period has come under closer scrutiny and is no longer seen, in certain cases at least, as sacrosanct. Thus, a nation committing genocide or other egregious human rights violations against its own people is no longer perceived as untouchable. Indeed, such situations are no longer automatically deemed a matter of "internal affairs."

While change is in the air (e.g., in certain notable cases, the international community did act in concert to stave off potential genocides), the jury is still out in regard to whether or not the international community is truly going to dedicate itself to genocide prevention. When all is said and done, between 1990 and 2005, there was more talk than action when it came to the prevention of genocide. And that is not only true of the leaders and bureaucrats of individual nations and international organizations, but also the developers of early warning systems, genocide scholars, and those NGOs concerned with the issue of genocide.

What the international community needs, desperately, is the development of a proactive and effective regime to prevent genocide. Whether the latter will ever become a reality remains a question mark.

(Note: For a discussion of recent and current efforts in the realm of genocide prevention, see Chapter "4" by Samuel Totten. Also see Chapter "11" by Greg Stanton.)

Notes

1. The "Somalia factor" resulted from a bloody fiasco in which the United States found itself in Somalia in October 1993. In an attempt to capture those responsible for killing over twenty Pakistani peacekeepers, elite U.S. forces engaged in a fierce battle with the militia troops of Mohammed Farah Aideed that resulted in the deaths of eight U.S. soldiers and the wounding of over seventy-three. Adding insult to injury, a dead U.S. soldier was stripped of his clothes and dragged through the streets of Mogadishu, a horrific image that was broadcast across the globe. The image and impact of the entire mission soured the leadership in Washington, D.C. on humanitarian missions. The backlash from the killings of the Pakistanis and the U.S. soldiers also cut into, if not partially gutted, the optimism of Boutros-Ghali's *Agenda for Peace*.
2. The Panel was chaired by former Algerian Foreign Minister Lakhdar Brahimi, and as a result the Panel's report is now commonly referred to as "The Brahimi Report." The rest of the Panel was composed of individuals with eclectic and significant experience in the areas of conflict prevention, peacekeeping and peace-building.

References

Aubrey, J. (Ed.) (1998). *Free East Timor: Australia's Culpability in East Timor's Genocide*. Sydney: Vintage/Random House Australia.

Barnett, Michael (2002). *Eyewitness to a Genocide: The United Nations and Rwanda*. Ithaca, NY: Cornell University Press.

Boutros-Ghali, Boutros (1992). *Agenda for Peace*. New York: United Nations.

Boutros-Ghali, Boutros (1995). *Supplement to an Agenda for Peace*. New York: United Nations.

Cotton, James (2001). "Against the Grain: The East Timor Intervention." *Survival: The IISS Quarterly*, Spring, 43(1):127-142.

Dallaire, Roméo (2003). *Shake Hands With the Devil: The Failure of Humanity in Rwanda*. New York: Carroll & Graf Publishers.

Des Forges, Alison (1999). *"Leave None to Tell the Story": Genocide in Rwanda*. New York: Human Rights Watch.

Fein, Helen (1994). "An Interview with Alison L. Des Forges: Genocide in Rwanda Was Foreseen and Could Have Been Deterred," pp. 21-31. In Helen Fein, Helen (Ed.) *The Prevention of Genocide: Rwanda and Yugoslavia Reconsidered*. New York: Institute for the Study of Genocide.

Gunn, G. C. (1997). *East Timor and the United Nations: The Case for Intervention*. Lawrenceville, NJ: Red Sea Press.

International Commission Intervention and State Sovereignty (2001). *The Responsibility to Protect: Report of the International Commission on Intervention and State Sovereignty*. Ottawa: International Development Research Centre.

Kaufman, Joyce P. (1999). "NATO and the Former Yugoslavia: Crisis, Conflict and the Atlantic Alliance." *The Journal of Conflict Studies*. Fall, 19(2): 5-38.

King, L. (1999). "Indonesian Pullout Marks End of Struggle, Dawn of Independence." September 31, *Northwest Arkansas Times*, p. A9.

Melvern, L. R. (2000). *A People Betrayed: The Role of the West in Rwanda's Genocide*. London: Zed Books.

Organization of African Unity (OAU) (2001). "International Panel of Eminent Personalities (IDEP): Report on the 1994 Genocide in Rwanda and Surrounding Events." *International Legal Materials*, 40:140-235.

Power, Samantha (2002). *"A Problem from Hell": America and Age of Genocide*. New York: Basic Books.

Robertson, Geoffrey (2000). *Crimes Against Humanity: The Struggle for Global Justice*. New York: The New Press.

United Nations Security Council (1993). "United Nations: Security Council Resolution on Establishing an International Tribunal for the Prosecution of Persons Responsible for Serious Violations of International Law (sic) Humanitarian Law Committed in the Territory of the Former Yugoslavia." *International Legal Materials*, 32, 1203-1205.

United Nations (2000). *Report of the Panel on United Nations Peace Operations*. New York: Author.

War Crimes Watch (1996). "Srebrenica: The Call for Justice." *War Crimes Watch*. 2 pp. members.tripod.com/~Bregava/SREBRENICA2

Weiss, Thomas G. (1993). "Intervention and Genocide." *The ISG* [Institute for the Study of Genocide] *Newsletter*, Fall, 11:6-7.

Weymouth, T., and Henig, S. (Eds.) (2001). *The Kosovo Crisis: The Last American War in Europe?* London: Reuters.

Annotated Bibliography

Prevention

Auerswald, Philip E., and Auerswald, David P. (2000). *The Kosovo Conflict: A Diplomatic History Through Documents*. The Hague: Kluwer Law International. 1285 pp.

This book is comprised of the following twelve chapters: 1. Nationalism, April 1987-1998; 2. Building the Sanctions Regime, February-July 1998; 3. "Looking for a Strategy," July-September 1998; 4. "Military Threats and Observer Mission, September 23-October 29, 1998; Chapter 5. "Renewed Violence, November 1998-January 28, 1999; 6. "Rambouillet: The Prelude to War, January 29-March 23, 1999"; 7. "NATO Begins Bombing Campaign, March 24-April 13, 1999"; 8. "NATO Campaign Under Scrutiny After Mistaken Bombings of Train and Civilian Convoy, April 13-April 19, 1999"; 9. "NATO Leaders Gather for 50th Anniversary Summit, Convey Unity on Bombing Campaign, April 22-May 7, 1999"; 10. "NATO Bombs Strike Chinese Embassy; 11. War Crimes Tribunal Indicts Milosevic, May 8-Mary 27, 1999"; and 12. "Yugoslavia Accepts G-8 Terms, Military Conflicts Ends, May 29-June 21, 1999." Among the hundreds of documents included herein are speeches by key actors; excerpts from press reports/releases; excerpts from communiqués; resolutions issued by various actors; government cables; reports; memoranda; excerpts from interviews; excerpts from government briefings; peace plans/agreements; pacts; and indictments.

Barnett, Michael (2002). *Eyewitness to a Genocide: The United Nations and Rwanda*. Ithaca, NY: Cornell University Press. 215 pp.

This is a thought-provoking and well written book that examines the history of the U.N's involvement in Rwanda prior to, during and following the 1994 Rwandan genocide. Barnett, a professor of political science at the University of Wisconsin at Madison, provides ample evidence as to how UN personnel were well aware of what was transpiring in Rwanda and yet failed to act—not, he claims, due to incompetence but reasoned choices "underlain by moral considerations." Ultimately, he argues that the bureaucratic culture of the UN resulted in the totally inadequate response to the numerous early warnings signals that a genocide was in the making as well as to the ongoing and desperate pleas by Roméo Dallaire, the force commander of the UN troops based in Rwanda, for a stronger mandate and more troops with which to stop the genocide.

Daalder, Ivo H., and O'Hanlon, Michael E. (2000). *Winning Ugly: NATO's War to Save Kosovo*. Washington, DC: Brookings Institution Press. 343 pp.

An in-depth examination of the causes, conduct and consequences of the war in Kosovo in which the United States and NATO ultimately bombed Serbian troops into submission, forcing them to withdraw from Kosovo, but in the end allowed the Serbs to continue to drive hundreds of thousands of Albanians from their homes and more than 800,000 from their country.

Dallaire, Roméo (2005). *Shake Heads with the Devil: The Failure of Humanity in Rwanda, 1993-1994*. New York: Carroll & Graf Publishers. 562 pp.
Dallaire, who served as the force commander of the UN troops in Rwanda prior to, during and following the 1994 genocide, provides an overview as to how Rwanda degenerated into genocide, detailed and horrifying descriptions of the atrocities, and key insights into the failure of the United Nations (the Security Council, UN Secretary General Boutros-Boutros Ghali, and others), individual nations (including the United States which refused to acknowledge that genocide was being perpetrated in Rwanda) and others to halt the genocide.

Genocide Studies and Prevention (2007). Special Issue ("The Prevention of Genocide: Ideas from International Politics and a Symposium on International Law") of *Genocide Studies and Prevention: An International Journal*, Spring, 2(1).

This special issue edited by Herb Hirsch, professor of political science at Virginia Commonwealth University, is comprised of the following articles: "Halting Genocide: Rhetoric Versus Reality" by Thomas Weiss; A Symposium on David Scheffer's "Genocide and Atrocity Crimes" ("Semantics or Substance? David Scheffer's Welcome Proposal to Strengthen Criminal Accountability for Atrocities" by William A. Schabas; "Naming Horror: Legal and Political Words for Mass Atrocities" by Martha Minow; "A Commentary on David Scheffer's Concepts of Genocide and Atrocity Crimes" by Sevane Garibian; "In the Footsteps of Raphael Lemkin" by Michael J. Bazyler; "What's in a Name? Reflections on Using, Not Using, and Overusing the 'G' Word" by Martin Mennecke); Critical Commentaries ("Proliferation of Terminology and the Illusion of Progress" by Payam Akhavan and "David Scheffer's 'Genocide and Atrocity Crimes': A Response" by Mark Levene); and David Scheffer Responds ("The Merits of Unifying Terms: 'Atrocity Crimes' and 'Atrocity Law'" by David Scheffer).

Power, Samantha (2002). *"A Problem from Hell": America and the Age of Genocide*. New York: Basic Books. 610 pp.

This Pulitzer Prize-winning book includes extremely insightful chapters on the U.S. reactions to genocides perpetrated throughout the twentieth century, including the following that were perpetrated in the 1990s: Bosnia, Rwanda, Srebrenica, and Kosovo.

Prunier, Gérard (1997). *The Rwanda Crisis: History of a Genocide*. New York: Columbia University Press. 424 pp.

Prunier, a journalist and Africa scholar, presents a thorough examination of the genesis and perpetration of the Rwandan genocide. In doing so, he discusses the ideological, political and economic aspects beyond the decision and actions that ultimately led to over 500,000 Tutsis and moderate Hutus being murdered in a three month period in 1994.

The book is comprised of the following ten chapters: 1. "Rwandese Society and the Colonial Impact: The Making of a Cultural Mythology (1894-1959)"; 2. "The Hutu Republic (1959-1990)"; 3. "Civil War and Foreign Intervention (October 1990-July 1991)"; 4. "Slouching Towards Democracy (July 1991-June 1992)"; 5. "The Arusha Peace Marathon (June 1992-August 1993)"; 6. "Chronicle of a Massacres Foretold (4 August 1993-6 April 1994)"; 7. "Genocide and Renewed War (6 April-14 June 1994)"; 8. "'Opération Turquoise' and Götterdämmerung in Central Africa (14 June-21 August 1994)"; 9. "Aftermath or New Beginning? (22 August-31 December 1994)"; and 10. Living in a Broken World."

Rohde, David (1997). *End Game: The Betrayal and Fall of Srebrenica: Europe's Worst Massacre Since World War II*. New York: Farrar, Straus and Giroux. 440 pp.

This Pulitzer Prize-winning book delineates in great detail the fall of Srebrenica in 1995. In doing so, Rhode provides a blow-by-blow account of the actions on the ground, the UN's totally inept handling of the situation, and the ways in which various nations (including the United States, France, Great Britain and the Bosnian government allowed 40,000 Muslims to fall into the hands of the Serbs during which 7,000 to 8,000 Muslim boys and men were slaughtered.

Totten, Samuel (Ed.) (2005). *Genocide at the Millennium: Genocide: A Critical Bibliographic Review*. New Brunswick, NJ: Transaction Publishers. 302 pp.

Numerous chapters in this book address various issues germane to the prevention and intervention of genocide (or lack thereof) in the 1990s: "Genocide in Bosnia and Herzegovina" by Eric Markusen and Martin Mennecke; "The Rwanda Genocide" by Howard Adelman; "Genocide in Kosovo" by Peter Ronayne; "The Role of Nongovernmental Organizations in Addressing the Prevention, Intervention and Punishment of Genocide in the 1980s, 1990s and Early 2000s" by Samuel Totten; "The United Nations and Genocide: Prevention, Intervention, and Prosecution" by Samuel Totten and Paul R. Bartrop; "The Role of Individual States in Addressing Case of Genocide" by Kenneth J. Campbell"; and "The International Legal Prohibition of Genocide Comes of Age" by William A. Schabas. Each chapter is comprised of an essay and an annotated bibliography germane to the focus of the essay

Totten, Samuel (Compiler/Editor) (2007). *The Prevention and Intervention of Genocide: An Annotated Bibliography*. New York: Routledge, 1153 pp.

This bibliography is comprised of 2,353 annotations. The annotations are placed under twenty-three headings: 1. United Nations Charter; 2. Chapter VI of the UN Charter; 3. Chapter VII of the UN Charter; 4. United Nations Convention on the Prevention and Punishment of Genocide (UNCG); 5. International Law and Genocide; 6. Sovereignty; 7. *Realpolitik*; 8. Potential Sources/Causes of Conflict and/or Violence (including Crimes Against Humanity and/or Genocide); 9. Prevention: Early Warning System; 10. Prevention: Early Warning Indicators/Signals of

Potential Crimes Against and/or Genocide; 11. Preventive Measures; 12. Prevention of Genocide; 13. Components of Intervention; 14. Intervention of Genocide; 15. The UN and the Prevention and Intervention of Genocide; 16. Post-Conflict; 17. Courts and Tribunals; 18. The International Criminal Court (ICC); 19. Organizations; 20. Education and Training; 21. Journals: A Select List; 22. Newsletters; and 23. Bibliographies.

Totten, Samuel, and Markusen, Eric (Eds.) (2006). *Genocide in Darfur: Investigating Atrocities in the Sudan.* New York: Routledge. 284 pp.

In this book, the contributors address different facets of the U.S. State Department's Atrocities Documentation Project in which twenty-four investigators were sent to refugee camps along the Chad/Sudan border to interview refugees about their experiences in Darfur at the hands of the Government of Sudan troops and the *Janjaweed* (Arab militia). The data collected by the investigators in their 1,130 interviews were analyzed by the U.S. State Department in order to ascertain whether genocide had been perpetrated against the black Africans. Based on an analysis of the data, Secretary of State Colin Powell announced, on September 9, 2004, that the GOS had committed genocide and was still possibly committing genocide.

The book is comprised of the following: Part 1: The Background (1. "Disaster in Darfur: Historical Overview" by Robert O. Colllins; 2. "Moving Beyond the Sense of Alarm" by Andrew S. Natsios); Part II: The Investigation (3. "Creating the ADT: Turning a Good Idea into Reality" by Nina Bang-Jensen and Stefanie Frease; 4. "Survey Methodology and the Darfur Genocide by Jonathan P. Howard; 5. "The Critical Link: Interpreters" by Helge Niska; 6. "Moving into the Field and Conducting Interviews: Commentary and Observations by the Investigators" by Samuel Totten and Eric Markusen); Part 3: The Genocide Determination (7. "Making the Determination of Genocide in Darfur" by Stephen A. Kostas; 8. "A New Chapter of Irony: The Legal Definition of Genocide and the Implications of Powell's Determination by Jerry Fowler"; and 9. "Prosecuting Gender Crimes Committed in Darfur: Holding Leaders Accountable for Sexual Violence" by Kelly Dawn Askin); Part 4. The Significance of the Darfur Atrocities Documentation Project: A Precedent for the Future? The Perspective of 'Outsiders': (10. "The Darfur Atrocities Documentation Project: A Precedent for the Future? A Perspective from Washington, D.C." by Taylor Seybolt; 11. "From Rwanda to Darfur: Lessons Learned?" by Gerald Caplan; 12.

"Proving Genocide in Darfur: The Atrocities Documentation Project and Resistance to Its Findings" by Gregory H. Stanton; 12. "'Atrocity' Statistics' and Other Lessons from Dafur" by Scott Straus); and Part 5: Analysis of the Rationale and Reasoning (14. "The U.S. Investigation into the Darfur Crisis and Its Determination of Genocide: A Critical Analysis").

Intervention

Abiew, Francis Kofi (1999). *The Evolution of the Doctrine and Practice of Humanitarian Intervention*. The Hague: Kluwer Law International. 325 pp.

The author defends the emergence of the right to humanitarian intervention, and argues that state sovereignty is not incompatible with the latter. Following a review of historical precedents, Abiew concludes by assessing contemporary developments in terms of sources and support for intervention humanitarian grounds.

The book is comprised of four chapters, plus an introduction and conclusion: 1. "The Traditional Doctrine and Practice of Humanitarian Intervention" (Historical Evolution of State Sovereignty and the Doctrine and Practice of Humanitarian Intervention: a. State Sovereignty, b. Humanitarian Intervention, and c. State Practice in the Nineteenth and Early Twentieth Century); 2. "The Right of Humanitarian Intervention in the Post-Charter Era (1945-1989)" (Evolving Norms: a. Principles of State Sovereignty and Non-Intervention, b. The Internationalization of Human Rights; c. The UN Charter's Effect on Humanitarian Intervention; Case Studies of State Practice from 1945-1989 -- The East Pakistan (Bangladesh) Intervention of 1971; The Tanzanian Intervention in Uganda of 1979, and Vietnam's Intervention in Cambodia (Kampuchea, 1978)); 3. "The Practice of Humanitarian Intervention in the Post Cold War Era" (Northern Iraq, Somalia, The Former Yugoslavia, Rwanda); and 4. "Assessing Humanitarianism in the Post Cold War Period: Sources of Consensus."

Beach, Hugh (2000). "Secessions, Interventions, and Just War Theory: The Case of Kosovo," pp. 11-36. In Pugwash Study Group (Ed.) *Pugwash Study Group on Intervention, Sovereignty and International Security.* Cambridge, MA: Council of the Pugwash Conferences on Science and

World Affairs.

A fascinating and informative essay on the issue of the evolution, justification and use of intervention in the so-called "internal affairs" of nations, using Kosovo (late 1990s) as a case study.

Bring, Ove (1999). "Should NATO Take the Lead in Formulating a Doctrine on Humanitarian Intervention?" *NATO Review*, Autumn, 47(3):24-27.

Bring, a professor of international law at the Swedish Defense College and Stockholm University, argues that there is an urgent need to formulate a doctrine on humanitarian intervention—one that builds on the emerging international norm that gives precedence to the protection of human rights over sovereignty in certain circumstances—and that NATO (the North Atlantic Treaty Organization) should take the lead on this.

Ciechanski, Jerzy (1997). "Enforcement Measures Under Chapter VII of the UN Charter: UN Practice After the Cold War," pp. 82-104. In Michael Pugh (Ed.) *The UN, Peace, and Force*. London: Frank Cass and Company.

This provocative essay is comprised of the following sections: Post-Cold War Resolutions Under Chapter VII; Chapter VII as Legitimizer of Legal Uses of Force; The Mistake of "Forcible Peacekeeping"; and International Legislation by the Security Council. Among the conflicts alluded to and/or discussed are those in the former Yugoslavia, the plight of the Kurds in northern Iraq, and the 1994 genocide in Rwanda.

Cotton, James (2001). "Against the Grain: The East Timor Intervention." *Survival: The IISS Quarterly*, Spring, 43(1):127-142.

In this thought-provoking essay, Cotton, a professor in the School of Politics at the Australian Defence Force Academy, University of New South Wales, argues that the 1999 intervention in East Timor was an anomaly in the region, and for that reason that intervention is not an indication of a change of principle regarding the "sanctity" of non-interference in the region.

Deng, Francis (Ed.) (1996). *Sovereignty as Responsibility: Conflict Management in Africa*. Washington, DC: Brookings Institution. 265 pp.

The collective authors herein address the question as to whether the international community should continue to abide by the longtime principle of nonintervention in the internal affairs of sovereign states, provided that their domestic politics do not constitute a "threat to international peace." All argue that it should not. Instead, they argue that sovereignty should be viewed as "conditional, for inherent in the concept of sovereignty is that of the responsibility to honor a social contract in which the legitimacy of leaders is based on their actions to ensure that their citizens' basic human rights are guaranteed" (p. 1). Furthermore, they argue that when those states, for whatever reason, fail to honor and protect such rights then they have no choice but to accept the right of other nations or international organizations to intervene in order to assist the endangered populations and to bring the conflict to a peaceful resolution.

Evans, Gareth, and Sahnoun, Mohamed (2002). "The Responsibility to Protect." *Foreign Affairs*, 81(6): 99-110.

Gareth (President and Chief Executive Officer of the International Crisis Group and former Foreign Minister of Australia) and Sahnoun (Special Adviser on Africa to the UN Secretary General and a former senior Algerian diplomat) argue that the dichotomy between those in favor of intervention when gross human rights are being violated in a country versus those who hold sovereignty to be sacrosanct needs to "be reframed not an as argument about the 'right to intervene' but about the 'responsibility to protect.' And it has to be accepted that although this responsibility is owed by all sovereign states to their own citizens in the first instance, it must be picked up by the international community if that first—tier responsibility is abdicated, or if it cannot be exercised" (p. 101). The article is comprised of the following sections: Sovereignty as Responsibility; Military Intervention: Setting the Bar; Operation Just Cause; Precautionary Principles; and The Problem of Political Will.

Gow, James (1998). "Nations, States, and Sovereignty: Meanings and Challenges in Post-Cold War International Security," pp. 171-210. In Christopher Dandeker (Ed.) *Nationalism and Violence*. New Brunswick, NJ: Transaction Publishers.

This essay is comprised of the following sections: The Sovereign State System; Nationalism, Sovereignty, and Self-Determination; The Serbian Snake; Sovereignty and Self-Determination: Yugoslavia and the Meaning of Nation; Chapter VII Measures: Intervention and Enforcement After the Cold War; and "Sovereignty and Security: New Bearings."

Gunter, Michael M. (1994). "The Kurdish Peacekeeping Operation in Northern Iraq, 1991," pp. 97-110. In David A. Charters (Ed.) *Peacekeeping and the Challenge of Civil Conflict Resolution*. New Brunswick: Centre for Conflict Studies, University of New Brunswick.

Gunter's conclusion to his essay is informative and telling:

> The imperfect, but effective, UN collective security operation against Iraq following that state's conquest of Kuwait in August 1990 eventually led to an equally flawed, but still useful, peacekeeping operation to help save the Kurds from the further depredations of Saddam Hussein after their failed uprising in March 1991. At a time when many were hailing the new effectiveness of the UN, it is ironic that world organization was forced into this peace-keeping operation only because the supposedly defeated Hussein was still able to triumph over the Kurds and then force them into a deadly flight into the mountains on the Iranian and Turkish borders.
>
> The UN's response proved to be a unique peace-keeping operation because, in effect, it was taking the side of the Iraqi Kurds and the allies against Iraq. This situation patently contrasted with the criterion of impartiality previous peacekeeping operations had possessed.
>
> What is more, for the first time, the UN had declared in Security Council 688 of 5 April 1991 that "the repression of the Iraqi civilian population, including most recently, Kurdish populated areas" could "threaten international peace and security." *In other words, the Council was saying that circumstances may arise in which extraordinary humanitarian needs would compel the world organization to intervene in the internal affairs of a sovereign state under the collective security provisions of UN Charter Chapter VII* (italics added). If so, this was certainly a precedent-setting declaration (p. 106).

The essay is comprised of the following sections: Origins, Safe Havens, The UN Begins to Move, Implementation, Finances, and Conclusions.

Holzgrefe, J. L., and Keohane, Robert (Eds.) (2003). *Humanitarian Intervention: Ethical, Legal and Political Dilemmas*. New York: Cambridge University Press. 400 pp.

The essays in this book address the various ethical, legal and political conditions under which humanitarian intervention can be justified. They also address the complexities inherent in such actions as well as the inherent dangers. Several of the essays discuss the ongoing legal discussions which, in part, deal with the identification of both principles and precedents for establishing new doctrines vis-à-vis humanitarian intervention, and in doing so, note the pros and cons of such actions and pay particular attention to the issue of sovereignty. The issue of the 1999 NATO Kosovo intervention is mentioned repeatedly as the authors discuss the tension between the protection of sovereignty and the perceived necessity of humanitarian action.

International Commission on Intervention and State Sovereignty (2001). *The Responsibility to Protect: Report of the International Commission on Intervention.* Two Volumes. Ottawa: International Development Research Centre. 110 pp. (Volume 1) and 426 pp. (Volume 2). Ottawa, ON, Canada: International Development Research Centre.

Volume One, *The Responsibility to Protect,* reflects the effort by the International Commission on Intervention and State Sovereignty (established by the government of Canada and a group of major foundations) to erect a conceptual bridge between issues related to intervention and sovereignty. In developing the book, the aim of the twelve member committee was to develop a framework that delineates (1) the complexities and problems inherent in intervention and (2) effective ways as to intervene in humanitarian crises. The committee consulted policy-makers, government leaders and scholars from across the globe, and the insights and suggestions of the latter are reflected in the report.

Volume Two, which was developed under the leadership of Thomas Weiss and Don Hubert, includes background information, research findings, and a major bibliography that addresses a wide range of issues (conceptual, ethical, legal, political, and operational) related to intervention.

What is particularly unique about the work of the International Commission is that it—following careful and close interpretation of the United Nations Charter, international law, and the sea-change in perspective as a result of the human rights regime of the latter half of the twentieth century—reconceptualized the concept of "sovereignty" to be understood as "the responsibility of a state to protect its citizens" (especially those most at risk)—and the case where a state fails to protect all of its citizens then—but only then—can the international community intervene for the express purpose of protecting the population at risk.

International Commission on Intervention and State Sovereignty. (2001). "State Sovereignty," pp. 5-13. In The International Commission on Intervention and State Sovereignty's *The Responsibility to Protect: Research, Bibliography, Background: Supplementary Volume to the Report of the International Commission on Intervention and State Sovereignty.* Ottawa, ON, Canada: International Development Research Centre.

This highly informative section of one of the most, if not the most, detailed and significant reports of late on the issues of intervention and state sovereignty addresses the following issues: Meaning and Purpose of Sovereignty; Limits of Sovereignty, and Emerging Challenges to Sovereignty.

Mays, Terry M. (2002). *The 1999 United Nations and 2000 Organization of African Unity Formal Inquiries: A Retrospective Examination of Peacekeeping and the Rwandan Crisis of 1994* (Paper Number 7 of the Pearson Papers). Clementsport, Nova Scotia: The Canadian Peacekeeping Press of the Pearson Peacekeeping Centre. 37 pp.

Several of the major factors regarding the failure of the peacekeeping operation in Rwanda are highlighted within the UN and OAU investigations, and each is explored in this study. Also discussed is whether the 2,000 member UN-peacekeeping operation in Rwanda could have halted the genocide had the political will existed to accomplish the task. Five options for the future are reviewed and a postscript includes a brief discussion of the relationship between state sovereignty and humanitarian intervention as delineated in the International Commission on Intervention and State Sovereignty.

Totten, Samuel (2004). "The Intervention and Prevention of Genocide: Sisyphean or Doable?" *Journal of Genocide Research*, 6(2):29-247.

Discusses such issues as detecting genocide early on, the tentativeness to intervene, the issue of state sovereignty, garnering the political will to act, the need for intervention forces to have a strong mandate, the critical need for a synergy of efforts amongst scholars in different fields, and the critical need to address systemic issues.

Wheeler, Nicholas J. (2001). "Reflections on the Legality and Legitimacy of NATO's Intervention in Kosovo," pp. 145-163. In Ken Booth (Ed.) *The Kosovo Tragedy: The Human Rights Dimension*. London: Frank Cass Publishers.

In this piece, Wheeler, Senior Lecturer in the Department of International Politics at the University of Wales, discusses whether NATO's actions in Kosovo "represent a watershed in the development of a new norm of humanitarian intervention, and how far this is to be welcomed or feared in a society of states built on the principles of sovereignty, non-intervention and non-use of force" (pp. 145-146). The sections of the essay are entitled: The Contested Legality of Humanitarian Intervention, NATO's Justification for Its Use of Force in Kosovo, A New Solidarist Norm of Humanitarian Intervention? and A Historical Watershed.

Wheeler, Nicholas J. (2000). *Saving Strangers: Humanitarian Intervention in International Society*. Oxford: Oxford University Press. 336 p.

Wheeler examines seven cases of intervention -- three in the 1970's (East Pakistan, Cambodia, and Uganda), one in the 1980's (Iraq), and three in the 1990's (Somalia, Rwanda, and the former Yugoslavia). Wheeler argues that it was only in the 1990's that a norm of humanitarian intervention began to come to the fore. Against the perspective of the international community that regards national sovereignty as inviolable, Wheeler argues that a concept of solidarity has emerged that combines order with (human rights-based) justice.

Wheeler, Nicholas, and Dunne, Tim (2001). "East Timor and the New Humanitarian Interventionism." *International Affairs*, October, 77(4):805-827.

In their abstract, Wheeler and Dunne, both of whom are senior lecturers in the Department of Politics at the University of Wales, write:

> The fate of East Timor provides a barometer for how far the normative structure of international society has been transformed since the end of the Cold War. In 1975, the East Timorese were abandoned by a Western bloc that placed accommodating the Indonesian invasions of the island before the protection of human rights. Twenty-five years later, it was the protection of the civilian population on the island that loomed large in the calculations of these same states. Australia, which had sacrificed the rights of the people of East Timor on the altar of good relations with Indonesia, found itself leading an intervention that challenged the old certainties of its "Jakarta

first" policy. The article charts the interplay of domestic and international factors that made this normative transformation possible. The authors examine the political and economic factors that led to the agreement in May 1999 between Portugal, Indonesia and the UN to hold a referendum on the future political status of East Timor.

The second part of the article looks at how the outbreak of the violence in early September 1999 fundamentally changed these political assumptions. The authors argue that it became politically possible to employ coercion against Indonesian sovereignty in a context in which the Habibie government was viewed as having failed to exercise sovereignty with responsibility. By focusing on the economic and military sanctions employed by Western States, the pressures exerted by the international financial institutions and the intense diplomatic activity at the UN and in Jakarta, the authors show how Indonesian political and military leaders were prevailed upon to accept an international force. At the same time, Australian reporting of the atrocities and how this prompted the Howard government to an intervention that challenged traditional conceptions of Australia's vital interests is considered. The conclusion reflects on how this case supports the claim that traditional notions of sovereignty are increasingly constrained by norms of humanitarian responsibility (n.p.)

3

The Development and Implementation of Genocide Early Warning Systems: Conceptual and Practical Issues[1]

Barbara Harff

From Risk Assessment to Early Warning

Risk assessment identifies countries and situations with substantial potential for genocidal violence. I have developed and tested a structural model that identifies the factors that preceded most of the 37 cases of genocides and politicides (political mass murders) that occurred between 1955 and 2000 (Harff 2003, 2004). This provides the basis for regular global risk assessments that identify those latent and low-level conflicts that may erupt into large-scale massacres or genocide. Risk assessment does not tell us when an episode is likely to occur; rather, what we do know is that, if the conditions persist and no countervailing international actions are taken, escalation can happen at any time.

Critics often assert in the aftermath of genocidal violence that there was no shortage of "early warnings," meaning that local observers and country experts "knew" that some kind of serious conflict was imminent. These kinds of warnings are of limited utility because they are more often late than early and typically focus on known crisis situations that may or may not lead to genocidal violence. Most such situations already attract international attention. In principle, risk assessment should identify potential cases of genocide early enough to prompt early remedial action.

This effort is comparable to examining an apparently healthy body and looking for precancerous conditions. The risk factors are then tabulated and presented in numerical format—identifying high, medium or low risk countries. Factors that contribute to the likely onset of genocides are identified prior to assessing risk and are based on existing theoretical arguments and empirical evidence on the preconditions of past genocides. Again, medical research provides a useful basis for comparison. Researchers are well aware that cancer sometimes runs in families. In the social sciences, we posit that certain types of political systems (the body politic) are more prone to deadly conflict and repression than others. Evidence from the last half-century shows that autocracies are almost always the culprits. Medical researchers know quite well that genetic dispositions alone do not trigger cancer; rather they interact with other factors such as exposure to carcinogenic agents. Similarly we know, for example, that ethnic, racial, religious or other societal cleavages are necessary preconditions for genocide. But cleavages by and of themselves yield few clues as to how and when they contribute to the onset of genocidal episodes. Almost all contemporary countries are ethnically divided. However, if one looks at ethnic divisions from an elite perspective, the assessment changes dramatically. Minority elites who dominate ethnic majorities are more likely to abuse their status. And, if such minority elites are motivated by exclusionary ideologies, the situation is risky enough to warrant close monitoring and international action.

So far we have described risk assessment but not early warning efforts, terms typically used interchangeably. Risk assessment relies on macro-structural indicators which do not tell us the whole story of conflict development, because they are comparable to snapshots taking at yearly intervals. And, as we know, conflicts can escalate rapidly to genocide, as in Rwanda in early 1994. To know why some conflicts rapidly transition from ethnic skirmishes to genocides, we need more time-sensitive models that can be used as tracking devices.

Good risk assessments are a precondition for reliable early warnings, partly because they focus our analytic attention on high-risk situations. Assume that Burundi is a high risk country. Given no or little international action and no changes in the direction of our predictors, the situation remains at high risk; that is, genocide may begin within the next one to two years. Two years gives policy makers time to pro-act, but often these warnings are not heeded. Only when the conflict escalates to serious levels do we hear requests for close monitoring. This is exactly where systematic early warning comes into play. It essentially means the monitoring of medium and high risk situations using models designed to detect the signals of impending genocide. The author has developed such a model, briefly described below, which identifies theoretically relevant factors that are measured using information on political events. Some of these events reflect changes in the structural risk conditions but more typically they trace variable conditions such as arms transfers or refugee movements that are subject to rapid, short-term fluctuation. Both domestic and international factors that either exacerbate or deescalate existing crises are monitored on a daily, near-real-time basis and then analyzed. To my knowledge this genocide early warning effort is the only empirically based system in operation, and unfortunately current results are neither complete nor publicly available. However, the model in use has been published in scholarly sources (for example in Harff and Gurr 1998). It is both desirable and feasible to transform this early warning model into a more qualitative system that can be used by local observers and nongovernmental organization (NGOs) to track and interpret conflict escalation.

Who is Working on Risk Assessment and Early Warning?[2]

A potent impetus for research on early warning of conflicts with grave humanitarian consequences came from the UN Secretary-General's *Agenda for Peace* of June 17, 1992 (UN General Assembly, 1992). Dr. Boutros Boutros-Ghali focused attention on threats to international security arising from "ethnic, religious, social, cultural or linguistic strife" (UN General Assembly, 1992, paragraph 11) and called for strengthening early-warning systems that incorporate information about natural disasters and "political indicators to assess whether a threat to peace exists and to analyze what action might be taken by the United Nations to alleviate it" (UN General Assembly, 1992, paragraph 26). In the following decade several UN agencies designed and employed early warning systems for international policy planning.

In New York, the UN's Office for the Coordination of Humanitarian Affairs (OCHA) developed the Humanitarian Early Warning System (HEWS) in the early 1990s, a database of quantitative and qualitative information on countries vulnerable to humanitarian crises. HEWS was used to support interpretive analyses and reports for decision-makers in UN operational agencies but was shut down in the late 1990s for lack of funding (see Ahmed and Kassinis 1998). A second project entitled ReliefWeb was established by OCHA's Geneva office and directed by an inter-agency UN working group. ReliefWeb is an internet-based compendium of current information and assessments on complex emergencies, ranging from civil wars to natural disasters. Its information is publically accessible and thus it is widely used by humanitarian organizations and private activists (see King 1998; the website is www.reliefweb.int). A third UN-related early warning project focuses on food crises rather than the civil conflicts that cause most humanitarian crises. The Global Information and Early Warning System (GIEWS), run by the Food and Agricultural Organization in Rome, monitors demand and supply for all basic foods throughout the world and provides alerts of imminent food crises. It is an exemplar of what could be done for conflict and genocide early warning given sufficient resources and political support from the UN's member states (see Rashid 1998; the website is www.fao.org/giews).

The European states also support early warning and preventive action programs. The Organization for Security and Cooperation in Europe (OSCE) maintains the research-oriented Conflict Prevention Center in Vienna while the office of the OSCE's High Commissioner on National Minorities, based in The Hague, has responsibility for reporting on and planning diplomatic responses to emerging ethnonational conflicts (see van der Stoel 1999). Though it issues some reports, most of its work consists of unpublicized diplomacy. The European Union (EU) supports the work of the Conflict Prevention Network of academic institutions and NGOs, designed to provide analytic and operational input to the EU system. The EU recently decided to establish a separate conflict early warning center directed by Niall Burgess (see Kronenberger and Wouters 2004). The British government also is planning a conflict and genocide early warning capacity under the guidance of a working group in the Office of the Prime Minister. Both the EU and British efforts are drawing on the conflict and genocide early warning research of this researcher's work and that of the U.S. Political Instability Task Force (previously known as the State Failure Task Force).

The Organization of African Unity (now the African Union) also initiated an early warning system in the mid-1990s, based in Addis Ababa, the first such effort by a regional organization outside Europe.

A number of Western governments have developed risk assessment and early warning systems to support post-Cold War policies of developmental and humanitarian assistance. While the long-run planning question for development administrators is how to design programs to forestall future crises, the short-run question is whether impending crises will destroy the gains of ongoing programs. The U.S. Agency for

International Development (USAID) makes such assessments, so does the British government (noted above), the Canadian Ministry of Foreign Affairs, the Swiss Foreign Ministry (under contract with the Swiss Peace Foundation), and the Foreign Ministry of the Netherlands (at its Clingendael center).

Beginning in the early 1990s, the U.S. Department of Defense and intelligence agencies began to shift their early warning efforts from the interstate conflicts, with which they were preoccupied during the Cold War, to intrastate conflicts and humanitarian crises that may call for U.S. rescue, assistance, and peace-keeping operations. A vivid illustration of increased U.S. concerns about humanitarian issues was the Clinton administration's (1992-2000) establishment, early in 1999, of an interagency center for early warning of atrocities based in the Department of State and headed initially by Ambassador for War Crimes David Scheffer.

Parallel to these national and international efforts at early warning are the research and action programs of numerous non-governmental organizations. The Carnegie Commission on Preventing Deadly Conflict carried out a major program of action research between 1994 and 2000, and its numerous books and reports dealt with the general causes of ethnonational and religious conflicts as well as with the means by which international entities could prevent mass violence and promote nonviolent problem-solving. The Center for Preventive Action, supported by the New York-based Council on Foreign Relations, had a more narrow focus. More specifically, it assembled expert teams for in-country assessments of conflict situations and increasingly emphasized preventive strategies (a good example is Rubin 1998).

The London-based Forum on Early Warning and Early Response (FEWER) is an umbrella organization that pursues similar objectives through a network of affiliated organizations. FEWER was founded in 1996 as a consortium of NGOs and academic research institutions and has built a global network for information exchange and action partnerships with governmental and private organizations. It has working links with regional early warning networks in Africa and the Commonwealth of Independent States (CIS), for example, the Moscow-based Network of Ethnological Monitoring on Early Warning of Ethnic Conflict, and distributes information from organizations doing early warning research. Examples of its work include early warning of the outbreak and escalation of conflicts in the Democratic Republic of Congo, and developing conflict and peace indicators for the Caucasus and Great Lakes regions (for current reports see www.alertnet.org).

The International Crisis Group (ICG) is the largest and best-funded private organization now working on conflict risk assessment and early warning. Founded in 1995 and currently (2007) directed by Gareth Evans, former Australian foreign minister, it aims to provide independent assessments of crises and emerging conflicts for officials, practitioners, and the media. It has a substantial Brussels-based staff plus eleven field offices—in the Balkans, Asia, and Africa—which prepare dozens of in-depth reports each year. A forty-two-page report entitled *Liberia: The Key to Ending Regional Instability*, issued in April 2002, is representative. It describes the origins of the anti-Taylor insurgency, assesses the internal political situation in Liberia, analyzes the conflict's international context, and sets forth recommendations for action by interested governments (Nigeria, the U.S., the U.K., and France), by the UN Security Council and UN Secretary General, and by international donors (for current reports see www.crisisweb.org).

The next link in the chain that begins with risk assessment and early warning is prevention. Whereas FEWER and ICG focus on assessment first and prevention second, other NGOs give priority to prevention. One very active umbrella organization is the Utrecht-based European Platform for Conflict Prevention and Transformation, which exchanges information and advocates prevention activities by participating NGOs. Its publication projects include a handbook that inventories conflict prevention centers world-wide and a series of regional Conflict Prevention Surveys (see its website, www.euconflict.org).

A great many other entities doing research related to early warning and preventive action might be cited. Annual tracking of armed conflicts are reported by university-based researchers in Sweden, Germany, and the United States. Periodic human rights assessments are prepared by Amnesty International, Human Rights Watch, the Human Rights Internet (Canada), and the U.S. Department of State. Political risk analyses are prepared for corporate clients by applied research groups in the U.S. and London. Refugees and the crises that generate them are assessed by university researchers and NGOs in North America, Europe, and Japan.

It is obvious from this overview that conflict early warners have diverse objectives and methods and work in different kinds of environments. The specific "bads" they warn about include civil wars, massive human rights violations, and refugee flows. Some collect and report data, others do case studies, and still others disseminate information. Some prepare rigorous risk assessments, others try to focus preventive efforts on impending crises. Some work in NGOs and university research programs, others provide staff support to national and international policy makers. Warning and prevention of genocide is one among many of their concerns.

The next section traces in detail the development of genocide risk assessment and early warning.

Architects of Genocide Early Warning

Israel W. Charny was the first genocide scholar who advocated the systematic observation and monitoring of particular problem situations. He believed that once such a system was established it was "conceivable that the major impact of the spotlight of world public opinion would be to reduce the number of fatalities" (Charny, 1982, p. 286). His chapter, "Toward a Genocide Early Warning System" (pp. 283-331) in *How We Can Commit the Unthinkable? Genocide: The Human Cancer* lays out the basic ideas on which later structural models, systematic risk assessment, and early warnings are based. The problem with the design of this "system" was Charny's ambition to capture every detail and nuance that would help us to understand why genocides are recurrent phenomena. However, much can be learned from his work. He correctly identified many structural factors that are used for risk assessment two decades later, and notes the processes and factors that are prone to rapid changes, many of them now used in early warning. He mentions briefly the potential problems that have to do with building models that use different systems level variables. Given the complexity of genocidal events, he suggests, we need to understand individual motives, group and societal factors, state systems characteristics, and those events that trigger a genocide. This is the dream of all social scientists who work on explanations of complex phenomena—to leave nothing out, to include everything. But we know that by doing so we may obfuscate a more parsimonious explanation, or explain one or two cases well but fail to develop general principles. However, students of risk assessment and early warning are well advised to look at Charny's list of possible factors that contribute to genocides. Some have found their way into the analytic literature that identifies common "causes," others have been tested in quantitative comparative studies and found to be significant—or not.

Hidden in Charny's 1984 book that reports proceedings of the International Conference on the Holocaust and Genocide is a fascinating proposal for an "applied science approach to a genocide early warning system." Authors Ephraim M. Howard and Yocheved Howard (1984) remind us of catastrophe theory, developed by mathematicians during the 1970s, and propose a model which assumes that genocide is a linear process. They point to Neil Smelser's idea of a value added process that identifies stages or phases in conflict evolution. Similar ideas appear in general models by Kuper (1985) Fein (1994) and Harff in which they identify phases of the genocidal process. The author of this chapter, with the help of gifted mathematicians and statistical wizards, has worked to develop an early warning model using mathematical and statistical tools for analysis of coded events data. Early versions of the accelerator model, as it is known, have been published in several chapters and articles (Harff and Gurr 1998) and partial analyses of four cases has also been reported (Harff 1996, 2001), but a full, complex analysis using the most advanced methods is not yet publicly available.

A number of problems have been identified in early warning research. Phases are essentially arbitrary devices superimposed on processes that may or may not develop in a linear fashion. So-called trigger events may disrupt linear development and throw the system into chaos—often this is the point at which conflicts do occur. And monitoring cases on a daily basis using a complex model—ours includes some seventy indicators—is forbiddingly expensive. Researchers now are working on automatic coding procedures that will make it possible to code thousands of pieces of information in minutes. On the more mundane level, information in some cases is spotty, which is a problem for daily monitoring.

There are a half-dozen other scholars whose ideas and research have contributed to risk assessment and early warning of genocide and similar events. More than anybody in the field, Helen Fein has contributed through her writings and active encouragement to the field at large. She also inspired me to pursue first and foremost collection of data on cases, and risk assessment and early warning. Her path-breaking work *Accounting for Genocide* (1979) and her 1984 chapter on modeling and phases provide us a wealth of information, ideas, and theoretical propositions that can be used to develop and test hypotheses. In 1993, T. R. Gurr and I convened a workshop on Early Warning of Communal Conflicts and Humanitarian Crises that resulted in a special issue of the *Journal of Ethno-Development*. In the latter, Fein compared and contrasted her and my theoretical frameworks (Fein 1994).

Research of ethnic conflict also is relevant to genocide. For example, Gurr and collaborators have developed and tested forecasting models for ethnic war (Gurr and Moore 1997, Gurr and Marshall 2000). Persistent protest, past repression directed at minorities, and group mobilization are major factors in the latest of these models. Other factors, I believe, that figure in explanations of ethnic conflict also are pertinent for genocide research. For example, mobilized ethnies in multi-ethnic societies facing an autocratic minority elite is a recipe for trouble. This brings us to an important issue. Any risk assessment and early warning research ultimately relies on the theoretical work done by scholars with in-depth knowledge. It is through comparative case studies that we discover patterned behavior, which allows us to generalize and develop testable hypotheses.

Howard Adelman is a prominent proponent of early warning through case studies. In the *Journal of Ethno-Development* he does a laudable job of comparing the different analytical approaches to early warning (Adelman 1993). Later, he and Suhrke examined the role of early warning in the Rwandan genocide (Adelman and Surke with Jones 1996). The case study approach to early warning is helpful as background material and, if combined with tracking, could provide us with important information on ongoing crises, but would not be able to detect a genocide in the making. In contrast, I use a model that is data-based and theory-driven. The model identifies six factors that are common antecedents of genocide and politicide (political mass murder). The universe of analysis consists of 129 instances of internal war and regime collapse that began between 1955 and 2000, as identified by the Political Instability Task Force. The model distinguishes -- with nearly 80 percent accuracy—the thirty-six serious civil conflicts that led to episodes of genocidal violence between 1955 and 2000 and ninety-three others that did not. The model then is applied to current data to assess the risks of future episodes in countries with ongoing conflict. The researchers involved in this project tested virtually every hypothesis proposed by genocide scholars, and the model described above had the greatest explanatory power (Harff 2003, 2004).

Of the younger researchers, Matthew Krain, Nicholas Sambanis, and Benjamin Valentino are familiar with both the theoretical literature and quantitative analysis. Krain was the first to systematically test hypotheses from the theoretical literature, including some of mine. He posits that openings in the political opportunity structure rather than the levels of concentration of power best predict the onset of genocides and politicides (Krain, 1997). Sambanis, a newcomer to the field and a gifted quantitative analyst, has systematically retested my risk assessment model adding different variables, which is of course the work that should be done to validate earlier findings. Most recently, Benjamin Valentino and collaborators ask why some wars result in the intentional killing of large numbers of civilians. This is not genocide per se, but their analysis includes most genocides of the last half-century (Valentino, Huth, and Balch-Lindsay, 2004).

Where are We Today

The author's risk assessment, described above, was the first of its kind and depended heavily on U.S. government funding. It was part of the ongoing State Failure effort, now renamed the Political Instability Task Force, of which I remain a member. In 1994, then Vice President Gore wanted some answers on why conflicts occur with some frequency. As a result, about a dozen scholars came together to propose theories, develop data, and test systematically the many hypotheses generated in the social sciences. My specific task was development of genocide models after the U.S. government decided, in 1998, that more reliable forecasts were needed than those provided by area experts. Over the years the Task Force put together the largest social science dataset ever developed including annual data for all countries since 1955 for nearly 1,000 indicators. This has made it possible to test a great many hypotheses, including those about the preconditions of genocide.

New Developments and Prevention

For all early warners the ultimate goal is prevention of conflict through early detection. For skeptics the most common counter argument is: What good is an early warning system when political will to intervene is missing? These are really two different issues. First, we never had any systematic, global early warning, so we cannot yet assess its impact. The obvious counterpoint is: Why does the U.S. government continue to invest heavily in risk assessment and early warning research if the findings have no policy use. From what I know for certain is that policymakers are now routinely briefed on findings, USAID uses them for long term planning, and, on the genocide front, it is worth pointing out that the U.S. was the first (and thus far only) country that declared the Darfur situation a genocide. Sudan has been on our high risk screen for a long time.

With regard to political will, in January 2004, the Stockholm Forum at which fifty-five-plus states pledged to prevent genocide was held.

A sampling of my risk assessments were presented at the Forum and ruffled the feathers of Rwanda's President Kagame. This is partly what we want to accomplish—to alert the global community and put potential perpetrators on the to-be-watched list. Equally important is the recent appointment by the UN Secretary-General of a Special Advisor on Genocide. Lastly, as mentioned above, early warning models can be modified to become a tool in the hands of NGOs for tracking high risk situations on the ground.

Notes

1. An earlier version of this section appears in T. R. Gurr and Barbara Harff (2003), "Early Warning Systems: From Surveillance to Risk Assessment to Action." In Cahill (Ed.) *Emergency Relief Operations*. New York: Fordham University Press and The Center for International Health and Cooperation, pp. 5-9.
2. The concept of early warning was first widely used during the Cold War by U.S. military and intelligence analysts who sought to anticipate East-West flashpoints. An account of empirical early warning research during this era is Edward Laurence's (1990) "Events Data and Policy Analysis: Improving the Potential for Applying Academic Research to Foreign and Defense Policy Problems." *Policy Sciences*, 23:111-132.

References

Adelman, Howard (1994). "Theoretical Approaches to Developing an Early Warning Model," pp. 124-131. In T. R. Gurr and B. Harff (eds.) Speical Issue (Early Warning of Communal Conflicts and Humanities Cases) of *The Journal of Ethno-Development*. College Park, MD: Center for International Development. July 4(1).

Adelman, Howard, and Suhrke, Astri with Brice Jones (1996). *Early Warning and Conflict Management in Rwanda. Study II of the Evaluation of Emergency Assistance to Rwanda*. Copenhagen: DANIDA, for the Michelsen Institute, Norway.

Ahmed, Adeel, and Kassinis, Elizabeth Voulieris (1998). "The Humanitarian Early Warning System: From Concept to Practice." In John L. Davies and T. R. Gurr (Eds.) *Preventive Measures: Building Risk Assessment and Crisis Early Warning Systems*. Lanham, MD: Rowman & Littlefield, pp. 203-211.

Alker, Hayward R.; Gurr, T. R.; and Rupesinghe, Kumer (Eds.) (2001). *Journeys Through Conflict: Narratives and Lessons. A Study of the Conflict Early Warning Systems Research Project of the International Social Science Council*. Lanham, MD: Rowman & Littlefield.

Charny, Israel W. (1982). *How Can We Commit the Unthinkable? Genocide: The Human Cancer*. Boulder, CO: Westview Press.

Charny, Israel W. (ed.) (1984). *Toward the Understanding and Prevention of Genocide: Proceedings of the International Conference on the Holocaust and Genocide*. Boulder, CO: Westview Press.

Davies, John L., and Gurr, T. R. (Eds.) (1998). *Preventive Measures: Building Risk Assessment and Crisis Early Warning Systems*. Lanham, MD: Rowman & Littlefield.

Fein, Helen (1979). *Accounting for Genocide: National Responses and Jewish Victimization During the Holocaust*. New York: Free Press.

Fein, Helen (1984). "Scenarios of Genocide: Models of Genocide and Critical Responses." In Charny, Israel W. (Ed.)*Toward the Understanding and Prevention of Genocide: Proceedings of the International Conference on the Holocaust and Genocide*. Boulder, CO: Westview Press, pp. 3-31.

Fein, Helen (1994). "Tools and Alarms: Uses of Models for Explanation and Anticipation." In T. R. Gurr and B. Harff (Eds.) Special issue of *Journal of Ethno-Political Development*, July, 4(1): 31-35.

Gurr, T. R., and Harff, Barbara (Eds.) (1994). "Early Warning of Communal Conflicts and Humanitarian Crises." Special issue of *Journal of Ethno-Political Development*, July, 4(1).

Gurr, T. R., and Moore, Will H. (1997). "Ethnopolitical Rebellion: A Cross-Sectional Analysis of the 1980s with Risk Assessments for the 1990s." *American Journal of Political Science*, October, 41(4):1079-1103.

Gurr, T. R., and Marshall, Monty G. (2000). "Assessing Risks of Future Ethnic Wars." In T. R. Gurr (Ed.) *Peoples Versus States: Minorities at Risk in the New Century*. Washington, DC: U.S. Institute of Peace Press, pp. 223-260.

Harff, Barbara (1996). "Early Warning of Potential Genocide: The Cases of Rwanda, Burundi, Bosnia, and Abkhazia." In T. R. Gurr and B. Harff (Eds.) *Early Warning of Communal Conflicts and Genocide: Linking Empirical Research to International Responses*. Tokyo: United Nations University Monograph Series on Governance and Conflict Resolution, pp. 47-78.

Harff, Barbara (2001). "Could Humanitarian Crises Have Been Anticipated in Burundi, Rwanda, and Zaire? A Comparative Study of Anticipatory Indicators." In H. R. Alker, T. R. Gurr and K. Rupesinghe (Eds.) *Journeys Through Conflict: Narratives and Lessons. A Study of the Conflict Early Warning Systems Research Project of the International Social Science Council*. Lanham, MD: Rowman & Littlefield. pp. 81-102.

Harff, Barbara (2003). "No Lessons Learned from the Holocaust? Assessing Risks of Genocide and Political Mass Murder Since 1955." *American Political Science Review*, February 97(1):57-73.

Harff, Barbara (2004). "Option Paper: Risk Assessment and Early Warning." *Stockholm International Forum 2004*, pp. 155-157.

Harff, Barbara, and Gurr, T. R. (1998). "Systematic Early Warning of Humanitarian Emergencies." *Journal of Peace Research*, September, 35(5):551-579.

Howard, Ephraim M., and Howard, Yocheved (1984). "From Theory to Application: Proposal for an Applied Science Approach to a Genocide Early Warning System." In Israel W. Charny (Ed.) *Toward the Understanding and Prevention of Genocide: Proceedings of the International Conference on the Holocaust and Genocide*. Boulder, CO: Westview Press, pp. 324-329.

King, Dennis (1998). "ReliefWeb: An International Information Management Tool." In John L. Davies and T. R. Gurr (Eds.)*Preventive Measures: Building Risk Assessment and Crisis Early Warning Systems*. Lanham, MD: Rowman & Littlefield, pp. 212-217.

Krain, Matthew (1997). "State-Sponsored Mass Murder: The Onset and Severity of Genocides and Politicides." *Journal of Conflict Resolution*, June 41(3):331-360.

Kronenberger, Vincent, and Wouters, Jan (Eds.) (2004). *The European Union and Conflict Prevention: Policy and Legal Aspects*. Cambridge, UK: Cambridge University Press.

Kuper, Leo (1985). *The Prevention of Genocide*. New Haven, CT: Yale University Press.

Laurence, Edward (1990). "Events Data and Policy Analysis: Improving the Potential for Applying Academic Research to Foreign and Defense Policy Problems." *Policy Sciences*, 23:111-132.

Rashid, Abdur (1998). "The Global Information and Early Warning System on Food and Agriculture." In John L. Davies and T. R. Gurr (Eds.) *Preventive Measures: Building Risk Assessment and Crisis Early Warning Systems*. Lanham, MD: Rowman & Littlefield, pp. 185-193.

Rubin, Barnett R. (Ed.) 1998. *Cases and Strategies for Preventive Action: Preventive Action Reports, Vol. 2, Report of the Carnegie Commission on Preventing Deadly Conflict*. New York: Century Foundation Press.

Government of Sweden (2004). *Stockholm International Forum 2004 26-28 January Proceedings: Preventing Genocide: Threats and Responsibilities*. Stockholm: Government of Sweden, Regeringskansliet.

Valentino, Benjamin, Huth, Paul and Balch-Lindsay, Dylan (2004). "Draining the Sea: Mass Killing and Guerrilla Warfare." *International Organization*, Spring, 58: 375-407.

Annotated Bibliography

Adelman, Howard (1994). "Theoretical Approaches to Developing an Early Warning Model." In T. R. Gurr and B. Harff (Eds.) (1994). "Early Warning of Communal Conflicts and Humanitarian Crises." Special issue of *Journal of Ethno-Political Development*, July, 4(1). pp. 124-131.

Distinguishes non-universalist from universalist approaches. Within this broad distinction Adelman contrasts narrative and correlation approaches; deductive and normative decision theories; and phenomenological and deconstructionist theories.

Adelman, Howard, and Suhrke, Astri with Brice Jones (1996). *Early Warning and Conflict Management in Rwanda. Study II of the Evaluation of Emergency Assistance to Rwanda*. Copenhagen: DANIDA, for the Michelsen Institute, Norway. 20 pp.

A detailed and critical descriptive study of the ways in which the international community did, or did not, take account of warnings before the Rwandan genocide, and how early warning could help planning assistance for its victims and survivors.

Ahmed, Adeel, and Kassinis, Elizabeth Voulieris (1998). "The Humanitarian Early Warning System: From Concept to Practice," pp. 203-211. In John L. Davies and T. R. Gurr (Eds.) *Preventive Measures: Building Risk Assessment and Crisis Early Warning Systems*. Lanham, MD: Rowman & Littlefield.

The HEWS system, designed by the UN's Office for the Coordination of Humanitarian Affairs, was used from the mid to late 1990s to provide early warnings of crises. This chapter describes its methodology and the mechanisms that supported the collection, analysis, and dissemination of information.

Alker, Hayward R., Gurr, T. R., and Rupesinghe, Kumar (Eds.) (2001). *Journeys Through Conflict: Narratives and Lessons. A Study of the Conflict Early Warning Systems Research Project of the International Social Science Council.* Lanham, MD: Rowman & Littlefield. 459 pp.

The CEWS project, funded by UNESCO, aimed to provide a theoretical and research-based approach to early warning of internal conflicts for international actors. Comparative case studies are reported, for example, of TransDniester and Chechnya, Slovakia and Kosovo, Angola and South Africa, and separatist conflicts in Southeast Asia. Special emphasis is given to alternative responses by nongovernmental organizations (NGOs) that might change conflict trajectories. It concludes with a detailed design for early warning networks.

Charny, Israel W. (1982). *How Can We Commit the Unthinkable? Genocide: The Human Cancer.* Boulder, CO: Westview Press. 430 pp.

A pioneering study of the origins of human destructiveness and the circumstances under which people can commit genocide, concluding with three hopeful chapters on non-aggression as an alternative to violence and how to design a genocide early warning system.

Charny, Israel W. (Ed.) (1984). *Toward the Understanding and Prevention of Genocide: Proceedings of the International Conference on the Holocaust and Genocide.* Boulder, CO: Westview Press. 396 pp.

Includes chapters on scenarios and types of genocide; case studies; analyses of the dynamics of genocide; and six chapters on intervention and prevention.

Davies, John L., and Gurr, T. R. (Eds.) (1998). *Preventive Measures: Building Risk Assessment and Crisis Early Warning Systems.* Lanham, MD: Rowman & Littlefield. 288 pp.

Provides an overview of academic research and policy-oriented programs that aim at early warning and prevention of humanitarian crises, refugee flows, ethnic war and state failures, and genocide. See the annotations in this bibliography of Ahmed and Kassinis, King, and Rashid.

Fein, Helen (1979). *Accounting for Genocide: National Responses and Jewish Victimization During the Holocaust*. New York: Free Press. 468 pp.

A classic comparative study whose hypotheses and conclusions have greatly influenced subsequent research on the causes and early warning of genocide.

Fein, Helen (1984). "Scenarios of Genocide: Models of Genocide and Critical Responses," pp. 3-31. In Israel W. Charny (Ed.)*Toward the Understanding and Prevention of Genocide: Proceedings of the International Conference on the Holocaust and Genocide*. Boulder, CO: Westview Press.

Distinguishes the causes and dynamics of four types of genocide, with hypothetical scenarios: developmental, despotic, retributive, and ideological genocides. Concludes with a discussion of responses that might disrupt these scenarios.

Fein, Helen (1994). "Tools and Alarms: Uses of Models for Explanation and Anticipation." In T. R. Gurr and Barbara Harff (Eds.) Special issue of *Journal of Ethno-Political Development*, July, 4(1): 31-35.

A point-by-point comparison of Fein's and Harff's models for explaining genocides and discussion of their uses for anticipation.

Gurr, T. R., and Harff, Barbara (Eds.) (1994). "Early Warning of Communal Conflicts and Humanitarian Crises." Special issue of *Journal of Ethno-Political Development*, July, 4(1).

Proceedings of a workshop with nineteen chapters covering such topics as theories and models of communal conflict and genocide; the development of systematic early warning models; and policy uses of such models. Chapters abstracted in this bibliography include those by Adelman (1994) and Fein (1994).

Gurr, T. R., and Moore, Will H. (1997). "Ethnopolitical Rebellion: A Cross-Sectional Analysis of the 1980s with Risk Assessments for the 1990s." *American Journal of Political Science*, October, 41(4):1079-1103.

Constructs a theoretical model built on both deprivation and resource mobilization arguments to explain ethnopolitical rebellion in the 1980s and to provide risk assessments for the early 1990s. The results help us explain why a number of groups that the analysis suggested would rebel in the early 1990s did not in fact do so.

Gurr, T. R., and Marshall, Monty G. (2000). "Assessing Risks of Future Ethnic Wars," 223-260. In T. R. Gurr (Ed.) *Peoples Versus States: Minorities at Risk in the New Century*. Washington, DC: U.S. Institute of Peace Press.

Develops empirical models of risks of future protest and rebellion by the 275 ethnopolitical groups surveyed by the Minorities at Risk project. Past conflict and state repression are major factors; international engagement can reduce risks. High-risk groups are identified in each world region.

Harff, Barbara (2001). "Could Humanitarian Crises Have Been Anticipated in Burundi, Rwanda, and Zaire? A Comparative Study of Anticipatory Indicators," pp. 81-102. In Hayward R. Alker, T. R. Gurr, and K. Rupesinghe (Eds.) *Journeys Through Conflict: Narratives and Lessons. A Study of the Conflict Early Warning Systems Research Project of the International Social Science Council*. Lanham, MD: Rowman & Littlefield.

Extends the analysis in Harff (1996) to Zaire, with close analysis of internal and international de-accelerating events that might have prevented mass killings in the three cases.

Harff, Barbara (1996). "Early Warning of Potential Genocide: The Cases of Rwanda, Burundi, Bosnia, and Abkhazia," pp. 47-78. In T. R. Gurr and Barbara Harff (Eds.) *Early Warning of Communal Conflicts and Genocide: Linking Empirical Research to International Responses*. Tokyo: United Nations University Monograph Series on Governance and Conflict Resolution.

Sketches a sequential model of internal and international conditions, intervening conditions, and seven types of accelerators of genocide and politicide. The cases are systematically compared and a graphic analysis of the buildup of accelerators during the year before the onset of each genocide provided—or in the case of Abkhazia, a genocide that did not occur.

Harff, Barbara (2003). "No Lessons Learned from the Holocaust? Assessing Risks of Genocide and Political Mass Murder Since 1955." *American Political Science Review*, February 97(1):57-73.

Reports statistical tests of a structural model of the antecedents of genocide and politicide, applied to 126 instances of state failure (internal wars and regime collapse) between 1955 and 1997. Six factors are shown to distinguish, with 74 percent accuracy, between the 35 failures that led to geno/politicide and the 81 that did not. Countries at risk in the near future are identified. Updated versions of this model are routinely used by the U.S. government to assess future risks of geno/politicide.

Harff, Barbara (2004). "Option Paper: Risk Assessment and Early Warning." *Stockholm International Forum 2004*, pp. 155-157.

An updated summary of Harff 2003 with comments on prevention.

Harff, Barbara, and Gurr, T. R. (1998). "Systematic Early Warning of Humanitarian Emergencies." *Journal of Peace Research*, September, 35(5):551-579.

The potential for communal rebellion is a joint function of group incentives, group capacity, and opportunities for collective action; 73 high-risk groups are identified. Geno/politicides are attributed to background and intervening conditions plus short-term increases in accelerators (see Harff 1996). Monitoring of accelerators and de-accelerators in potential crisis situations provides a link between risk assessments based on structural models and early warnings of use to policymakers.

Howard, Ephraim M., and Howard, Yocheved (1984). "From Theory to Application: Proposal for an Applied Science Approach to a Genocide Early Warning System," pp. 324-329. In Israel W. Charny (Ed.)*Toward the Understanding and Prevention of Genocide: Proceedings of the In-*

ternational Conference on the Holocaust and Genocide. Boulder, CO: Westview Press.

Genocide does not necessarily result from a linear process. Catastrophe theory, developed by mathematicians during the 1970s, provides an alternative approach. The authors also make use of Neil Smelser's idea of a value added process that identifies stages or phases in the evolution of conflict.

King, Dennis (1998). "ReliefWeb: An International Information Management Tool," pp. 212-217. In John L. Davies and T. R. Gurr (Eds.)*Preventive Measures: Building Risk Assessment and Crisis Early Warning Systems*. Lanham, MD: Rowman & Littlefield.

Describes the purposes and structure of a decentralized, public access, information management system for complex emergencies, a concept that ranges from natural disasters to civil wars and genocide.

Krain, Matthew (1997). "State-Sponsored Mass Murder: The Onset and Severity of Genocides and Politicides." *Journal of Conflict Resolution*, June 41(3):331-360.

An empirical study of the preconditions of geno/politicides prior to 1995 whose key proposition is that openings in the political opportunity structure rather than the levels of concentration of power best predict the onset of genocides and politicides. Results support the general argument and identify other causal factors.

Kronenberger, Vincent, and Wouters, Jan (Eds.) (2004).*The European Union and Conflict Prevention: Policy and Legal Aspects*. Cambridge, UK: Cambridge University Press. 644 pp.

Twenty-five chapters on conflict-prevention work by researchers and policy-makers in the European Union. Of particular interest is Niall Burgess' description, in Chapter 2, of the early warning procedures being established by the Council of Europe.

Kuper, Leo (1985). *The Prevention of Genocide*. New Haven, CT: Yale University Press. 286 pp.

Analyzes obstacles to effective UN preventive action, then proposes a general campaign for prevention based on the cooperation of international NGOs.

Laurence, Edward (1990). "Events Data and Policy Analysis: Improving the Potential for Applying Academic Research to Foreign and Defense Policy Problems." *Policy Sciences*, 23:111-132.

The concept of early warning was first widely used during the Cold War by US military and intelligence analysts who sought to anticipate East-West flashpoints. The author describes empirical early warning research during this era and suggests why it was of limited utility for policymakers.

Rashid, Abdur (1998). "The Global Information and Early Warning System on Food and Agriculture," pp. 185-193. In John L. Davies and T. R. Gurr (Eds.) *Preventive Measures: Building Risk Assessment and Crisis Early Warning Systems*. Lanham, MD: Rowman & Littlefield.

Describes the structure and operations of the Global Information and Early Warning System (GIEWS) operated by the Food and Agricultural Organization in Rome, which monitors demand and supply of all basic foods throughout the world and provides alerts of imminent food crises.

Rubin, Barnett R. (Ed.) (1998).*Cases and Strategies for Preventive Action: Preventive Action Reports, Vol. 2, Report of the Carnegie Commission on Preventing Deadly Conflict*. New York: Century Foundation Press. 247 pp.

Case studies of major internal conflicts of the 1980s and 1990s and the preventive strategies that were brought to bear on them.

Government of Sweden (2004). *Stockholm International Forum 2004 26-28 January Proceedings: Preventing Genocide: Threats and Responsibilities*. Stockholm: Government of Sweden, Regeringskansliet. n.p.

Summarizes the events, speeches, and working papers of a conference attended by delegations from 55 states and ten international organizations, as well as most of the world's leading practitioners and experts in the field of genocide prevention. The participants adopted a final declaration committing themselves to early warning and monitoring of genocidal threats and to early preventive action.

Valentino, Benjamin; Huth, Paul; and Balch-Lindsay, Dylan (2004). "Draining the Sea: Mass Killing and Guerrilla Warfare." *International Organization*, Spring, 58: 375-407.

A quantitative comparative study of 147 wars between 1945 and 2000 whose results show that mass killing of civilians—including many instances of genocide and politicide—is often a calculated military strategy used in attempts to defeat guerrilla insurgencies. The greater the popular support for guerrillas, and the greater the military threat posed by the insurgency, the more likely that mass killings will occur.

Note: With thanks to T. R. Gurr for contributing to the annotations.

4

The Prevention of Genocide: Missed Opportunities, Complexities, and Possibilities

Samuel Totten

Introduction

Over the past decade and a half or so, people across the globe basically read about and/or passively watched (via television and Internet sites) as three major genocides unfolded before their eyes: the 1994 Rwandan genocide, the 1995 genocide in Srebrenica, and the current genocide in Darfur (2003 to the present). They also witnessed two major attempts that were ostensibly undertaken to prevent genocide: Kosovo in 1999 and East Timor in 1999. Both involved, at first, preventive diplomacy, and, then, when the latter failed to bring about the desired results (e.g., halting the Serbs' vicious attacks on the Albanians, and stopping the Indonesian forces and militia attacks on the East Timorese, respectively), military intervention. In the case of Kosovo, instead of sending in ground troops, NATO chose to attempt to pummel the Serbs into submission by bombing them. Ironically, such an approach allowed the Serbs to expel tens of thousands more Albanians than they would have been able to do otherwise. As for East Timor, by the time the preventive efforts got underway, hundreds, if not thousands, of innocent people had already been killed by Indonesian forces and scores of towns throughout East Timor had been utterly destroyed.

In regard to the situation in the former Yugoslavia, Ronayne (2005) notes the following:

> While it is tempting to laud NATO's intervention as a sea change event, as a powerfully important and first-ever "pre-emptive humanitarian intervention," it only constitutes a partial change. The unwillingness to use ground forces and the insistence that Allied

planes fly at 15,000 feet--reducing both their vulnerability and their accuracy--calls into questions the actual depth of commitment to genocide prevention demonstrated by the U.S. and its NATO allies. Indeed, the lack of Allied ground forces initially allowed the Serbs to continue, and even accelerate, their brutal campaign of ethnic cleansing in Kosovo despite the high-tech armada flying overhead (p. 67).

Despite the fact each intervention was far from being ideal, they seemingly prevented what appeared to be potential genocides in the making. Each, in their inimitable ways, also contributed hard-earned knowledge about what works and does not work when it comes to the prevention and intervention of genocide.

Stating the obvious, the prevention of genocide is not an easy task. Indeed, it is time-consuming, at times extremely frustrating, always politically complex, and extremely costly. It is also critical to note that each case is unique and thus requires its own set of preventive actions, which range across a wide spectrum of choices.[1]

Addressing Systemic Problems

If there is to be any hope at all to solve the set of problems that frequently lead to violent conflict (and sometimes genocide) then it is imperative to address the systemic issues that may, and often do, constitute the seeds of mass violence. In this regard, UN Secretary General Kofi Annan (1999) asserted that "...most researchers agree that it is useful to distinguish 'structural' or long-term factors, which make violent conflict more likely, from 'triggers,' which actually ignite it. The structural factors all have to do with *social* and *economic* policy, and the way that societies govern themselves" (italics added) (p. 47). Continuing, Annan (1999) noted, significantly, that

> What is highly explosive is..."horizontal" inequality: when *power* and *resources* are unequally distributed between groups that are also differentiated in other ways—for instance, by race, religion or language. So-called "ethnic" conflicts occur between groups which are distinct in one or more of these ways, when one of them feels it is being discriminated against, or another enjoys privileges which it fears to lose.... As resources get scarcer, competition for them gets fiercer, and elites use their power to retain them at everyone else's expense. And when economic decline is prolonged —especially when it starts from an already low base—the result can be a steady degeneration of the State's capacity to govern, until the point where it can no longer maintain public order (italics added) (p. 51).

While the twentieth century has been deemed by some "the century of genocide," unless humanity is proactive in addressing such systemic issues across the globe, the twenty-first century may earn itself an equally depressing sobriquet. In that regard, in an essay entitled "Genocide and Scarcity," Smith (1998) argued as follows:

> If current trends continue, a combination of environmental degradation, loss of agricultural land, depletion of fish stocks, dwindling of fuel resources, and a doubling of population to about 11 billion in the latter part of the twentieth-first century will lead to extreme hardship, even disaster, in many areas of the world.... Genocide, with some exceptions..., has seldom been the result of material scarcity, whereas material scarcity has often been a direct result of genocide. Nevertheless, in a world that in the twentieth century has displayed an unparalleled capacity for mass slaughter, it would be surprising if severe shortages would not exacerbate existing tendencies toward resolving social and political problems through the elimination of the groups thought to constitute the problem (pp. 200, 201).

In light of the complexity, breadth and depth of the latter problems, such issues may be the most intractable of all vis-à-vis the prevention of potential genocide. These are not matters, of course, that can simply be left to individual states to attempt to solve on their own. Indeed, it is going to take a Herculean effort by various intergovernmental organizations (IGOs), regional organizations, nongovernmental organizations (NGOs), think tanks and individual states to address such problems in an effective *and* timely manner.

Genocide Early Warning Signals

Genocide early warning signals are those statements, actions, events that suggest, in one way or another that a situation is possibly slouching towards genocide. Since the early 1980s a great deal of research has been conducted into the factors that contribute to the possibility of an outbreak of genocide. Among some of the many factors scholars have delineated are: the perpetration of an earlier genocide within a nation (e.g., Rwanda); an exclusionary ideology or legitimization of victimization by the perpetrators (e.g., the Ottoman Turks genocide of the Armenians between 1915 and 1923; the Nazis genocide of the Jews, Gypsies and handicapped during the Holocaust years; and the Hutu genocide of the Tutsis in Rwanda in 1994); authoritarian or totalitarian rule (e.g., Nazi Germany's genocide of the Jews and others, the Iraqi attacks against their Kurdish populations in the late 1980s); "the level of violence in a society and other institutional processes" (Charny, 1999, p. 258) (e.g., Nazi Germany, the U.S.S.R. under Stalin, Kampuchea under the Khmer Rouge, the gassing of the Iraqi Kurds during the reign of Saddam Hussein);

ethnic minority rule (e.g., the situation in Burundi in 1972 involving the Tutsis and Hutus); the perception of the target group as dangerous (e.g., the perceived status of the Tutsis prior to and during the 1994 Rwandan genocide); political upheaval during war or revolution (e.g., the Ottoman Turk genocide of the Armenians, the Nazi genocide of the Jews and others, the Khmer-Rouge perpetrated genocide); periods of transition (especially from autocratic governments to democratic ones) (Gurr, 2000); the sealing off of borders (e.g., Kampuchea from 1975 to 1979); and the lack of or refusal to engage in international trade (e.g., the case of the Khmer Rouge in Kampuchea between 1975 and 1979).

Genocide scholar Greg Stanton has devised an eight stage developmental model of genocide that he asserts is capable of assisting in detecting early warning signals. For example, the detection of actions committed by the potential perpetrators during some of the eight stages (e.g., "classification--'us vs. them'"); symbolization, dehumanization; organization (the formation of hate groups); polarization; preparation (the identification, expropriation, rounding up, and transportation of victims) (Stanton, 2004) are all capable of providing key information vis-à-vis early warning efforts. Some critics suggest that Stanton has created a model that that is "linear" in its approach; that is, some interpret the model as suggesting that crises evolving into genocide basically adhere to a set pattern of events whereas, they argue, there is no set pattern.

Among the scores of genocide early warning signals that have been delineated are the following: a society signaling out groups as being, in genocide scholar Helen Fein's words, "outside its universe of obligation"; the dehumanization (via dehumanizing language) of a specific group of people within a society; the creating of "others" within a society as scapegoats; ongoing and increasingly severe discrimination against and/or disenfranchisement of a target group; the targeting of groups by the media (newspapers, radio and/or television), calling for their expulsion or worse; systematic human rights violations carried out against a particular group of people; ethnic cleansing of a specific group; and sporadic massacres against a specific group of people.

As Huttenbach (2002) has argued, "By definition, then, any threat to and endangerment of a group's existence can serve as a signal of potential (possible if not immediately probable) genocide; it can serve as a sign of the deterioration of a group's ability to sustain itself in the face of an aggressively unfriendly foe such as a rival ethnic group. Thus, a careful monitoring of the granting or denying of a group's basic rights can act as a barometer of its existential condition at various times" (p. 124).

Over the past several decades, many situations slouching towards potential genocide have been noted early on by various organizations and agencies. Such reports have been issued, for example, by UN peacekeeping forces on the ground, UN Special Rapporteurs, the Central Intelligence Agency, diplomats (especially ambassadors) assigned to states or regions where violent conflict has flared up, the U.S. State Department, regional specialists working both inside and outside government agencies, various NGOs, and journalists. Unfortunately, the detection and dissemination of such knowledge has largely been conducted in a rather unsystematic, if not haphazard, manner. And even in those cases where certain intelligence agencies have systematically tracked a potential genocide, the forwarding of such critical information to the leaders of their own nation, the United Nations, and/or press has ranged from issuing the information in a timely fashion to the slow leaking of such information to not issuing it at all.

Due to the less than systematic manner in which potential and/or actual genocides have been detected and/or duly reported, many genocides have been in full tilt before the international community has chosen to act. The result is often the mass murder of tens if not hundreds, of thousands. This situation, of course, speaks to the need for a genocide early warning system capable of collecting, analyzing and disseminating information about early warning signals in a systematic, thorough and timely manner.

Ultimately, those who develop and operate genocide early warning systems will not only need to decide which signals are likely to be of most use in assessing whether a genocide is on the horizon, but how to most accurately analyze them *and* fashion reports that catch the attention of the powers that be.

Early Warning Systems

Over the past thirty some years there has been a great deal of discussion about the need for the development and implementation of a genocide early warning system. The purpose of such a system would be the collection of genocide early warning signals, the analysis of such data, and the dissemination of such data to the United Nations, member states of the UN, nongovernmental organizations whose focus is the protection of human rights and/or the prevention of genocide, the press, and the general public. As Rupesinghe (1999) has asserted, there is "a growing realization that successful conflict prevention is heavily dependent on the development of an effective early warning system. Without adequate forewarning of an impending crisis, the task of preventing the dispute from escalating into armed conflict becomes that much more difficult" (p. 265). Concomitantly, as Gurr and Harff (1999) noted, "Effective early warning systems would enable observers to differentiate among impending conflicts and to monitor on a daily basis the turning point events (accelerators) that lead to rapid escalation" (p. 272).

The development of such early warning systems is being undertaken by a diverse set of actors, including but not limited to: university based-researchers; nongovernmental organizations (NGOs) such as the Forum on Early Warning and Early Response (FEWER), Genocide Watch, and the International Crisis Group; the United Nations; the European Union; and the governments of some individual nations (including the United States). Addressing the development of such systems, Stanton (2005) has written that

> The early warning of threats to national interests has long been a job of the intelligence agencies that inform government policy makers. Threats of genocide were added to that task by the U.S. Central Intelligence Agency (CIA) in 1994, when that organization inaugurated its "State Failure Task Force," whose mission includes the analysis of factors that predispose states to genocide. Efforts to develop systems of early warning on the part of think tanks and university officers have also been funded by governments--in the United Kingdom, the Netherlands, Denmark, Sweden and Germany.
>
> At the UN, the Framework of Coordination was established within the Department of Political Affairs to convene high-level planners from UN departments to discuss and plan responses to crises that are judged to be capable of generating genocidal aggression (p. 272).

While some proposed genocide early warning systems would be limited to collecting and analyzing data and disseminating the findings of the analysis, others, such as the Forum for Early Warning and Emergency Response (FEWER), go beyond that:

> FEWER distinguishes itself from other early warning initiatives in a number of important ways. Firstly, it is highly action-oriented, directly linking conflict early warning to early action. Secondly, it works to provide decision makers with balanced, timely and reliable information and analysis on conflict-threatened countries and regions as well as possible policy responses based on and tailored to local needs and capacities for peace. Finally, and perhaps most significantly, FEWER is a collaborative effort on a global scale encompassing existing early warning projects and capitalizing on expertise from both the Northern and Southern Hemispheres (Rupesinghe, 1999, p. 265).

Preventive Diplomacy: A Wide Array of Early Measures to Ease Tensions, Stave Off Violence, and Bring a Modicum of Stability to a State or Region

Preventive measures should be taken early on when a government (or other body) begins to single out a specific group of people as "other" and/or "outside its [the government's] universe of obligation." The latter often results in particular groups being singled out solely based on who they are (e.g., their nationality, religion, ethnicity, race or political affiliation) and being treated in a variety of negative ways, including but not limited to being referred to in dehumanizing terms, ostracized, discriminated against, expelled from their homes and the areas in which they reside, and/or harmed or killed. It is always an unknown, of course, whether incipient actions against a targeted group will result in genocide, but *the primary goal should be to head off that possibility by taking action early on*. Action can be undertaken by the UN, regional organizations, nongovernmental organizations, and/or individual nations--and often is. The trouble, though, is that most preventive measures have not proved as effective as they could or should be, and that is because they have often been anemic, haphazard, and/or consisted of too little, too late.

Jentleson (2000), for one, argues that "the optimal conceptualization of preventive diplomacy" is that

> *It involves situations in which the likelihood of violent mass conflict is imminent--not yet existing, but also not low or just potential; the time frame is short to medium term--not immediate, but also not just a matter of ongoing relations over the long-term; and the objectives are to take the necessary diplomatic action within the limited time frame to prevent those crises...which seem imminent* (italics added) (p. 296).

Different researchers and practitioners perceive and/or define "preventive diplomacy" in radically different ways. Some, for example, state that preventive diplomacy is comprised of "nonviolent interactions that lead to constructive dialogue between adversaries...explicitly excluding the use of armed forces" (Thompson and Gutlove, 1994, p. 5), while certain others argue that it must be comprised of "both coercive and noncoercive measures" (Boutros-Ghali, 1995; Jentleson, 2000, p. 297). In regard to the latter, Jentleson (2000) asserts that "preventive diplomacy, no less than other forms of diplomacy, often needs to be backed by the threat if not the actual use of force" (p. 296). Continuing, he states that "[t]he parties to the conflict must know both that cooperation has its benefits and that those benefits will be fully equitable, and that noncooperation has its consequences and that the international parties are prepared to enforce those consequences differentially as warranted by who does and does not do what. Accordingly, although the preference may be to avoid having to use military force or economic sanctions or other coercive measures, the firmness of credible coercive measures need to be projected more often and more quickly than has tended to be the case thus far" (Jentleson, 2000, p. 309).

Preventive diplomacy has also, variously, been said to be comprised of a wide range of possibilities, including, for example, the following: conflict resolution, crisis-prevention mediation, the use of sanctions to induce change in the policies and actions of a targeted regime, the use of "carrots and sticks" (incentives and punitive measures), providing economic assistance contingent on a nation respecting and upholding basic human rights, the implementation of confidence building measures, the termination of violence, and, ultimately, when all else fails, preventive military deployment. A number of these actions seemingly cross over into intervention but, technically, if they contribute to the goal of staving off mass violence they constitute preventive efforts.

There are, of course, pros and cons to using each of the aforementioned means. For example, the efficacy of imposing sanctions is contingent upon a host of factors, including: selecting the appropriate type of sanction(s) vis-à-vis the context in which they will be imposed; implementing the sanctions in a sound manner; and thoroughly monitoring and evaluating the effects of the sanctions on a regular basis and, when needed, revising the type and/or implementation of the sanctions. Not surprisingly, the imposition of sanctions has met with mixed results. Sanctions are ineffective, if not counterproductive, when carelessly selected, haphazardly implemented (e.g., in a way that does not induce compliance), erratically enforced, and/or either evaluated in a haphazard manner or not at all.

A great deal of research has been (and continues to be) conducted into the way in which sanctions can be applied in the most effective manner. Much of this work has focused on what is commonly referred to as "smart sanctions." In regard to the issue of the efficacy of sanctions, as well as that which constitutes "smart sanctions," Cortright and Lopez (2002) note that

Surely, sanctions must be effective if they are to be smart. Here, [though,] the experience of the past decade has prompted doubts.... The meager results of so many sanctions episodes have promoted a search for more effective means of exerting pressure. This too has become part of the meaning of smart sanctions: to find methods of...pressure that can more effectively convince elites to change objectionable policies.

The twin impulses [of sanctions]—to reduce unintended humanitarian consequences and enhance political effectiveness—have led to the use of targeted and selective sanctions.

Targeting is intended to focus coercive pressure on those responsible for wrongdoing, while minimizing unintended negative impacts. Targeting means applying pressure on specific decision-making elites and the companies or entities they control.

Targeting can also mean selectively sanctioning specific products or activities that are vital to the conduct of an objectionable policy....While some see a distinction between targeted and selective sanctions, we view the two as inseparably linked. In our definition, a smart sanctions policy is one that imposes coercive pressures on specific individuals and entities and that restricts selective products or activities, while minimizing unintended economic and social consequences for vulnerable populations and innocent bystanders (p. 2).

On a different but related note, while coercive force may be effective in certain instances, it can also have counterproductive consequences. In some cases, "such measures may harden the situation and elicit punitive counter-reactions, leading to an escalation of violence" (Väyrynen, 2002, p. 141). That said, Jentleson (1998) is correct in his assertion that "...policymakers need [to] take more seriously the 'Rubicon' problem: that as difficult as preventive diplomacy is, the onset of mass violence transforms the nature of the conflict in ways that make resolution and even limitation even more difficult" (p. 315).

Post-Conflict Peacebuilding

Post-conflict peacebuilding is an integral component of conflict prevention. Fortunately, scholars in the areas of peace and conflict studies, along with many practitioners, appreciate the critical nature of post-conflict peacebuilding and have contributed a good amount of attention to it.

A plethora of issues need to be addressed in a post-genocidal situation, among them being: the signing of peace agreements that are perceived as just by both sides (which, then, must be closely monitored to ensure that such agreements are adhered to); a disarmament and demobilization plan; the integration and transformation of the armed forces; the establishment of law and order, including the creation of a fully functioning and fair criminal justice system; elections that are truly representative *and* conducted fairly; economic reconstruction and recovery; the successful return of any internally displaced persons and refugees; timely and fair trials for the alleged perpetrators of the genocide; and national reconciliation. When any one of these components is either not addressed or addressed in a perfunctory manner, the door is left open for serious, and possibly deadly, repercussions--including the eruption of another genocidal act.

Sticky and Sticking Issues

Preventing genocide is obviously easier said than done. In those nations where a crisis is possibly slouching towards genocide (including those where certain groups have been targeted for "ethnic cleansing," and/or where sporadic massacres and other crimes against humanity have taken place) many governments are likely to perceive any attempt to prevent genocide as an encroachment upon their state sovereignty and thus interference in their so-called "internal affairs." Indeed, in their eyes, there may be little to no difference between preventive measures and intervention. To support their contention of intrusiveness, such nations are likely to cite the so-called sanctity of each and every nations' sovereignty and the so-called (but sorely misinformed stance) of a state's "implied right" to do as it chooses within its own borders. In making such a claim they are likely to cite the Treaty of Westphalia.

In recent years, though, the concept of sovereignty and its perceived sanctity has come under scrutiny, as has the concept and claim of absolute sovereignty, especially in regard to the perpetration of genocide within one's borders. More specifically, the focus of the International Commission on Intervention and State Sovereignty's (ICISS) (2001) report, *The Responsibility to Protect*, which was conducted under the auspices of the United Nations and sponsored by the government of Canada, basically argues that "sovereign states have a responsibility to protect their own citizens from avoidable catastrophe—from mass murder and rape, from starvation—*but that when they are unwilling or unable to do so, that responsibility must be borne by the broader community of states*" (emphasis added) (p. viii). More specifically, in Part 3 of the report ("The Responsibility to Prevent"), the authors state that "This Commission strongly believes that the responsibility to protect implies an accompanying responsibility to prevent. And we think that it is more than high time for the international community to be doing more to close the gap between rhetorical support for prevention and tangible commitment. The need to do much better on prevention, and to exhaust prevention options before rushing to embrace intervention, were constantly recurring themes in our worldwide consultations..." (p. 19). Continuing, the authors state that

> ...conflict prevention is not merely a national or local affair. The failure of prevention can have wide international consequences and costs. Moreover, for prevention to succeed, strong support from the international community is often needed, and in many cases may be indispensable. Such support may take many forms. It may come in the form of development assistance and other efforts to help address the root cause of potential conflict; or efforts to provide support for local initiatives to advance good governance, human rights, or the rule of law; or good offices, missions, mediation efforts and other efforts to promote dialogue or reconciliation. In some cases, international support for prevention efforts may take the form of inducements; in others, it may involve a willingness to apply tough and perhaps even punitive measures (p. 19).

While the ICISS's report constitutes a major statement vis-à-vis a state's responsibility to protect its own citizens from such tragedies as genocide, whether it shall constitute a watershed event in international relations and move beyond simply being an ideal to actually influencing practice is still to be seen. There are many, it must be noted, who look askance at "softening" state sovereignty in any way at all and argue that it has been and continues to be the bedrock on which international stability (between and amongst nations) exists.

As for those organizations and nations that have the power to implement preventive actions, various reasons often deter them from taking such action, including the following:

- a plain lack of interest (they simply do not care about the fate of a group of people far from their own borders);

- various national leaders simply do not see it as their job to act to attempt to prevent or stanch genocide (and this may be so even though their nation has ratified the UN Convention on the Prevention and Punishment of the Crime of Genocide);

- a quasi-like triage situation is at work in regard to those problems/issues a nation chooses to tackle. That is, the world is plagued with so many major problems that nations pick and choose those that they have the greatest interest in or concern about (including the impact it might have on their own citizens, their government and the larger international community); those they believe they can have the greatest impact on; and/or perceive as the least taxing on their own resources.

- *realpolitik* is certainly one of the main, if not *the main*, reasons as to why individual nations—including, of course, members of the UN Security Council—do not act to halt genocide early on, or when they do act, it is only half-heartedly and, thus, largely ineffective. That is, their own national interests—political, social, economic—drive their decisions and responses;

- a lack of political will by a country's leaders. In such cases, a nation's leaders may believe (or want to believe) that their constituents (the voters) are not willing to support or pay for such an endeavor and/or not willing to risk the lives of their country's troops, and thus the leaders are not willing to take a political risk by supporting such efforts. Leaders may also fear becoming entangled in an intractable problem, and/or feel or believe that they are already over-stretched vis-à-vis their commitments; and,

- a nation's leaders may misinterpret—sometimes inadvertently, sometimes purposely—the seriousness of a crisis/situation.

Hand-in-hand with the above, Fein (2000) has observed that many situations possibly slouching towards genocide are "distanced by framing them with a neutral label that avoid the perception of the criminal causes of such events: refugee or humanitarian crises, complex humanitarian emergencies, or ethnic conflict, implying there are two equally culpable parties. This serves to obscure both cause and perpetrator; thus, there is no crime, such as genocide, requiring international attention" (p 42). A classic case of this phenomenon was evident during the early period of the Rwandan genocide in 1994.

As for the issue of *realpolitik*, genocide scholar Alex Alvarez (2001) has written as follows:

> The difficulty with diplomacy and diplomats is that they are often held hostage to *Realpolitik* strategies that place a higher value on protecting national security than on protecting an oppressed group. Just before Indonesia invaded East Timor in 1975 and began its brutal repression of the East Timorese population, the Australian ambassador to Indonesia wrote that Australia should assume "a pragmatic rather than a principled stand," because "that is what national interest and foreign policy is all about." American diplomats were similarly directed to avoid the issue of East Timor and, just days before the invasion, [U.S. Secretary of State] Henry Kissinger and [U.S. President] Gerald Ford met with Indonesian President Suharto and essentially gave him the go-ahead for the invasion. Approximately two hundred thousand East Timorese have been killed under the Indonesian occupation.
>
> [...In early 1994,] James Woods, a U.S. deputy assistant secretary of defense, placed Rwanda-Burundi on a list of potential trouble spots just before the killing [in Rwanda] began but was told by a superior, "If something happens in Rwanda-Burundi, we don't care. Take it off the list.... U.S. national interest is not involved.... [W]e

can't put all these silly humanitarian issues on lists like important problems like the Middle East and North Korea and so on" (p. 137).

Over and above the latter concerns/issues, far too many leaders and policymakers to do not see a need to act, if in fact they ever do, *until a crisis is "officially" deemed to be genocide*. In other words, far too often massive, violent human right violations (e.g., crimes against humanity) are not perceived as something worthy of the world's attention, let alone immediate action to halt them. Such a situation, of course, constitutes an acute misunderstanding of the critical value of early prevention. As Staub (2002) perspicaciously argues:

> While good theory can specify how to predict the likelihood of group violence, its exact form is probably impossible to predict. If we want to focus on genocide only, we can only focus on events that have already taken place. Until, and if ever, further research identifies different origins of genocide and mass killing, it is reasonable to conclude that prevention can only aim at avoiding group violence, not genocide specifically (pp. 103-104).

That is a lesson that policymakers and leaders at the UN and individual nations need to both learn *and* act upon.

Three recent and "classic" examples of *realpolitik* are evident in China's, Russia's and the United States' response to the ongoing genocide in Darfur. China and Russia have both threatened to veto any vote sanctioning Sudan, as China has huge petroleum interests in Sudan and Russia has petroleum interests as well as a large and lucrative arms deal with Sudan. As for the United States, even though it declared, in September 2004, that genocide was being perpetrated in Darfur by Government of Sudan (GOS) troops and the *Janjaweed* (Arab militia), in early 2005 it (the United States) backed off applying pressure on Sudan to cease and desist from its genocidal actions, and that was due to the fact that Sudan's President al-Bashir promised to assist the U.S. in tracking down and capturing terrorists in the latter's war against terrorism. From that point onward, the United States government has vacillated between calling on Sudan to rein in gos troops and the *Janjaweed* to claiming the situation in Darfur has improved.

Recommendations

Numerous researchers and scholars, intergovernmental organizations (including the UN), NGOs, and individual states have made recommendations in regard to how the international community can become more effective in preventing potential genocidal events. Among some of the many are as follows:

- If there is to be any hope whatsoever of developing effective means to prevent genocide, genocide scholars and those in adjunct fields must come together in an effort to synergize their efforts. That means those who specialize in genocide studies, conflict prevention, conflict management, conflict resolution, peacekeeping, peacemaking, peace enforcement, international law, sanctions, the development of early warning systems, post-conflict development, et al. need to collectively address a host of issues (e.g., international law (accords, covenants, conventions, treaties); information-gathering and analysis; early warning signals; data risk bases; early warning systems; intelligence sharing; conflict resolution; conflict prevention; conflict management; peacekeeping, diplomatic peacekeeping; peacemaking; peace enforcement; sanctions; partitioning; coercive inducements; and institution building) (Totten, 2004, p. 243) for the express purpose of designing an effective anti-genocide regime.

    Basically corroborating the latter approach, Lt. General (retired) Romeo Dallaire (Canada), who served as the commander of the UN Assistance Mission in Rwanda from 1993-1994 and saw genocide up close, argues that "there is absolutely no way that we will find effective and lasting solutions to these conflicts if we work from different plans. Unless we move to one integrated plan of the political, the humanitarian, the military, the security, the economics the nation-building, the sustainable capabilities, with all these components working together with different emphases at different times depending on the scenario, we will continue to be wrapped up in...classic responses [to crimes against humanity and genocide]" (quoted in Rittner, Roth, and Smith, 2002, p. 72).

- Individual nations, regional organizations and the United Nations must focus *their greatest attention on prevention* (versus intervention, which is often carried out only after tens of thousands of people have already been murdered). What that means is: (1) There is a critical need, as mentioned earlier, to address the various systemic issues that can and have served as the catalyst for violent conflict. Until such issues are addressed, it is almost a certainty that genocide will continue to erupt in various parts of the world. As Weiss (1993) has perspicaciously argued: [E]ffective prevention should include basic investment in economic and social development as well as reforms to distribute the benefits of future growth more equitably. It would also include changing the global financial and trading systems" (p. 7); (2) When mass violence is threatened and/or massive human rights abuses begin to occur, the international community (or at least portions of it) needs to act immediately--*and not wait for some organization or official body to declare the crisis to constitute a case of "genocide."* As Staub (2002) has cogently argued, this means not only working to halt significant violence that is not yet genocidal, but implementing "preventive actions when the conditions for group violence exist.... Relevant UN agencies should be reformed and governmental agencies should be established everywhere with this specific responsibility. Their task should not be only early warning, which is of great recent interest, but early action" (p. 106); (3) Early on in a conflict, both conflict resolution and mediation should play a significant role, along with political diplomacy; if the latter fails, a tougher approach must be implemented along with tough, targeted sanctions as well as a show of political will to act swiftly and directly (e.g., militarily) if need be; and (4) Weiss (1993) argues wisely that "What is required [for effective prevention] is nothing less than a shift in the dominant way that we attack problems. Our new policy lenses should be tinted with preventive peacebuilding rather than post-conflict intervention and management" (p. 7).

- A sophisticated genocide early warning system (equipped with the latest technology, including satellites, and operated by independent researchers who specialize in early warning, human rights, crimes against humanity, genocide, and data analysis) that collects data on a minute-by-minute basis from around the world, analyzes the data, and disseminates key information to the United Nations, individual nations, NGOs, and the press must become a major priority. Such a system has been discussed for at least thirty years but a comprehensive system such as this has not yet come to fruition.

- A fully operational anti-genocide regime needs to be developed and implemented as soon as possible. Its various purposes, in part, would, ideally, constitute the following: (1) conduct research into all aspects of genocide; (2) conduct research into such sticky issues as overcoming *realpolitik*, the lack of political will, and a self-imposed slowness by the UN, regional organizations and states to act to halt crimes against humanity and genocide; (3) develop research-based and highly effective methods vis-à-vis the prevention and intervention of genocide; (4) maintain a sophisticated genocide early warning system; (5) disseminate the latest information regarding situations that may be slouching towards genocide; (6) generate attention regarding pre-genocidal situations that can serve as a clarion call for action; (7) create a robust (well trained with a substantial number of troops that is adequately funded and provided institutional support) rapid action anti-genocide force.[2]

- Human rights and anti-genocide organizations, major broadcasting systems, NGOs and the UN need to develop concrete plans of action to offset the use of media by potential (and actual) perpetrators of genocide to incite and/or direct genocide (see Chalk, 1999, pp. 198-200); and

- The establishment of a sizable, well-financed, highly qualified and thoroughly independent genocide investigative team must be established. Working in conjunction with human rights organizations, NGOs in the field, genocide early warnings specialists, and, ideally, an anti-genocide regime, the investigative team's express purpose would be to deploy teams to "hotspots" early on in order to conduct the most comprehensive and objective investigation into whether a crisis situation is slouching towards crimes against humanity and/or genocide. "Upon completion of the investigation and documentation of the situation, the investigative group should disseminate its report to the United Nations and other intergovernmental organizations, major governments of the world, key nongovernmental organizations, and the media (e.g., newspapers, radio and television), and work in tandem with the latter to issue calls to act to prevent the crimes from being perpetrated" (Totten, 2002, pp. 172-173).

Likelihood of Success

The likelihood of making the prevention of genocide a given versus a hope is mixed. Any likelihood of success is bound to be based on a wide array of factors, including: a reformed United Nations that takes its mandate to prevent genocide much more seriously than it currently does, a true synergy of efforts amongst and between an eclectic group of organizations and individuals with deep and broad expertise in a wide array of fields, and an ongoing effort by the nations of the world to nurture and abide by the notions of "the responsibility to protect" and "a responsibility to prevent."

Some movement in this regard provides glimmers of hope. One is the establishment and implementation of various investigations by the United States, the United Nations, and Physicians for Human Rights, Even this progress, though, has been tainted in that the investigations have come late in the killing process and the outcomes and ultimate impact of the investigations by the U.S. and the UN have been adversely impacted by politics and *realpolitik* in one way or another (see Totten, 2006). It is also true, though, that overall progress in preventing genocide has been excruciatingly slow, when it need not be (and this is especially so in regard to the development of a sophisticated and fully functioning genocide early warning system). And when one looks at the genocidal tragedies of the past decade (e.g., the 1994 genocide in Rwanda, the 1995 genocide at Srebrenica, and the current (2003-present) genocide in Darfur, Sudan), it is hard to believe that much *real* progress has been made at all.

In July 2004, UN Secretary General Kofi Annan named Juan E. Méndez (a human rights advocate, lawyer and former political prisoner from Argentina) as his first special adviser on the prevention of genocide. Initially, many heralded the establishment of such a position as a positive step forward. However, the UN's tepid and totally ineffectual response to the ongoing violence in Darfur has to make one wonder about the value of there even being a UN special adviser on the prevention of genocide.

On May 3, 2006, Annan established an advisory group to provide support to his special adviser on the prevention of genocide and to contribute to the broader efforts of the UN to prevent massive human rights violations, including crimes against humanity and genocide. The Advisory Committee on Genocide Prevention is composed of seven well-known individuals with a wide range of backgrounds and experience: Monica Anderson (Department for International Human Rights and Treaty of Law within Sweden's Foreign Ministry); Zackari Ibrahim (former foreign minister of Nigeria); Roméo Dallaire (senator, Canadian Parliament and former UN force commander in Rwanda); Gareth Evans (president of the International Crisis Group and former foreign minster of Australia); Roberto Garreton (former representative for the High Commissioner for Human Rights in Latin America and special rapporteur on human rights in the Democratic Republic of Congo); David Hamburg (president emeritus of the Carnegie Corporation of New York); Sadako Ogata (co-chair of the UN Commission on Human Security and former High Commission of Refugees); and Bishop Desmond Tutu (Nobel Peace Prize laureate, South Africa).

The ultimate value of both the advisor's position and the advisory committee is yet to be determined. It is possible, but hardly a certainty, that the special adviser on the prevention of genocide and the Advisory Committee on Genocide Prevention will eventually address many of the aforementioned issues germane to the prevention of genocide.

As previously noted, the area which is least likely to see significant progress is that of systemic issues. In light of the abysmal and unconscionable inequity among nations, peoples and various groups in different societies, it is more than a little difficult to be optimistic concerning the possibility of systemic change vis-à-vis such deeply rooted problems--the brutish poverty, abject hunger, lack of clean water, lack of even minimal health care, wages so minimal that they can only be equated with indentured servitude, the lack of adequate educational opportunities, and governments with political systems that perpetuate extreme injustice. The lives of hundreds of millions are so sordid in so many ways that it is almost, if not, in fact, beyond the imagination of the average person in the West--and possibly that is one of the many reasons why there has been little to no real movement vis-à-vis the amelioration of these problems.

Currently, the efforts to address such systemic issues constitute more of a band-aid-like approach than a well-thought out, thorough and systematic effort to address the roots of the problem(s). That is not to say that some approaches are not helpful to certain people for they are. Indeed, as a result of the dedication and efforts of various arms of the United Nations, hundreds of NGOs, and various philanthropic groups, glimmers of "success" certainly arise from small scale efforts, e.g., providing potable water for villages; teaching a region's farmers new ways of land use; establishing innovative loan and repayment programs, et al. But, it is also true that many of the current efforts of the World Bank, United Nations programs and NGOs are not *the* answer. In far too many cases, the efforts of such organizations are addressing problems that states once attempted to address but have chosen to relinquish, for whatever reason(s). Furthermore, money is frequently "thrown" at projects and groups; and when this is done time and again, instead of helping the needy build a foundation on which to build, it turns them into "charity cases." Finally, systemic changes need to be made in the world's economic systems that confine tens of millions of peoples' dreams, hopes, needs, and lives to abject and obscene poverty.

It seems as if the systemic issues that plague so many societies and often degenerate into violent conflict, including (though to a lesser extent) genocide, will not be altered without a huge investment of time, thought, innovation and dedication by scholars and activists across the globe. Concomitantly, it is also going to take awakening the "haves" to the miserable plight of the "have nots" and the ramifications of the latter for the entire world.

It also seems as if it is going to take a Manhattan-like project (the development of the first atomic bomb during World War II by the United States) to devise a highly sophisticated and effective anti-genocide regime, one built upon a foundation that thoroughly and effectively addresses the systemic issues plaguing many parts of the world today *and* does its all to address crisis situations early on in a real attempt to stave off violence.

In attempting to address *all* of the aforementioned concerns, the international community must work arduously to *avoid* applying old--and often ineffective--"remedies" to tortuously complex and/or new and difficult problems.

And so where does that leave us in regard to all of the aforementioned concerns? With the age-old cliché, I fear, that "only time will tell."

Notes

1. The "popular" view is that there is a clear distinction between prevention and intervention. Huttenbach (2002), for example, asserts that "What needs to be understood is that...a clear distinction must be made, in the context of genocide prevention, between heading off a suspected genocide and intervention in ongoing genocide.... [I]involvement in a genocide in progress is not prevention but genocide termination" (p. 125). In reality, however, such a division constitutes a false dichotomy. That is true, for, first, until a genocide is actually perpetrated and all but over, it is often difficult, if not impossible, to ascertain, whether a violent conflict is going to evolve into genocide. Second, if sanctions (be they arms embargoes, the freezing of assets, travel bans or trade bans) are imposed against a government for "violating a group's rights," they are, at least from the alleged perpetrator's perspective, interventive measures, but could be--and often are--considered preventive measures by those who impose them. It is also true that there are military actions that can be, and are, perceived as preventive in nature (e.g., a Chapter VII mandate of peace enforcement) and yet such actions imposed against a nation's will will undoubtedly be perceived as intervention. The point is, the distinction(s) between prevention and intervention is/are not as clear as some want to make it/them out to be.

2. A potential problem facing the creation of such a force is that currently, and well into the future, is the likelihood it will be placed, if anywhere, under the auspices and control of the UN Security Council. That means, of course, that the force will be buffeted by the winds of *realpolitik* as just about everything is that the Security Council considers and then either acts or does not act upon. Furthermore, such a force will inevitably be constrained by the UN's bureaucratic inertia and numerous other constraints that typify UN policy and actions.

   On a different but significant note, since individual nations are, more often than not, hesitant to commit military personnel and resources to stave off and/or combat genocide, it seems imperative to develop a force that is comprised of volunteer troops versus those that are on loan from various nations. Such a force must be well-staffed, well-equipped, well-financed, well-trained and highly qualified for various types of preventive (and interventive) assignments. Ideally, volunteers would come from virtually any area of the globe, be highly trained by qualified officers with solid field experience, and be well-paid. This is an idea that has been written about extensively (e.g., Alvarez, 2001, pp. 100-107; Mendlovitz and Fousek, 2000, pp. 105-122; and Stanton (Chapter in this book), but it is still far from being realized.

References

Alvarez, Alex (2001). *Governments, Citizens, and Genocide: A Comparative and Interdisciplinary Approach.* Bloomington and Indianapolis: Indiana University Press.

Annan, Kofi A. (1999). "Development is the Best Form of Conflict Prevention," pp. 47-56. In Kofi A. Annan's *The Question of Intervention: Statements by the Secretary General.* New York: United Nations.

Bedjaoui, Mohammed (2000). "The Fundamentals of Preventive Diplomacy," pp. 29-50. In Kevin M. Cahill (Ed.) *Preventive Diplomacy: Stopping Wars Before They Start.* New York: Routledge.

Chalk, Frank (1999). "Radio Broadcasting in the Incitement and Interdiction of Gross Violations of Human Rights, Including Genocide," pp. 185-200. In Roger W. Smith (Ed.) *Genocide: Essays Towards Understanding, Early Warning, and Prevention.* Williamsburg, VA: Association of Genocide Scholars.

Charny, Israel W. (1999). "Genocide Early Warning System," pp. 253-261. In Israel W. Charny (Ed.) *Encyclopedia of Genocide.* Santa Barbara, CA: ABC Clio Press.

Cortright, David, and Lopez, George A. (2002). "Introduction: Assessing Smart Sanctions from the 1990s," pp. 1-22. In David Cortright and George A. Lopez (Eds.) *Smart Sanctions: Targeting Economic Statecraft.* Lanham, MD: Rowman & Littlefield Publishers.

Fein, Helen (2000). "The Three P's of Genocide Prevention: With Application to a Genocide Foretold--Rwanda," pp. 41-66. In Neal Riemer (Ed.) *Protection Against Genocide: Mission Impossible?* Westport, CT: Praeger.

Gurr, Ted Robert (2000). *Peoples Versus States: Minorities at Risk in the New Century.* Washington, DC: U.S. Institute of Peace Press.

Gurr, Ted Robert, and Harff, Barbara (1999). "Minorities and Genocide: Early Warning and Minorities At Risk Around the World," pp. 267-272. In Israel W. Charny (Ed.) *Encyclopedia of Genocide.* Santa Barbara, CA: ABC Clio Press.

Huttenbach, Henry (2002). "Anticipating Genocide," pp. 123-126. In Carol Rittner, John K. Roth, and James M. Smith (Ed.) *Will Genocide Ever End?* St. Paul, MN: Paragon House.

International Commission on Intervention and State Sovereignty (2001). *The Responsibility to Protect.* Ottawa, ON: International Development Research Centre.

Jentleson, Bruce W. (1998). "Preventive Diplomacy and Ethnic Conflict: Possible, Difficult, Necessary," pp. 293-316. In David A. Lake and Donald Rothchild (Eds.) *The International Spread of Ethnic Conflict.* Princeton, NJ: Princeton University Press.

Mendlovitz, Saul, and Fousek, John (2000). "A UN Constabulary to Enforce the Law on Genocide and Crimes Against Humanity," pp. 105-122. In Neal Riemer (Ed.) *Protection Against Genocide: Mission Impossible?* Westport, CT: Praeger.

Rupesinghe, Kumar (1999). "Forum for Early Warning and Emergency Response (FEWER)," pp. 265-267. In Israel W. Charny (Ed.) *Encyclopedia of Genocide.* Volume I. Santa Barbara, CA: ABC CLIO Press.

Smith, Roger W. (1998). "Scarcity and Genocide," pp. 199-219. In Michael N. Dobkowski and Isidor Wallimann (Eds.) *The Coming Age of Scarcity: Preventing Mass Death and Genocide in the Twenty-First Century.* Syracuse, NY: Syracuse University Press.

Stanton, Greg H. (2005). "Early Warning," pp. 271-273. In Dinah L. Shelton (Ed.) *Encyclopedia of Genocide and Crimes Against Humanity.* New York: Macmillan

Stanton, Gregory (2004). "Could the Rwandan Genocide Have Been Prevented?" *Journal of Genocide Research,* 6(2):211-228.

Staub, Ervin (2002). "Understanding Genocide," pp. 103-109. In Carol Rittner, John K. Roth, and James M. Smith (Eds.) *Will Genocide Ever End?* St. Paul, MN: Paragon House.

Totten, Samuel (2004). "The Intervention and Prevention of Genocide: Sisyphean or Doable?" *Journal of Genocide Research*, 6(2):229-247.

Totten, Samuel (2004). "A Task Whose Time Has Come," pp. 167-175. In Carol Rittner, John K. Roth, and James M. Smith (Eds.) *Will Genocide Ever End?* St. Paul, MN: Paragon House.

Totten, Samuel (2006). "The U.S. Investigation into the Darfur Crisis and Its Determination of Genocide: A Critical Analysis," pp. 199-222. In Samuel Totten and Eric Markusen (Eds.) *Genocide in Darfur: Investigating Atrocities in the Sudan*. New York: Routledge.

Annotated Bibliography

Bibliographies

Totten, Samuel (Compiler/Editor) (2006). *Prevention and Intervention of Genocide: An Annotated Bibliography*. New York: Routledge. 1,153 pp.

A major annotated bibliography comprised of over two thousand annotations on such topics as: prevention of genocide (theories and practices), preventive diplomacy, conflict resolution, genocide early warning systems, sanctions, and the United Nations efforts vis-a-vis the prevention of genocide,

Genocide Prevention: Possibilities, Measures, Failures

Ackerman, Alice (2000). *Making Peace Prevail: Preventing Violent Conflict in Macedonia*. Syracuse, New York: Syracuse University Press. 217 pp.

The book is comprised of the following sections, and chapters: "Introduction"; 1. "An Ounce of Prevention..."; 2. "Preventive Diplomacy: 'Successes' and 'Failures'"; 3. "Macedonia and the Balkans"; 4. "The Domestic Politics of Prevention"; 5. "The Preventive Role of International Organizations"; 6. "The CSCE/OSCE in Macedonia"; 7. "Nongovernmental Organizations and Long-Term Conflict"; 8. "The Art of Conflict Prevention"; and "Epilogue."

Adelman, Howard (1999). "Preventing Genocide: The Case of Rwanda," pp. 161-182. In Roger W. Smith (Ed.) *Genocide: Essays Toward Understanding, Early Warning, and Prevention*. Williamsburg, VA: Association of Genocide Scholars, and Department of Government, College of William and Mary. Adelman, co-author of *Early Warning and Conflict Management: The Genocide in Rwanda* (1996), discusses why the United Nations failed to prevent the 1994 Rwandan genocide from being perpetrated.

Annan, Kofi (2002). *Prevention of Armed Conflict: Report of the Secretary General.* New York. United Nations Publications. 106 pp.

Annan basically pledges to move the United Nations from a culture of reaction to a culture of prevention vis-a-vis violent conflict. In doing so, he presents a series of practical actions that he claims the UN is attempting to implement.

Avruch, Kevin (1998). *Culture and Conflict Resolution.* Washington, DC: United States Institute of Peace Press. 153 pp.

Avruch challenges both scholars and practitioners not only to develop a clearer understanding of what culture is, but also to take that understanding and incorporate it into more effective conflict resolution processes. The book is divided into four parts: I. Culture, II. Conflict Resolution, III. Frames for Culture and Conflict Resolution, and IV. Discourses of Culture and Conflict Resolution.

Babbitt, Eileen F. (1997). "Contributions of Training to International Conflict Resolution," pp. 365-387. In I. William Zartman and J. Lewis Rasmussen (Eds.) *Peacemaking in International Conflict: Methods & Techniques.* Washington, DC: United States Institute of Peace Press.

Among the issues the author addresses are: reframing the parties' conception of their conflict; reframing the parties' conception of their own side and the other side; skills for dialogue and problem solving; ethical concerns and other criticism (exporting models that are not culturally relevant, perpetuating dependence on outsiders, creating dramatic change in individuals, but not structures); and evaluation.

Bedjaoui, Mohammed (2000). "The Fundamentals of Preventive Diplomacy," pp. 29-50. In Kevin M. Cahill (Ed.) *Preventive Diplomacy: Stopping Wars Before They Start.* New York: Routledge.

The sections and subsections of this essay are comprised of the following: The Geopolitics of Preventive Diplomacy; Preventive Diplomacy to Promote Development (Underdevelopment: A Threat to International Peace and Security; Development: The Best Contraceptive; and The Severe Disappointments of Preventive Diplomacy in the Area of Development); Preventive Diplomacy Through World-Wide Education; and Preventive Diplomacy and Human Rights (Preventive Diplomacy and Security; Prevention as a Matter of Necessity, and Diplomacy as a Gesture of Humility).

Brown, Michael E., and Rosecrane, Richard N. (1999). *The Costs of Conflict: Prevention and Cure in the Global Arena*. Lanham, MD: Rowman & Littlefield. 280 pp. Written under the auspices of the Carnegie Commission on Preventing Deadly Conflict, this book is comprised, in part, of the following: Chapter 1. "Comparing Costs of Prevention and Costs of Conflict: Toward a New Methodology"; Part One: Failed Prevention (Chapter 2: "Bosnia"; Chapter 3: "Rwanda"); Part Two: Initial Prevention (Chapter 7: "Macedonia"; Chapter 8: "Slovakia"); and Part Three: Mid-Course Prevention.

Campbell, Kenneth J. (2001). *Genocide and the Global Village*. New York: Palgrave. 178 pp.

In Chapter 8 ("Remedy"), Campbell comments on the failure of the international community to halt contemporary genocide and then comments on "signs of progress" and "the limits of progress." He briefly discusses the need to build political will, "enhance international capacity," and "consolidate normative consensus" vis-a-vis preventing/halting genocide.

Carnegie Commission on Preventing Deadly Conflict (1997). *Preventing Deadly Conflict: Final Report with Executive Summary*. Washington, DC: Author. 257 pp.

This book is comprised, in part, of the following: Prologue: Conflict Prevention in the Twenty-First Century (The Legacy of Rwanda; Is Prevention Possible?; Toward a New Commitment to Prevention); Chapter 1: "Against Complacency" (From Cold War to Deadly Peace, A World Transforming, Rapid Population Growth; The Cost of Deadly Conflict; A

Historic Opportunity: Toward Prevention); Chapter 2: "When Prevention Fails" (How and Why Deadly Conflict Occurs; Understanding Violent Conflict; Conflict within States; What Are the Tasks?; What Works?); Chapter 3: "Operational Prevention" (Strategies in the Face of Crisis; A Framework for Engagement; A Comprehensive Political-Military Response; Early Warning and Early Response; What Kind of Warning Is Most Useful?; Who Can Best Provide Useful Early Warning?; Who Should Be Warned?; Preventive Diplomacy Economic Measures; Forceful Measures; Peacekeeping and Maintaining Civil Order; "Thin Blue Line" Preventive Deployments; "Fire Brigade" Deployments); Chapter 4: "Structural Prevention" (Strategies To Address the Root Causes of Deadly Conflict; Regional Contingencies; Helping from Within: Development Revisited; Making Development Sustainable; Helping from Outside: Development Assistance; Justice in the International Community; Humanitarian Law; Nonviolent Dispute Resolution; Justice within States; Transition to Democracy); Chapter 5: "Preventing Deadly Conflict" (The Responsibility of States, Leaders, and Civil Society); Chapter 6: "Preventing Deadly Conflict" (The Responsibility of the United Nations and Regional Arrangements; Strengths of the UN; Limitations of the UN; Strengthening the UN for Prevention; Reform of the Security Council; The UN's Role in Long-Term Prevention; The International Financial Institutions; Economic Organizations); and Chapter 7: "Toward A Culture of Prevention."

Charny, Israel W. (1988). "Intervention and Prevention of Genocide," pp. 20-38. In Israel W. Charny (Ed.) *Genocide: A Critical Bibliographic Review*. London and New York: Mansell Publishers and Facts on File, respectively.

This essay and critical annotated bibliography (which includes 53 citations), provides an overview, in part, of some of the many critical issues vis-a-vis prevention.

Crocker, Chester A.; Hampson, Fen Osler; and Aall, Pamela (Eds.) (1999). *Herding Cats: Multiparty Mediation in a Complex World*. Washington, DC: United States Institute of Peace Press. 735 pp.

Among some of the many chapters included in this book are: "The Role of the OSCE High Commissioner in Conflict Prevention" by Max van der

Stoel; "Burundi: A Case of Parallel Diplomacy" by Fabienne Hara;"Peace to Cambodia" by Richard H. Solomon; "The Road to Sarajevo" by Richard Holbrooke; and "Rising to the Challenge of Multiparty Mediation" by Crocker, Hampson, and Aall.

Crocker, Chester A.; Hampson, Fen Osler; and Aall, Pamela (Eds.) (1999). "Multiparty Mediation and the Conflict Cycle," pp. 19-45. In Chester A. Crocker, Fen Osler Hampson, and Pamela Aall (Eds.) *Herding Cats: Multiparty Mediation in a Complex World*. Washington, DC: United States Institute of Peace Press.

The authors provide an extended discussion of key issues vis-à-vis mediation theory. The subsections of the essay are as follows: Two Paradigms of Mediation; The Structuralist Paradigm of Mediation; Social-Psychological Approaches; Toward a Synthesis of Perspectives; Comparative Advantage of Different Kinds of Mediations; The Wars in the Balkans: An Illustration; and Challenges of Multiparty Mediation.

Cushman, Thomas (2003). "Is Genocide Preventable? Some Theoretical Considerations." *Journal of Genocide Research*, December, 5(4): 523-542.

Theoretical and empirical reflections on the problems and prospects of the prevention of genocide in the twenty first-century."

Dorn, A. Walter, and Matloff, Jonathan (2000). "Preventing the Bloodbath: Could the UN Have Predicted and Prevented the Rwandan Genocide?" *The Journal of Conflict Studies*, 20(1): 9-52.

The essay is comprised of the following sections: Background (Historical Review, and UN Mandate for Monitoring and Prevention); Early Warning Signals; Preventive Action; and Political Will. The essay also includes an appendix entitled: "The Genocide Fax": Cable from UNAMIR Force Major Romeo Dallaire to UN Headquarters.

Fein, Helen (Ed.) (1992). *Genocide Watch*. New Haven, CT: Yale University Press. 204 pp.

The essays in this volume most germane to the prevention of genocide are: "Recognizing Genocides and Politicides" by Barbara Harff; "Refugees: Contemporary Witnesses to Genocide" by Bill Frelick; "Newspaper Responses to Reports of Atrocities: Burundi, Mozambique, Iraq" by Walter K. Ezell; "Reflections on the Prevention of Genocide" by Leo Kuper; and "A Campaign to Deter Genocide: The Bahá'í Experience" by Katherine R. Bigelow.

Fein, Helen (1993). "Never Again? A Ten Step Program to Stop Genocide." *The ISG* [Institute for the Study of Genocide] *Newsletter*, Fall, 11:8-10.

The ten steps that Fein suggests and briefly discusses are: "1. Penalize perpetrators of gross violations of human rights promptly and reward states which rectify past policies of violation; 2. Tie political legitimacy to protecting human rights; 3. [C]hange the political environment of the potential perpetrators; 4. Prevent escalation of conflict wherever possible; 5. Enable independent investigators, social scientists, lawyers, and mediators to evaluate human rights violations and risks and help countries seeking to change their ways; 6. Take prompt and forceful action to move the perpetrator to stop, or consider means of humanitarian intervention; 7. When we can't stop the perpetrators, help the victims fight back if defense is possible; 8. Enable the victims of genocide, persecution and indiscriminate killing to flee by providing means of rescue and giving asylum promptly; 9. Recognize the victims publicly and shame the perpetrators of past genocides; and 10. Create an international criminal court to prosecute acts of genocide and other international crimes in order not only to prosecute offenders but to get some restitution for the victims" (pp. 8, 9, 10).

Fein, Helen (1999). "Patrons, Prevention and Punishment of Genocide: Observations on Bosnia and Rwanda," pp. 5-13. In Helen Fein (Ed.) *The Prevention of Genocide: Rwanda and Yugoslavia Reconsidered*. New York: Institute for the Study of Genocide.

Basically, Fein suggests the following: "We need to heighten the awareness of the patrons and press them to prevent genocide by (a) coordinating the promises of donors, re., withdrawing aid and making further aid contingent on observing life-integrity rights (not tolerating massacres, extrajudicial executions, 'disappearances,' or torture); (b) isolating and suppressing extremist parties which use violence; (c) promoting interdependent solutions; and (d) warning the instigators that genocide will not pay" (p. 9).

Fein, Helen (Ed.) (1994). *The Prevention of Genocide: Rwanda and Yugoslavia Reconsidered.* New York: Institute for the Study of Genocide. 44 pp.

This "working paper" is comprised of the following essays: "Patrons, Prevention and Punishment of Genocide: Observations on Bosnia and Rwanda" by Helen Fein; "Ethnic Nationalism, Breakdown, and Genocide in Yugoslavia: Comment on 'Patrons, Prevention, and Punishment for Genocide' and Proposal for the Future" by Steven L. Burg; "An Interview with Alison L. Des Forges: Genocide in Rwanda was Foreseen and Could have Been Deterred" by Helen Fein; and "U.S. and UN Actions Escalate Genocide and Increase Costs in Rwanda" by Milton Leitenberg.

Freeman, Michael (1999). "The Role of Institution Building in the Prevention of Genocide," pp. 205-222. In Roger W. Smith (Ed.) *Genocide: Essays Toward Understanding, Early-Warning, and Prevention.* Williamsburg, VA: Association of Genocide Scholars and the Department of Government, College of William and Mary.

Freeman argues that "Genocide scholars have generally pinned their hopes for the prevention of genocide on third-party intervention..., [but] that is not the only option and not always the most promising one. The development of democratic social institutions is at least as important" (p. 218).

Gowing, Nik (2000). "Media Coverage: Help or Hindrance in Conflict Prevention?" pp. 203-226. In Stephen Badsey (Ed.) *The Media and International Security.* London: Frank Cass Publishers.

Among the many conflicts the author addresses herein are the Balkans Crisis in the 1990s, the 1994 genocide in Rwanda, Burundi in the mid-1990s, and Kosovo in the mid- to late-1990s.

Hampson, Fen Osler (2002). "Preventive Diplomacy at the United Nations and Beyond," pp. 139-157. In Fen Osler Hampson and David M. Malone (Eds.) *From Reaction to Conflict Prevention: Opportunities for the UN System.* Boulder, CO: Lynne Rienner Publishers.

An overview of some of the key scholarly and policy literature published in the 1990s on preventive diplomacy, and a discussion of "some of the key fault lines in the debate over the definition [of preventive diplomacy], the range of techniques available, and the utility/feasibility of preventive diplomacy" (p. 139).

International Commission on Intervention and State Sovereignty (2001). *The Responsibility to Protect. Report of International Commission on Intervention and State Sovereignty.* Ottawa, ON: Author. 240 pp.

In his 2000 UN General Assembly report, UN Secretary-General Kofi Annan challenged the international community to try to forge a consensus around the principle and process of carrying out intervention in the face of major human rights atrocities. Subsequently, the independent International Commission on Intervention and State Sovereignty was established by the Government of Canada to respond to that challenge. The Commission carried out a major research effort over a twelve month period and produced *The Responsibility to Protect* which delineates the Commission's findings. The report is comprised of eight chapters: 1. "The Policy Challenge"; 2. "A New Approach: 'The Responsibility to Protect'"; 3. "The Responsibility to Prevent"; 4. "The Responsibility to React"; 5. "The Responsibility to Rebuild"; 6. "The Question of Authority"; 7. "The Operational Dimension"; and 8. "The Responsibility to Protect: The Way Forward." It also includes a major annotated bibliography on a wide array of issues germane to the issues of prevention and intervention.

Jakobsen, Peter Viggo (2000). "Reinterpreting Western Use of Coercion in Bosnia-Herzegovina: Assurances and Carrots Were Crucial." *The Journal of Strategic Studies*, June, 23(2): 1-22.

The author argues that Western policymakers need to come to an understanding and appreciation that diplomacy that uses "assurance and carrots accompanied by credible threats" (p. 1) is much more likely to be effective than diplomacy that simply uses threats and/or use of force.

Jentleson, Bruce W. (2000). *Coercive Prevention: Normative, Political, and Policy Dilemmas*. Washington, DC: United States Institute of Peace. 43 pp. This report is comprised of the following sections: 1. "Introduction: Coercive Prevention"; 2. "The Realism of Conflict Prevention"; 3. "Coercive Prevention: Argument and Evidence"; 4. "Normative Dilemma: Sovereignty as Rights versus Sovereignty as Responsibility"; 5. "The Dilemma of Political Will: How Fixed, How Malleable the Domestic Constraints?"; 6. "Policy Dilemmas: Constituting Credible Coercive Threats and Wielding Effective Preventive Force"; and 7. "Conclusion: Difficult, but Possible."

Jentleson, Bruce W. (Ed.) (2000). *Opportunities Missed, Opportunities Seized: Preventive Diplomacy in the Post-Cold War World*. Lanham, MD: Rowman and Littlefield. 431 pp.

The collective authors in this book assess the value and likelihood of success in using preventive diplomacy to effectively address conflict by focusing on ten highly complex post-Cold War cases (including conflicts in Chechnya, Croatia and Bosnia, Macedonia, and Rwanda).

Jentleson, Bruce W. (1998). "Preventive Diplomacy and Ethnic Conflict: Possible, Difficult, Necessary," pp. 293-316. In David A. Lake and Donald Rothchild (Eds.).*The International Spread of Ethnic Conflict: Fear, Diffusion, and Escalation*. Princeton, NJ: Princeton University Press.

A discussion of specific ways to "refine the concept of preventive diplomacy, de-reifyng any remaining promises of panacea, and otherwise moving from an appealing idea to usable foreign policy strategies. After first developing a working definition for the term preventive diplomacy, I then address each of [three] postulates—possible, difficult, necessary—drawing both on theoretical-conceptual arguments and empirical evidence from recent major cases" [e.g., Somalia, the former Yugoslavia, and the 1994 genocide in Rwanda] (p. 293).

Jentleson, Bruce W. (2003). "The Realism of Preventive Statecraft," pp. 26-46. In David Carment and Albrecht Schnabel (Eds.) *Conflict Prevention: Path to Peace or Grand Illusion?* New York: United Nations University Press.

This chapter is comprised of four sections: 1. A discussion of the empirical and analytic bases supporting the claim that preventive statecraft is possible; 2. An explanation of the strategic logic of preventative statecraft; 3. An evaluation of the problems related to the issue of political will; and 4. The delineation of specific policy recommendations (e.g., diplomatic strategies, credible preventive military force, and establishing the norm of sovereignty as responsibility).

Kuper, Leo (1992). "Reflections on the Prevention of Genocide," pp. 135-161. In Helen Fein (Ed.) *Genocide Watch*. New Haven, CT: Yale University Press.

The first part of the chapter focuses on the setting of standards that might contribute to the prevention of genocide. The second part addresses what Kuper refers to as "active campaigning" against genocide by nongovernmental organizations (NGOs) and others. The chapter concludes with a section entitled "Potentialities for Preventive Action."

Mthembu-Salter, Gregory (2002). "Mediation and Genocide in Rwanda." *Track Two: Constructive Approaches to Community and Political Conflict*, October, 11 (5 and 6):5-20.

This article discusses why the mediation conducted by the Tanzanian government to end the civil war between the Rwandan armed forces and the guerrilla Rwandan Patriotic Front (RPF) ultimately failed, and examines whether the failure can be ascribed to the deficiencies in the confidence building approach that was used.

Nafziger, E. Wayne, and Väyrynen, Raimo (Eds.) (2002). *The Prevention of Humanitarian Emergencies*. New York: Palgrave. 320 pp.

This book is comprised of: 1. "The Political Economy of Preventing Humanitarian Emergencies—Asking the Questions" by E. Wayne Nafziger; Part I: International Economic Responses (2. "Macroeconomic Stabilization and Structural Adjustment" by Christopher Cramer and John Weeks; 3. "Global Linkages, Vulnerable Economies and the Outbreak of Conflict" by Valpy FitzGerald); Part II: Domestic Economic Responses (4. "State Legitimacy, Tax Reform, and the Provision of Basic Service" by John Toye; 5. "Agrarian Reform, Land Redistribution and Small-Farm

Policy" by R. A. Berry; 6. "Protecting Environmental Resources and Preventing Land Degradation" by Gaim Kibreab); Part III. Governmental and non-Governmental Strategies (7. "Preventing Humanitarian Emergencies: Human Security and Strategic Action" by Raimo Väyrynen; 8. "Democratization and Institutional Reform" by Richard Sandbrook; 9. "Donor Governments" by Helge Hveem; 10. "Transnational Non-Governmental Organizations: The Edge of Innocence" by William E. DeMars; 11. "Multilateral Military Responses" by Thomas G. Weiss; 12. "Human Rights" by Andrew Clapham; 13. "The Geopolitics of Mercy: Humanitarianism in the Age of Globalization" by Antonio Donini; and "Conclusion: Lessons for Preventative Action" by Raimo Väyrynen).

Natsios, Andrew (1997). "An NGO Perspective," pp. 337-361. In I. William Zartman and J. Lewis Rasmussen (Eds.) *Peacemaking in International Conflict: Methods & Techniques*. Washington, DC: United States Institute of Peace Press.

Natsios critiques the strengths, weaknesses and limitations of NGOs vis-a-vis the issue of conflict resolution as the latter pertains to international conflict.

Orth, Rick (1997). "Four Variables in Preventive Diplomacy: Their Applications in the Rwanda Case." *The Journal of Conflict Studies*. Spring, 17(1): 79-100.

A thought-provoking critique of the international community's reaction to the genocide in Rwanda and the ways in which the use of preventive diplomacy could possibly have prevented the mass killing.

Ould-Abdallah, Ahmedou (2000). *Burundi on the Brink, 1993-95. A U.S. Special Envoy Reflects on Preventive Diplomacy*. Washington, DC: United States Institute of Peace Press. 170 pp.

The book is comprised of the following chapters: 1. "Understanding Burundi"; 2. "A Mandate for Burundi, November 1993-March 1994"; 3. "Bringing Burundi Back from the Brink, April 1994-October 1995"; 4. "The Peace Process Fragments, October 1995-July 1998"; and 5. "Drawing Lessons from Burundi: Some Guidelines for Preventive Diplomacy."

Rotberg, Robert I. (Ed.) (1996). *Vigilance and Vengeance: NGOs Preventing Ethnic Conflict in Divided Societies.* Washington, DC, and Cambridge, MA: Brookings Institution Press and the World Peace Foundations, respectively. 277 pp.

The book is comprised, in part, of the following parts and chapters: International Preventive Action ("Introduction" by Emily MacFarquhar, Robert I. Rotberg, and Martha A. Chen; "International Preventive Action: Developing a Strategic Framework" by Kalypso Nicolaïdis); Guatemala ("The Search for Peace and Justice in Guatemala: NGOs, Early Warning, and Preventive Diplomacy" by Tom Lent); "International NGOs in Preventive Diplomacy and Early Warning: Macedonia" by Eran Fraenkel; "Making Noise Effectively: Lessons from the Rwandan Catastrophe" by Alison L. Des Forges; and "Humanitarian Assistance and Conflict Prevention in Burundi" by Richard A. Sollom and Darren Kew.

Rubin, Barnett R. (2002). "Targeted Prevention," pp. 161-184. In Barnett R. Rubin's *Blood on the Doorstep: The Politics of Preventive Action.* New York: The Century Foundation Press.

Among the many issues Rubin discusses herein are: strategies; structural prevention: development and governance (development; governance; and regional structures); and operational prevention: conflict management, and coercive diplomacy.

Rupesinghe, Kumar with Sanam Naraghi Anderlini (1998). *Civil Wars, Civil Peace: An Introduction to Conflict Resolution.* London: Pluto Press. 179 pp.

Rupesinghe presents what he deems is a radical new approach to conflict prevention, resolution, and diplomacy. In doing so, he provides an overview of conflict in the post-Cold War world, covering such topics as identifying and assessing early warnings of conflict, and the need to take early action; information gathering and analysis; and the need for preventive diplomacy. In particular, the role of nongovernmental organizations and other third party mediators in conflict resolution is considered.

Schabas, William A. (2006). "The 'Odious Scourge': Evolving Interpretations of the Crime of Genocide." *Genocide Studies and Prevention: An International Journal*, September, 1 (2):93-106.

Schabas discusses the fact that "although the text of the definition [of genocide in the UN Convention on the Prevention and Punishment of the Crime of Genocide] remains the same, judicial interpretation has broadened it significantly" (p. 93). He goes on to discuss how the broadening of the definition can and has "influenced the determination of genocide."

Scheffer. David (2006). "Genocide and Atrocity Crimes." *Genocide Studies and Prevention: An International Journal, December*, 1(3):229-250. Scheffer, former U.S. Ambassador at Large for War Crimes Issues (1997-2001), makes two basic arguments herein: "First, there is a critical need to liberate governments and international organizations from the genocide factor, by which I mean to enable them to readily identify precursor of genocide without being constrained by the legal requirement that must be met to properly identify the crime of genocide. Second, I believe it is essential that we transform the terminology used in scholarship, public documents, and public dialogue regarding the crime of genocide, crimes against humanity, and war crimes" (p. 229). The term he argues in favor of is "atrocity crimes."

Schnabel, Albrecht (2002). "Post-Conflict Peacebuilding and Second-Generation Preventive Action." *International Peacekeeping*, Summer, 9(2):7-30.

This essay "evolves around three core arguments: first, peacebuilding is only sustainable if it embraces core principles of conflict prevention; second, preventive action is more feasible (yet more complex) in the post-conflict environment; and third, lessons from post-conflict preventive action must encourage and inform preconflict prevention—still the most effective stage of preventive action" (p.7).

Smith, Roger W. (Ed.) (1999). *Genocide: Essays Toward Understanding, Early-Warning, and Prevention*. Williamsburg, VA: Association of Genocide Scholars and Department of Government, College of William and Mary. 240 pp.

Four chapters in particular focus on aspects of the prevention of genocide: "Preventing Genocide: The Case of Rwanda" by Howard Adelman; "Radio Broadcasting in the Incitement and Interdiction of Gross Violations of Human Rights Including Genocide" by Frank Chalk"; "The Role of Institution Building in the Prevention of Genocide" by Michael Freeman; and "Preventing Genocide in the Post-Cold War World" by Herbert Hirsch.

Sriram, Chandra Lekha, and Wermester, Karin (Eds.) (2003). *From Promise to Practice: Strengthening UN Capacities for the Prevention of Violent Conflict*. Boulder, CO: Lynne Rienner Publishers. 434 pp.

Examines how the United Nations, regional and subregional organizations, government donors, and other policymakers could best apply the tools of conflict prevention to the wide range of intrastate conflict situations found in the field. The detailed case studies and analytical chapters are presented with the goal of providing operational lessons for fashioning strategy and tactics to meet the challenges of specific conflicts, both potential and actual. The book includes chapters on the situations in East Timor and Burundi, among others.

Strozier, Charles B., and Flynn, Michael (Eds.) (1996). *Genocide, War, and Human Survival*. Lanham, MD: Rowman & Littlefield Publishers. 343 pp.

Includes the following chapters: "To Prevent or to Stop Mass Murder" by Ronnie Dugger; "Meeting the Challenge of Genocide in Bosnia: Reconciling Moral Imperatives with Political Constraints" by Richard Falk; and "The Prevention and Punishment of the Crime of Genocide" by Saul Mendlovitz and John Fousek.

Totten, Samuel, and Markusen, Eric (Eds.) (2006). *Genocide in Darfur: Investigation of Atrocities Perpetrated in the Sudan*. New York: Routledge. 284 pp.

This book examines the genesis, implementation and ramifications of the U.S. State Department's 2004 Atrocities Documentation Project in which State sent 24 investigators to refugee camps along the Chad/Sudan border for the express purpose of conducting interviews with refugees to collect data for analysis in order to ascertain whether genocide had been, and/or was continuing to be, perpetrated in Darfur. It includes chapters by U.S. State Department officials and researchers, USAID officials, the Coalition of International Justice personnel who coordinated the project, investigators, and others.

Touval, Saadia (2002). *Mediation in the Yugoslav Wars: The Critical Years, 1990-95*. New York: Palgrave. 211 pp.

This book is comprised of the following nine chapters: 1. "Introduction"; 2. "Failed Attempts to Prevent War"; 3. "The Entry of Mediators"; 4. "The Cease-fire in Slovenia"; 5. "The Search for a Comprehensive Settlement"; 6. "The Cease-fire in Croatia"; 7. "Collective Mediation in Bosnia, 1992-94"; 8. "U.S. Policy and the Making of the Dayton Accords"; and 9. "Priorities."

van Walraven, Klaas (Ed.) (1998). "Inter-governmental Organizations and Preventing Conflicts: Political Practice Since the End of the Cold War," pp. 19-44. In Klaas van Walraven (Ed.) *Early Warning and Conflict Prevention: Limitations and Possibilities*. The Hague: Kluwer Law International. 204 pp.

The subtitles in this chapter provide a good sense of the specific focus of the piece: Early Warning and Conflict Prevention in Politics: Conceptual Fluidity; Early Warning Systems in Practice; Conflict Prevention: Official Policies Versus the Practice: When Do International Organizations Respond?; Signals of Conflict and Concepts of Security; and Responses to Potential Violence: Procedures and Institutional Arrangements (OSCE, ASEAN, UN, OAS, OAU, CMCA).

Väyrynen, Raimo (2003). "Challenges to Preventive Action: The Cases of Kosovo and Macedonia," pp. 47-69. In David Carment and Albrecht Schnabel (Eds.) *Conflict Prevention: Path to Peace or Grand Illusion*. New York: United Nations Press.

Examines two interdependent case studies, Kosovo and Macedonia, in order to attempt to ascertain which factors contribute to the success and failure of conflict prevention. Additionally, the author analyzes how horizontal and vertical prevention efforts interact and how such interaction is shaped by the different phases of a conflict.

Väyrynen, Raimo (1997). "Preventive Action: Failure in Yugoslavia," pp. 31-42. In Michael Pugh (Ed.) *The UN, Peace and Force*. London: Frank Cass and Company.

The author discusses the resurrection of preventive action in the 1990s, the positive aspects of preventive diplomacy in helping to avoid or minimize the "costs" of collective violence, and the failure of the international community to effectively prevent many humanitarian crises.

Wallensteen, Peter (Ed.) (1998). *Preventing Violent Conflicts: Past Record and Future Challenges*. Uppsala, Sweden: Department of Peace and Conflict Research, Uppsala University. 307 pp.

Among the chapters likely to be of most interest to genocide scholars are: 1. "Preventive Security: Direct and Structural Prevention of Violent Conflicts" by Peter Wallensteen; 2. "Preventive Action and Preventive Diplomacy" by Jan Eliasson and Robert Rydberg; 3. "The Security Council in Preventive Action" by Jüergen Dedring; 4. "Conflict Prevention as Strategic Interaction: The Spoiler Problem and the Case of Rwanda" by Stephen John Stedman, 5. "Conflict Prevention in Burundi: A Case Study" by Lennart Wohlgemuth; 8. "Not Only When to Act, But How: From Early Warning to Rolling Prevention" by Michael S. Lund; 9. "New Threats and New Security: The Post-Cold War Debate Revisited" by Carl Johan Asberg and Peter Wallensteen; 10. "Peacebuilding and Human Security: Frameworks for International Responses to Internal Conflict" by John C. Cockell; 11. "Preventing Deadly Conflicts: The Contribution of International Mediation" by Jacob Bercovitch; 12. "Preventing Violent Conflict Through Kantian Peace" by Bruce M. Russett; 13. "Legitimacy, Justice and Preventive Intervention" by Dan Smith; and 14. "Security for the Next Century: Towards a Wider Concept of Prevention" by Anders Bjurner.

Wallensteen, Peter (2002). "Reassessing Recent Conflicts: Direct vs. Structural Prevention," pp. 213-228. In Fen Osler Hampson and David M. Malone (Eds.) *From Reaction to Conflict Prevention: Opportunities for the UN System*. Boulder, CO: Lynne Rienner Publishers.

Wallensteen examines and clarifies the relationship between direct and structural conflict prevention (the latter referring to measures such as the promotion of democracy, ethnic integration, international regional cooperation, arms control, and disarmament). The chapter "takes direct prevention as its point of departure, analyzes the measures involved, and then delineates the potential role of structural prevention" (p. 214). In doing so, Wallensteen discusses the issues of predicting escalation and taking early action, as well as different forms of preventive action.

Weissman, Stephen (1998). *Preventing Genocide in Burundi: Lessons from International Diplomacy.* Washington, DC: Institute of Peace. 36 pp.

This booklet is comprised of the following: 1. "Introduction"; 2. "Burundi: The Politics of Genocide"; 3. "The United Nations and Humanitarian Military Intervention" 4. "Regional African Diplomacy for a Negotiated Political Settlement"; 5. "'Second-Track' Unofficial Diplomacy and Other Nongovernmental Initiatives"; and 6. "Five Lessons from International Diplomatic Peacemaking in Burundi."

Wolfrum, Rüdiger (2005). "Prevention," pp. 820-825. In Dinah Shelton (Ed.) *Encyclopedia of Genocide and Crimes Against Humanity.* New York: Macmillan.

Addresses the following issues: factors likely to induce genocide, factors likely to prevent genocide, preventive measures under the UN Convention on Genocide, and preventive measures under various human rights agreements.

Woodhouse, Tom, and Ramsbotham, Oliver (Eds.) (2000). *Peacekeeping and Conflict Resolution.* London and Portland, OR: Frank Cass Publishers. 269 pp.

This volume considers the contribution that conflict resolution can make to the development of the new concepts and practices of peacekeeping called for by the United Nations peacekeeping forces.

The book is comprised of the following chapters by the following authors: "Conflict Resolution and Peacekeeping: Critiques and Responses" by Tom Woodhouse; "United Nations Peacekeeping: A Matter of Principles?" by Stephen Ryan; "Defining Warlords" by John MacKinlay; "Sharpening the Weapons of Peace: Peace Support Operations and Complex Emergencies" by Philip Wilkinson; "Organizing for Effective Peacebuilding" by David Last; "Working with Ethno-political Conflict: A Multi-modal

Approach" by Sean Byrne and Loraleigh Keashly; "NGOs, Conflict Management and Peacekeeping" by Pamela Aall; "Cultural Issues in Contemporary Peacekeeping" by Tamara Duffey; "Reflections on UN Post-Settlement Peacebuilding" by Oliver Ramsbotham; "Peacekeeping, Conflict Resolution and Peacebuilding: A Reconsideration of Theoretical Frameworks" by A. B. Fetherston; and "Conflict Prevention: Options for Rapid Deployment and UN Standing Forces" by H. Peter Langille.

Zartman, I. William (Ed.) (2001). *Preventive Negotiation: Avoiding Conflict Escalation*. Lanham, MD: Rowman & Littlefield Publishers. 336 pp.

The contributors to this book present an examination of the way in which preventive negotiation has been practiced, delineate its characteristics, and suggest how lessons can be transferred from one area to another (only, though, when particular conditions warrant such a transfer). The contributing authors treat eleven basic issues: boundary problems, territorial claims, ethnic conflict, divided states, state disintegration, cooperative disputes, trade wars, transboundary environmental disputes, global natural disasters, global security conflicts, and labor disputes.

Early Warning Indicators and Systems

Adelman, Howard (1998). "Difficulties in Early Warning: Networking and Conflict Management," pp. 51-81. In Klaas van Walraven (Ed.) *Early Warning and Conflict Prevention: Limitations and Possibilities*. The Hague: Kluwer Law International.

Among the issues Adelman discusses are: the definition of early warning, the symbiosis of early warning and conflict management, structural and precipitating factors that might lead to violence, problems inherent in early warning systems and related structural dimensions, and the "labeling" of a crisis—"Lessons from the 1994 genocide in Rwanda."

Adelman, Howard (1999). "Early Warning and Prevention: The United Nations and Rwanda," pp. 289-309. In Frances Nicholson and Patrick Twomey (Eds.) *Refugee Rights and Realities: Evolving International Concepts and Regimes*. New York: Cambridge University Press.

The chapter is comprised, in part, of the following sections: UN Peacekeeping in Rwanda; Early Warning; The Information Available; Direct Observations; Communications; Structural Problems; Timeliness; Toward a Comprehensive Explanation for Failure; and Normative Factors.

Adelman, Howard (1998). "Humanitarian and Conflict-oriented Early Warning: A Historical Background Sketch," pp. 45-49. In Klaas van Walraven (Ed.) *Early Warning and Conflict Prevention: Limitations and Possibilities*. The Hague: Kluwer Law International.

A short but informative piece on the development and status of various early warning systems devised by the United Nations, nongovernmental organizations (NGOs), academic institutions, and states. Among the early warning systems Adelman comments on are: the Office for Research and the Collection of Information (ORCI) and its Humanitarian Early Warning System (HEWS); The Department of Humanitarian Affairs (DHA) and its Integrated Regional Information Network (IRIN); the University of Maryland's Global Event Data System (GEDS); and the International Alert (IA) facilitated Working Groups on Early Warning and Conflict Prevention, and its Forum for Early Warning and Emergency Response (FEWER).

Alker, Hayward R.; Gurr, Ted Robert; and Rupesinghe, Kumar (Eds.) (2001). *Journeys Through Conflict: Narratives and Lessons*. Lanham, MD: Rowman & Littlefield Publishers. 462 pp.

This collection is comprised of essays about the Conflict Early Warning Systems (CEWS) project of the International Social Science Research Council—including its empirically grounded approach to anticipating violent conflict.

Cockell, John G. (2003). "Early Warning Analysis and Policy Planning in UN Preventive Action," pp. 182-206. In David Carment and Albrecht Schnabel (Eds.) *Conflict Prevention: Path to Peace or Grand Illusion?* New York: United Nations University Press.

"In outlining the basic elements of a composite analytical method for UN early warning, certain features of conflict analysis theory which either facilitate or hinder the contemporary need to evolve pragmatic strategies and instruments for the prevention of protracted violent conflict [are] highlighted" (pp. 182-183).

Gurr, Ted Robert (2000). "Early-Warning Systems: From Surveillance to Assessment to Action," pp. 243-262. In Kevin M. Cahill (Ed.) *Preventive Diplomacy*. New York: Routledge.

Presents a discussion of those organizations working on the development of early warning systems and discusses evidence from early-warning research concerning ethnic conflict situations at high risk of escalation at the outset of the twenty-first century.

Harff, Barbara (2001). "Could Humanitarian Crises Have Been Anticipated in Burundi, Rwanda and Zaire? A Comparative Study of Anticipatory Indicators," pp. 81-102. In Hayward R. Alker, Ted Robert Gurr, and Kumar Rupesinghe (Eds.) *Journeys Through Conflict: Narratives and Lessons*. Lanham, MD: Rowman & Littlefield Publishers.

Harff addresses the following issues: systematic monitoring, risk assessment, and early warning; structural conditions of genocide and politicide; accelerators, triggers, and de-accelerators; conflict phases and interventions; Burundi: massacres and repression; Rwanda: genocide; and Zaire: autocratic leadership and democratization.

Harff, Barbara (2003). "No Lessons Learned from the Holocaust? Assessing Risks of Genocide and Political Mass Murder Since 1955." *American Political Science Review*, February, 97(1):57-73.

Reports the findings of a study in which the author tested a structural model of the antecedents of genocide and politicide (political mass murder).

Last, David (2003). "Early Warning and Prevention of Violent Conflict: The Role of Multifunctional Observer Missions," pp. 157-181. In David Carment and Albrecht Schnabel (Eds.) *Conflict Prevention: Path to Peace or Grand Illusion?* New York: United Nations Press.

The author notes that "the limitations and strengths of traditional [both UN and civilian) fact-finding and observation missions suggest the need for expanding the concept of observer missions to include political, social, economic, and psychological dimensions of the conflict" (p. 157).

The chapter is comprised of the following sections: Information for Early Warning; Fact-Finding and Military Observers; How Can Early Warning and Prevention Work?; Collecting Information (Political and Social Information, Economic Information, Information About the Media, Military Information); Establishing a Multifunctional Mission; and From Information to Action.

Lund, Michael S. (1998). "Not Only When to Act, But How: From Early Warning to Rolling Prevention," pp. 155-166. In Peter Wallensteen (Ed.) *Preventing Violent Conflicts: Past Record and Future Challenges*. Uppsala, Sweden: Department of Peace and Conflict Research, Uppsala University.

The purpose of this essay is to attempt to answer the following questions posited by the author: 1. "What kinds of knowledge do would-be preventive policymaker needs for responding effectively to early warnings?"; 2. "To what extent does most current warning work provide that knowledge?"; 3. "What are some ways to fill the evident gap?"; and 4. "What knowledge do early responders need?"

Rowlands, Dane, and Joseph, Troy (2003). "The International Monetary Fund and Conflict Prevention," pp. 207-230. In David Carment and Albrecht Schnabel (Eds.) *Conflict Prevention: Path to Peace or Grand Illusion?* New York: United Nations University Press.

The role of the International Monetary Fund (IMF) vis-à-vis conflict early warning, prevention, and resolution and reconstruction is examined.

Rupesinghe, Kumar with Sanam Naraghi Anderlini (1998). *Civil Wars, Civil Peace: An Introduction to Conflict Resolution*. London: Pluto Press. 179 pp.

Section three of the book deals primarily with early warning systems: "From Early Warning to Early Action" (The Continuum of Conflict; Sounding the Alarm—Devising a System for Early Warning; Information Gathering; Information Analysis; Responding Appropriately; Reasons for Failure—Lessons from Early Warning Systems; Generating Early Action; Taking Action; A Range of Options; Skeptics and Critics).

Rupesinghe, Kumar, and Nyheim, David with Maha Kahn (2001). "A Review of Research and Practice in Early Warning and Early Response: Lessons Learned and Policy Issues," pp. 397-420. In Hayward R. Alker, Ted Robert Gurr, and Kumar Rupesinghe (Eds.) *Journeys Through Conflict: Narratives and Lessons*. Lanham, MD: Rowman & Littlefield Publishers.

The authors state that "The chapter looks at definitions of early warning, provides a rough overview of the historical milestones in the early warning literature, situates early warning in relation to different kinds of responses to conflict, and reviews lessons learned in early warning methodology and practice. It concludes with a review of policy implications and future directions for the field."

Schmid, Alex P. (2001). "A Comparative Look at Early Warning Indicators: PIOOM, the State Failures Project, and CEWS Cases," pp. 291-317. In Hayward R. Alker, Ted Robert Gurr, and Kumar Rupesinghe (Eds.) *Journeys Through Conflict: Narratives and Lessons*. Lanham, MD: Rowman & Littlefield Publishers.

Schmid's chapters is comprised of the following subheadings, which provide a solid sense of the various issues he addresses: "Definition and Focus of Early Warning"; "The U.S. Government's State Failure Study" ("Indicators Used in the State Failure Project," and "Forecasting with the State Failure Model"); "Forecasting State Failure with Alternative Indicators"; "Comparing the Top Six Indicators of the SF [State Failure] and PP [Pierson/PIOOM] Sets"; and "Redefining 'State Failure."

van Walraven, Klaas (Ed.) (1998). *Early Warning and Conflict Prevention: Limitations and Possibilities*. The Hague: Kluwer Law International. 204 pp.

Includes numerous chapters that address a wide array of issues germane to early warning, including but not limited to: "Humanitarian and Conflict-oriented Early Warning: A Historical Background Sketch" by Howard Adelman; "Difficulties in Early Warning: Networking and Conflict Management" by Howard Adelman; "Acting Early: Detection, Receptivity, Prevention, and Sustainability: Reflecting on the First Post-Cold War Period" by Peter Wallensteen; "From Information to Political

Action: Some Political Prerequisites" by Ruddy Doom; and "Early Warning and Conflict Prevention: The Role of the United Nations" by James S. Sutterlin.

Addressing Systemic/Structural Issues: Poverty, Economics, Trade, Injustice(s)

Alger, Chadwick F. (Ed.) (1998). *The Future of the United Nations System: Potential for the Twenty-First Century.* Tokyo: United Nations University Press. 450 pp.

Twenty-two scholars from across the globe contribute twelve chapters that address such issues as prevention of violence, and creating economic and social structures that sustain human fulfillment. Included in the text are sixty-six recommendations for new institutions and programs on issues that include, among others, human rights, economic policies, and refugees.

Anderson, Mary B. (1999). *Do No Harm: How Aid Can Support Peace —or War.* Boulder, CO: Lynne Rienner Publishers. 161 pp.

Among some of the key chapters in this book are: "Aid's Impact on Conflict Through Resource Transfers"; "Aid's Impact on Conflict Through Implicit Ethical Messages"; "Framework for Analyzing Aid's Impact on Conflict"; and "Reflecting on the Role of Aid."

Dobkowski, Michael N., and Wallimann, Isidor (Eds.) (1998). *The Coming Age of Scarcity: Preventing Mass Death and Genocide in the Twenty-First Century.* Syracuse, NY: Syracuse University Press. 350 pp.

The contributors to this volume address how scarcity and "surplus populations" can lead to catastrophes, including genocide.

Eliasson, Jan (2000). "Establishing Trust in the Healer: Preventive Diplomacy and the Future of the United Nations," pp. 215-239. In Kevin M. Cahill (Ed.) *Preventive Diplomacy: Stopping Wars Before They Start.* New York: Routledge.

The chapter is comprised of the following sections and subsections: Steps to Prevent and Handle Post-Cold War Conflicts; Is Prevention Possible —and When?; The Role of the UN in Conflict Prevention; and Beyond the Crisis: A Program for Preventive Action (Carry Out Financial and Structural Reform, Define a Rational Division of Labor with Regional and Other Organizations, Work Together with NGOs and Civil Society, Address the Root Causes of Conflict, Integrate Disarmament into Preventive Action, Reform the Security Council, Strengthen the Capacity of the Secretariat in Preventive Diplomacy, Make Better Use of Article 99, Develop the Instruments for Peaceful Settlement of Disputes, Keep Open the Possibility of Preventive Deployment of Peacekeepers, Develop Concrete Preventive Tasks for the General Assembly, and Mobilize All of the UN System).

Falk, Richard (2000). "The Challenge of Genocide and Genocidal Politics in an Era of Globalization," pp. 177-194. In Tim Dunne and Nicholas J. Wheeler (Eds.) *Human Rights in Global Politics*. New York: Cambridge University Press.

Falk, Professor of International Law and Practice at Princeton University, notes that he "...considers two clusters of interrelated contemporary developments that are responsible for the most widespread and acute human suffering in the world: genocidal politics and economic globalization. In both settings the fundamental ordering arrangements of international society and prevailing realist mentality seem unable and unwilling to protect vulnerable peoples" (p. 182).

Klare, Michael T. (2001). *Resource Wars: The New Landscape of Global Conflict*. New York: Henry Holt. 277 pp.

Klare asserts that much of the ethnic and sectarian conflict engulfing parts of the globe in the 1990s has been instigated by clashes over natural resources, especially oil, water, timber and minerals. He further asserts that while many of the conflicts may seem to be ethnic in nature—and may have evolved into such—scholars and policymakers would be remiss if they overlooked the conflict origins as they relate to resource disputes. Ultimately, Klare proposes the creation of new international bodies whose goal would be to prevent conflict and, if need be, allocate resources in periods of scarcity.

Lake, David, and Rothchild, Donald (Eds.) (1998). *The International Spread of Ethnic Conflict: Fear, Diffusion, and Escalation.* Princeton, NJ: Princeton University Press. 392 pp.

The editors and contributors argue that ethnic conflict is not caused directly by intergroup differences or centuries-old feuds. They argue, instead, that anxieties over security, competition for resources, breakdown in communication with the government, and the inability to make enduring commitments lead ethnic groups into conflict.

Muscat, Robert J. (2002). *Investing in Peace: How Development Aid Can Prevent or Promote Conflict.* Armonk, NY: M. E. Sharpe. 265 pp.

The book is comprised of the following parts and chapters: Part 1. Conflicts, Causes, and Economic Development (I. "Introduction: Conflicts, Causes, and Economic Development"; 2. "Conflicts Fought, Conflicts Avoided: Nine Cases" [including Rwanda and Yugoslavia]; 3. "Development and Conflict: Connections and Precursors"); and Part II. Toward an Agenda for Conflict Prevention (4. "Relevance and Assessment"; 5. "Inducing Nonviolent Politics and Conflict Management"; 6. "Economic and Sector Policies: Reforms, Preferences, and Harmonization of Interests"; and 7. "Persuasion, Leverage, and Sanctions").

Nafziger, E. Wayne, and Auvinen, Juha (2003). *Economic Development, Inequality and War: Humanitarian Emergencies in Developing Countries.* New York: Palgrave. 256 pp.

This book is comprised of the following chapters: "A Humanitarian Emergency: War, Genocide, and Displacement"; "Poverty, Stagnation, Unemployment, and Inflation"; "Ethnicity, Political Economy, and Conflict"; "Inequality, Exclusivity, and Relative Deprivation"; "Stagnation, Inequality, Adjustment, and Elite Interests"; "Authoritarianism, Democratization, and Military Centrality"; "The Failure of Agriculture: Food Entitlements, Elite Violence, and Famines"; "The Conflict over Land and Natural Resources"; and "Preventing Humanitarian Emergencies: Policy Implications."

Nafziger, E. Wayne, and Väyrynen, Raimo (Eds.) (2002).*The Prevention of Humanitarian Emergencies.* New York: Palgrave. 320 pp.

This book is comprised of the following parts and chapters: 1. "The Political Economy of Preventing Humanitarian Emergencies—Asking the Questions" by E. Wayne Nafziger; Part I: International Economic Responses (2. "Macroeconomic Stabilization and Structural Adjustment" by Christopher Cramer and John Weeks; 3. "Global Linkages, Vulnerable Economies and the Outbreak of Conflict" by Valpy FitzGerald); Part II: Domestic Economic Responses (4. "State Legitimacy, Tax Reform, and the Provision of Basic Service" by John Toye; 5. "Agrarian Reform, Land Redistribution and Small-Farm Policy" by R. A. Berry; 6. "Protecting Environmental Resources and Preventing Land Degradation" by Gaim Kibreab); Part III. Governmental and non-Governmental Strategies (7. "Preventing Humanitarian Emergencies: Human Security and Strategic Action" by Raimo Väyrynen; 8. "Democratization and Institutional Reform" by Richard Sandbrook; 9. "Donor Governments" by Helge Hveem; 10. "Transnational Non-Governmental Organizations: The Edge of Innocence" by William E. DeMars; 11. "Multilateral Military Responses" by Thomas G. Weiss; 12. "Human Rights" by Andrew Clapham; 13. "The Geopolitics of Mercy: Humanitarianism in the Age of Globalization" by Antonio Donini; and "Conclusion: Lessons for Preventative Action" by Raimo Väyrynen).

Prendergast, John (1996). *Frontline Diplomacy: Humanitarian Aid and Conflict in Africa*. Boulder, CO: Lynne Rienner. 165 pp.

Making use of the insights of dozens of aid agency personnel with many years of experience in various parts of Africa, the author discusses how aid can actually increase conflict and delineates how such an adverse impact can be lessened by an accurate needs assessment and by avoiding the many problems inherent in "blind involvement."

Rubin, Barnett R. (2002). "Targeted Prevention," pp. 161-184. In Barnett R. Rubin's *Blood on the Doorstep: The Politics of Preventive Action*. New York: The Century Foundation Press.

The chapter includes a section entitled "Strategies; Structural Prevention: Development and Governance." It addresses the critical issues of development, governance, and regional structures.

Säve-Söderbergh, Bengt, and Lennartsson, Izumi Nakamitsu (2002). "Electoral Assistance and Democratization," pp. 357-377. In Fen Osler Hampson and David M. Malone (Eds.) *From Reaction to Conflict Prevention: Opportunities for the UN System.* Boulder, CO: Lynne Rienner Publishers.

The essay is comprised of the following sections: Root Causes and Structural Sources of Contemporary Violent Conflict; Emerging Linkage Between Peace, Development, and Democratization: The Reality of UN Missions; Key Challenges of Democratization Assistance in Conflict Prevention; and Designing and Supporting Democratic Institutions as Conflict Management Instruments.

Smith, Roger (1998). "Scarcity and Genocide," pp. 199-219. In Michael N. Dobkowski and Isidor Wallimann (Eds.) *The Coming Age of Scarcity: Preventing Mass Death and Genocide in the Twenty-First Century.* Syracuse, NY: Syracuse University Press.

This chapter is comprised of the following sections: Scarcity; Relationships Between Genocide and Scarcity: The Basic Patterns (Genocide That Leads to Scarcity; Genocide and Direct Conflict over Resources; Natural Disaster, Advertent Omission, and Genocide; Genocide with Scarcity as a Principal Means; Scarcity as a Contributing Factor in Genocide); and Preventing Genocide (Reducing Scarcities, and Institutional and Political Means).

Stewart, Frances (2002). "Horizontal Inequalities as a Source of Conflict," pp. 105-136. In Fen Osler Hampson and David M. Malone (Eds.) *From Reaction to Conflict Prevention: Opportunities for the UN System.* Boulder, CO: Lynne Rienner Publishers.

Stewart argues that horizontal inequalities (e.g., inequality in political, economic, and/or social conditions among culturally and/or geographically distinct groups) are one of the major causes of conflict. In her introduction she states that "the aim [of this chapter] is to suggest how introducing crisis prevention into policymaking would alter the normal design of policy for low-income countries. Among the many conflicts she mentions are the Iraq's "suppression" of the Kurds, 1994 genocide in Rwanda, and the ongoing killings in Burundi.

5

Sanctions as Counter-Genocide Instruments

George A. Lopez and Kathryn Stuhldreher

In late April, 2006, the United Nations Security Council passed SCR 1672, which imposed travel and financial sanctions on four specific Sudanese individuals for their role in the on-going genocidal violence in the Darfur region of Sudan and along the Chad-Sudan border. The passage of these economic penalties provides a glimpse into the bittersweet duality of sanctions as instruments for countering genocide.

On the one hand, the ability to target individuals—not national governments—indicates a level of sophistication in sanctions formulation and implementation that results from fifteen years of experience and detailed policy development. On the other hand, the resolution, came almost two years after the Security Council had originally engaged the issue of Darfur violence when, via SCR 1556 (July, 2004), it imposed an arms embargo on "all non-governmental entities." This resolution, and the four that were to follow, were simply far too little and much too late in deterring genocide in Darfur.

In this chapter we explore the thinking that gave rise to economic sanctions as diplomatic tools in the contemporary era. Although sanctions have been increasingly successful in achieving a number of objectives in the peace and security realm of the United Nations, the reality is that they have been much less effective in countering or deterring genocide. If sanctions are to be a more effective tool in the future, the development of more targeted or smart sanctions may be the key. We will examine the potential of such sanctions measures and conclude with the challenges which face sanctions policy in dealing with genocide.

Post-Cold War Sanctions Development

Since 1990 United Nations sanctions have become frequently used instruments of multilateral action. With the imposition of comprehensive trade sanctions on Iraq in Resolution 661 (August, 1990), the Security Council opened a new era in the use of these collective coercive economic measures as a means of responding to violations of international norms. Although the Security Council had employed sanctions only twice in its first forty-five years of existence—first, in Southern Rhodesia in 1966 and then in South Africa, in 1977—the sixteen years since 1990 have witnessed an active phase of Security Council sanctions.

Sanctions emerged as a preferred form of action by the Council for a number of reasons. First, sanctions permitted big power cooperation as the UN entered the post-cold war era. The fact that sanctions were being imposed mostly against states which were not critical allies of the former superpowers made this cooperation feasible. Secondly, unlike earlier times in which the dynamics of international trade provided benefits—at least in the short term—to states subverting embargoes, the post-cold war era of rapidly expanding global trade brought rewards to nations that joined and supported international economic coalitions. Finally, in a world where vocal domestic concerns and transnational advocacy networks push governments and the United Nations "to do something" about war and human rights abuses, sanctions served as a public indicator that the Council was prepared to take action (Cortright and Lopez, 2000, pp. 1-13).

Over the course of the past sixteen years, dozens of sanctions resolutions have been levied against sixteen distinct targets, including such non-governmental entities as Al Qaeda and the Taliban, the National Union for the Total Independence of Angola (UNITA), and militias in eastern Congo. Sanctions were imposed to serve a range of objectives: to reverse aggression, restore democratically elected governments, protect human rights, end international and civil wars, to bring suspected terrorists to justice and, more recently, to counter the threat of international terrorism.

UN sanctions rely on Chapter VII of the Charter for their legal authority, specifically on Article 41 which provides that the Council may call upon states to impose nonmilitary measures such as the interruption of economic and diplomatic relations to protect international peace and security. The political logic of sanctions lies in the desire of policymakers to have options other than war for applying pressure on

Sanctions as Counter-Genocide Instruments 133

targeted states, entities, and individuals accused of violating international norms. Indeed, their attraction rests in a number of benefits they offer to multilateralists:

- They comprise a middle course lying "between war and words" by avoiding the costs of military action, yet they provide policy options more forceful than diplomatic remonstrance;

- When employed effectively, they can exert significant pressure on those targeted; and

- When designed and applied astutely, sanctions can serve as the basis for a bargaining dynamic in which the promise of lifting sanctions becomes an incentive to encourage political concessions and cooperation (Cortright and Lopez, 2000, pp. 27-32).

The record of Security Council sanctions since 1990, though, is one of striking contrasts, if not contradictions. As the Council moved forcefully to use sanctions as a means for advancing the UN mandate to preserve peace and security, most particularly in Iraq (as a result of the international community's concern that it was developing weapons of mass destruction), it found that the outcomes of these measures were undermining other dimensions of the UN agenda, especially the goal of improving the human condition. As the number of Iraqis died of preventable disease, and seemingly from malnutrition, concern grew about the humanitarian impact of sanctions on Iraq. The "sanctions cause genocide" assertion, however short-lived and isolated to the Iraq case, was championed by Church-based and humanitarian non-governmental organizations (NGOs) and was significant in leading to the creation of both the Oil-for-Food relief program and the search for smart sanctions on Iraq (Cortright and Lopez, 2002a, pp. 27-34; Lopez, 2000, pp. 76-78).

What We Know About Sanctions' Success and Failure

In examining the various cases in which the UN has imposed sanctions since 1990, scholars have been able to develop clear generalizations as to what does and does not work (Wallensteen and Staibano, 2005). More specifically, UN sanctions are most successful when:

- The Security Council details a very clear and limited number of demands in the sanctions resolution;

- The sanctions adopted by the Council and its members are one component of a more multifaceted means of persuasion/coercion aimed at the target;

- The Sanctions Committee charged with oversight of the sanctions has an active and creative chair, especially regarding travel to the sanctioned state/area;

- An internal or external expert committee monitors sanctions' effectiveness and recommends improvements which are acted upon by the Council early in the sanctions episode;

- The Council has made provisions for humanitarian exemptions, if needed;

- The Council can accomplish the sanctions' objectives within two years of the date of the original resolution;

- The Council and its member states have established a strong border or contra-band monitoring and capturing system to enforce the sanctions;

- Sanctions violators are identified and held accountable;

- A certain, more informal, bargaining process emerges between the UN—either via the Council or its member states—and the target, regarding compliance;

- Member states provide the target or actors within the target, with some incentives for sanctions compliance that are consistent with the goal of the sanctions;

- Member states have the capacity, and of course the willingness, in their domestic legislation and legal enforcement mechanisms to implement the sanctions; and

- The target believes that sanctions are fully supported by military force should sanctions fail.

Because we can posit conditions for sanctions success, it is not surprising that we also know when sanctions are destined for failure. In addition to not meeting the conditions consistent with sanctions success, failure of UN sanctions occur when:

- Sanctions are so excessively punitive that they isolate a target from continued bargaining with either the Council or member states;

- Sanctions provide leaders in the target-nation with a classic "rally around the flag" situation whereby they can successfully portray the Council and its members as the offending party and deflect the focus from their own behavior;

- The Council or its members fail to recognize and engage a target manifesting partial compliance with sanctions;

- Certain member states overtake the voice and role of the Council as leader of the sanctions process; and

- Successful application of economic coercion on the target produces no change in the political behavior or compliance of the target.

Sanctions and Cases of Genocide

The unfortunate, but accurate, generalization is that UN sanctions have been a general failure in deterring genocide. But understanding the distinct reasons for this failure across cases is significant in increasing the chances of success in the future. This may be especially important as a number of the new reforms brought to the imposition of sanctions increase the capacity of sanctions to deter and punish genociders, should the political will of national leaders be mobilized to impose such instruments.

Before 1990, the Cold War stalemate that paralyzed all Security Council actions combined with the general under-development of regional organizations to produce no real action, much less economic sanctions, on those perpetrators of suspected and/or actual crimes against humanity and genocide. From the killing fields of Cambodia in the early 1970s through the case of the genocide and forced migration of thousands of Kurds in northern Iraq in the late 1980s, no international action vis-à-vis sanctions occurred.

With the increase of UN action post-1990, the pattern of response to genocide varied in relation the nature of the genocide episode itself and the attitude of the UN itself. The first case faced by the international community came in the massacres of civilian Bosnian Muslims in the context of the war that ravaged the former Yugoslavia from 1991-1995. The Security Council imposition of an arms embargo in SCR 713 in September 1991 began a half-decade of measures which suffered from a series of problems: they lagged behind the pace and brutality of the unfolding violence; they were cast rather broadly and not aimed at key perpetrators; until early 1994 they were weakly enforced and monitored by surrounding states; and, they were not bolstered by UN peace-keeping units in the area, which themselves had too narrow a mandate for response and too few personnel.

The complexity of the Yugoslav civil war certainly added pressure to the prospect that sanctions could be effective. At first glance, it would appear that an arms embargo would be a critical step in ending the killing, even as the scope and ethnic dimensions of it were becoming clearer. But the Belgrade regime had easy access to black markets through porous borders, while the Bosnian Muslim communities had virtually no weapons with which to defend themselves. Rather then helped by the embargo, it appeared that Muslims were its victims, however unintended that effect. Moreover, UN sanctions took a rather blanket-like until September 1994 when SCR 942 demanded that economic and arms denial be focused on the Bosnian Serbs. From then on, the sanctions effort gained strength as a result of both (a) the commitment and rigor of European enforcement and (b) the search in Belgrade for ways to have the sanctions lifted (Lopez, 2000, pp. 73-76).

Ultimately the recalibration of sanctions by the UN and the tightening of their effectiveness on both the Belgrade government and the Milosevic regime played some role in the signing of the Dayton Peace Accords ending the war. But they were too unfocused and too weak to prevent the violent ethnic cleansing that so distinguished the killing in that war.

As the linkage between mass violence and Milosevic came to the fore again in early 1998, the UN Security Council, in SCR 1160, again imposed an arms embargo, this time to halt the killings that had begun in Kosovo. This embargo was marginally more successful in accomplishing its goal because it was enforced by a fairly robust troop contingent, the UN Preventive Deployment Force. But the mandate of this force was not renewed in February 1999 and the Kosovo crisis was finally resolved both by the use of NATO air bombing and the defeat of Milosevic in the 2000 elections.

The tragic lack of response by the international community to the rapidly unfolding genocide in Rwanda from April through June 1994 was a result of many failures beyond weak and belated sanctions. It is generally acknowledged that the unwillingness of UN member states to provide sufficient resources to accomplish the commitments it had made to preserving peace in Rwanda via the UN Assistance Mission for Rwanda (UNAMIR) meant that this first line of defense against genocide was non-existent. When the Council finally passed a comprehensive arms and military material embargo in May of 1994 in the form of SCR 918, its implementation would not occur until some 800,000 people had already been slaughtered (Lopez, 2000, pp. 72-73).

UN inaction to the plight of black Africans in Darfur, Sudan, repeats the trend found in the two cases of the 1990s: even if effective arms embargoes and economic measures are passed against killing regimes, this does not readily translate into a political success that ends the genocide.

United States, European, and UN attempts to halt genocidal violence in Darfur via targeted sanctions have failed for many of the same reasons that incapacitated various UN sanctions attempts for the past fifteen years—a lack political will on the part of the permanent five nations and other states. This produced compromised designs, targeting, delays and less biting sanctions than might have been imposed. Had a strong and unified set of targeted coercive measures been imposed on nearly every Sudanese government and military official in September 2004, rather than the limited sanctions which did not pass until March 2005, tens of thousands of lives would have been saved in Darfur. More to the point, had the smart, targeted sanctions passed in April 2006 been used by the Council against a wide range of Sudanese officials in mid-2004, much of the Darfur crisis would have been stifled. As a result of this failure, not only does the human devastation continue in the region, but the international community, vacillating again about its aims and purpose, now must resort to more costly military measures.

Ironically, a decade ago (1996) the UN did have moderate success in multilateral, targeted sanctions against Sudan's support for terrorism. But in that case, a set of factors different from those present in the UN-Sudan-Darfur case helped to make sanctions successful. In the Darfur case, the Sudanese government kept the UN at bay by veiled threats to scrap the long-awaited and UN-brokered peace accord which ended the Sudanese twenty-year-old civil war. Khartoum also used its relationship with a key Security Council member (China) and a systematic campaign of deception and denial to limit the reach of sanctions when they were imposed. These lessons for future sanctions policy in stifling genocide are quite discouraging.

Adapting and Reforming Sanctions

The strongest reason for placing some hope in the arena of economic sanctions as an effective diplomatic tool is that over the past decade groups of diplomats, sanctions specialists, representatives of international governmental and non-governmental organizations, and a wide array of experts (e.g., in banking, commodities trade, law enforcement, transportation, comparative legislative behavior) have worked in concert to define, develop, and revise substantial proposals for the formulation and implementation of targeted sanctions (which are often referred to as "smart" sanctions). These efforts, in turn, have been further refined in the practice of the Council itself and through the development of legislative model laws for national member states. These new formulations are the subject of on-going exploration and consultation by a select group of specialists in the US, in Europe, and within the UN Secretariat.

Sanctions deemed smart or targeted are comprised of two key dimensions: (1) they take as their target specific economic actors (companies, entities, or individuals) deemed most responsible for the policies or actions considered by the international community as illegal or abhorrent; and (2) they narrow the focus of economic coercion to a micro-activity that constrains the target in unique and painful ways (Cortright and Lopez, 2002b, pp. 23-40). Since the late 1990s, targeted financial sanctions have been the cornerstone of effective UN sanctions imposition (Wallensteen and Staibano, 2005).

The impetus for smart sanctions came from increased concern about the inefficiencies and negative humanitarian consequences of comprehensive trade sanctions. This prompted the search for more effective means of economic coercion that were within the bounds and spirit of action that the UN might take under Chapter VII of the UN Charter.

For example, in 1998 and 1999, the Swiss government convened two international seminars at Interlaken. The meetings brought together financial experts and regulators, bankers, international practitioners, lawyers and academic researchers from about two dozen nations to develop concrete proposals for instituting and improving financial sanctions. Special attention was devoted to exploring how to increase the technical capacity of the UN system and member states in locating and locking down assets and in harmonizing financial terminology (such as what comprises an "asset" in various national banking systems). This led to the development of model Security Council resolutions and the exploration of how to strengthen national member state capacity to implement targeted financial sanctions. From 2000 until the present, refinement of these techniques has been greatly assisted by the research of scholars at the Watson Institute for International Studies at Brown University.

Concomitantly, in a series of workshops and practitioner oriented sessions, the German Foreign Ministry asked the Bonn International Center for Conversion (BICC) to spearhead an initiative on the refinement of travel bans, aviation sanctions, and the strengthening of arms embargoes. Expert meetings were held in Bonn in 1999 and Berlin in 2000, with follow-up work continuing through 2006 at the BICC and the Joan B. Kroc Institute for International Peace Studies at the University of Notre Dame, both of which will be involved in the analysis of the effectiveness of arms embargoes.

The Bonn-Berlin process was especially effective in that its designers aimed to link distinct types of targeted measures within a similar framework vis-a-vis both policy and implementation. Special attention was devoted to arms embargo monitoring. The outcome was the development of model language to guide future Security Council resolutions and national legislation to enhance arms embargo enforcement (Brzoska, 2001).

In October 2001, Sweden announced its initiation of a third process, which would focus on the implementation of targeted sanctions. The Stockholm process was comprised of an intense series of seminars and commissioned research papers that made detailed recommendations for each type of targeted sanctions. Beyond the critically important advancement of best practices in each area of targeted sanctions, the Stockholm process explored significant issues coming out of new UN practices with smart sanctions, such as those developing in the UN Counter-Terrorism Committee. It also developed comprehensive recommendations for improved implementation and monitoring of sanctions. To this day, the Department of Peace and Conflict Research at Uppsala University continues to conduct research and convene seminars examining these themes (Wallensteen and Staibano 2005).

Ultimately, the three aforementioned reform processes were dynamically interactive and resulted in innovations introduced by the Security Council in the 1990s in each category of targeted sanctions. More specifically, there has been considerable refinement in the technique of imposing sanctions, which has, in turn, increased their impact. Significantly, it has also influenced the sharpening of the monitoring process. Interestingly, too, it has also contributed to improving the quality and attention devoted to national laws that are needed to support effective Security Council sanctions. For example, efforts were made to encourage member states to criminalize violations of UN arms embargoes and strengthen export control laws and regulations. These initiatives helped to create a firmer foundation in the domestic law of member states for penalizing those who supply arms and military related goods in violation of UN arms embargoes.

In 2004, the Security Council directed UN peace-keeping forces in the Democratic Republic of Congo and Côte d'Ivoire to assist with the monitoring of arms embargoes in those countries. This added significant responsibilities to the mission of UN peace-keepers in those countries, but it might also help prevent the devastating killing in genocide in the future.

Critical Challenges Facing Sanctions Policy

The prospect of preventing governmental elites from committing genocide by imposing external coercive instruments such as smart sanctions is more technically possible than ever before. But are sanctions strong enough to deter genocide? In the history of the so-called Oil-for-Food scandal, one pattern is clear: The powerful members of the Security Council will do what they believe is in their national interest. As they acted during the Oil-for-Food era, they will make exceptions to Council resolutions, fail to take action on recommendations provided by the Secretariat, and hold control of the sanctions enterprise close to their own decision-making center. In other words, the unique mix of professionalism and politics that characterizes the UN at its core will likely continue to influence the imposition of economic sanctions unless others step into the fray. As the critical and dominant third UN component beyond the Security Council and the Secretariat, only the member states of the Council and the wider UN can guarantee that sanctions are actually implemented. Furthermore, in order to have any hope of preventing the most egregious crime against humanity, genocide, sanctions must be implemented in the early stages of a conflict, impose significant costs on the target government, and maintain widespread support among member states.

Thus, the ongoing task of sanctions reform is to increase member states' capacity, and thereby to positively influence their willingness, to implement the measures which the wider global community have deemed necessary to preserve peace and security. The use of smart, targeted sanctions provides some confidence that this can be accomplished, even as it places before the member states, the Council, and the Secretariat a new set of important practical, legal and ethical challenges that will doubtless be central to continued sanctions success in this decade.

References

Brzoska, Michael (Ed.) (2001). *Design and Implementation of Arms Embargoes and Travel and Aviation Related Sanctions: Results of the Bonn-Berlin Process.* Bonn, Germany: The Bonn Center for Conversion.

Cortright, David and George A. Lopez (2000). *The Sanctions Decade: Assessing UN Strategies in the 1990s.* Boulder, CO: Lynne Rienner.

Cortright, David and George A. Lopez (2002a). *Sanctions and the Search for Security: Challenges to UN Action.* Boulder, CO: Lynne Rienner.

Cortright, David and George A. Lopez (Eds.) (2002b). *Smart Sanctions: Targeting Economic Statecraft.* Lanham, MD: Rowman & Littlefield.

Lopez, George A. (2000). "Economic Sanctions and Genocide: Too Little, Too Late, and Sometimes Too Much," pp. 67-84. In Neal Riemer (Ed.) *Protection Against Genocide: Mission Impossible?* Westport, CT: Praeger Press.

Wallensteen, Peter and Staibano, Carina (Eds.) (2005). *International Sanctions: Between Words and Wars in the Global System.* New York: Frank Cass.

Annotated Bibliography

Brzoska, Michael (Ed.) (2001). *Design and Implementation of Arms Embargoes and Travel and Aviation Related Sanctions: Results of the Bonn-Berlin Process.* Bonn, Germany: The Bonn Center for Conversion. 129 pp.

This volume includes chapters delineating the results of a two year UN-sponsored set of meetings held in Bonn and Berlin among experts and policy makers interested in improving the efficacy of design and implementation of UN arms embargoes. Its recommendations were significant for subsequent arms sanctions imposed by the Council after 2000.

Cortright, David, and Lopez, George A. (2000). *The Sanctions Decade: Assessing UN Strategies in the 1990s.* Boulder, CO: Lynne Rienner. 273 pp.

Considered by many the definitive casebook of the fourteen cases of UN multilateral sanctions of the 1990s. In addition to examining each of the cases in detail, the authors assess the strengths and weaknesses of the design, implementation and evaluation of the cases within the UN system. They conclude that a bargaining model, rather than a coercion model, has worked best to produce target compliance and they chart the future agenda in research and policy on sanctions. The book won a *Choice* magazine award for academic excellence in 2000.

Cortright, David, and Lopez, George A. (2002a). *Sanctions and the Search for Security: Challenges to UN Action.* Boulder, CO: Lynne Rienner. 249 pp.

The authors examine the past dozen years of UN sanctions by focusing primarily on overarching themes such as humanitarian impact and arms and commodity embargoes. The book devotes special attention to the emergence of smart sanctions and to the prospects for reform of UN sanctions in light of experience.

Cortright, David, and Lopez, George A. (Eds.) (2002b). *Smart Sanctions: Targeting Economic Statecraft.* Boulder, CO: Rowan & Littlefield. 259 pp.

A collection of essays that emerged from a series of UN-sponsored conferences on how to develop and implement smart, targeted sanctions. Chapters include an examination of the logic and success of smart sanctions as well as discrete areas such as financial resource flows, travel and aviation bans, arms embargoes and selective cultural and sports bans.

Drezner, Daniel (2000). *The Sanctions Paradox.* London: Cambridge University Press. 342 pp.

Drezner advances a theory that sanctions can have unintended consequences on targets and can essentially lead to strengthening their resolve to pursue their course of action rather than compliance. He examines cases of the former Soviet Union and Russia in imposing embargoes on states within its former political control.

Haass, Richard N., and O'Sullivan, Meghan L. (Eds.) (2000) *Honey and Vinegar: Incentives, Sanctions and Foreign Policy.* Washington, DC: The Brookings Institution. 211 pp.

This volume results from a study group sponsored by Brookings to assess the utility of economic measures of coercion in US and multilateral foreign policy. A number of the cases focus on export controls of high technology goods for curtailing the ability of states (Pakistan, India, Iran) to produce prohibitive weapons systems. The volume also addresses the significant flip-side of sanctions, incentives that can be provided for altering state behavior.

Kaempfeer, William H., et al. (2004) "International Economic Sanctions Against a Dictator." *Economics & Politics*, March, 16(1):29-51.

This article illustrates the "rally 'round the flag" dimension of sanctions when a dictator tries to translate the impact of sanctions into a power base to support his own rule. The article also considers how sanctions can result in a competition for loyalty within the regime and an opportunity for repression.

Wallensteen, Peter, and Staibano, Carina (Eds.) (2005). *International Sanctions: Between Words and Wars in the Global System*. New York: Frank Cass Publishers. 251 pp.

This volume essentially provides an overview of the ideas discussed and discussions held at the Stockholm Process for Implementing Targeted Sanctions. It includes contributions by some of the best technical and thematic experts who contributed to the meetings of the process. The strength of the volume is its threefold division of themes across sanctions: capacity, actors and effectiveness.

Weiss, Thomas G.; Cortright, David; Lopez, George A.; and Minear, Larry (Eds.) (1997). *Political Gain and Civilian Pain: Humanitarian Impacts of Economic Sanctions*. Lanham, MD: Rowan & Littlefield. 277 pp.

This book provides a framework and methodology for assessing the negative humanitarian impacts of sanctions on vulnerable populations in targeted nations. The cases examined include Iraq, Haiti, the former Yugoslavia and South Africa. It served as the basis for much of the United Nations assessments of the humanitarian impact of sanctions for the remainder of the 1990s and early 2005 (up through 2004).

6

The Tension between Sovereignty and Intervention in the Prevention of Genocide

Bruce Cronin

Introduction

Efforts by international organizations to prevent and punish genocide are hampered by a fundamental tension that exists within international relations, that between sovereignty and responsibility. On the one hand, as a matter of international law and diplomatic practice, all states are entitled to a high degree of autonomy in governing their domestic affairs. This includes managing the relationships between their governments and citizens and between the various groups in society. Implicit in this entitlement is the right to be free from external interference in matters that are deemed to be domestic. On the other hand, all states have an interest in ensuring that governments adhere to basic principles of governance, including the protection of their population's security and well-being. While the definition of proper governance changes over time, there has been a strong consensus that deliberate attempts to eliminate entire groups goes well beyond this standard.

This chapter is concerned with how the international community tries to protect populations who are the victims of this most extreme form of brutality without threatening the principle of state sovereignty, a principle that has been the bedrock of international order and stability since the early days of the nation-state system. The accompanying bibliography will provide additional readings for those interested in this debate.

Sovereignty versus Responsibility

The principle of sovereignty holds that states are not subject to the authority of any higher institution or principle and that the state itself is the ultimate source of political authority within its territory. Following this basic principle of international organization, international law and diplomatic practice are clearly biased in favor of state autonomy in matters that are considered to be domestic. At its most basic level, autonomy implies freedom from unrequested external interference in the internal affairs of the state, particularly if this interference is of a coercive nature. This institution has provided a measure of stability, predictability and order within the anarchic system of nation-states for several centuries. For this reason, the jurisdiction of international organizations has traditionally been limited to regulating the relations between states, not within them. Under most conditions, states tend to be jealous of these rights and resist accepting rules that significantly limit their freedom of action. This is equally true for both strong and weak states.

For weak states, the institution of sovereignty provides a political and legal deterrent against the imposition of values and policies by more powerful states. In extreme cases, it may be the only protection against territorial conquest by a stronger entity. It is the single equalizer in a world of great inequality. Thus, even in cases where most political leaders agree that a particular practice is abhorrent—such as genocide—governments from weaker states strongly hesitate granting to great powers the authority to intervene in another state's internal affairs. For strong states, sovereignty provides a legal justification that allows them to define and pursue their interests unilaterally, without being subjected to the will of a majority. This relieves the strong and wealthy of the obligation to help the weak and poor. Consequently, great powers can avoid accepting responsibility for helping the victims of genocide when they do not believe it to be in their interests to do so. In both cases, sovereignty enables each society to develop its own domestic institutions based on its own political values and principles.

At the same time, while sovereignty provides wide latitude for governments to pursue their own interests and control their own domestic affairs, states also participate in a complex pattern of relationships that impose limitations on their will to be independent. Most political leaders recognize that a stable, predictable and functional international order requires formal rules that define acceptable behavior, regulate political interaction and facilitate the resolution of conflicts. Since states receive their sovereignty, at least in part, from their recognition as legitimate political actors in international affairs, the international community has long claimed the right to place limits on state action. Thus, since the early days of the nation-state system, multilateral treaties and international organizations have long provided for collective action in situations where governments violate generally-accepted norms of behavior.

Diplomats and politicians have long understood sovereignty to encompass both rights and responsibilities. Acceptance of these responsibilities has been the cost of membership in the international society of states. Chief among a state's responsibility is to provide for the security and well-being of its population. Obviously genocide and other forms of mass state violence are the ultimate negation of this responsibility. At the same time, sovereignty also means that the broader international community of states and diplomats has certain collective responsibilities. Since states have exclusive authority over their territories, they are responsible for ensuring that conditions within their borders do not threaten international peace and security. When they abdicate this responsibility, the broader community is obligated to take action aimed at rectifying the situation. Genocide not only grossly abuses the victims. It also tends to produce massive refugee flows, spawn cross-border guerrilla movements, and create tensions with neighboring states. Thus the line between domestic policies and international consequences is blurred.

These competing concepts of sovereignty as autonomy and sovereignty as responsibility have produced tensions within the institution of international relations. When governments are engaged in massive abuses of their population the tension becomes far more pronounced, leading to a fundamental dilemma: when the two concepts of sovereignty clash, which one should dominate and who is entitled to make this decision?

Problems with Intervention

Since the end of World War II, there has been an overwhelming international consensus among political leaders, diplomats, and the general public that genocide is an unacceptable practice regardless where it is perpetrated—including when it is confined within the borders of a sovereign state. The conclusion of the 1948 UN Convention on the Prevention and Punishment of the Crime of Genocide (UNCG) created a legal framework for states to override the rights of sovereignty whenever genocide was committed. Yet the UNCG went beyond annulling a state's sovereign right to commit extreme human rights abuses; it also challenged the sovereign right of outside states to remain uninvolved in cases of mass violence against ethnic, religious, or national groups. This turned the issue of sovereignty on its head by suggesting not only a right to intervene in cases of genocide, but a responsibility to do so.

This has produced a new set of tensions. Despite an overwhelming consensus on the need to stop genocide, political leaders still hesitate supporting intervention even when the act of genocide has been confirmed. The UNCG grants individual governments the right and responsibility to intervene, but it does not provide any check on this right. Thus, in cases where intervention has been undertaken either unilaterally by a single state or in alliance by a self-selected coalition, some states have questioned the motives of the interveners. For example, most practitioners and scholars agree that the aims of India's 1971 intervention in West Pakistan and NATO's 1999 intervention in Kosovo were not limited to stopping the slaughter of the Bengalis and Kosovar Albanians, respectively. In both cases, humanitarian concerns were only one factor in the decision to intervene, prompting fears from other states that the interveners were using the atrocities as an opportunity to pursue other interests. For this reason, many states in the developing world (as well as competing great powers such as China) have viewed specific cases of intervention as an unjustified violation of sovereignty, making it difficult to gain a consensus on the need for action.

At the same time, the ability of the international community to oppose genocide has also been hampered by the opposite problem rooted in the principle of sovereignty: even when most states agree that acts of genocide have occurred and that such acts are violations of international law, those with the ability to act have refused to do so, drawing on their sovereign right not to put their own citizens at risk in order to protect a foreign population Sovereignty also means the right not to act. Thus in Bosnia, Rwanda, and most recently Sudan, the institution of sovereignty provided a cover for the great powers to avoid their responsibilities when they did not believe it to be in their interest to intervene.

In neither case has the problem been one of principle. After many years of disagreement over the issue, there is now a general consensus that states do in fact have both the right and the responsibility to intervene in cases of genocide (although there may be differences over specific cases). Rather, the problem is one of collective action. As the cases cited above suggest, states continue to be suspicious of each other's motives, while at the same time balk at themselves paying the cost in lives and treasure to protect another country's population. This problem is particularly acute because even in the course of stopping genocide, the interveners are supposed to protect the sovereignty of the offending state. That is, such intervention is supposed to be limited to alleviating the humanitarian crisis, not defeating an enemy or altering the political makeup of the government. This raises at least three concerns.

First, most political leaders and scholars agree that the most effective way to stop genocide is to prevent it before it occurs. In most cases, genocide is neither spontaneous nor unexpected, but rather emerges out of an ongoing internal conflict. Indicators such as the stigmatization and discrimination of ethnic minorities, the creation of heavily armed militias, and the broadcasting of chauvinistic and hate-filled political speeches can strongly suggest the possibility of an impending genocide. Yet, in and of themselves, such actions do not legally justify external intervention by an outside power. Thus, preventing a genocide requires a state or international organization to breach the sovereignty of another state before it has actually committed any violation. In effect, taking preventative action calls for intervening states to declare guilt before the crime has been committed. This raises the possibility of abuse by powerful states seeking to justify actions taken for reasons that have little to do with humanitarian concern. In effect, humanitarian claims could have the potential of becoming an all-purpose justification for any form of great power intervention.

Second, since in most cases the intervening states have neither been threatened nor attacked by the perpetrators of the genocide, their right to breach the sovereignty of the target state is limited to alleviating the humanitarian crisis. This often requires the intervening states to place the protection of the victim population over the minimization of casualties among their own soldiers. This, of course, contradicts established military doctrine. In practice, humanitarian interventions to prevent genocide and other atrocities tend to be fought according to military objectives—that is, to use overwhelming force to defeat an enemy. This often results in high civilian casualties, often the very people the interveners are trying to save. Thus, for example, when NATO intervened in Kosovo to stop the ethnic cleansing of the Kosovar Albanians, NATO and its allies refused to send in ground forces to protect the victims. Instead, they relied on massive bombing of Serbian cities, thereby avoiding placing their own soldiers at risk. This not only caused civilian casualties in Serbia, but it also led to an acceleration of the genocide in Kosovo by Serbian militias.

Third, the right of intervention is predicated on the principle that military force is necessary to protect the population. This necessarily limits the actions of the interveners to stopping the atrocities; technically, then, the interveners must withdraw once their goal is accomplished. Yet, even if the interveners can put aside their own strategic interests (a doubtful proposition) it is neither realistic nor politically or morally possible for them to allow the abusive government to remain in power after it has left. Thus, humanitarian intervention to stop genocide usually results in the ultimate assault on state sovereignty: the overthrow of the existing regime and an occupation of the perpetrator's territory by outside forces.

Critical Challenges Facing the Field

Following the end of World War II, foreign policy officials and "norm entrepreneurs" from non-governmental organizations undertook a number of efforts to change the balance from an emphasis on sovereignty as autonomy toward sovereignty as responsibility, particularly in cases where mass atrocities were committed. The UNCG, the Universal Declaration on Human Rights, and the Refugee Convention were all efforts to create a political and legal framework for increasing the involvement of the international community in alleviating domestic humanitarian crises. This initial movement was soon overshadowed by the Cold War and the growing North-South conflict. The former made cooperation by the great powers very difficult. In most cases, the powerful states were far more concerned with alliance loyalties than with the behavior of governments toward their own citizens. Reflecting this, the United States did not even ratify the UNCG until 1987, even though it was one of the original signatories. The North-South divide created an environment of extreme suspicion of great power motives among newly independent states in the developing world, making them highly unlikely to support any form of intervention in the internal affairs of a sovereign state.

The end of the Cold War brought forth both opportunity and crisis in this regard. For the first time in forty years, the great powers began to cooperate on a regular basis on a wide variety of areas related to international peace and security. The absence of the East-West conflict also allowed states to at least consider their collective responsibility for protecting the victims of egregious human rights abuses, without regard to alliance patterns. Moreover, the decline of the North-South conflict reduced fears that international intervention to stop atrocities would feed the imperialist designs of the advanced industrial countries.

At the same time, the breakup of the Soviet Union, the revolutions in Eastern Europe, and the accompanying decline of superpower support for weak and corrupt governments in the developing world led to conflict and instability. The violent breakup of Yugoslavia and the brutal application of state violence in Eastern Europe, the former Soviet republics, and Africa shocked the international community, particularly the great powers. Genocide and "ethnic cleansing" became state policy in Bosnia, Rwanda, Kosovo, and later East Timor and Sudan. This challenged the international community to put into practice its newfound political commitment to protect those who fell victim to atrocities perpetrated by the state. Ultimately, the United Nations (UN) began to shift its approach toward internal state violence. This was significant in that the sovereignty/responsibility tension is particularly acute within the UN, inasmuch as the organization represents both the institutionalization of state sovereignty and the notion of international responsibility toward the broader global community. On the one hand, the United Nations was the driving force behind the Universal Declaration of Human Rights and the UNCG. Moreover, the UN Charter (legally a binding multilateral treaty) requires its member states to cede at least a portion of their sovereignty to the collective, at least in the area of international peace and security. On the other hand, the UN decision making bodies are comprised solely of representatives of sovereign states. Article 2 (7) clearly states that aside from enforcement measures by the Security Council, the UN does not have the authority to intervene in matters which are essentially within the domestic jurisdiction of any state. This has been confirmed in practice. Traditionally, the UN membership (represented by the General Assembly) has strongly supported state sovereignty over international involvement in matters that they deemed to be internal to a state.

In the post-Cold War environment, however, the balance shifted toward greater UN intervention in cases of extreme state violence and human suffering. Although the Security Council reacted slowly and offered weak (Bosnia) or non-existent (Rwanda) assistance, it did establish a precedent for direct involvement in the internal affairs of states when there was a widespread and consistent pattern of atrocities. In 1993, the Security Council declared Srebrenica and five other Bosnian towns and cities to be "safe havens," a designation that prohibited armies from operating within that territory. Although the United Nations failed to enforce this by confronting Serbian militias (resulting in a massacre in Srebrenica and other safe havens), the designation of the "safe areas" was, in and of itself, one more indication that the international community was willing to override, at least to a certain extent, one of the most basic tenets of sovereignty—territorial integrity—in order to prevent genocide.

Most notably, the Council decided to directly challenge the practice of genocide by creating international tribunals to prosecute and punish those accused of committing such atrocities in the Balkans (the International Criminal Tribunal for the Former Yugoslavia), Rwanda (the International Criminal Tribunal for Rwanda), and Sierra Leone (the Special Court for Sierra Leone). These tribunals represented the most direct challenge to the doctrine of sovereignty. Traditionally, the Act of State Doctrine and the customary principle of sovereign immunity protected state leaders from being judged for their official acts in the courts of another state or by an international tribunal. Yet these international courts not only stripped accused leaders of this immunity, but also required all states to extradite them for trial. The use of international tribunals as deterrents and instruments of justice in cases of extreme state violence received a strong boost with the creation of the International Criminal Court (ICC). Although it is too early to assess its success, it has received widespread support. Even the United States, which currently opposes the ICC, agreed to refer cases from Sudan's genocide to this international body.

At the same time, the international community remains ambivalent over the degree to which states and international organizations can intervene in the internal affairs of sovereign states. NATO's intervention in Kosovo in 1999 made this abundantly clear. Initially, the Kosovo issue was supposed to be brought before the Security Council, however it was clear that its members were divided and were unlikely to approve a resolution in support of direct military intervention. NATO acted without explicit Council authority, raising charges that it was acting unilaterally, and some argued, illegally.

The Real Probabilities of Progress in the Field

The experiences of the past two decades has led to a deluge of scholarly and policy-oriented literature addressing the tension between sovereignty and intervention. This debate has raged within academic institutions, national governments, and international organizations. Politically, the balance here has also shifted toward greater intervention in cases where there is "a consistent pattern of gross, flagrant, or mass violations" that "shock the conscience" of humankind (these phrases have been drawn from treaties and U.N. resolutions).

The most comprehensive attempt to address the sovereignty/responsibility dilemma was initiated in response to a plea by Secretary-General Kofi Annan in 2000. The Secretary-General asked the member states to establish a set of principles that would justify humanitarian intervention without assaulting the institution of sovereignty. The Canadian government responded by establishing a high-level task force of political leaders and scholars, dubbed the International Commission on Intervention and State Sovereignty (ICISS). The resulting report, *The Responsibility to Protect*, set out to (a) establish clearer rules, procedures and criteria for determining whether, when and how to intervene; (b) ensure that military intervention, when it occurs, is carried out only for the purposes proposed, is effective, and is undertaken with proper concern to minimize the human costs and institutional damage that will result; and (c) help eliminate, where possible, the causes of conflict while enhancing the prospects for durable and sustainable peace.

The report is notable not for developing new ideas on the issue, but rather, for articulating what has been a growing consensus among a wide range of government leaders, diplomats, scholars, and non-governmental organizations. The report suggests how mass atrocities can be identified in advanced, prevented (when possible), and opposed (when necessary). It also discusses the many other responsibilities for members of the international community in creating conditions that make genocide unlikely, and directly addresses the question of who has the authority to act, under what circumstances, and in what manner. Most importantly, it reconceptualizes the dilemma in regard to the conditions under which there is a "right to intervention" to a "responsibility to protect."

In establishing the criteria that could justify a violation of state sovereignty, the report draws from just war doctrine, as well as customary international law and stipulates the following: right authority, just cause, right intention, last resort, proportional means, and reasonable prospects for success. Most important from this list is right authority, since the other criteria are in many ways influenced by this. To the extent that actions to prevent genocide are initiated by international or regional organizations (which are the bodies that are legally authorized to undertake them), there are established deliberative processes inherent in their structures that allow for discussion and debate over these very factors. For example, whether a particular set of actions by a government amounts to genocide is a question that multilateral organizations can determine according to the decision making procedures already accepted by the members. This provides a check against the ambitions of a single state or self-selected coalition of the willing. It also enables smaller and weaker states—who tend to be more sensitive to violations of sovereignty—to participate in the decision.

Conclusion

Over the past decade the debate over whether states or international organizations are justified in violating a state's sovereignty to prevent or stop genocide has shifted sharply in favor of external involvement. Few if any states currently argue that governments have a sovereign right to commit genocide and most agree that the international community has both a right and a responsibility to respond when such actions occur. Although there is still no consensus on how to deal with routine human rights violations committed by states, there is little controversy over the sovereignty/responsibility dilemma when such violations reach the level of genocide. The problem is in the details. Collective action requires individual participation. For any system of legitimate intervention to prevent or stop genocide to work, individual states must be willing to consider the collective good even if this does not coincide with their parochial state interest. This not only means agreeing to sanction a friend or ally, but also accepting the responsibility of providing resources to do so. This is something governments continue to balk at.

At the same time, as the ICISS report points out, preventing and stopping genocide has to be approached differently from a typical military mission. The object is usually not victory, but to save the victims, something that often involves placing one's soldiers in harm's way.

Annotated Bibliography

Brown, Chris (2002). *Sovereignty, Rights and Justice: International Political Theory Today*. Cambridge, UK: Polity Press. 276 pp.

Herein, Brown, professor of international relations at the London School of Economics and Political Science, examines the relationship between international relations theory and political theory. In doing so, he shows how they are very much interrelated.

Initially, Brown provides a historical overview of the international political theory based on the "Westphalia system." He then examines international theory in the twentieth century, concluding with a discussion of key issues germane to late-twentieth century international relations. In the latter part, he discusses such issues as the right of political communities, the ethics of force in international relations, human rights, humanitarian intervention, social justice, the moral relevance of borders, among other issues.

Collins, Cindy and Weiss, Thomas (2000). *Humanitarian Challenges and Intervention: World Politics and the Dilemmas of Help*. Boulder, CO: Westview Press. 248 pp.

This book analyzes the ends, means and consequences of humanitarian intervention in conflict areas, by closely examining a number of post-Cold War cases. The authors argue that institutional humanitarian challenges and intervention concerns often produce policies that are counterproductive to the immediate requirements of victims. They focus on the conflicting interests, resources, and organizational structures within humanitarian institutions, and examine how they can blunt the effectiveness of efforts on behalf of war victims.

Cronin, Bruce (2002). "Multilateral Intervention and the International Community," pp. 147-168. In Donald Sylvan and Michael Keren (Eds.) *International Intervention: Sovereignty vs. Responsibility*. London: Frank Cass.

This article examines how the "paradox of sovereignty" simultaneously protects the right of states to control their own internal affairs, while allowing the international community to place conditions limiting that right. It argues that the existence of a pluralistic international community provides a political and legal foundation for collective intervention on behalf of domestic populations when fundamental norms are threatened, but at the same time creates a highly restrictive set of conditions under which this can occur.

Cronin, Bruce (1998). "Changing Norms of Sovereignty and Multilateral Intervention," pp. 159-180. In Joseph Lepgold and Thomas G. Weiss (Eds.). *Collective Conflict Management and Changing World Politics*. Albany: State University of New York Press.

The author traces how the norms of sovereignty change over time and discusses how this influences the foundation upon which legitimate multilateral intervention is based. He argues that as our definitions of legitimate sovereignty change, the distinction between a domestic and an international issue changes as well. This in turn determines the conditions under which international institutions will consider an intervention to be justified. With the end of the Cold War, the "will of the people" as the foundation for sovereign authority has been granted a higher status, enabling states to legally intervene on behalf of human rights.

Friedman, Elisabeth Jay; Hochstetler, Kathryn; and Clark, Ann Marie (2005). *Sovereignty, Democracy, and Global Civil Society: State-Society Relations at UN World Conferences*. Albany: State University of New York Press. 221 pp.

This book explores the ever-increasing power of nongovernmental organizations (NGOs) by analyzing a microcosm of contemporary global state-society relations at UN World Conferences. It is comprised of the following six chapters: 1. "Global State-Society Relations"; 2. "Global Civil Society: Emergence and Impact"; 3. "Global Civil Society and Latin America in the UN Conferences"; 4. "Sovereignty in the Balance"; 5. "Sovereignty Bargains and Challenges at the Conferences on Population and Development, Social Development; and Human Settlements"; and 6. "Global Civil Society: Transforming Sovereignty and Building Democracy?"

International Commission on Intervention and State Sovereignty (2002). *The Responsibility to Protect*. Ottawa, Ontario: International Development Research Center. 91 pp.

This is the final report issued by the International Commission on International and State Sovereignty, a blue-ribbon panel of eminent political leaders and scholars charged with establishing clear rules, procedures and criteria for determining whether, when and how multilateral organizations should intervene for humanitarian purposes.

Holzgrefe, Jeff and Keohane, Robert (2003). *Humanitarian Intervention: Ethical, Legal and Political Dilemmas*. Cambridge: Cambridge University Press. 362 pp.

This book of articles offers a comprehensive examination of "the dilemma of humanitarian intervention" that was raised during the Kosovo action: Is it legitimate for a regional organization to use force without a UN mandate or international consensus in cases where there are gross and systematic violations of human rights? Written by leading analysts of international politics, ethics, and law it seeks to identify strategies that may reduce the current tension between human rights and state sovereignty.

Krasner, Stephen (1999). *Sovereignty: Organized Hypocrisy*. Princeton, NJ: Princeton University Press. 248 pp.

The author challenges the notion that sovereignty protects states from intervention, arguing that from the beginning of the nation-state system, states have routinely violated the sovereignty of other states when they deemed it in their interest to do so. Using historical cases, he specifically examines international intervention to protect both minority rights and human rights, as well as the external involvement of financial institutions in the domestic affairs of states. He tries to demonstrate that such interventions are the result of power and interests, not principles and norms.

Lyons, Gene and Mastanduno, Michael (Eds.) (1995). *Beyond Westphalia? State Sovereignty and International Intervention*. Baltimore, MD: Johns Hopkins University Press. 360 pp.

The authors of this collection of essays explore whether recent political changes have shifted the balance between the sovereign rights of states and the authority of the international community to take action when global norms are violated. Specifically, they make a distinction between multilateral and unilateral intervention (the former is legitimate while the latter is not) and address the question of whether intervention can be justified in order to promote humanitarian goals.

Maogoto, Jackson Nyamuya (2003). *State Sovereignty and International Criminal Law: Versailles to Rome*. Ardsley, NY: Transnational Publishers. 311 pp.

In this book, the author discusses the progression of international criminal law from, as the subtitle suggests, Versailles to the establishment of the International Criminal Court. The book is comprised of the following seven chapters: 1. "The Concept of Sovereignty and the Development of International Law"; 2. "World War I: Sowing the Seeds of Challenge to State Sovereignty"; 3 "World War II: Reaping the Fruits of the Challenge to State Sovereignty"; 4. "The Cold War: The 20th Century's Third Hegemonic Struggle"; 5. "The Yugoslav Tribunal: State Sovereignty in the Shadow of International Justice"; 6. "The Rwandan Tribunal: Gaining Ground in the Diminution of State Sovereignty"; and 7. "The International Criminal Court: Challenges and Concessions to the Westphalian Model."

Mills, Nicolaus and Brunner, Kira (Eds.) (2002) *The New Killing Fields: Massacre and the Politics of Intervention.* New York: Basic Books. 288 pp.

A group of war reporters and analysts revisit four of the worst instances of state-sponsored killing in the last half of the twentieth century (Cambodia, Yugoslavia, Rwanda, and East Timor) in order to reconsider the success and failure of U.S. and U.N. humanitarian interventions. It is one of the few books that examine the results of an intervention several years after its completion by evaluating postwar reconstruction concerns.

Moore, Jonathan (Ed.) (1998). *Hard Choices: Moral Dilemmas in Humanitarian Intervention.* Lanham, MD: Rowman and Littlefield. 336 pp.

This book, sponsored by the International Committee of the Red Cross, offers a variety of articles by practitioners and scholars, each of whom examines the conflicting moral pressures present in different kinds of interventions. The study covers a wide range of cases including Rwanda, Somalia, Cambodia, and Bosnia. From their various cultural and professional perspectives, the authors examine a host of issues, including: human rights, sanctions, arms trade, refugees, and the media. As a whole, the authors argue that humanitarian actions often result in increased suffering, and advocate moral reflection as a way to improve the quality of decision-making and intervention in internal conflicts.

Murphy, Sean (1996). *Humanitarian Intervention: The United Nations in an Evolving World Order.* Philadelphia: University of Pennsylvania Press. 427 pp.

The author offers a detailed examination of the historical development of constraints on the use of force and humanitarian intervention prior to, during, and after the Cold War. In doing so, he suggests that the central challenge for the twenty-first century rests in reconciling the norms against territorial intervention with the increasing desire to protect innocent persons from human rights deprivations that often take place during civil wars or that result from persecution by autocratic governments.

Mychajlyszyn, Natalie and Shaw, Timothy M. (2005). *Twisting Arms and Flexing Muscles: Humanitarian Intervention and Peacebuilding in Perspective*. Burlington, VT: Ashgate. 151 pp.

The authors examine the complexities and dynamics associated with the application of military force for humanitarian assistance and peacebuilding. In this way, it moves beyond the military/interventionary aspects and explores issues related to reconstruction. It specifically focuses on case studies of recent crises in Africa and the Balkans.

Power, Samantha (2002). *"A Problem From Hell": America and the Age of Genocide*. New York: Basic Books. 610 pp.

Power charges that the United States has no history of intervening to stop genocide or even condemning it as it occurred. She suggests that U.S. leaders were quite aware of the horrors as they were occurring against Armenians, Jews, Cambodians, Iraqi Kurds, Rwandan Tutsis, and Bosnians during the past century, and argues that much human suffering could have been alleviated through a greater effort by the U.S. She attributes this failure to a lack of political will.

Thakur, Ramesh, and Malcontent, Peter (Eds.) (2004). *From Sovereign Impunity to International Accountability: The Search for Justice in a World of States*. New York: United Nations University Press. 305 pp.

This book of essays examines a host of issues germane to sovereign impunity and international accountability, including but not limited to: forces of transformation and the changing international human rights context; the limits of international criminal accountability, the individual within international law; gender related crimes; international criminal courts and the admissibility of evidence, balancing the rights of the accused with the imperatives of accountability; looking beyond individual responsibility to the responsibility of organizations, corporations and states; the value of the International Criminal Court; and the relationship between human rights and peace.

Welsh, Jennifer (Ed.) (2004). *Humanitarian Intervention and International Relations*. Oxford: Oxford University Press. 280 pp.

The authors in this collection of essays examine the challenges to international society posed by humanitarian intervention in the affairs of sovereign states. They address the pros and cons of such intervention and explore how far sovereignty can protect a state that causes or refuses to stop humanitarian crises. The volume includes several key case studies to highlight these questions.

Wheeler, Nicholas (2000). *Saving Strangers: Humanitarian Intervention in International Society*. Oxford: Oxford University Press. 352 pp.

The author explores the changing legitimacy of humanitarian intervention by comparing the international response to cases of humanitarian intervention in the cold war and post-cold war periods. Wheeler argues that contemporary norms help to legitimize such interventions, even when the intervenors themselves deny this as their motive for taking action. Indeed, he demonstrates that these norms both empower and constrain potential intervenors and that the lack of humanitarian motives does not necessarily jeopardize the possibility of positive outcomes.

7

The Intervention of Genocide

Samuel Totten

Over the past several centuries a common belief among political theorists and governmental leaders is that a sovereign state's border is inviolate when it comes to domestic jurisdiction. Such a belief, of course, is a direct result of the Treaty of Westphalia. As of late, though, an ever-increasing number of scholars and practitioners have collectively and seriously questioned the putative "sanctity" of the traditional concept of sovereignty. In that regard, some argue that the world is "witnessing the emergence of a customary law of humanitarian intervention" (Caplan, 2003, p. 141). Such a position though is not uncontested, and the debate and battle over the issue is far from over as a broad spectrum of scholars (stretching from those on the far right to those on the far left) and practitioners weigh in on the issue. In fact, some argue, persuasively, that even those leaders of governments and international governmental organizations who have voiced support of the concept of humanitarian intervention often do so more rhetorically than in reality. Others have asserted that the concept of humanitarian intervention is simply a "Trojan horse used by the powerful to legitimize their interference in the affairs of the week" (Bellamy, 2005, p. 32). Among the many critics of the so-called "new interventionism," those on the far left are among the most vehement in their disdain, calling it, among other things, an attempt at "a new colonial 'age of empire'" (Selfa, 2002) and yet another attempt to maintain hegemony by the West. Tellingly, even some liberals are beginning to perceive humanitarian intervention in the same light (Rieff, 2005). Still others are taking a cautionary approach, arguing that humanitarian intervention on the behalf of those whose human rights are being trampled can cause a whole new set of problems: "Policymakers can also overlook the dark sides of their work and treat initiatives which take a familiar humanitarian form as likely to have a humanitarian effect" (Kennedy, 2004, p. 112).

Defining "Humanitarian Intervention"

Traditionally, "international law has defined 'intervention' as 'forcible interference in the domestic affairs' of another state" (Smith, 2000a, p. 124). "Humanitarian intervention" has been defined in a variety of ways by different scholars. Nicholas Wheeler (2000), a scholar of international politics, defines "humanitarian intervention" as "the use of force to end appalling abuses of human rights" (p. 2). Providing a more detailed but similar definition, Jennifer Welsh (2004), University Lecturer in International Relations at Oxford, defines "humanitarian intervention "as "coercive interference in the internal affairs of a state, involving the use of armed force, with the purpose of addressing human rights violations or prevention of widespread human suffering" (p. 3). Similarly, Martin Frank (2004), a professor of international studies at the University of Bremen (Germany), defines "humanitarian intervention" as "an intervention in the internal political affairs of another state with (military) force against the will of the government of that state for reasons of stopping gross human rights violations" (p. 97). In *The Responsibility to Protect: Report of the International Commission on Intervention*, the International Commission on Intervention and State Sovereignty (2001) define "humanitarian interventions" as being "classically seen as coercive action by one or more states involving the use of armed force in another state without the consent of its authorities, and with the purpose of preventing widespread suffering or death among the inhabitants" (p. 79).

The key components/phrases related to humanitarian intervention, then, are "force," "internal affairs of a state," "against the will," and "halting gross human rights violations and widespread suffering." Humanitarian intervention is not carried out to defeat another state, per se, or acquire new territory; rather, it is to quell major human rights infractions that have caused, and will continue to cause if not stanched, the horrific suffering of innocents.

Intervention: A Shift from the Cold War Years to the Post-Cold War Years

Military intervention to prevent or halt a potential or actual genocide was relatively rare during the Cold War years. Generally, the U.S. and Soviet Union ignored major human rights violations that were taking place in the states of their allies and "clients"; and, at one and the same time, the U.S. and the USSR were wary, due largely to nuclear tensions, of "interfering" in those states that were under the protective wing of their major antagonist. That is, each used proxies to fight various battles for various reasons in different parts of the world. Furthermore, with the possible exception of human rights activists, most seemed partial to the concept of noninterference in the "internal affairs" of sovereign states. That is not surprising in light of the fact that "ever since the idea of humanitarian intervention was born in the minds of pre-Westphalian writers like Grotius, Gentili and Suarez, it has been disputed in the theory and practice of international relations on the grounds that it threatens the institutional bases of international order" (Kundsen, 1997, p. 246).

Some have claimed that two notable exceptions during the Cold War years were India's intervention during the 1971 Bangladesh genocide and Vietnam's late intervention in Kampuchea (Cambodia) during the Khmer Rouge-perpetrated genocide (1975-1979). But the fact is, neither intervention was undertaken for the express purpose of halting genocide. Rather, there were, as is often the case, ulterior reasons for intervening when each did. More specifically, India certainly had strategic reasons for wanting to see the dismantling of East Pakistan and the rise of a state (Bangladesh) friendly to the Indians. As for Vietnam's intervention, it was largely initiated as a result of the Khmer Rouge's attacks carried out across the Kampuchean/Vietnamese border in Vietnamese territory.

With the end of the Cold War and the radically altered geopolitical landscape in which the vast majority of conflicts and crises shifted from being mainly interstate to intrastate there evolved a greater tendency by individual nations, regional organizations and the United Nations to carry out humanitarian interventions. Such interventions were carried out in vastly different parts of the world, including Northern Iraq, the former Yugoslavia, Rwanda, East Timor, and currently in Darfur (Sudan). Be that as it may, many of the latter interventions have been enmeshed in controversy—and the vast majority could hardly be considered resounding successes. In fact, more often than not, the interventions came late in the killing process, had weak mandates, and were under-manned and under-resourced.

In 2000, UN Secretary-General Kofi Annan challenged the international community to try to "endeavor to build a new international consensus on how to respond in the face of massive violations of human rights and humanitarian law" (International Commission on Intervention and State Sovereignty, 2001, p. 341). Canada accepted the challenge and established the International Commission on Intervention and State Sovereignty (ICISS) for the purpose of conducting a study into the aforementioned issues. In its report, *The Responsibility to Protect*, the ICISS (2001) asserted that it had "reconceptualized" the concept of sovereignty to be understood as the responsibility of a state to protect its citizens and prevent them from harm, and that when a state failed to do so the international community not only has the right but the responsibility to intervene for the express purpose of protecting the population at risk.

While this report was welcomed by many as a major milestone in the long, evolving path of human rights protection, it was also looked askance at by others. Thus, for example, while Thakur (2002), among others, hailed the ICISS report as "a new normative and operational consensus on the role of military intervention for humanitarian purposes" (p. 323), those on the far left took a much more negative position, asking such questions as: "With a few powerful states dominating the world, can there be any doubt that they will determine whose human rights abuses will be punished and whose will be excused?" (Selfa, 2002, p. 11) and "What is more, can anyone seriously accept the idea that the most powerful nations in the world will agree to be held to the same standards that they hold the rest of the world?" (Selfa, 2002, p. 11).

Numerous reasons have been offered for the ostensible shift in theory (though, it must be noted, not necessarily in reality or at least not to the extent some had hoped for) towards a "norm of intervention," including: the emergence of an ever-stronger worldwide human rights regime (which has resulted in "changing international expectations regarding the responsibilities of states and of the international community for halting gross and systematic violations of human rights with grave humanitarian consequences," Karns and Mingst, 2001, p. 216); Dag Hammarskjold's interpretation of a "Chapter Six and a Half" mandate as a justification of peacekeeping and humanitarian intervention (which of course, does not exist in the UN Charter); the end of the Cold War, which allowed for interventions without the fear of causing a catastrophic (read, nuclear) war; the ever-increasing interdependence of nations; various UN proposals, including Secretary General Boutros Boutros-Ghali's "Agenda for Peace" and his "Supplement to the Agenda for Peace"; the UN's creation of its Department of Peacekeeping Operations (UNDPKO); UN Secretary-General Kofi Annan's call for the "development of international norms" to protect civilians from slaughter," which the UN Security Council supported, and thus legitimized (Wheeler, 2002, p. 127); "the complete disregard for international humanitarian law by war criminals," which incensed large portions of the international community (Weiss, 2003, p. 84); the prevalent "use of foreign aid to fuel conflicts and war economies" and the backlash against such (Weiss, 2003, p. 84); and "the protracted nature of many so-called emergencies" (Weiss, 2003, p. 84).

That said, Krasner and Froats (1996) cogently argue that

> The view that developments [in the world] signal a fundamental change in how international relations are ordered in fact—rather than theory—is myopic both empirically and analytically.... Relations between ruler and ruled have been an enduring international concern. The principles of nonintervention and territoriality, which define the Westphalian model, have persistently been challenged by alternative principles such as universal human rights, toleration, and ethnic determination. Every major peace settlement of the modern period has addressed the fate of minorities, defined in terms of religious affiliation and later ethnic identity. With the end of the Cold War, minority rights have ["simply," once] again become a focus of international concern (pp. 227-228).

Similarly, Nardin (2002) first observes and then asserts that

> [h]umanitarian intervention is usually discussed as an exception to the nonintervention principle. According to this principle, states are forbidden to exercise their authority, and certainly to use force, within the jurisdiction of other states. The principle finds firm support in the United Nations Charter, which permits a state to defend itself from attack but forbids the use of armed force against the territorial integrity or political independence of other states. Taken literally, these provisions prohibit armed intervention, including intervention to protect human rights. And in general, humanitarian intervention finds scant support in modern international law.
>
> There is, however, a much older tradition in which the use of force is justified not only in self-defense but to punish wrongs and protect the innocent. This tradition is in some tension with modern international law and especially with the UN Charter. It holds that armed intervention is permissible to enforce standards of civilized conduct when rulers violate these standards, and finds expression today in the widely held opinion that states, acting unilaterally or collectively, are justified in enforcing respect for human rights. It is this enduring tradition, not current international law, that best explains the moral basis of humanitarian intervention.... [In] other words, humanitarian intervention is justified within a powerful reformulation of natural law

worked out by philosophers influenced by Immanuel Kant. This post-Kantian version of natural law, which I follow Alan Donagan in calling" common morality," suggests why humanitarian intervention remains morally defensible despite modern efforts to make it illegal (pp. 57-58).

Still, and not surprisingly, there are those (various scholars, government leaders, and personnel in intergovernmental organizations) who are adamantly against any type of change that challenges the so-called "traditional" position on nonintervention. Indeed, they vehemently question the legality of intervening in another state's "internal affairs" (which they consider a breach of a nation's sovereignty), even in the face of mass killing. Be that as it may—and no matter how the current climate is described (be it a shift in theory, a new focus, a refocusing, a more pronounced perspective, legitimate or not, legal or illegal, and/or moral or immoral), the fact of the matter is there has been and is a propensity by both the UN and various states to more overtly challenge, at least in words, the traditional conception of the so-called sanctity of state sovereignty. Whether such a challenge eventually results in a radical change of behavior by nation states and the UN is yet to be determined.

Most of the recent interventions have hardly been, as their name suggests, altruistic in nature. Most, in fact, were undertaken when the intrastate conflict seemed to pose an imminent danger to its neighbors and/or region. Nor, as stated earlier, have the interventions been as effective as they could or should have been—and that is a gross understatement.[1]

Notably, almost every single case of intervention undertaken by the United Nations, NATO, or a coalition of independent nations was implemented *only after the conflict had erupted and resulted in the murder and deaths of tens— if not hundreds—of thousands of people.* Indeed, this was true in regard to the intervention in response to the Iraq's gassing of the Kurds (McDowall, 1996); the Hutu genocide of the Tutsis in Rwanda in 1994 (Des Forges, 1999; Melvern, 2004); the slaughter perpetrated in the former Yugoslavia in the 1990s (Thompson and De Luce, 2002, p. 201; Weiss, 1996, pp. 59-96); the ethnic cleansing and murder of the Albanians in Kosovo; and the Government of Sudan's and *Janjaweed's* genocidal actions against the black Africans of Darfur (Totten and Markusen, 2006). Even in East Timor (1999), which has been deemed a relative "success story" vis-à-vis humanitarian intervention efforts, a horrific amount of killing and destruction was committed prior to Australia's intervention.

Many of the interventions have been mired in controversy, albeit for different reasons. The intervention in Rwanda, for example, has been lambasted as being "too little, too late." The UN Assistance Mission in Rwanda (UNAMIR) was not only constrained by a Chapter VI (or peacekeeping mandate), but the force was badly under-manned and under-resourced. The catastrophic result was the murder of over 500,000 Tutsi men, women, children and babies and moderate Hutus by extremist Hutus in a 100 day period between April and July 1994.

The 1999 intervention in Kosovo was something altogether different. While Tomes (2000), for one, suggests that NATO's bombing campaign of Kosovo in 1999 should be considered legitimate, and concludes with a *jus cogens* argument (similar to a natural law argument) in support of intervention to stop gross violations of human rights, Falk (2001) asserts that it was not legitimate. More specifically, Falk (2001) argues as follows:

> One of the most important efforts of international law is to restrict uses of force to defensive modes or under UN auspices....Under [the latter] circumstances, the claim to prevent genocide or to stop the commission of crimes against humanity is the essential basis for the legitimacy of the operation. But recourse to war even under these exceptional circumstances can only be treated as a permissible departure from normal restraints on the use of force if a maximal effort was made to achieve a diplomatic solution. The NATO countries contend that the combination of the efforts at Rambouillet and the shuttle diplomacy of Richard Holbrooke exhausted all reasonable efforts to reach an acceptable political settlement of the dispute. Critics, however, are not convinced. They wonder why the terms offered Belgrade at Rambouillet seemed so rigidly insistent on highlighting the NATO role, which could only be understood as a slap in the face of Yugoslav sovereignty....
>
> ...The exclusive reliance on air power to achieve "victory" in a war concerning arrangements internal to a sovereign state was a novelty in the long history of warfare....The civilian infrastructure in former Yugoslavia was targeted directly after the initial target list composed of military sites was exhausted after the first few days of bombing without achieving the expected response in Belgrade.
>
> Such tactics raise future doubts about the claim of a humanitarian war. First of all, to shift the risks of casualty to the side that is being assisted, tarnishes at the very least the humanitarian dimension of the undertaken. Such an impression is strengthened by the total absence of battle casualties on the NATO side, and the estimated death of some 2,000 Kosovar and Serb civilians (pp. 329, 330).

Even the rationale behind the intervention in Kosovo is in dispute. Both NATO officials and the Clinton Administration argued that the purpose of the intervention was to put an end to the vicious ethnic cleansing taking place. In praising both the purpose and "success" of NATO's operation in Kosovo, Javier Solana (1999), former Secretary-General of NATO, argued that the Kosovo intervention was the first time a defense alliance conducted a military campaign to attempt to prevent a humanitarian tragedy outside its borders. He also asserted that "after 77 days, with no casualties of its own, NATO had prevailed. A humanitarian disaster had been averted. About one million refugees could now return in safety. Ethnic cleansing had been reversed" (Solana, 1999, p. 118). Various critics of the NATO bombing of Kosovo, though, question the validity of such a claim and/or the notion that the intervention was such a resounding "success." Whitman (2001), for example, asserts that the intervention in Kosovo was a classic case of self-interest:

> The NATO intervention in Kosovo has been hailed in some quarters as a "victory"; as principled action in defense of human rights; and as a triumphant defense of the rights of refugees. [However,] the unprecedented response to the Kosovo crisis was animated less by human rights principles than by a concern to contain the refugees within the region and to maintain political support for the military campaign against Serbia. NATO humanitarianism was an emergency response to an unanticipated refugee crisis of historic proportions in which the rights of the refugees themselves and the larger issue of human rights in Kosovo did not interfere with the strategic and political concerns of Western European states (p. 164).

Also arguing that the intervention was hardly the success Solana claimed it was, Mandelbaum (1999) argues that NATO's bombing of Kosovo constituted a "gross error in political judgment" (p. 2). Continuing, he asserts

> At the outset of the bombing campaign, the Clinton Administration said that it was acting to save lives. Before NATO intervened on March 24, approximately 2,500 people had died in Kosovo's civil war between the Serb authorities and the ethnic Albanian insurgents of the Kosovo Liberation Army (KLA). During the 11 weeks of bombardment, an estimated 10,000 people died violently in the province, most of them Albanian civilians murdered by Serbs.
> An equally important NATO goal was to prevent the forced displacement of the Kosovar Albanians. At the outset of the bombing, 230 were estimated to have left their homes. By its end, 1.4 million were displaced.... (p. 2).

Interventions to prevent crimes against humanity and/or genocide are bound to be contentious for one reason or another, and nothing in the short term is going to change that. Be that as it may, *ideally* they should be carried out for alteristic purposes. What can and must be changed, though, are both the timing *and* the way in which the international community, regional organizations and/or individual states make the decision to intervene and then act on such a decision. That, of course, is easier said than done.

The Complexities of Intervention

The complexities surrounding humanitarian interventions are many, and no doubt that is why, at least in part, most have not been as effective as they could or should have been. For example, in an essay entitled "The Intervention and Prevention of Genocide: Sisyphean or Doable?" Totten (2004) noted and commented on all of the following: the difficulty of ascertaining whether a situation is going to result in genocide or not, and thus the tentativeness of "outsiders" to act in a timely fashion; the availability of only fragmented information about a conflict; conflicting reports from various sources (including those issued by the media, NGOs, IGOs, government officials and others) concerning the status of a crisis; the lack of a central, fully operational and highly sophisticated genocide early warning system; the longtime and resilient notion of the sanctity of sovereignty that many nations still hold sacrosanct; the lack of an adequate mandate for the interventionary force; the ongoing impediment of *realpolitik;* a general lack of political will by most nations to intervene in a violent conflict (due to various reasons, including financial concerns, a concern for the safety of a nation's troops, a concern as to how political constituents may perceive the effort, etc.); a lack of support by the UN Security Council (which gets back to the issue of *realpolitik*); and, as callous as it may sound, a total lack of concern about "those others" in an "insignificant" part of the world.

Based on first-hand experience and research, Barnett (2002) further asserts that the bureaucratic nature of the UN directly and adversely impacts the effectiveness of its intervention and peacekeeping efforts. Bureaucratic inertia, in-fighting, and miscommunication and/or lack of communication at the UN (between and amongst the UN Secretary General and the Security Council, the various department's of the UN, and between UN headquarters and its field commanders) invariably results in the proverbial situation where the right hand doesn't know what the left hand is doing and vice versa.

Then there is the problem posed by those states that contribute troops to a peace enforcement or peacekeeping mission that tend to send poorly trained forces with inadequate equipment or that which is in poor repair. This was a major frustration for Lt. General Romeo Dallaire, force commander of the UN troops in Rwanda prior to, during and following the 1994 genocide. (See his book, *Shake Hands with the Devil: The Failure of Humanity in Rwanda.* New York: Carroll & Graf Publishers, 2005.)

Over and above the latter, Maley (2002), Associate Professor of Politics at the University of New South Wales Australian Defence Force Academy, has delineated twelve theses that he asserts adversely impact the success of external military intervention (whether authorized by the UN Security Council or not): "I. Interventions will more readily and rapidly address symptoms than underlying causes of political disorder; II. Interventions will have significant, and quite possibly unintended, effects on the value to particular individuals of positional and distributional goods; III. Intervention will bring a range of new actors to the political landscape; IV. Interventions may foster warlordism; V. Some new actors may be intent on settling old scores; VI. Interventions will be merely the starting points in complex processes of change; VII. Intervening forces will find it difficult to confront problems of political culture, elite structure, institutional design and institutionalization; VIII. Post-intervention peace processes may be faced with serious 'spoiler' problems, with vulnerable civilians on occasion the principal targets; IX. Interventions may have significant potential impact on trust, social capital and the character of society, but it is difficult to produce positive effects directly; X. Progress towards a civil economy will be difficult if the intervening powers perversely distort local incentive structures, create an unaccountable 'rentier state' or inadvertently provide space for criminality to flourish; XI. Interventions may end up being under-resourced; and XII. A coalition of intervening powers may fragment over some of these issues" (pp. 266-274). While not all twelve of the theses were evident in each and every humanitarian intervention undertaken in the 1990s, one or more of the theses were evident in each of the interventions. Those who carry out interventions and fail to seriously consider the aforementioned concerns are handicapping themselves at the outset and, more than likely, setting themselves and the victim population they are attempting to assist for great disappointment and misery.

Is Inaction and/or Ineffectiveness Solely a Lack of Political Will?

Time and again when a genocide is perpetrated and little to nothing is done to prevent it and/or the international community fails to intervene in a timely and effective manner, prognosticators assert that it is largely a result of a "lack of political will." The charge has become so common that it verges on being a cliché. Two key questions loom over this issue: "First, is such inaction truly a case of a lack of political will—or something else altogether?" and, "If the situation is a result of a lack of political will, how can it be overcome—if, in fact, it can be?"

In many cases, the inaction by individual states, regional organizations, and/or the United Nations *is*, at least in part, a lack of political will. Governmental officials, for example, may not be sure if their constituents would support sending troops into a situation that ostensibly has no direct bearing on their country, and thus hesitate doing so. A nation's leaders may feel that their military is already over-committed, if not over-extended, and cannot spare additional troops or supplies for another mission. Some national leaders may also perceive a situation as "hopeless," and thus unwilling to put their nation's military troops at risk. The point is, there are a host of contingencies that may add up to a lack of political will.

Political will, however, is not the sole reason in regard to why states, regional organizations, and/or the United Nations are tentative, at best, and unwilling, at the extreme, to attempt to prevent or halt a genocidal situation. Thus, while it may appear as if a dearth of concern and/or action constitutes a lack of political will, it may be something else altogether. More specifically, it may be due to any and/or a combination of the following: (1) a true lack of understanding as to whether the situation constitutes genocide or not (at least in the early stages of the genocidal action) (Power, 2002, pp. 300, 318-319, 321-324, 359-360). (This, of course, broaches a whole other issue, and that is: "Why is there the ostensible need to wait until mass killing is deemed "genocide" to stanch it?"); (2) certain nations may wish to act but not have the imprimatur of the UN Security Council to do so, and do not wish to risk the wrath of the UN and individual states by acting unilaterally; (3) certain members of the UN Security Council may wish to act but are prevented from doing so by the veto(es) of other members; and/or (4) it may be a case of *realpolitik*.

Realpolitik

Despite the fact that the international community and individual nations have been increasingly involved in interventions of late, *realpolitik*[2] still plays a key role in regard to who decides to intervene when, where, why, and to what extent. Indeed, the tentativeness to intervene, the slowness to carry out interventions, the lack of support for specific interventions, and the weak mandates provided for various interventions have all been impacted, in one way or another, by *realpolitik*. In this regard, Sadkovich (1996) argues that

> The United Nations and other international and regional organizations act to contain and manage, not end or resolve, such phenomena as aggression and genocide [and] the proponents of state sovereignty and *realpolitik* rule the day (p. 283).
>
> The years [1991-1995] may have marked the victory of the proponents of state sovereignty and the practitioners of bureaucratic barbarism and power politics over the advocates of individual and collective rights, [...but] there has been a tendency to reassert the *realpolitik* of the nineteenth century without the humanistic principle of the period. So foreign policies are now less "hypocritical" in that the naked self-interest of states is repeatedly invoked to justify action or inaction, but elites have become morally insensitive. Governments will not intervene to stop aggression or genocide so long as doing so presents any risk of serious conflict (p. 294).

Various statements, decisions, and actions (and, in actuality, inactions) by the United States in the face of various genocidal situations during the 1990s provide classic examples of the "ways" of *realpolitik*. More specifically, in regard to the unfolding human rights disaster in Bosnia, Secretary of State James Baker (a member of the 1988-1992 Bush administration), asserted that the United States did not "have a dog in this fight" (inferring that the United States had no interests there and thus was not about to get involved) (Power, 2002, p. 267). In a similar vein, six days into the 1994 Rwandan genocide, Republican Senate minority leader Robert Dole commented that "I don't think we have any interest there.... The Americans are out, and as far as I'm concerned, in Rwanda, that ought to be the end of it" (Power, 2002, p. 352).

A Lack of Care

For the most part, when scholars and others have discussed why members of the international community have either not attempted to prevent a genocide and/or why interventions have been so ineffective, the primary explanations have centered on the lack of political will and/or *realpolitik*. There is, however, another reason, and that is the simple but profound fact that governmental and/or intergovernmental officials have simply not cared about certain crisis situations. (There are those who are bound to assert that a lack of care and *realpolitik* are one and the same but the lack of care constitutes, in a very real sense, an even more heartless and base element at work.) Power (2002) provides numerous examples that corroborate this point. For example, "when James Woods of the U.S. Defense Department's African Affairs Bureau suggested that the Pentagon add Rwanda-Burundi to its list of potential trouble spots, his bosses told him, in his words, 'Look if something happens in Rwanda-Burundi, we don't care. Take it off the list. U.S. national interest is not involved and we can't put all these silly humanitarian issues on lists.... Just make it go away'"(Power, 2002, p. 342). Yes, realpolitik was at work but so was a total lack of care about the safety of other human beings.

Also, at the beginning of the Rwandan genocide in April 1994, Secretary of State Warren Christopher, a member of the Clinton Administration, cavalierly dismissed the tragedy unfolding on the ground. Speaking of his attitude, Power (2002) reports the following: "Secretary of State Warren Christopher knew little about Africa. At one meeting with his top advisers, he pulled an atlas off his shelf to help him locate the country. Belgian foreign minister Willie Claes recalls trying to discuss Rwanda with his American counterpart and being told, 'I have other responsibilities'" (p. 352). Who know how many leaders and bureaucrats in other powerful nations have voiced similar thoughts and sentiments.

Gradations of Intervention

Assuming that preventive efforts have failed and there is a need for intervention, there are numerous stages and degrees of intervention that can be implemented prior to carrying out humanitarian (military) intervention. At a minimum, the former includes but is not limited to the following: the threat and/or implementation of sanctions, information intervention, the threat of force, and/or coercive inducement.

There is a wide variety of sanctions available for use, and among these are: diplomatic sanctions; arms embargoes; oil embargoes; flight bans; travel bans; economic sanctions (e.g., trade bans, the freezing of financial assets, the prohibition of financial transactions, bans on transshipment of strategic goods through or across the targeted nation); and bans on sporting and cultural events. There is also a broad range in which sanctions can be imposed: unilaterally, bilaterally, regionally, comprehensively, coercively, incremental versus rapid imposition of such, targeted or smart sanctions, and a stick and carrot approach (i.e., the imposition of negative sanctions followed by positive incentives).

The imposition of sanctions, though, has proved to be controversial, and that is true for numerous reasons: (1) sanctions often don't result in the desired effect (e.g., they do not bring to bear the desired pressure on a perpetrators' economy, and/or a halt in the ethnic cleansing of an area or the perpetration of massacres); (2) sanctions often result in unintended consequences (e.g., they often penalize and hurt the nation's general population more than the leaders of the government they're aimed at); and (3) at times, they inadvertently enrich the very individuals (e.g., governmental leaders) the sanctions are aimed at coercing.

That said, over the past decade the threat and/or imposition of sanctions have had varying degrees of success. For example, the sanctions imposed on Yugoslavia during the 1990s met with partial success. The success that did result was due, in large part, to the fact that "comprehensive sanctions" were imposed and tightly enforced. The sanctions against Rwanda in 1994 were a dismal failure, due in part to the fact that the sanctions were limited and poorly enforced. Time and again (from summer 2004 through fall 2006), the UN threatened to impose sanctions against Sudan for its—and the *Janjaweed's* –attacks against Darfur's black African population, but the threats did little to nothing to stanch the killing. That was largely due to the fact that the threats were never acted upon. (For a detailed and insightful examination of the imposition of sanctions in the post-Cold War period, see *The Sanctions Decade: Assessing UN Strategies in the 1990s* by David Cortright and George A. Lopez. Boulder, CO: Lynne Rienner Publishers, 2000; see also Chapter 5 in this book by George A. Lopez and Kathryn Stuhldrehe.)

Outside forces can (and often do) conduct information intervention prior to, during and following military intervention. Such intervention involves various actions, including the blocking or scrambling of propagandistic and/or hate-filled messages aired over television and radio stations. Significantly, it also involves the broadcasting of counter messages. (During the course of a military intervention, full-scale bombardment of television and radio stations and/or the confiscation of transmitters is another viable option.) In the post genocidal period, new laws and a regulatory regime over broadcast transmissions can (and should) be established (Price and Monroe, 2002).

Commenting on the threat of military action, Michael Joseph Smith (2000a) correctly notes that "a credible threat of force made in advance may well obviate the necessity actually to use force, or at least may require a lesser degree of force" (p. 133). The key term here, though, is "credible." When threats are made time and again with no effect on the perpetrators' actions and the threats are not carried out, they quickly lose their credibility.

Complementing but upping the threat of an attack is the concept of "coercive inducement," a term UN Secretary General Kofi Annan coined when he was UN Under-secretary General for Peacekeeping. "Coercive inducement" is a form of coercive diplomacy that involves the deployment and demonstration of military power versus the actual use of the power. In other words, it constitutes a warning that an outside force (the international community) is ready, willing and able to use force if the belligerent neglects to heed the demands of the international community to cease and desist from its abhorrent actions. As Daniel, Hayes and Oudraat (1999) note,

> The coercive side of coercive diplomacy...is a function of their credibility, of whether they are physically up to the task of intimidation and whether political leaders are committed to employing them violently if necessary....Military efficiency would take second place to politio-diplomatic concerns, the most important of which is not military victory but change in the target state's behavior.
> ...Even when highly capable and endowed with Chapter VII authority to employ "all necessary means," the long-under-lying presence of an inducement force is to be more reactive than initiatory, employ when possible essentially defensive measures...and focused violence such as striking only at specific weapons causing death or injury (pp. 22, 23).

When all else fails and there is clear evidence that attacks on a population are being prepared for (or are actually starting to be carried out), a full-blown Chaper VII intervention becomes a must.

Humanitarian Intervention

As noted at the outset of this chapter, humanitarian intervention is, ideally and theoretically, carried out to quell major human rights infractions that have caused, and will continue to cause, if not halted, horrific suffering of innocents.

As commented on earlier, between 1990 and 2007 many efforts to quell ethnic cleansing, crimes against humanity, and genocide have involved peacekeeping missions with weak and inadequate mandates that were unable to stanch the crimes being perpetrated. "Peacekeeping" is basically "the deployment of a U.N. [or regional organization] presence in the field, with the consent of all parties concerned, to allow contending forces that wish to stop fighting to separate with some confidence that they will not be attacked in order to create conditions conducive to a political settlement" (Congressional Research Service, 1995, n. p.). When a peacekeeping mission is placed in the middle of a war or full-blown genocide, the ultimate result is disastrous for both the peacekeepers and those the mission is attempting to protect. Three recent genocides provided "classic" and irrefutable evidence of that: Rwanda (1994), Srebrenica (1995) and Darfur (2003-present).

As previously mentioned, in Rwanda, the UN Assistance Mission for Rwanda was limited to a peacekeeping mission in which military personnel served as monitors/observers under extremely tight (e.g., restricted) rules of engagement versus a Chapter VII mandate or peace enforcement operation in which the mission would have been allowed to use force in an attempt to bring about a cessation of violent activity. Protective engagement (the use of the military to provide safe havens) was implemented in Srebrenica but with disastrous results due to a limited mandate and a undermanned force. (Srebrenica will be discussed in more detail below.) As for Darfur, a small, undermanned, under-resourced mission of African Union troops with an inadequate mandate (Chapter VI versus Chapter VII) was deployed to an area the size of France and thus was basically forced to watch as Government of Sudan troops and the *Janjaweed* had their way with both the black Africans under attack as well as the human rights monitors on the ground (not to mention the AU troops themselves).

Many scholars and practitioners assert that one of the most successful interventions was conducted in East Timor in 1999. Alan Ryan (2002), a Senior Research Fellow with Australian Army's Land Warfare Studies Centre, goes so far as to argue that the way in which the intervention was conducted serves as a model of sorts for future interventions along this line. More specifically, he asserts that

> the speed with which the International Force in East Timor (INTERFET) was deployed and the rapidity with which it was able to establish conditions of security in East Timor make this operation an excellent model for future ad hoc, complex, multinational deployments. In large part, the success of the operation was due to the troop-contributing nations' acceptance of the imperfections inherent in such a disparate force. Operational responsibility was distributed according to the capabilities of the forces assigned to the mission. The need for a robust command-and-control architecture was realized in the strong-lead-nation model that INTERFET adopted. Short-notice deployments of "coalitions of the willing" in the future will benefit from a consideration of the clear, simple, and unified command structure that characterized *Operation Stablise* in East Timor (Ryan, 2002, p. 23).

One, though, cannot be too sanguine about the intervention in East Timor for it came late in the killing process (estimates ranged from 600 to 7,000 people who had already been murdered) *and* not until after the destruction of the entire region and its infrastructure. An estimated 300,000 also had already been driven from their homes and villages.

There are numerous reasons as to why various interventions were either minimal successes or abject failures: some missions were issued inadequate mandates (e.g., the previously mentioned peacekeeping (Chapter

VI) mandate versus a peace enforcement (Chapter VII) mandate; the tentativeness of potential interveners to make decisive and critical decisions early on that would have resulted in saving thousands, if not tens and/or hundreds of thousands, of lives (e.g., Rwanda, 1994; the former Yugoslavia, throughout the 1990s; Darfur, Sudan, 2003-2007); certain troops were ill-prepared for the mission (e.g., the Bangladeshi contingent was highly unprofessional in its conduct and appeared to fear contact with the perpetrators in Rwanda in 1994 (Dallaire, 2005, pp. 204-205, 243-244, 269-271, 323-324); various troops lacked adequate resources (e.g., the entire contingent of UNAMIR in Rwanda in 1994, and the current African Union mission in Darfur, Sudan); the military approach failed to protect the victim population (Kosovo, 1999); and, in certain cases, intervening parties developed exit strategies and made decisions about exit dates *prior* to the implementation of the intervention.

As for conducting an intervention under a weak and inadequate mandate, Mockaitis (1999) has argued that his analysis of the peace operation missions in the former Yugoslavia between 1992 and 1995 reveals a

> consistent pattern...of the inadequacy of peacekeeping models for intrastate conflict.... [The] UN deployed a peace-keeping force under Chapter 6, only to discover that such a force could accomplish little in the face of an active civil war.
> ...Because the UN and its member states insisted on applying traditional peacekeeping methods to the unique conditions of civil conflict, [the] mission responded to an escalating crisis on a reactive, rather than on a proactive, basis. This ad hoc approach reduced the effectiveness of each intervention and led to greater loss of life than might *otherwise have occurred. The limited effectiveness of the missions suggests the need for a new approach to such intervention.* Intervening in an active civil war is neither a peacekeeping activity nor a collective security action. Troops inserted in an active civil war must be prepared for a range of contingencies from combat to policy work (emphasis added) (pp. 6-7).

Mockaitis' comments vis-à-vis a peacekeeping versus a peace enforcement are germane to virtually any intervention mission deployed on the behalf of those facing genocidal actions.

Weiss (1993) has also provided trenchant commentary on the West's and the United Nation's tentative, half-hearted, and often disastrous, interventions that were carried out in various crisis-situations in the early 1990s. Here he, too, addresses those that were implemented in the former Yugoslavia:

> Incremental measures under the United Nations auspices paradoxically fostered Serbia's genocidal war aims. Given their traditional constraints and operating procedures, UN soldiers were not strong enough to deter the Serbs. But they deterred the international community from more assertive intervention because the troops, along with aid workers, were vulnerable targets. While assistance to refugees saved

lives, it also helped foster ethnic cleansing by stimulating movement of unwanted populations. Air-drops of food made it seem as if people counted; while massive and unspeakable human rights abuses and war crimes continued unabated.

Inadequate military and humanitarian action, combined with half-hearted sanctions and a negotiating charade, thus constituted a powerful diversion. They collectively impeded more vigorous Western diplomatic and military pressure or lifting the arms embargo for Muslims to help level the killing fields (Weiss, 1993, p. 7).

Over the past fifteen years or so, interveners have established a wide array of so-called safe locations, including "safe havens"[3] (e.g., in northern Iraq in 1991 to protect the Kurdish populations from the ongoing attacks by Iraqi forces), and "safe areas" (e.g., Srebrenica, Sarajevo, Tuzla, Zepa, Gorazde, and Bihac in the former Yugoslavia in the early 1990s). An ancillary to safe areas is the use of "no fly zones," which were, for example, established in both Bosnia in the 1990s and Iraq in 1991.

"Safe havens" and "safe areas" are useful and can work, but only when they are well protected by an adequate number of troops that are well armed and have a mandate that allows them to take strong actions to deter hostile forces. Concomitantly, they need to have ready access to additional firepower, including fighter aircraft, if the situation calls for it. The danger of not providing an adequate mandate, enough manpower and adequate military support became horrifically clear when the Serbs overran numerous safe areas, including Srebrenica where approximately 7,000 Muslim men and boys were ultimately murdered by the Serbs. Due in large part to the latter situation, the term "safe area" has become an oxymoron.

At various times over the past decade and a half (1990-2006), individual nations, as well as the United Nations, have opted to "do something," no matter how ineffective it might be, so that at least the appearance of concern was portrayed to the wider world. While some have referred to this as the "fig leaf" approach, I refer to it as the "mirage effect." Such actions, in effect, are "illusory" and a "delusional." Not only is such an approach unconscionable, it can have (and has had) deleterious, if not catastrophic, results. A classic case involves the numerous threats of sanctions issued by the U.N. against the Government of Sudan (GOS) in a futile attempt to prod the GOS and *Janjaweed'* to halt their killing of the black African population in Darfur. Time and again such threats were ignored by Khartoum and the killing continued, unabated.[4]

On a related but somewhat different note, Smith (2000b) wisely notes that

[I]ntervention should come early, before blood is spilled and the situation badly polarized. This observation directly contradicts today's doctrine...which has the disadvantage of waiting so long for diplomatic efforts or economic embargoes to work that when force is finally used it must come in large amounts for long periods of time. "Peacekeeping" and "preventive diplomacy" must have a military arm if they are to be successful. The failure to insist clearly enough on such a commitment has cost lives in...the Balkans, Central Africa, and Southeast Asia (p. 22).

As alluded to earlier, a thorny issue that arose as a result of so many interventions in the 1990s was that of predetermined exit strategies and exit dates established *at the outset* of the intervention. It is virtually impossible for any intervener to know how an intervention is going to play out prior to conducting the intervention. Indeed, it is impossible to accurately predict with any type of certainty the types of barriers likely to impede progress, the determination of the perpetrators/foes to stand their ground, and/or how long it will take to control and stabilize the situation on the ground until well into the process. Thus, to design an exit strategy and/or decide upon an exit date early on is bound, in most cases, to result in an arbitrary set of plans that may have little to nothing to do with the realities on the ground (Rose, 1998).

Conclusion

It is all but a foregone conclusion that many of the most complex and difficult challenges noted above will not be solved in the near future. That is true for the simple but profound reason that *realpolitik* still "governs," at least to a large extent, the way in which most nations act and react to crises—and *that* is not likely to change any time soon. That is not to say that some, or even most, of the issues will go unaddressed.

Certainly one of the major challenges—Herculean-like, in fact—is the need for a major overhaul of the UN system in order to make it more proactive vis-à-vis the prevention and intervention of genocide. The UN's Byzantine ways, however, seem to be all but impregnable. A major problem is that the system is so huge, so ostensibly resistant to change, and "sclerotic," as one wag put it, that changes at the United Nations are, more often than not, undertaken in piecemeal fashion and, in many cases, the "reforms" never "take."

Since the early 1990s there has been a plethora of talk at the UN about the need to reform its bureaucracy and operation procedures, but most attempts have been little more than cosmetic. Indeed, little to nothing has been done thus far to address in a systematic and thorough manner the various systemic problems/issues (e.g., the unwieldy bureaucracy, the overarching power of several states in the UN Security Council, the lack of clear communication channels within various units of the UN and the UN and its field operations) that could help it become a more effective body

That said, it is worthy of note that on November 31, 2004, a United Nations panel issued a report that proposed wide-sweeping reforms that included a recommendation to "overhaul its decision-making organ, the Security Council" (Hoge, 2004, p. 2a). In actuality, two proposals were set forth. Both proposals called for an increase in the membership of the Security Council. One proposal suggested increasing the permanent membership from five (Great Britain, China, France, Russia, and the United States) to eleven. The other suggested adding "eight semi-permanent members chosen for renewable four-year terms" (Hoge, 2004, p. 2A). The panel also expanded the understanding of "global threats" that could require military action to include the protection of civilians from genocide and other atrocities. In fact, the authors of the report asserted that "'nightmare scenarios' facing the international community may justify the use of force, 'not just reactively but preventively'" (Hoge, 2004, p. 2A). Only time will tell whether the proposals are acted upon and then result in positive, systemic changes that streamline the work of the UN and make it more efficient and effective in addressing potential and/or actual genocides.[5]

In order for the UN to be as effective as possible when it comes to interventions to stave off or interrupt a potential or actual genocide, there are numerous areas, over and above the bureaucracy of the UN, that demand serious attention: 1. the development and full implementation of an effective UN genocide early warning system; 2. the development of effective methods for detecting, early on, various types of genocide warning signals; 3. "enhance[ment] of the UN's capacity for local political risk analysis" (Kolodziej, 2000, p. 139); 4. the development and adherence to regulations requiring the issuance of clear and sound mandates that are most applicable to the type of conflict a mission's troops will face; 5. "clarification of the criteria for applicable responses under Chapter VI and VII of the UN Charter" (Kolodziej, 2000, p. 139); 6. the development of sound procedures for strengthening "the earmarking of military forces from national contingents for Chapter VI and VII security operations" (Kolodziej, 2000, p. 139); 7. the establishment of "the standards for and the development of competent command and control for complex military operations" (Cook, 2003, p. 147); 8. "the development of closer liaison and joint planning operations between the United Nations and regional security organizations and their member states" (Kolodziej, 2000, p. 139); 9. the development of a set of procedures for strengthening military input at the strategic level; 10. the development and implementation of stronger policies related to the coordination of civilian and military tasks; 11. the development and implementation of a much stronger military training program for all troops involved in UN peace operations; and 12. the development and implementation of a strong, well-equipped rapid reaction force that is truly quick and effective. (Hopefully, the latter will help to alleviate—at least to some extent—the need to rely on individual nations, which are often tentative about supporting an intervention or committing troops due to the fact that their decisions are based more on "domestic calculations and pressures" (Woodward, 1995, p. 147) and/or their national interests vis-à-vis foreign relations than in the belief that any genocide anywhere must be stanched as quickly as possible.) All of these issues are, minimum in the talking stage, and some are beyond that.

Part and parcel of the latter components is the critical need for the development of a research-based, fully funded, and strongly supported anti-genocide regime in which a main component would be the effective detection of genocidal situations followed by the rapid and efficient dispatching of well-resourced, well-trained troops with a strong mandate to quell the genocide.

At a minimum, an effective anti-genocide regime must be comprised of the following: (1) an early warning system, operated by "handlers" who are objective and not under the watch or thumb of any political organization; (2) an effective procedure, along with the means, for applying pressure on individual nations, regional organizations, and the UN to *generate the political will* to act to prevent a genocide before it breaks out and, in the case of a genocidal event, to act in an efficient and effective manner to implement a mission to put an end to the genocide; and (3) an efficient anti-genocide rapid action force.

The United Nations continues to be more than a little tentative about developing, funding, and operationalizing a rapid action force (Sarooshi,

2001). And while such a force has been discussed, what has not been addressed in any detail is the organization that would have oversight responsibilities for such a force. If the UN Security Council had oversight duties then there is the likelihood that the force's use would be as politicized as ever. But it is not likely, at least at this point in time, that the Security Council would allow some other agency within the UN to serve in an oversight capacity. Some have suggested the need for a totally independent force, but still under the auspices of the UN. That is an interesting idea, but it is likely that the UN Security Council would veto that idea as well. Such objections and barriers, of course, are not reasons to forego the effort of creating such a force.

Most of the challenges (with the major exception being the restructuring of the United Nations) mentioned above are much more likely to be addressed today than ever before, and that is due, in part, to the following: the ever-increasing strength of the human rights regime which began to flourish with the establishment of the United Nations in 1948; the influence of the new and burgeoning field of genocide studies; efforts by nongovernmental organizations (NGOs), individual nations and the United Nations to development an effective genocide early warning system; the ongoing efforts of scholars and human rights practitioners to develop key parts of what could become an anti-genocide regime; and the fact that an ever-increasing number of NGOs in a wide array of fields (e.g., human rights, refugee rights, international law, peace operations, humanitarian relief, development) have begun to appreciate the fact that their efforts are greatly hindered and diminished by ongoing genocidal assaults, and thus they are becoming more intent on addressing the horror of genocide across the globe.

At this point in time there obviously has not been a true sea change vis-à-vis the international community's position on the intervention of genocide—and there won't be until the international community commits itself to acting early on, rapidly, efficiently and effectively whenever the possibility of genocide arises. For now—and possibly far into the future—*realpolitik*, selfishness, and a *willed* lack of political will shall likely rule international relations, and as long they do targeted groups are bound to suffer horrifically. The hope by many, though, is that over time state sovereignty will truly come to be equated with responsibility—not only a responsibility to do no harm to one's own citizens but also a responsibility to intervene when another nation violates what should be a sacrosanct principle. That is a gigantic hope, but glimmers of progress have been made, and that, in and of itself, is vitally significant.

All that said, it is also true that intervention to prevent genocide has, as a result of the recent Iraq war in which the United States deposed Saddam Hussein only to see Iraq splinter and descend into a state of internecine chaos, become entangled in the debate over the so-called "altruistic nature" of so-called humanitarian intervention. Possibly the most articulate observer of this debate is David Kennedy (2004), a former legal advisor to the United Nations High Commissioner for Refugees and other international governmental and nongovernmental humanitarian agencies, who asserts, in *The Dark Sides of Virtue: Reassessing International Humanitarianism*, that the major problem with the humanitarian impulse vis-à-vis major human rights violation comes to the fore "the moment the humanitarian averts his eyes from his own power" (p. 329). More specifically, he argues that "We will need to lay down the tools of pragmatic renewal which block our experience of responsibility from rulership, and lead us to false certainty about what humanitarianism can mean. To confront the dark sides of humanitarian policy making, we need a policymaking style which welcomes, rather than obscures, the hard choices of governance. We need to develop a new posture or character of international humanitarianism—informed by the vertiginous experience of disenchantment, of seeing that one is responsible and yet does not already know" (Kennedy, 2004, p. 347).

Only time will tell if humanity has learned anything from the few successes, numerous failures, and new insights gleaned over the past fifteen years or so vis-à-vis humanitarian intervention.

Notes

1. Granted, some of the interventions did, in fact, save great numbers of people (some in the hundreds of thousands) but that does not diminish the fact that they could have been much stronger than they were and thus even more effective.
2. There are, of course, variations of *realpolitik*, including neorealism, neoclassical realism, defensive and offensive, but space precludes addressing each of these. Defining each adequately would require ample space and discussing how each impacts a state's decisionmaking process vis-à-vis intervention would take even more.
3. The safe locations established in Iraq were called safe "havens" in order to "not impugn Iraq's territorial rights over the region" (Ramsbotham and Woodhouse, 1999, p. 217).
4. Once the international community actually did act, it chose to send in a minuscule initial force of 300 African Union troops to patrol an area (Darfur) that is roughly the size of Texas. And even though the number of troops was increased over the next several years to some 7,000 troops, it never approached the number of troops (between 15,000 to just over 20,000) that experts clearly stated needed to be on the ground in order to take control of the situation.
5. Simply adding members to the UN Security Council is not likely to streamline its decisionmaking process. In fact, it may make it more cumbersome. A more radical change is needed in order to free it from its tendency to deal with matters via *realpolitik*.

References

Barnett, Michael (2002). *Eyewitness to a Genocide: The United Nations and Rwanda.* Ithaca, NY: Cornell University Press.

Bellamy, Alex, J. (2005). "Responsibility to Protect or Trojan Horse? The Crisis in Darfur and Humanitarian Intervention After Iraq." *Ethics & International Affairs,* 19(2):31-53.

Caplan, Richard (2003). "Humanitarian Intervention: Which Way Forward?" pp. 131-144. In Anthony F. Lang, Jr. (Ed.) *Just Intervention.* Washington, DC: Georgetown University Press.

Congressional Research Service (1995). *CRS Report for Congress* (Appendix I). Washington, DC: Author. Issued June 29th.

Cook, Martin L. (2003). "'Immaculate War': Constraints on Humanitarian Intervention," pp. 144-154. In Anthony F. Lang, Jr. (Ed.) *Just Intervention.* Washington, DC: Georgetown University Press.

Daniel, Donald C. F.; Hayes Bradd C.; and Oudraat, Chantal de Jonge (1999). *Coercive Inducement and the Containment of International Crises.* Washington, DC: United States Institute of Peace Press.

Des Forges, Alison (1999). *Leave None to Tell the Story: Genocide in Rwanda.* New York: Human Rights Watch.

Falk, Richard (1999). "'Humanitarian Wars,' Realist Geopolitics, and Genocidal Practices: 'Saving the Kosovars'," pp. 325-334. In Ken Booth (Ed.) *The Kosovo Tragedy: The Human Rights Dimensions.* London: Frank Cass.

Frank, Martin (2004). "The Dilemmatic Structure of Humanitarian Interventions," pp. 97-113. In Georg Meggle (Ed.) *Ethics of Humanitarian Interventions.* Frankfurt: Ontos Verlag.

Hoge, Warren (2004). "Report Proposes Reforms for U.N." *Arkansas Democrat Gazette*, December 1, p. 2A.

Karns, Margaret P., and Mingst, Karen A. (2001). "Peacekeeping and the Changing Role of the United Nations: Four Dilemmas," 215-237. In Ramesh Thakur and Albrecht Schnabel (Eds.) *United Nations Peacekeeping Operations: Ad Hoc Missions, Permanent Engagement*. Tokyo: United Nations University Press.

Kennedy, David (2004). *The Dark Sides of Virtue: International Humanitarianism*. Princeton, NJ: Princeton University Press.

International Commission on Intervention and State Sovereignty (2001). "About the Commission," pp. 341-347. In The International Commission on Intervention and State Sovereignty's *The Responsibility to Protect: Research, Bibliography, Background: Supplementary Volume to the Report of the International Commission on Intervention and State Sovereignty*. Ottawa, ON, Canada: International Development Research Centre.

International Commission on Intervention and State Sovereignty (2001). "Interventions After the Cold War," pp. 79-126. In The International Commission on Intervention and State Sovereignty's *The Responsibility to Protect: Research, Bibliography, Background: Supplementary Volume to the Report of the International Commission on Intervention and State Sovereignty*. Ottawa, ON, Canada: International Development Research Centre.

Kolodziej, Edward A. (2000). "The Great Powers and Genocide: Lessons from Rwanda." *Pacifica Review*, 12(2):121-145.

Krasner, Stephen D., and Froats, Daniel T. (1998). "Minority Rights and the Westphalian Model," pp. 227-250. In David A. Lake and Donald Rothchild (Eds.) *The International Spread of Ethnic Conflict: Fear, Diffusion, and Escalation*. Princeton, NJ: Princeton University Press.

Layne, Christopher (2000). "Collateral Damage in Yugoslavia," pp. 51-58. In Ted Galen Carpenter (Ed.) *NATO's Empty Victory: A Postmortem on the Balkan War*. Washington, DC: CATO Institute.

Maley, William (2002). "Twelve Theses on the Impact of Humanitarian Intervention." *Security Dialogue*, 33(3): 265-278.

Mandelbaum, Michael (1999). "A Perfect Failure: NATO's War Against Yugoslavia." *Foreign Affairs*, September/October, 78(5): 2-8.

Maxwell, Dayton L. (1998). "Facing the Choice Among Bad Options in Complex Humanitarian Emergencies," pp. 179-191. In Max G. Manwaring and John T. Fishel (Eds.) *Toward Responsibility in the New World Disorder: Challenges and Lessons of Peace Operations*. London: Frank Cass Publishers.

McDowall, David (1996). "The Road to Genocide," 1975-1988," pp. 343-367. In McDowall's *A Modern History of the Kurds*. New York: I.B. Tauris.

Melvern, Linda (2004). *Conspiracy to Murder: The Rwanda Genocide*. New York: Verso.

Mockaitis, Thomas R. (1999). *Peace Operations and Intrastate Conflict: The Sword or the Olive Branch?* Westport, CT: Praeger Publishers.

Peck, Connie (1996). *The United Nations as a Dispute Settlement System: Improving Mechanism for the Prevention and Resolution of Conflict*. The Hague: Kluwer Law International.

Price, Monroe E., and Thompson, Mark (Eds.) (2002). *Forging Peace: Intervention, Human Rights and the Management of Media Space*. Bloomington and Indianapolis: Indiana University Press.

Nardin, Terry (2002). "The Moral Basis of Humanitarian Intervention." *Ethics & International Affairs*, 16(1):57-70.

Power, Samantha (2002). *"A Problem from Hell": America and the Age of Genocide.* New York: Basic Books.

Rieff, David (2005). *At the Point of a Gun: Democratic Dreams and Armed Intervention.* New York: Simon & Schuster.

Rose, Gideon (1998). "The Exit Strategy Delusion." *Foreign Affairs*, January/February, 56-67.

Ryan, Alan (2002). "The Strong Lead-nation Model in an ad hoc Coalition of the Willing: Operation *Stablise* in East Timor." *International Peacekeeping*, 9(1): 23-44.

Sadkovich, James J. (1996). "The Former Yugoslavia, the End of the Nuremberg Era, and the New Barbarism," pp. 282-303. In Thomas Cushman and Stjepan G. Mestrovic (Eds.) *This Time We Knew: Western Responses to Genocide in Bosnia.* New York: New York University Press.

Sarooshi, Danesh (2001). *The United Nations and the Development of Collective Security: The Delegation by the UN Security Council of its Chapter VII Powers.* Oxford: Oxford University Press.

Selfa, Lance (2003). "A New Colonial 'Age of Empire'?" *International Socialist Review*, Issue 23, May-June 2002.

Smith, Michael Joseph (2000a). "On Humanitarian Intervention," pp. 123-140. In Neal Riemer (Ed.) *Protection Against Genocide: Mission Impossible?* Westport, CT: Praeger Publishers.

Smith, Tony (2000b). "Morality and the Use of Force in a Unipolar World: The 'Wilsonian Moment'?" *Ethics and International Affairs*, 14:11-22.

Solana, Javier (1999). "NATO's Success in Kosovo." *Foreign Affairs*, November/December, 87(6):114-120.

Thakur, Ramesh (2002). "Intervention, Sovereignty and the Responsibility to Protect: Experiences from ICISS." *Security Dialogue*, 33(3):323-340.

Thompson, Mark, and De Luce, Dan (2002). "Escalating to Success? The Media Intervention in Bosnia and Herzegovina," pp 201-235. In Monroe E. Price and Mark Thompson (Eds.) *Foreign Peace: Intervention, Human Rights and the Management of Media Space.* Bloomington and Indianapolis: Indiana University Press.

Tomes, Robert (2000). "Operation Allied Force and the Legal Basis for Humanitarian Interventions." *Parameters,* Spring, 30(1): 38-50.

Totten, Samuel (2004). "The Intervention and Prevention of Genocide: Sisyphean or Doable?" *Journal of Genocide Research*, June, 6(2):229-247.

Totten, Samuel, and Markusen, Eric (Eds.) (2006). *Genocide in Darfur: Investigating Atrocities in the Sudan.* New York: Routledge.

Weiss, Thomas G. (1996). "Collective Spinelessness: UN Actions in the Former Yugoslavia," pp. 59-96. In Richard H. Ullman (Ed.) *The World and Yugoslavia's Wars.* New York: Council on Foreign Relations.

Weiss, Thomas G. (1993). "Intervention and Genocide." *The ISG* [Institute for the Study of Genocide] *Newsletter*, Fall, 11:6-7.

Weiss, Thomas G. (2003). "Principles, Politics, and Humanitarian Action," pp. 84-103. In Anthony F. Lang, Jr. (Ed.) *Just Intervention.* Washington, D.C.: Georgetown University Press.

Wheeler, Nicholas J. (2002). "Decision-making Rules and Procedures for Humanitarian Intervention." *The International Journal of Human Rights*, Spring, 6(1):127-138.

Wheeler, Nicholas J. (2000). *Saving Strangers: Humanitarian Intervention in International Society.* New York: Oxford University Press.

Whitman, Jim (2001). "The Kosovo Refugee Crisis: NATO's Humanitarianism versus Human Rights," pp. 164-183. In Ken Booth (Ed.) *The Kosovo Tragedy: The Human Rights Dimension.* London: Frank Cass.

Woodward, Susan L. (1995). "Western Intervention," pp. 146-198. In Susan Woodward's *Balkan Tragedy: Chaos and Dissolution After the Cold War.* Washington, D.C.: The Brookings Institution.

Annotated Bibliography

Totten, Samuel (2007). *The Prevention and Intervention of Genocide: An Annotated Bibliography.* New York: Routledge.

This major bibliography addresses a host of issues, including but not limited to: The UN Charter, Chapter VI, Chapter VII, The UNCG, International Law, Sovereignty, *Realpolitik*, Prevention, Peace Operations, Intervention, Sanctions, and Rapid Action Forces.

Books, Chapters, and Articles

Advisory Council on International Affairs and Advisory Committee on Issues of Public International Law (2000). *Humanitarian Intervention.* The Hague: Author. N. p.

This report basically constitutes a reassessment of the concept of humanitarian intervention and an exploration of the varied issues raised by the various interventions conducted throughout the 1990s.

Anglin, Douglas (2002). *Confronting Rwanda Genocide: The Military Options: What Could and Should the International Community Have Done?* (Paper Number 6 of the Pearson Papers). Clementsport, Nova Scotia: The Canadian Peacekeeping Press of the Pearson Peacekeeping Centre. 49 pp.

This essay "explores promising courses of action that, given the necessary political will, would have been military feasible and morally justifiable. It assesses realistically their prospects of success in checking the hemorrhage in Rwandan lives and identifies the circumstances and significance of the opportunities missed. Particular attention is paid to the time frame [of the events]."

Annan, Kofi A. (1999). *The Question of Intervention: Statements by the Secretary-General.* New York: United Nations. 58 pp.

This booklet contains five speeches that U.N. Secretary-General Kofi Annan gave on the issue of intervention. The titles of the talks are: "Reflections on Intervention"; "Standing Up for Human Rights"; "Unifying the Security Council in Defense of Human Rights"; "Two Concepts of Sovereignty"; and "Development is the Best Form of Conflict Prevention." The speeches basically affirm the legitimacy of intervention when the latter is conducted to protect innocent victims of violence committed by sovereign states or where sovereign states are unable or unwilling to protect their citizens.

Ayoob, Mohammed (2002). "Humanitarian Intervention and State Sovereignty." *The International Journal of Human Rights*, Spring 6(1):81-102.

The author discusses the ongoing tension between those who favor humanitarian intervention in the case of flagrant and serious human rights violations (including genocide) and those who are more tentative to act in light of the belief that the best way to maintain international order is by honoring sovereign authority.

Beach, Hugh (2000). "Secessions, Interventions, and Just War Theory: The Case of Kosovo," pp. 11-36. In Pugwash Study Group (Ed.) *Pugwash Study Group on Intervention, Sovereignty and International Security*. Cambridge, MA: Council of the Pugwash Conferences on Science and World Affairs.

A fascinating and informative essay on the issue of the evolution, justification and use of intervention in the so-called "internal affairs" of nations, using Kosovo (late 1990s) as a case study.

Bhatia, Michael V. (2003). *War and Intervention: Issues for Contemporary Peace Operations*. Bloomfield, CT: Kumarian Press. 222 pp.

This book is comprised, in part, of the following chapters: "Background: The United Nations, the United States, and Ground Intervention"; "The Operational Environment"; Contemporary Peace Operations"; and "The Military Dimension: Methods and Emerging Capabilities." Among the genocides discussed herein are those that were committed in Rwanda and the former Yugoslavia. The 1999 intervention in East Timor is also discussed.

Both, Norbert (2000). *From Indifference to Entrapment: The Netherlands and the Yugoslav Crisis 1990-1995*. Amsterdam: Amsterdam University Press. 265 pp. Examines how the Netherlands dealt with the Yugoslav crisis during the years 1990-1995, a period when the crisis erupted into areas of conflict and genocidal massacres. It was during this period that the Netherlands supplied the peacekeeping presence in Srebrenica (a so-called safe area where the Serbs killed some 7,000 Muslim men and boys).

Brown, Chris (2002). "Humanitarianism and Humanitarian Intervention," pp. 134-150. In Chris Brown's *Sovereignty, Rights and Justice: International Political Theory Today*. Cambridge (UK): Polity.

The chapter is comprised of the following sections: Humanitarian Intervention and the Westphalia System; the Emergence of a Strong Norm of Non-Intervention; Intervention in the 1990s: An Overview; and Reflections on Humanitarian Intervention in the 1990s.

Chesterman, Simon (2001). *Just War or Just Peace? Humanitarian Intervention and International Law*. Oxford: Oxford University Press. 326 pp.

In an examination of the legality of humanitarian intervention, the author discusses the genesis of the concept and asserts that as a legal concept it does not make sense. He delineates what he considers to be the weaknesses inherent in the arguments supporting a doctrine of unilateral humanitarian intervention in international society, and argues that states do not have a legal right to carry out such intervention even if it is supported by an UN Security Council resolution (and not even if they believe that it is the only way to halt a genocide).

Coady, C. A. J. (2002). *The Armed Ethics of Humanitarian Intervention*. Washington, DC: United States Institute of Peace. 45 pp.

This report is comprised of the following sections and subsections: Definitions and Cautions (The Meaning of "Intervention"; The Meaning of "Humanitarian"; The Nature of Ethics; Realist Caution; Humanitarian Violence: A Paradox?); The Just War Tradition and Defense Against Aggression (Grounding the Paradigm; Challenging the Paradigm: The Case for Intervention; The Sovereignty Debate; and The Theory of Aggression); Just War and Humanitarian Intervention: The Burden to Be Met (Just Cause; Right Authority: Who Is to Intervene?; Proportionality and Its Ambiguities; Last Resort: Exploring the Alternatives; The Prospects for Success); and Facing the Future (Moral Legitimacy, the United Nations, and International Collaboration; Arrangements for Peacekeeping and Peacemaking; The Need for a UN Intervention Force; Holistic Solutions; and Cooperative Multilateral Action).

Cotton, James (2001). "Against the Grain: The East Timor Intervention." *Survival: The IISS Quarterly*, Spring, 43(1):127-142.

In this thought-provoking essay, the author argues that the 1999 intervention in East Timor was an anomaly in the region, and for that reason the intervention does not constitute a change of principle regarding the "sanctity" of non-interference in the region.

Daalder, Ivo, and O'Hanlon, Michael E. (2000). *Winning Ugly: NATO's War to Save Kosovo*. Washington, DC: Brookings Institution Press. 343 pp.

The authors analyze the causes, conduct, and consequences of the United States and NATO's actions in the Kosovo war. They argue that while the cause to save Kosovo was worthy, the strategy that NATO used was "deeply flawed." They suggest that the Kosovo crisis is a cautionary tale for those who believe force can be used easily and in limited increments to halt genocide, mass killing, and the forceful expulsion of entire populations.

Damrosch, Lori Fisler (Ed.) (1993). *Enforcing Restraint: Collective Intervention in Internal Conflicts*. New York: Council on Foreign Relations Press. 403 pp.

Edited by a Professor of Law at Columbia University, *Enforcing Restraint* presents an examination of the role of the international community in resolving internal conflict where it threatens international stability. Among the chapters germane to the prevention and intervention of genocide are: Chapter 1. "International Involvement in the Yugoslavia Conflict" by James B. Steinberg; Chapter 6. "The United Nations in Cambodia: A Model for Resolution of International Conflicts" by Steven R. Ratner; Chapter 7. "The Civilian Impact of Economic Sanctions" by Lori Fisler

Damrosch; and Chapter 8. "A Paradigm of Legitimate Intervention" by Tom J. Farer.

Destexhe, Alain (1995). *Rwanda and Genocide in the Twentieth Century*. Washington Square, NY: New York University Press. 92 pp.

Destexhe provides a powerful examination of the international community's failure to halt, let alone prevent, the 1994 genocide in Rwanda. The book is comprised of the following: 1. "The Unlearned Lessons of History"; 2. "Three Genocides in the Twentieth Century"; 3. "The Hutu and Tutsi"; 4. "From Indifference to Compassion"; and 5. "Justice Must be Done."

Dickens, David (2002). "Can East Timor Be a Blueprint for Burden Sharing?" *The Washington Quarterly*, Summer, 25(3):29-40.

Dickens suggests that the international intervention East Timor in 1999, which was led by Australia, could possibly serve as a model for how other nations could take the lead in intervening in humanitarian crises in their region of the world. The article is comprised of the following sections: "Why Did the East Timor Model Work?"; "Identifying Leadership Candidates"; "How Would Others Measure Up?"; and "Policy Implications for Washington [DC]."

Finnemore, Martha (2003). *The Purpose of Intervention: Changing Beliefs About the Use of Force*. Ithaca, NY: Cornell University Press. 173 pp.

This book presents an examination of the use of military intervention for various purposes, including humanitarian crises. It is comprised of the following chapters: 1. The Purpose of Force; 2. Sovereign Default and Military Intervention; 3. Changing Norms of Humanitarian Intervention; 4. Intervention and International Order; and 5. How Purposes Change.

Frye, Alton (2000). *Humanitarian Intervention: Crafting a Workable Doctrine*. Washington, DC: Council of Foreign Relations Press. 94 pp.

This Council Policy Initiative addresses the dilemmas of humanitarian intervention through three diverse arguments, emphasizing, respectively, the moral imperative to intervene against massive abuses, the strategic case to refrain from intervention except in the extreme circumstance of genocide, and the political prerequisite to balance moral and strategic claims on American power. The diverse assessments are presented to provoke and inform the debate over future U.S. decisions regarding humanitarian intervention.

Garrett, Stephen A. (1999). *Doing Good and Doing Well: An Examination of Humanitarian Intervention*. Westport, CT: Praeger. 213 pp.

This book is comprised of the following eight chapters: 1. "Initial Considerations"; 2. "The Realm of Philosophy"; 3. "The Realm of Law"; 4. "Issues and Ambiguities"; 5. "How Governments Decide"; 6. "Judging Decisions, Judging Results"; 7. "Going It Alone or Going It With Others"; and 8. "Humanitarian Intervention Reconsidered."

Glennon, Michael J. (2001). *Limits of Law, Prerogatives of Power: Interventionism After Kosovo*. New York: Palgrave. 239 pp.

The author presents a "critical, top down reassessment of the whole use-of-force edifice" (p. 4). As his starting point, Glennon discusses how the 1999 Kosovo bombing campaign by NATO violated Article 2(4) of the UN Charter--that is, the prohibition of "the threat or use of force against the territorial integrity or political independence of any state." He rejects the arguments that have been put forth that "humanitarian intervention" is consonant with the UN Charter. Here he argues that such interventions as India's 1971 intervention in Bangladesh and the 1979 intervention by Tanzania in Uganda, as well as others, all are problematic as precedents. Ultimately, Glennon argues that the UN Charter has lost its relevance when it comes to the whole use of force issue and goes on to challenge the legal justifications for the UN Security Council's authorization to use force to deal with intrastate violence.

Gow, James (1997). *Triumph of the Lack of Will: International Diplomacy and the Yugoslav War*. New York: Columbia University Press. 343 pp.

Gow examines why the major Western powers failed to resolve the "War of Dissolution" in Yugoslavia. In doing so, he evaluates the various attempts by diplomats, UN peacekeepers, and world leaders to devise a workable peace, and identifies four factors that contributed to the subversion of the peace process: bad timing, bad judgment, poor cohesion, and, above all, the absence of political will, especially concerning the use of force.

Holzgrefe, J. L., and Keohane, Robert (Eds.) (2003). *Humanitarian Intervention: Ethical, Legal and Political Dilemmas.* New York: Cambridge University Press. 400 pp.

The essays in this book address the various ethical, legal and political conditions under which humanitarian intervention can be justified. They also address the complexities and dangers inherent in such interventions.

Honig, Jan Willem, and Both, Norbert (1996). *Srebrenica: Record of a War Crime.* London: Penguin. 204 pp.

The authors provide a detailed account of the genocide perpetrated by Bosnian Serbs in Srebrenica--a so-called "safe area"--in July 1995. In addition to delineating the specifics of the genocide, the authors examine the incoherent Western plans that led up to the slaughter and the failure of the "safe areas" policy and Western intervention as a whole.

International Commission on Intervention and State Sovereignty (2001). "Intervention," pp. 15-26. In The International Commission on Intervention and State Sovereignty's *The Responsibility to Protect: Research, Bibliography, Background: Supplementary Volume to the Report of the International Commission on Intervention and State Sovereignty.* Ottawa, ON, Canada: International Development Research Centre.

A highly informative section of one of the most significant reports of late vis-à-vis the issues of intervention and state sovereignty. Among the topics addressed are: the meaning of intervention, the concept of humanitarian intervention, military intervention and the UN Charter, nonmilitary interventions, and the contemporary debate over intervention.

International Commission on Intervention and State Sovereignty (2001). "Interventions After the Cold War," pp. 79-126. In The International Commission on Intervention and State Sovereignty's *The Responsibil-*

ity to Protect: Research, Bibliography, Background: Supplementary Volume to the Report of the International Commission on Intervention and State Sovereignty. Ottawa, ON, Canada: International Development Research Centre.

Among some of the many interventions discussed herein are: Northern Iraq, 1991; The Former Yugoslavia (1990s); Somalia, 1992-1993; Rwanda and Eastern Zaire, 1994-1996; Kosovo, 1999; and East Timor, 1999.

International Commission on Intervention and State Sovereignty (2001). *The Responsibility to Protect: Report of the International Commission on Intervention*. Two Volumes. Ottawa: International Development Research Centre. 110 pp. (Volume 1) and 426 (Volume 2).

Volume One, *The Responsibility to Protect,* is a valuable book that reflects the effort by the International Commission on Intervention and State Sovereignty to erect a conceptual bridge between issues related to intervention and sovereignty. In developing the book, the aim was to develop a framework that delineates (1) the complexities and problems inherent in intervention and (2) effective ways to intervene in humanitarian crises.

Volume Two, which was developed under the leadership of Thomas Weiss and Don Hubert, includes background information, research findings, and a major bibliography that addresses a wide range of issues (conceptual, ethical, legal, political, and operational) related to intervention.

International Journal of Human Rights (IJHR) (2003). "Forum: The International Commission on Intervention and State Sovereignty." *The International Journal of Human Rights*, Autumn, 7(3).

Includes three articles about the 2001 report by the International Commission on Intervention and State Sovereignty (ICISS): "Intervention: One Step Forward in the Search for the Impossible" by Adam Roberts; "Responsibility to Protect and the Limits of Imagination" by Daniel Warner; and "Reply in Defense of the Responsibility to Protect" by Ramesh Thakur.

Jentleson, Bruce W. (1997). "Who, Why, What, and How: Debates Over Post-Cold War Military Intervention," pp. 39-70. In Robert J. Lieber

(Ed.) *Eagle Adrift: American Foreign Policy at the End of the Century.* New York: Longman.

Jentleson, a noted political scientist, "...reviews and analyzes the debates on four fundamental questions as they have played out in the [U.S.] Clinton Administration from 1992 to 1997: 1. *Who* among the president, Congress, and public opinion should have what voice in deciding whether the United States should use military force?; 2. *Why* should the United States even consider such action? *What* are the vital interests and values that warrant it?; 3.*What* strategies are needed to make military force effective when it is used?; and 4. *How* should such strategies be carried out in terms of the respective roles of the United States, other major powers, the United Nations, and regional multilateral organizations?" (pp. 40-41).

Kaufman, Joyce P. (1999). "NATO and the Former Yugoslavia: Crisis, Conflict and the Atlantic Alliance." *Journal of Conflict Studies.* Fall, 19(2): 5-38.

An essay highly critical of when and how NATO carried out its intervention in Kosovo ("waiting until armed conflict erupted before getting involved, and counting on the efficacy of diplomacy long after it was evident that it was a hopeless effort).

Keren, Michael, and Sylvan, Donald A. (Eds.) (2001). *Dilemmas of International Intervention.* London: Frank Cass Publishers. 224 pp.

This collection of essays is interdisciplinary in nature and presents a balance between scholarly approaches and humanitarian concerns vis-à-vis the issue of intervention. Among the many questions that the various contributors address are: "Should sovereignty be respected under all conditions, or are there instances in which interference in a state's internal affairs becomes not only a right, but a duty?"; "What responsibility do striking violations of international norms committed within a sovereign state pose to the international community?"; "What constitutes an international 'community' in this regard, and under what conditions and restraints should it intervene?"; and "What should be the role of domestic forces and international bodies in defining the need to intervene and how can justified intervention be distinguished from sheer breach of sovereignty?"

Knudsen, Tonny Brems (1997). "Humanitarian Intervention Revisited: Post-Cold War Responses to Classical Problems," pp. 146-165. In Michael Pugh (Ed.) *The UN, Peace and Force*. London: Frank Cass and Company.

This essay is comprised of the following sections: The Grotian Doctrine of Humanitarian Intervention, The Problems of Humanitarian Intervention, The Post-Cold War Doctrine of Humanitarian Intervention, and The Pros and Cons of the Post-Cold War Doctrine of Humanitarian Intervention.

Kober, Stanley (2000). "Setting Dangerous International Precedents," pp. 107-119. In Ted Galen Carpenter (Ed.) *NATO's Empty Victory: A Postmortem on the Balkan War*. Washington, DC: CATO Institute.

In his conclusion, the author argues that nations that pursue unilateral intervention without the imprimatur of the UN Security Council are likely to set in process a highly dangerous situation that will possibly, if not certainly, result in "a world [that] will divide once again, and the century will end the way it began, primed for major conflict" (p. 117).

Kolodziej, Edward A. (2000). "The Great Powers and Genocide: Lessons from Rwanda." *Pacifica Review*, 12(2):121-145.

This article is comprised of three main sections: 1. A summary of the "prevailing, if circumscribed, moral and legal consensus against genocide--accompanied with three lines of argument to broaden the foundation of this consensus" (p. 120); 2. An examination of the Rwandan genocide and the identification of the main political and strategic constraints that were at play in the failure of the United Nations and the great powers to, both in the past as well as in the present, adequately address the matter of genocide; and 3. A proposal that suggests how the UN's capacity could be strengthened in order to create an effective anti-genocide regime.

Kuperman, Alan J. (2001). *The Limits of Humanitarian Intervention: Genocide in Rwanda*. Washington, DC: Brookings Institute Press. 162 pp.

An extremely thought-provoking book that is a must read for those interested in the issues of the intervention and prevention of genocide. While many of his points are worthy of serious consideration, controversy and counter-arguments have called into question the validity of some of Kuperman's key claims/assertions.

The book is comprised of the following chapters: 1. "The Common Wisdom"; 2. "Roots of the Rwandan Tragedy"; 3. "Mechanics of the Genocide"; 4. "When Did We Know?"; 5. "The Military Science"; 6. "Transporting Intervention Forces"; 7. "Plausible Interventions"; 8. "Contending Claims"; 9. "Early Warning and Preventive Intervention" and 10. "Lessons."

Kurth, James (2001). "Lessons from the Past." Special issue (The Can and Can'ts of Humanitarian Intervention") of *Orbis: A Journal of World Affairs*, Fall, 45(4):569-578.

The author assesses various U.S. military interventions (e.g., Somalia, Bosnia, and Kosovo) with an eye to the future role military operations should play in global relations. The essay is comprised of the following sections: A Century of Humanitarian Intervention, A Variety of Interventions and Perspectives, The Abstention Model, The Relief Model, The Relief-Plus Model, The Reconstruction Model, and Words versus Deeds.

Lang, Anthony F., Jr. (Ed.) (2003). *Just Intervention*. Washington, DC: Georgetown University Press. 229 pp.

This collection of essays explores the moral dimensions of humanitarian intervention. Some of the contributors discuss whether outside nations have an obligation to protect citizens of other nations, and whether it is alright to kill in order to save potential victims, while others delineate conceptual approaches for addressing many of the conflicting values inherent in humanitarian intervention. Some also draw specifics lessons from recent cases of intervention.

Layne, Christopher (2000). "Collateral Damage in Yugoslavia," pp. 51-58. In Ted Galen Carpenter (Ed.) *NATO's Empty Victory: A Postmortem on the Balkan War*. Washington, DC: CATO Institute.

The author notes and then asserts that "A central argument that President Clinton and his advisers invoked to justify their decision to use force against Yugoslavia was that NATO bombing was needed to prevent a Serbian military offensive in Kosovo and its concomitant 'ethnic cleansing.' The bombing campaign was disastrously counterproductive with regard to that goal. Indeed, it helped to cause, and greatly magnified, the human tragedy in Kosovo and throughout the rest of Yugoslavia" (p. 51).

Lohman, Diederik (2000). "The International Community Fails to Monitor Chechnya Abuses." *Helsinki Monitor*, 3: 73-82.

This is a thought-provoking essay on the human rights abuses by the Russians in Chechnya--many of which are "similar to those the Serbs committed in Kovoso prior to NATO's military intervention--summary executions, torture, rape, and the systematic destruction of civilian property" (p. 73).

Lyons, Gene M., and Mastanduno (Eds.) (1995). *Beyond Westphalia? State Sovereignty and International Intervention.* Baltimore, MD: The Johns Hopkins University Press. 360 pp.

Beyond Westphalia? brings together a distinguished group of scholars to explore the question of whether recent political changes have shifted the balance between the sovereign rights of states and the authority of the larger international community. Among the many contributors are Jarat Chopra, Jack Donnelly, Robert H. Jackson, Stephen D. Krasner, and Thomas G. Weiss.

Maley, William (2002). "Twelve Theses on the Impact of Humanitarian Intervention." *Security Dialogue, 33*(3): 265-278.

The twelve theses are posited and then briefly discussed. While most are commonsensical (though often overlooked during the course of actual interventions), all merit serious thought and discussion.

Mandelbaum, Michael (1999). "A Perfect Failure: NATO's War Against Yugoslavia." *Foreign Affairs*, September/October, 78(5):2-8.

In this hard-hitting essay, Mandelbaum argues that NATO's bombing of Kosovo constituted a "gross error in political judgment" (p. 2). (For an almost totally opposite perspective of the Kosovo operation, see Javier Solana's "NATO's Success in Kosovo.")

Martin, Ian (2001). *Self-Determination in East Timor: The United Nations, the Ballot, and International Intervention.* Boulder, CO: Lynne Rienner Publishers. 169 pp.

In this report, Martin, the former Secretary-General of Amnesty International and Special Representative of the UN Security-General for the East Timor Popular Consultation, traces events in East Timor from the negotiations that led to the May 1999 agreements among Indonesia, Portugal, and the United Nations to the mandating of international intervention to check the violence that wracked the country following the elections. His discussion includes an analysis of the intense negotiations that led to the Indonesian government's reluctant acceptance of intervention.

Mayall, James (2000). "The Concept of Humanitarian Intervention Revisited," pp. 319-333. In Albrecht Schnabel and Ramesh Thakur (Eds.) *Kosovo and the Challenge of Humanitarian Intervention.* Tokyo: United Nations University Press.

Mayall notes that his purpose "is to re-examine the political and intellectual background to the debate on humanitarian intervention that has waxed and waned since the end of the Cold War, before considering if there are any new lessons to be learned as a result of the Kosovo Crisis" (p. 319).

Mayall, James (Ed.) (1996). *The New Interventionism: United Nations Experience in Cambodia, Former Yugoslavia, and Somalia.* New York: Cambridge University Press. 238 pp.

This is a valuable assessment of the three major U.N. interventions in the 1990's. In his introduction, Mayall comments that major weaknesses of the "new interventionism" were: (1) the U.N. peacekeeping bureaucracy's make-up itself interfere[d] with its effectiveness in attempting to address complex political and military operations; (2) the member states [were] not committed to open-ended efforts to nation-building; and (3) there [was] an aversion to both injury and death to military personnel and monetary costs by the general public and politicians in members states.

McInnes, Colin, and Wheeler, Nicholas J. (2002). *Dimensions of Western Military Intervention.* London: Frank Cass Publishers. 224 pp.

This book explores how military power both has been and might be used by the West to help protect those who are in danger in other parts of the world. In doing so, it looks at: the political context in which force is used (including the West's intolerance for casualties and the role of the media); limits on the use of force; and how monitoring and verification of cease-fires can be effectively implemented to stop force from being used.

McRae, Rob, and Hubert, Don (Eds.) (2001). *Human Security and the New Diplomacy: Protecting People, Promoting Peace.* Montreal: McGill-Queen's University Press. 279 pp.

Among the most pertinent chapters germane to genocide and intervention are: "Case Study: Bosnia-Herzegovina" by Sam Hanson; "Case Study: Guatemala" by Daniel Livermore; "Humanitarian Military Intervention" by Don Hubert and Michael Bonser; "The Evolution of International Humanitarian Law" by Darryl Robinson and Valerie Oosterveld; and "Case Study: The Security Council and the Protection of Civilians" by Ellissa Golberg and Don Hubert.

Metzl, Jamie F. (1997). "Information Intervention: When Switching Channels Isn't Enough." *Foreign Affairs*, November/December, 76(6):15-21.

Metzl, a former UN Human Rights Officer, argues that the international community should seriously consider new measures to combat gross human rights violations (including genocide), and one that he is in favor of is monitoring, countering, and blocking radio and television broadcasts that incite widespread violence in zones of conflict.

Murphy, Sean D. (1996). *Humanitarian Intervention: The United Nations in an Evolving World Order.* Philadelphia: University of Pennsylvania Press. 427 pp.

A major study of the complexities of humanitarian intervention, this book addresses the following questions: "Should states be allowed to intervene militarily in the affairs of other states to prevent human rights deprivation--an action commonly referred to as 'humanitarian intervention'?"; and "If so, under what conditions should such intervention occur?" In regard to cases of genocide, it examines cases of intervention in Bosnia and Rwanda.

Nardin, Terry (2002). "The Moral Basis of Humanitarian Intervention." *Ethics & International Affairs*, 16(1):57-70.

Nardin states that "My strategy in this article is to relocate discussion of humanitarian intervention, moving it out of the familiar discourse of sovereignty and self-defense and into the discourse of rectifying wrongs and protecting the innocent.... This post-Kantian version of natural law, which I follow Alan Donagan in calling 'common morality,' suggests why humanitarian intervention remains morally defensible despite modern efforts to make it illegal" (pp. 57-58).

Odom, William E. (2000). "Making NATO Intervention Work: An American Viewpoint." *Strategic Review*. Summer, 28(2): 13-18.

In this provocative piece, retired U.S. Army General William E. Odom argues that the most effective way for the North Atlantic Treaty Organization (NATO) to intervene in crises (including the perpetration of genocide) is to be "selective [and] decisive in its execution of the intervention (e.g., complete and utter defeat of the enemy)," along with the aim of developing a "new society committed to rejoining the international order" (p. 15).

O'Hanlon, Michael (2003). *Expanding Global Military Capacity for Humanitarian Intervention*. Washington, DC: Brookings Institution. 125 pp.

O'Hanlon presents a blueprint for developing sufficient global intervention capacity to save more lives through force than have been saved in the past. He contends that, at least for now, individual countries rather than the United Nations "should develop the aggregate capacity to address several crises of varying scale and severity," and that many more countries should share in the effort.

O'Hanlon, Michael (1997). *Saving Lives With Force: Military Criteria for Humanitarian Intervention*. Washington, DC: Brookings Institution. 86 pp.

O'Hanlon provides a framework for understanding the military dimensions of humanitarian intervention such as those undertaken in Rwanda (following the 1994 genocide) and Bosnia in the 1990s. He also analyzes operations likely to be conducted under Chapter VII of the UN Charter for the purpose of restoring order in nations plagued by violence.

Pasic, Amir, and Weiss, Thomas G. (1998). "The Politics of Rescue: Yugoslavia's Wars and the Humanitarian Impulse," pp. 296-333. In Joel H. Rosenthal (Ed.) *Ethics and International Affairs: A Reader.* Washington, DC: Georgetown University Press.

This essay addresses the following issues: the politics of rescue, the regime of the displaced from Yugoslavia's wars, and the issues of humanitarianism and sovereignty.

Pellet, Alain (2000). "State Sovereignty and the Protection of Fundamental Human Rights; An International Law Perspective," pp. 37-45. In Pugwash Study Group (Ed.) *Pugwash Study Group on Intervention, Sovereignty and International Security.* February, 1(1): 37-45. Cambridge, MA: Council of the Pugwash Conferences on Science and World Affairs.

Pellet's purpose is to show that sovereignty, properly defined, is not a defense for breaches of gross violations of fundamental human rights" (p. 37). It includes an instructive discussion of "simply binding" versus "peremptory norms of general public international law," and the ramifications of each in relation to the issues of sovereignty and "internal affairs." Pellet concludes with an application of his argument to the situation in Kosovo in early 1999.

Pieterse, Jan Nederveen (Ed.) (1998). *World Order in the Making: Humanitarian Intervention and Beyond.* Basingstoke: Macmillan. 276 pp.

The book is comprised, in part, of the following:" "Humanitarian Action in War Zones: Recent Experience and Future Research" by Thomas G. Weiss; "Containing Systemic Crisis: The Regionalization of Welfare and Security Policy" by Mark Duffield; "Human Rights and Intervention: A Case for Caution" by Caroline Thomas and Melvyn Reader; "Rethinking Humanitarian Intervention" by Bhikku Parekh; "Humanitarian Intervention: A Military View" by Major-General Rtd J. W.Brinkman; "The Media and the Rwanda Crisis: Effects on Audiences and Public Policy" by Greg Philo, Lindsey Hilsum, Liza Beattie and Rick Holliman; and "Sociology of Humanitarian Intervention: Bosnia, Rwanda and Somalia Compared" by Jan Nederveen Pieterse.

Power, Samantha (2002). *"A Problem from Hell": America and the Age of Genocide*. New York: Basic Books. 611 pp.

This highly acclaimed book provides a critical analysis of the United States' reaction to genocide during the course of the twentieth century. Drawing upon exclusive interviews with many of Washington's top policymakers, access to thousands of pages of newly declassified documents, and her own reporting, Power shows how U.S. citizens inside and outside government looked away from genocide by convincing themselves that refugees were lying, that intervention would be futile, or that contemporary genocide did not measure up to the crime they said they would "never again permit."

Pugwash Study Group (2000). *The Pugwash Study Group on Intervention, Sovereignty, and International Security*. February, 1(1): 1-63.

This booklet contains three essays: "Secessions, Interventions and Just War Theory: The Case of Kosovo" by Hugh Beach; "State Sovereignty and the Protection of Fundamental Human Rights: An International Law Perspective" by Alain Pellet; and "The Politics of Intervention" by Gwyn Prins.

Pugwash Study Group (2001). *The Pugwash Study Group on Intervention, Sovereignty, and International Security*. January, 2 (1): 1-92.

This booklet contains four essays: "Humanitarian Intervention: Russian Perspectives" by Vladimir Baranovsky; "China, Asia and Issues of Intervention and Sovereignty" by Chu Shulong; "Sovereignty and Intervention: Opinions in South Asia" by Radha Kumar; and "The Heirs of Nkrumah: Africa's New Interventionists" by Adekeye Adebajo and Chris Landberg.

Ramsbotham, Oliver P., and Woodhouse, Tom (1996). *Humanitarian Intervention in Contemporary Conflict: A Reconceptualization*. Cambridge: Polity Press. 284 pp.

This book constitutes an assessment of the international response to violent conflicts that transpired in the 1990s. Following a thorough survey of the traditional debates over the legitimacy of intervention, the authors analyze various conflicts, using examples from a wide range of post-Cold

War examples, including those in Bosnia and Rwanda (where genocide was perpetrated). Various options -- including non-intervention, peacekeeping, and forcible humanitarian intervention -- are examined.

Rosenthal, Joel H. (1999). *Ethics & International Affairs: A Reader*. Washington, DC: Georgetown University Press. 484 pp.

Part III of this book--"Issues"--contains a number of essays related to the issues of intervention of genocide: "Humanitarian Intervention: An Overview of the Ethical Issues" by Michael J. Smith; "The Politics of Rescue: Yugoslavia's War and the Humanitarian Impulse" by Amir Pasic and Thomas G. Weiss; "NGOs and the Humanitarian Impulse: Some Have It Right" by Andrew Natsios; "An Emergency Response System for the International Community: Commentary on 'The Politics of Rescue'" by Morton Winston; "Holding Humanitarianism Hostage: The Politics of Rescue" by Alain Destexhe; and "When Is It Right to Rescue?: A Response to Pasic and Weiss" by David R. Mapel.

Rothchild, Donald, and Lake, David A. (1998). "Containing Fear: The Management of Transnational Ethnic Conflict," pp. 203-226. In David A. Lake and Donald Rothchild (Eds.) *The International Spread of Ethic Conflict: Fear, Diffusion, and Escalation*. Princeton, NJ: Princeton University Press.

This chapter is comprised of the following sections: Coping with Fear; Confidence-Building Measures (Demonstrations of Respect, Power Sharing, Elections, Regional Autonomy and Federalism, and Confidence-Building Measures Evaluated); and External Intervention (Noncoercive Intervention, Coercive Intervention, Third-Party Mediation, and the Limits of Intervention).

Rothert, Mark (2000). "U.N. Intervention in East Timor." *Columbia Journal of Transnational Law*, 39(1):257-282.

The author examines the three resolutions (passed by the U.N. Security Council between May and October 1999) authorizing intervention in East Timor as well as the subsequent intervention that took place. In doing so, the author examines the status of East Timor under international law; the principles of non-intervention, humanitarian intervention, and self-determination; and the question as to whether intervention was justified--and whether the intervention set a precedent.

Sadkovich, James J. (1996). "The Former Yugoslavia, the End of the Nuremberg Era, and the New Barbarism," pp. 282-303. In Thomas Cushman and Stjepan G. Mestrovic (Eds.) *This Time We Knew: Western Responses to Genocide in Bosnia*. New York: New York University Press.

Arguing that "the United Nations and other international and regional organizations act to contain and manage, not end or resolve, such phenomena as aggression and genocide," (p. 282), the author further asserts that the proponents of state sovereignty and *realpolitik* rule the day.

Schnabel, Albrecht, and Thakur, Ramesh (Eds.) (2000). *Kosovo and the Challenge of Humanitarian Intervention: Selective Indignation, Collective Intervention, and International Citizenship*. Tokyo: United Nations University Press.

A detailed analysis of the intervention in Kosovo by scholars and practitioners from across the globe. Among the many informative and thought-provoking chapters in this book are: "Policy Brief: Lessons from the Kosovo Conflict" by Albrecht Schnabel and Ramesh Thakur; "Kosovo in the Twentieth Century: A Historical Account" by Marie-Janine Calic; "The Costs of Victory: American Power and the Use of Force in the Contemporary Order" by G. John Ikenberry; "NATO: From Collective Defence to Peace Enforcement" by Nicola Butler; "The United Nations System and the Kosovo Crisis" by A. J. R. Groom and Paul Taylor; "The Concept of Humanitarian Intervention Revisited" by James Mayall; "The Concept of Sovereignty Revisited" by Alan M. James; and "Force, Diplomacy and Norms" by Coral Bell.

Seybolt, Taylor B. (2004). *Humanitarian Military Intervention: Causes of Success and Failure*. New York: Oxford University Press. 300 pp.

This study focuses on the question of when and how military intervention can achieve humanitarian benefits. It uses the standard that an intervention should do more good than harm to evaluate the successes and failures. As a minimalist measure, the author develops a methodology to determine the number of lives saved. The analysis of nineteen military operations in six case studies (Iraq, Somalia, Bosnia, Rwanda, Kosovo, and East Timor) reveals both successful and unsuccessful interventions.

Sisk, Timothy D. (2001). "Violence: Intrastate Conflict," pp. 534-563. In P. J. Simmons and Chantal DeJonge Oudraat (Eds.) *Managing Global Issues: Lessons Learned.* Washington, DC: Carnegie Endowment for International Peace.

This chapter is comprised of the following sections: Civil Wars: Causes, Characteristics, and Consequences; International Intervention in Civil Wars (Actors, and Instruments); Track Record; Lessons Learned (Agenda Setting, Negotiation, Implementation and Compliance, Reactions to Noncompliance); and Conclusions and Recommendations.

Among the many situations the author comments on are: the collapse of the Yugoslav federation; the Rwandan genocide; NATO's intervention in Bosnia; and the Australian-led intervention in East Timor.

Smith, Michael J. (1998). "Humanitarian Intervention: An Overview of the Ethical Issues," pp. 271-295. In Joel H. Rosenthal (Ed.) *Ethics and International Affairs: A Reader.* Washington, DC: Georgetown University Press.

Smith presents a succinct overview of the changes in "the broader milieu of international relations as they relate to humanitarian intervention" (p. 272), surveys and analyzes the arguments justifying as well as opposing the concept of humanitarian intervention from both the realist and liberal perspectives, and presents his own views regarding the great difficulty in effectively implementing humanitarian intervention.

Solana, Javier (1999). "NATO's Success in Kosovo." *Foreign Affairs*, November/December, 87(6):114-120.

In praising NATO's Kosovo operation, Solana, former Secretary-General of NATO, asserts that it was the first time a defense alliance conducted a military campaign to attempt to prevent a humanitarian tragedy outside its border. (For an almost totally opposite perspective of the Kosovo operation, see Michael Mandelbaum's "A Perfect Failure: NATO's War Against Yugoslavia.")

Sörensen, Jens Stilhoff (2002). "Balkanism and the New Radical Interventionism: A Structural Critique." *International Peacekeeping*, Spring, 9(1): 1-22.

The author presents a critique of the theory behind the "new radical interventionism, both in its military disciplining form and in the form of a radical aid policy that attempts to change and control whole processes of social life by targeting mentalities and attitudes" (p. 1). The author's main contention is that the new interventionism, while appealing to moral and civil values, is as "realist" oriented as ever. Moreover, Sörensen asserts that "the moralist discourse behind 'cosmopolitan policing' and 'humanitarian bombing' is shared within both the 'left' and the 'right' enabling a merger into a neo-liberal agenda with radical interventionist ambitions. This, in turn, has become possible by drawing on elements from three other discourses ('balkanism', 'universalism' and 'cultural nihilism'), thus creating a formula for a hegemonic project" (p. 1).

Stanley Foundation (2001). *Using "Any Means Necessary" for Humanitarian Response*. Muscatine, IA: Author. n.p.

"This is the report of the 26th annual United Nations of the Next Decade Conference that brought together experts wrestling with the political, legal, and practical challenges the world community faces when intrastate conflicts escalate into massive violence. While a broad consensus emerged supporting forceful intervention in the worst cases, the questions of who should intervene, when, and how was the subject of lively debate."

Tesón, Fernando (1997). *Humanitarian Intervention: An Inquiry into Law and Morality*. Irvington-on-Hudson, NY: Transnational Publishers, Inc. 378 pp.

This book is comprised of the following parts and chapters: Part One: A Philosophical Defense of Humanitarian Intervention (1: "International Law, Humanitarian Intervention, and Moral Theory"; 2. "The Assumptions of the Interventionist Model"; 3. "The Hegelian Myth"; 4. "The International Legitimacy of Governments"; 5. "Utility, Rights and Humanitarian Intervention"; 6. "A Moral Framework for Humanitarian Intervention"); and Part Two: Humanitarian Intervention in International Law; 7. "The Concept of Humanitarian Intervention in International law"; 8. "Humanitarian Intervention: State Practice"; 9. "Collective Humanitarian Intervention" (which includes the following sections: I. Introduction, II. Collective Humanitarian Intervention: 1. General Principles; 2. The Cause of Iraq's Treatment of the Kurds, 1991; 3. The Operation in Somalia, 1992-1993; 4. The Case of Haiti, 1994; 5. The Case of Rwanda, 1994; and 6. A Note on the Intervention in Bosnia, 1994).

Thomas, Raju G. C. (Ed.) (2003). *Yugoslavia Unraveled: Sovereignty, Self-Determination, Intervention.* Lanham, MD: Lexington Books. 386 pp.

A collection of essays that are highly critical of the "West's" and the United Nations' involvement and approach to the Yugoslavia crisis.

Thompson, Mark, and Price, Monroe E. (2003). "Intervention, Media and Human Rights." *Survival: The IISS Quarterly*, Spring, 45(1):183-202.

The authors examine how international peace operations in the 1990s faced the problem of developing a capacity for tackling the problem of media manipulation in societies racked by violence (such as the former Yugoslavia and Rwanda) or recovering from massive conflict (such as Cambodia).

Tomes, Robert (2000). "Operation Allied Force and the Legal Basis for Humanitarian Interventions." *Parameters*, Spring, 30(1):38-50.

This article presents a discussion of international law arguments against NATO's bombing campaign of Kosovo in 1999, suggests that the operation should be considered legitimate, and concludes with a *jus cogens* argument--similar to a natural law argument--in support of intervention to stop gross violations of human rights.

Totten, Samuel (Ed.) (2005). *Genocide at the Millennium. Volume 5: Genocide Bibliographical Series.* New Brunswick, NJ: Transaction Publishers. 302 pp.

This volume is comprised, in part, of the following sections and chapters: "Genocide in Kosovo?" by Peter Ronayne; "The Role of Nongovernmental Organizations in Addressing the Intervention, Prevention and Punishment of Genocide in the 1980s, 1990s, and Early 2000s" by Samuel Totten; "The United Nations and Genocide: Prevention, Intervention, and Prosecution" by Samuel Totten and Paul R. Bartrop; "The Role of Individual States in Addressing Cases of Genocide" by Kenneth J. Campbell; and "The International Legal Prohibition of Genocide Comes of Age" by William A. Schabas.

Totten, Samuel (2004). "The Intervention and Prevention of Genocide: Sisyphean or Doable?" *Journal of Genocide Research*, June, 6(2): 229-247.

Among the issues discussed herein are: detecting genocide early on; the issues of sovereignty and "internal affairs"; the problem of political will; the need for a strong mandate, a well-trained and well-resourced force; the critical need to address systemic issues, and the need for a synergy of efforts amongst scholars in different fields.

Trachtenberg, Marc (1993). "Intervention in Historical Perspective," pp. 15-36. In Laura W. Reed and Carl Kaysen (Eds.) *Emerging Norms of Justified Intervention: A Collection of Essays from a Project of the American Academy of Arts and Sciences*. Cambridge, MA: American Academy of Arts and Sciences.

A succinct but informative overview of the concept and practice of intervention and the controversies that surrounded the latter over the course of the nineteenth and twentieth centuries.

von Hippel, Karin (2000). *Democracy by Force: U.S. Military Intervention n the Post-Cold War World*. New York: Cambridge University Press. 224 pp.

This book contains three chapters particularly germane to the issue of intervention: 1. "Introduction: Dangerous Hubris?"; 4. "UNPROFOR, IFOR, and SFOR: Can Peace Be Forced on Bosnia?"; and 6. "Hubris or Progress: Can Democracy be Forced?"

Walter, Barbara F., and Synder, Jack (Eds.) (1999). *Civil Wars, Insecurity, and Intervention*. New York: Columbia University Press. 331 pp.

The collective essays in this book present an examination of four interventions in the 1990s (Bosnia and Herzegovina, Somalia, Cambodia, and Rwanda) in order to draw lessons for ongoing policy debates.

Weiss, Thomas G. (1996). "Collective Spinelessness: UN Actions in the Former Yugoslavia," pp. 59-96. In Richard H. Ullman (Ed.) *The World and Yugoslavia's Wars*. New York: Council on Foreign Relations.

In his introduction, Weiss states that "This chapter details the painful dithering and ineffectiveness of UN actions from the beginning of the end of Yugoslavia on June 25, 1991, until the agreement on November 21, 1995, that partitioned Bosnia-Herzegovina into a Muslim-Croat federation and a Bosnia-Serb entity while reserving the fiction of a central government of a multi-ethnic state with its seat in Sarajevo" (p. 59).

Weiss, Thomas G. (1993). "Intervention: Whither the United Nations?" *The Washington Quarterly*, 17(1):109-128.

Weiss analyzes various interventions conducted in the early 1990s, examines five key policy propositions, and concludes with three policy recommendations. The three policy recommendations are: 1. Give priority to prevention; 2. Do it right or not at all; and 3. Be prepared for triage.

Weiss, Thomas G. (1999). *Military-Civilian Interactions: Intervening in Humanitarian Crises*. Lanham, MD: Rowman and Littlefield. 281 pp.

This book is comprised, in part, of the following chapters: "Armed Forces and Humanitarian Action: Past and Present"; "Framework for Estimating Military Costs and Civilian Benefits from Intervention"; "Northern Iraq, 1991-1996: A Difficult Act to Follow?"; "Somalia, 1992-1995: The Death of Pollyannaish Humanitarianism?"; "Bosnia, 1992-1995: Convoluted Charity?"; "Rwanda, 1994-1995: Better Late than Never?"; and 8. "Humanitarian Intervention: Costs, Benefits, Quandaries."

Weiss, Thomas G., and Collins, Cindy (2000). *Humanitarian Challenges and Intervention*. Boulder, CO: Westview Press. 222 pp.

Weiss and Collins delineate how institutional humanitarian challenges and intervention concerns within the international humanitarian system combined with the domestic context of armed conflict often yield policies that do not serve the immediate requirements for protection of rights, stabilization, or reconstitution. Based on case studies of the post-Cold War experiences in Central America, Northern Iraq, the former Yugoslavia, and the African Great Lakes region, the authors make recommendations for a more effective international humanitarian system.

Wheeler, Nicholas J. (2001). "Reflections on the Legality and Legitimacy of NATO's Intervention in Kosovo," pp. 145-163. In Ken Booth (Ed.)

The Kosovo Tragedy: The Human Rights Dimension. London: Frank Cass Publishers.

Wheeler discusses whether NATO's actions in Kosovo "represent a watershed in the development of a new norm of humanitarian intervention, and how far this is to be welcomed or feared in a society of states built on the principles of sovereignty, non-intervention and non-use of force" (pp. 145-146).

Wheeler, Nicholas J. (2000). *Saving Strangers: Humanitarian Intervention in International Society.* Oxford: Oxford University Press. 336 p.

In this book, Wheeler examines seven cases of intervention—three in the 1970's (East Pakistan, Cambodia, and Uganda), one in the 1980's (Iraq), and three in the 1990's (Somalia, Rwanda, and the former Yugoslavia).

Wheeler, Nicholas, and Dunne, Tim (2001). "East Timor and the New Humanitarian Interventionism." *International Affairs*, October, 77(4):805-827.

In their abstract, Wheeler and Dunne, write: "The fate of East Timor provides a barometer for how far the normative structure of international society has been transformed since the end of the Cold War.... The article charts the interplay of domestic and international factors that made this normative transformation possible" (p. 805).

Welsh, Jennifer M. (Ed.) (2004). *Humanitarian Intervention and International Relations.* New York: Oxford University Press. 220 pp.

This book is comprised, in part, of the following parts and chapters: Part One: International Relations Theory and Humanitarian Intervention ("Limiting Sovereignty" by Henry Shue; "The Humanitarian Responsibilities of Sovereignty: Explaining the Development of a New Norm of Military Intervention for Humanitarian Purposes in International Society" by Nicholas J. Wheeler; "Taking Consequences Seriously: Objections to Humanitarian Intervention" by Jennifer M. Welsh); Part Two: The Politics and Practice of Humanitarian Intervention ("The United Nations and Humanitarian Intervention" by Sir Adam Roberts; "Humanitarian Intervention in the Balkans" by Nicholas Morris; "Humanitarian Intervention and International Society: Lessons from Africa" by James Mayall; and "International Intervention in East Timor" by Ian Martin).

Whitman, Jim (2001). "The Kosovo Refugee Crisis: NATO's Humanitarianism versus Human Rights," pp. 164-183. In Ken Booth (Ed.) *The Kosovo Tragedy: The Human Rights Dimensions*. London: Frank Cass Publishers.

The argument of this essay is "that the unprecedented response to the Kosovo crisis was animated less by human rights principles than by a concern to contain the refugees within the region and to maintain political support for the military campaign against Serbia" (p. 164).

8

Peace Operations and their Ramifications vis-à-vis the Prevention and Intervention of Genocide

Lawrence Woocher[1]

Introduction

"Peace operations" is a general term used to describe a range of military and police actions, typically taken under multilateral auspices, with non-traditional military goals such as monitoring cease fires, securing the provision of humanitarian assistance, supporting implementation of peace treaties, protecting minorities from persecution, and so forth. An outgrowth of the long-standing concept of United Nations peacekeeping, peace operations encompass missions variously described as traditional peacekeeping, peace enforcement, humanitarian intervention and post-conflict peace building. They can vary widely in their context, resources and strategies, especially in the type and extent of military force used.

The relationship between peace operations and genocide prevention is complex. Multilateral military action is probably the most commonly publicly debated policy option for preventing or halting cases of mass atrocities. Yet, missions have typically been dispatched for purposes other than genocide prevention, and have frequently lacked the capabilities and/or mandate to intervene effectively when civilians have become imperiled. In the worst cases, peace operations have more closely resembled bystanders to genocide than effective tools for prevention.

Meanwhile, the number of peace operations in the field continues to grow, as does the range of tasks these missions are charged with (many of which increasingly include civilian protection) (Holt, 2005).

The pace of progress in addressing political and capacity-related challenges to effective peace operations, however, has not matched that of these changing demands. Thus, continued improvements are needed to make peace operations an effective instrument for genocide prevention. Without these improvements, the deployment of peace operations can risk offering false comfort to the international community and, worse, to local populations at risk.

The Changing Nature of Peace Operations

Peacekeeping was an invention of the UN Security Council in seeking to fulfill its unique responsibility for the maintenance of international peace and security. What is now known as classical or traditional peacekeeping entails positioning a lightly armed multinational force between previously warring armies of sovereign states to monitor a cease fire or armistice; e.g., deployment between Israeli and Egyptian forces in the Sinai. The core principles of classical peacekeeping missions include consent of the parties, neutrality/impartiality, and use of force only in self-defense. Classical peacekeeping is sometimes associated with Chapter VI of the UN Charter, which describes peaceful means of resolving international conflicts; in fact, peacekeeping was not envisaged in 1945 and can be found nowhere in the Charter.

The end of the Cold War brought major changes in political and military circumstances with huge consequences for peace operations (Cockayne and Malone, 2005). Armed conflicts became overwhelmingly intra-state rather than inter-state, many had a religious or ethnic element and most were associated with large scale humanitarian crises, violence against civilians and forced migration (Boutros-Ghali, 1995). No longer deadlocked by the East-West rivalry and optimistic that the UN could finally be a major force for peace, the UN Security Council authorized new peace operations at an unprecedented rate. These new missions were deployed into more difficult circumstances and for more varied and ambitious purposes than ever before.

For the first time, UN peacekeeping missions were being authorized and deployed when there was no sturdy peace to keep. In some cases, lacking consent from local governments, new peace operations were mandated under Chapter VII of the UN Charter, which grants the UN Security Council enforcement power. Chapter VII "peace enforcement" missions are associated with less permissive environments and require more robust force. Since the UN relies on voluntary troop contributions from member states, in many cases the Security Council "subcontracted" enforcement missions to an individual lead nation (e.g., Australia for East Timor in 1999), an ad hoc coalition (e.g., the US-led coalition in 1991 in Iraq) or a regional organization (e.g., NATO in Bosnia) because of their superior capabilities.

In addition, the Security Council began deploying peace operations to serve wider ranging functions, e.g., enabling the provision of humanitarian assistance, protecting minorities, promoting human rights and the rule of law, supporting post-conflict reconstruction, etc. These aims, in contrast to more modest monitoring of cease fires, required more varied and significant capabilities than was easily found, as well as new degrees of coordination among civilian and military, UN and non-UN actors. The concept of complex or multidimensional peace operations emerged to reflect the multiplicity of functions peace operations were being called on to fulfill (United Nations Peacekeeping Best Practices Unit, 2003).

Along with the changing demands of individual peace operations, the overall global demand in terms of numbers of missions, troops and police has continued to rise. As of September 2005, the UN Department of Peacekeeping Operations supported sixteen active peace operations—five of which were authorized in the prior two years—totaling about 67,000 military and civilian police personnel. This level of activity is significantly stretching both the management capability of the UN and the ability of the Secretary-General to find states willing to contribute capable troops for new missions.

Selected Cases of Peace Operations and Genocide

A brief, selective review of peace operations highlights strategies used, outcomes and major lessons learned vis-à-vis the prevention of genocide.

Iraq

No multilateral military action was launched to respond to the 1988 Iraqi Anfal campaign, which killed at least 50,000 Kurdish people. In the aftermath of the Gulf War of 1991, however, a Kurdish uprising followed by a violent government response against Iraq's Kurdish population caused massive flight, which in turn led the UN Security Council to demand that Iraq cease its repression and cooperate with humanitarian operations. This spawned the U.S.-led Operation Provide Comfort, which coordinated the imposition of a no-fly zone with an enormous humanitarian assistance effort in a "safe zone" of Northern Iraq, backed up by credible threat of overwhelming force. Many thousands of Iraqi Kurds were saved. This case illustrates the effective use of safe zones and successful civil-military coordination (Haspeslagh, 2003).

Rwanda

A small, lightly armed UN peace operation (UNAMIR) was on the ground to monitor implementation of the Arusha Accords, which had ended Rwanda's civil war, when warning signs of genocide began to mount. Famously, UNAMIR's commanding officer, Canadian Gen. Romeo Dallaire cabled his superiors at UN headquarters that an organized campaign of killings on ethnic lines was imminent and requested reinforcements and authorization to suppress the violence. Instead, most of his force was withdrawn while the genocidal killings proceeded apace. Several weeks into the genocide, the UN Security Council authorized France to intervene to create a safe area for the provision of humanitarian assistance. But many question France's motives, and in practice this deployment provided limited relief because the French did not demilitarize the safe area (Haspeslagh, 2003). In 100 days, roughly 500, 000 to 800,000 Rwandans were killed. Rwanda demonstrated how ill equipped a classical UN peacekeeping mission—by mandate as much as by manpower—was to prevent genocide, clearly no substitute for political agreement among powerful states to take more forceful action.

Srebrenica

The massacre of more than 7,000 Bosnian Muslims at Srebrenica in 1995 is another case of peace operations failing in the face of genocide. The Security Council initially dispatched the UN Protection Force (UNPROFOR) with a minimal mandate, but this was gradually expanded beyond UNPROFOR's means as Bosnia's bloody civil war worsened. Moreover, lack of consensus among Security Council members left UNPROFOR with no clear strategic guidance (Annan, 1999). The Security Council declared Srebrenica, and later five other towns, safe areas. But in the face of Serb aggression, UNPROFOR had inadequate military assets—NATO bombing was not effectively coordinated—and no clear plan to defend the safe areas. Serb forces easily overran UN personnel, took control of Srebrenica and massacred its men and boys. Like Rwanda, this case painfully illustrates the dangers of political conflict in a peace operation's authorizing body, and how a peacekeeping force with an ambiguous mandate and without the means to respond to exigencies could be more dangerous than no peace operation at all. In addition, the failure of coordination between the UN and NATO demonstrates the importance of unity of command.

Darfur

The international response to the conflict and atrocities that have taken place in the Darfur region of Western Sudan since 2003 has been particularly sobering. As in numerous earlier situations, the Darfur crisis has been marked by a recalcitrant government, political conflict in the UN Security Council, and a shortage of quickly deployable military and police forces. Over the course of this slowly progressing crisis, experts have advocated immediate deployment of a robust force of 10,000 or more with a strong mandate to protect civilians (e.g., International Crisis Group, 2005). At the time of this writing, the African Union had deployed a mission to Darfur with the consent of the Sudanese government and a mandate that stressed monitoring. Western governments have assisted with transport of these African troops, but deployment has been slow. The Darfur experience illustrates the continued challenge of finding the political agreement and the means sufficient to mount an effective genocide prevention operation.

Efforts to Strengthen Peace Operations: Benefits for Genocide Prevention

The rapid changes in the mandated functions of UN peacekeeping missions along with some stark failures of the 1990s spurred efforts to rethink and strengthen peace operations.

An Agenda for Peace and Its Supplement

UN Secretary-General Boutros Boutrous Ghali's *An Agenda for Peace* (1992) reflected the optimism of the immediate post-Cold War period. He articulated an expansive vision of UN peace and security activities, including preventive diplomacy, peacemaking, peace enforcement, peacekeeping and post-conflict peace building. Boutros-Ghali's more sober *Supplement to An Agenda for Peace* (1995), less than three years later, more fully grasped the profound challenges facing UN peace operations. Reflecting failures in Somalia, Bosnia and Rwanda, he urged action to remedy problems, including the failure to distinguish between peacekeeping and peace enforcement, lack of unity of command, and lack of available troops and equipment.

The Brahimi Report

Five years on, UN Secretary-General Kofi Annan charged a panel led by former Algerian Foreign Minister Lakhdar Brahimi to carry out a thorough review of UN peace and security activities. The Panel's report—known ubiquituously as the "Brahimi Report"—has become the touchstone for nearly all subsequent efforts to reform and strengthen the UN's activities in this area. Its criticism was pointed, concluding that "the United Nations has repeatedly failed—and it can do no better today," calling for "significant institutional change, increased financial support, and renewed commitment on the part of Member States."

The Panel stressed that there is no substitute for the ability to project credible force, in terms of numbers, capabilities, mandate and rules of engagement. It sharply criticized strict adherence to impartiality in cases where there is a clear victim and aggressor, going so far as to say this can "amount to complicity with evil." Moreover, the Panel concluded that peacekeepers should be presumed to be authorized to stop violence against civilians regardless of the mission's mandate, and that "operations given a broad and explicit mandate for civilian protection must be given the specific resources to carry out that mandate." Regarding military capabilities, the Panel recommended further developing standby arrangements to include several multinational, brigade-size forces. An NGO study in 2003 found the UN had made "clear progress in implementing a majority of reforms" called for by the "Brahimi Report" (Durch et al., 2003).

In parallel with these UN-led efforts, groups of governments and regional organizations have taken steps toward expanding capacity for peace operations. For example, several countries joined together to create a Stand-By High Readiness Brigade (SHIRBRIG) to serve as a "well-prepared, rapidly deployable capability for peacekeeping operations mandated by the UN Security Council." In addition, the African Union has pledged, with G8 support, to establish by 2010 an African Standby Force capable of rapid deployment to keep or enforce the peace (Kent and Malan, 2003). The European Union has also decided to develop a rapid reaction force with the ultimate aim of being able to deploy 60,000 troops within sixty days. These capacity building efforts received political endorsement in the wide-ranging statement by more than 150 heads of state and government at the 2005 World Summit: "Stressing the need to mount operations with adequate capacity to counter hostilities and fulfill effectively their mandates, we urge further development of proposals for enhanced rapidly deployable capacities to reinforce peacekeeping operations in crises" (United Nations General Assembly, 2005).

Critical Challenges Facing the Field

Rapidly deployable, robust military force, which can be threatened or used to deter or halt genocidal crimes is an essential, if ideally seldom used, tool for prevention. There are several prominent obstacles to ensuring that this is consistently a viable option.

Political Dissension

The first—and often highest—hurdle to an effective peace operation is forging political agreement among powerful governments. Lack of agreement on fundamental questions can quash a peace operation before it begins or threaten its success by producing confusing, or worse yet, feckless mandates. Political dissension tends to be most visible in debates at the UN Security Council. In the case of Kosovo, anticipated opposition by at least one of the Council's five permanent, veto-wielding members led the U.S. and Europe to bypass the Council, raising questions about the intervention's legitimacy and legality. In the case of Darfur, the sluggish, attenuated international response similarly reflects resistance by permanent members of the Council (International Crisis Group, 2005).

Capacity Constraints

Despite long-standing attention to the lack of standby capacity, it is still the norm that troops and materiel for peace operations must be gathered on a case-by-case basis. This is especially problematic in cases of genocide prevention since speed of deployment tends to carry particularly large consequences. Moreover, the demand for capable troops and police for peace operations continues to outstrip the global supply. This gap is all the more pronounced where more robust forces and/or advanced transport, logistics and communications are required as is often the case for civilian protection missions.

Limits of the Military Option

Much of the public debate about using peace operations to prevent genocide ignores the practical challenges to accomplishing this goal even when an appropriate force is authorized and deployed. Standard warfighting doctrine, strategies and skills of even the most capable military forces must typically be jury-rigged for genocide prevention/intervention. In addition, environmental factors can limit the potential for armed intervention to protect at risk populations. For example, even the world's best military force will struggle to prevent a rapidly developing genocide in a vast, isolated and unfamiliar area.

Demands of the Post-Conflict Period

The situation in Iraq—the United States' toppling of Saddam Hussein and the bitter internecine fighting and war carried on against the U.S. troops—is only the latest and most dramatic case of the difficulty and high costs of assisting a country through physical, political and economic reconstruction following armed conflict. Though the international community has increasingly accepted that the post-conflict process should be driven by locals, there remains a presumptive responsibility for external interveners to assure at least minimally decent conditions before disengaging. As long as political leaders perceive that launching a peace operation to prevent or halt genocide would also mean a long, costly commitment to post-conflict peace building, they will be more hesitant to intervene militarily.

The Probability of Progress

There are a number of reasons to fear these challenges will remain significant for the foreseeable future. First, overcoming political obstacles probably requires a shift in the underlying distribution of political power internationally or domestically in key states. This is not impossible, but also not easily done. Second, overcoming obstacles related to capacity to carry out peace operations will require significant investment in advance of a crisis—no easy task in most political systems. Further enhancement of collective capacity is feasible and worth pursuing, but a great leap forward is unlikely. Third, military operations will always be a risky and costly option. Therefore, political leaders will rarely deploy their nation's armed forces unless they judge vital national interests to be at stake. Few states have defined genocide in this way.

Conclusion

Current trends point to peace operations playing an ever-growing role with respect to genocide prevention. The frequent deployment of multidimensional peace operations to internal conflicts that have a national, ethnical, racial or religious dimension means that missions will often already be on the ground when warning signs of genocide emerge. In these cases, as history has shown, it is imperative to appreciate the limitations of typical peace operations in protecting populations at risk from large-scale violence. In other cases, governments may choose to deploy peace operations specifically as preventive measures. Political differences and capacity constraints will continue to make these operations difficult. But if properly designed and resourced, peace operations can be an important tool for genocide prevention.

Note

1. I thank John Stanton Haddock for his research assistance.

References

Annan, Kofi (1999). *Report of the Secretary-General Pursuant to General Assembly Resolution 53/55: The Fall of Srebrenica*. New York: United Nations.

Boutros-Ghali, Boutros (1995). *An Agenda for Peace, 1995: With the New Supplement and Related UN Documents*. New York: United Nations.

Cockayne, James, and Malone, David M. (2005). "The Ralph Bunche Centennial: Peace Operations Then and Now." *Global Governance*, 11 (3).

Durch, William J.; Holt, Victoria K.; Earle, Caroline R.; and Shanahan, Moira K. (2003). *The Brahimi Report and the Future of UN Peace Operations*. Washington, DC: The Henry L. Stimson Center.

Haspeslagh, Sophie. (2003). "Safe Havens," n. p. In Guy Burgess and Heidi Burgess (Eds.) *Beyond Intractability*. Boulder, CO: Conflict Research Consortium, University of Colorado.

Holt, Victoria K. (2005). *The Responsibility to Protect: Considering the Operational Capacity for Civilian Protection*. Washington, DC: The Henry L. Stimson Center.

International Crisis Group (2005). *Darfur: The Failure to Protect*. Nairobi/Brussels: International Crisis Group.

Kent, Vanessa and Malan, Mark (2003). "The African Standby Force: Progress and Prospects." *African Security Review*, 12 (3), 71-87.

United Nations General Assembly (2005). *2005 World Summit Outcome*. New York: United Nations.

United Nations Peacekeeping Best Practices Unit (2003). *Handbook on United Nations Multidimensional Peacekeeping Operations*. New York: United Nations.

Annotated Bibliography

Annan, Kofi (1999). *Report of the Secretary-General Pursuant to General Assembly Resolution 53/55: The Fall of Srebrenica.* New York: United Nations. 113 pp.

This report details the events leading up to the massacres in the "safe area" of Srebrenica and concludes by addressing two questions: "How can this have been allowed to happen?" and "How will the United Nations ensure that no future peacekeeping operation witnesses such a calamity on its watch?" Annan attributes much of the failure to the fact that UN "tried to keep the peace and apply rules of peacekeeping when there was no peace to keep."

Black, George (1993). *Genocide in Iraq: The Anfal Campaign Against the Kurds.* New York: Human Rights Watch. 370 pp.

This report details the Iraqi government's campaign to exterminate the Kurdish population of northern Iraq. It concludes these crimes constituted genocide.

Boulden, Jane (2005). "Mandates Matter: An Exploration of Impartiality in United Nations Operations." *Global Governance*, 11 (2): 147-160.

The author argues that "the impartiality of a UN mandate needs to be considered separately from the impartiality of the implementation of that mandate." Based on this analysis, the author finds contradictions in many UN peace operations that threaten their success.

Boutros-Ghali, Boutros (1995). *An Agenda for Peace, 1995: With the New Supplement and Related UN Documents.* New York: United Nations. 159 pp.

UN Secretary-General Boutros Boutros-Ghali produced his original *An Agenda for Peace* in 1992 to help improve the UN's peace and security activities during this period of rapid change and escalating demand for peacekeeping missions. He developed a conceptual framework for the broader set of UN peace-related activities, including preventive diplomacy, peacemaking, peace enforcement, peacekeeping and post-conflict peacebuilding. Boutros-Ghali's more sober *Supplement to An Agenda for Peace (1995)*, less than three years later, more fully grasped the profound challenges facing UN peace operations. Reflecting intervening failures in Somalia, Bosnia and Rwanda, he urged action to remedy problems including the blurring of the distinction between peacekeeping and peace enforcement, lack of unity of command, and lack of available troops and equipment.

Carlsson, Ingvar; Han, Sung-Joo; and Kupolati, Rufus M. (1999). *Report of the Independent Inquiry into the Actions of the United Nations During the 1994 Genocide in Rwanda*. New York: United Nations. 82 pp.

This report to the UN Secretary-General reviews the chronology of UN actions and failures to act related to the Rwandan genocide. It concludes that each part of the UN system shares responsibility for the overall failure: the Secretary-General, the Secretariat, the Security Council and member states. The inquiry found that a lack of resources and political commitment was the fundamental failure.

The Challenges Project (2002). *Challenges of Peace Operations: Into the 21st Century—Concluding Report 1997-2002*. Stockholm, Sweden: Elanders Gotab. 295 pp.

This report offers a thorough review of current issues based on a collaborative project launched by the Swedish government. It covers topics including doctrine, integrating the human rights perspective, preventive action, civil-military relations, etc. For additional reports, see HYPERLINK "http://www.peacechallenges.net"

Cockayne, James and Malone, David M. (2005). *The Ralph Bunche Centennial: Peace Operations Then and Now*. Global Governance, 11 (3).

The authors review major changes in UN peace operations since their inception. They cite six causal factors: "the end of the Cold War; engagement with 'internal' conflicts; rising regional organizations; North-South politics; the U.S.-UN relationship; and changes in peace operation mandates." They also identify three future challenges: "state building, the reconception of sovereignty, and the need for realism."

Dallaire, Romeo (2003). *Shake Hands with the Devil: The Failure of Humanity in Rwanda.* Toronto: Random House Canada. 562 pp.

This is the detailed account of the former head of the UN peacekeeping mission in Rwanda during the 1994 genocide.

Des Forges, Alison (1999). *"Leave None to Tell the Story": Genocide in Rwanda.* New York: Human Rights Watch. 789 pp.

This indispensable study on the Rwandan genocide by a Human Rights Watch researcher includes, among other things, a detailed account of the actions of the UN peacekeeping mission in Rwanda.

Donald, D. (2002). "Neutrality, Impartiality and UN Peacekeeping at the Beginning of the 21st Century." *International Peacekeeping*, 9 (4), 21-38.

This article examines the UN effort to clarify and update the principles of neutrality and impartiality. The author finds continued confusion, thus posing a threat to UN peace operations in difficult political contexts.

Durch, William J.; Holt, Victoria K.; Earle, Caroline R.; and Shanahan, Moira K. (2003). *The Brahimi Report and the Future of UN Peace Operations.* Washington, DC: The Henry L. Stimson Center. 142 pp.

This report was authored by the former staff director of the Brahimi panel in order to provide an analysis of the implementation of the recommendations found in the "Brahimi Report" three years on. The authors concluded that the UN had "demonstrated clear progress in implementing a majority of reforms" and that "more concrete and operational recommendations, implementable by the UN bureaucracy, fared better than those pitched at the level of doctrine or strategy or those addressed to the member states themselves." The review is organized by doctrine and strategy, capacity for operations, and rapid and effective deployment.

Feil, Scott R. (1998). *Preventing Genocide: How the Early Use of Force Might Have Succeeded in Rwanda.* Washington, DC: Carnegie Corporation of New York. 70 pp.

This report, based on the proceedings of a conference sponsored by the Carnegie Commission on Preventing Deadly Conflict, analyzes the details of a military response aimed at halting the genocide in Rwanda: mandate, type and size of force, and operational plans. It elaborates on the much-discussed request by Lt. General Romeo Dallaire for a force of 5,000 well armed troops as well as an alternative operational plan. Conference participants concluded, "The hypothetical force described by General Dallaire could have made a significant difference."

Findlay, Trevor (2002). *The Use of Force in UN Peace Operations*. New York: Oxford University Press. 486 pp.

This book reviews how UN peacekeeping missions have managed the use of force, from the UN's first mission through East Timor and Sierra Leone. He finds mandates, rules of engagement, operational guidelines, etc. concerning the use of force have generally been ineffective and concludes with a wide-ranging set of recommendations.

Haspeslagh, Sophie (2003). "Safe Havens," n.p. In Guy Burgess and Heidi Burgess (Eds.) *Beyond Intractability*. Boulder: Conflict Research Consortium, University of Colorado.

A study of the use of safe havens and safe areas as a response to refugee crises, including brief case studies on Iraq, Rwanda and Bosnia.

Holt, Victoria K. (2005). *The Responsibility to Protect: Considering the Operational Capacity for Civilian Protection*. Washington, DC: The Henry L. Stimson Center. 62 pp.

Following on the work of the International Commission on Intervention and State Sovereignty, this working paper explores a single, important and complex question: "What current doctrines, training programs, simulation exercises, rules of engagement or other tools prepare forces to intervene and protect civilians from mass killings, ethnic cleansing or genocide in non-permissive, Chapter VII environments?" The analysis, based on dozens of interviews with official and unofficial experts on peace operations, seeks to identify gaps in the international community's capacity and points to preliminary strategies for narrowing these. The paper also includes a useful matrix excerpting key information on UN

Security Council resolutions for missions involving aspects of civilian protection.

International Commission on Intervention and State Sovereignty (2001). *The Responsibility to Protect: Report of the International Commission on Intervention and State Sovereignty*. Ottawa, Canada: International Development Research Centre. 91 pp.

Established by the Canadian government, this panel studied the tensions between state sovereignty and what was argued to be a right of the international community to intervene in cases of genocide or mass atrocities. Co-chaired by former Australian Foreign Minister Gareth Evans and former senior Algerian diplomat Mohammed Sahnoun, the Commission developed the idea of "responsibility to protect" as an alternative to the right of intervention versus sovereignty debate. Chapter 7 discusses "The Operational Dimension," including recommendations on mandate, resources, command structure, rules of engagement, etc.

Kuperman, Alan J. (2001). *The Limits of Humanitarian Intervention: Genocide in Rwanda*. Washington, DC: Brookings Institution Press. 162 pp.

The author argues that even had the United States launched a maximal military intervention to stop the 1994 genocide in Rwanda, at best it could have saved 125,000 Tutsi lives or one-quarter of the total actually killed. His conclusion is based mainly on four premises: the delay before the U.S. president could have confidently judged that genocide was underway; the time required to airlift an intervention force to remote, landlocked Rwanda; the speed of the genocide; and the incentives for the perpetrators to accelerate their killing if armed intervention was being mobilized.

O'Hanlon, Michael, and Singer, P.W. (2004). "The Humanitarian Transformation: Expanding Global Intervention Capacity." *Survival*, 46 (1), 77-100.

The authors find the global supply of "projectable military forces" suitable for humanitarian protection missions to be inadequate to foreseeable future needs. By the authors' count, the US accounts for 62 percent of quickly deployable forces, while non-NATO countries account for just six percent. They analyze what would be required to narrow the gap between military capabilities and humanitarian needs and outline an action agenda that they characterize as "difficult, but not so daunting or expensive as to excuse inaction." Specifically, they call on European countries and Japan to enhance their capabilities and to make use of private military service contractors for transport, logistics, etc.

O'Neill, John Terence, and Rees, Nick (2005). *United Nations Peacekeeping in the Post-Cold War Era*. London: Routledge. 256 pp.

Case studies of UN peace operation in the Congo, Cyprus, Somalia, Angola, Sierra Leone and East Timor and a conclusion examining reforms following the "Brahimi Report."

Posen, Barry R. (1996). "Military Responses to Refugee Disasters." *International Security*, 21 (1), 72-111.

The author argues that military action will generally be significantly less successful at preventing or halting forced refugee crises, which often result from genocidal crimes, than is commonly assumed. He discusses military actions such as punitive bombing, truce enforcement, and the establishment of safe zones or safe havens.

Power, Samantha. (2002). *"A Problem from Hell": America and the Age of Genocide*. New York: Basic Books. 640 pp.

An important analysis of American responses to genocide in the 20th Century, Power's book includes detailed case studies of policy deliberations related to crises in Armenia, Cambodia, Iraq, Bosnia, Rwanda and Kosovo. Her analysis of primary documents and interviews with American policymakers offers unique insight into how the U.S. government formulated its response, including how peace operations were perceived and used.

Schnabel, Albrecht and Thakur, Ramesh (Eds.) (2000). *Kosovo and the Challenge of Humanitarian Intervention: Selective Indignation, Collective Action and International Citizenship*. Tokyo: United Nations University Press. 536 pp.

This edited volume produced soon after the Kosovo crisis contains twenty short essays organized into seven parts, including reflections on the NATO intervention and its implications from a variety of national and political perspectives.

Slaughter, Anne-Marie (2005). "Help Develop Institutions and Instruments for Military Intervention on Humanitarian Grounds." In Open Society Institute and Security and Peace Institute (Eds.) *Restoring American Leadership: 13 Cooperative Steps to Advance Global Progress.* New York: Open Society Institute and The Century Foundation. pp. 37-43.

This short essay calls on the Bush administration to take steps to create instruments and institutions specifically for military intervention to protect civilians, e.g., explore the feasibility of "a NATO rapid-reaction force specially trained and ready for intervention in humanitarian crises."

Stephens, Dale (2005). "The Lawful Use of Force by Peacekeeping Forces: The Tactical Imperative." *International Peacekeeping*, 12 (2), 157-172.

This article analyzes difficulties in assuring that tactical guidelines for the use of force in UN peace operations are appropriate, consistent with Security Council mandates and adhered to by national contingents. The author proposes reforms to address these highly consequential tactical level issues.

Task Force on the United Nations (2005). *American Interests and UN Reform: Report of the Task Force on the United Nations.* Washington, DC: United States Institute of Peace. 145 pp.

This report of a congressionally mandated study led by former House Speaker Newt Gingrich and former Senate Majority Leader George Mitchell is an important statement of bipartisan American views on the UN. Its second chapter, "Saving Lives, Safeguarding Human Rights, and Ending Genocide," includes recommendations to the US government on general policies for genocide prevention and on Darfur specifically, (e.g., that the US should assist in establishing a no-fly zone over Darfur). Chapter 5 includes analysis and recommendations for UN peace operations.

United Nations (2000). *Report of the Panel on United Nations Peace Operations*. New York: United Nations. 74 pp.

Known as the "Brahimi Report" for the chair of the high level panel that UN Secretary-General Kofi Annan commissioned, this detailed report analyzes the ability of the UN to conduct peace operations effectively and makes wide ranging recommendations to strengthen this ability. The report has become the touchstone for nearly all subsequent analysis and reform efforts related to UN peace operations. It begins with a forthright argument that the UN must change the way it thinks about and conducts peace operations to meet changing demands, particularly to take account of the complex or multidimensional peace operations that were becoming more prevalent at the time. The report urges specific actions in four broad areas: doctrine, strategy and decision-making; UN capacities to deploy operations rapidly and effectively; headquarters resources and structure for planning and supporting peacekeeping operations; and peace operations and the information age.

United Nations High-Level Panel on Threats, Challenges, and Change (2004) *A More Secure World: Our Shared Responsibility: Report of the High-Level Panel on Threats, Challenges, and Change*. New York: United Nations. 129 pp.

UN Secretary-General Kofi Annan commissioned this study following the sharp debate about the U.S.-led war in Iraq in 2003, judging that the world needed to forge a new consensus on collective security. He charged this panel with analyzing current security threats and recommending actions to strengthen collective responses. This report offers no less than 101 recommendations, including calling on the UN General Assembly to endorse the "responsibility to protect" and a number in the area of peace operations.

United Nations Peacekeeping Best Practices Unit (2003). *Handbook on United Nations Multidimensional Peacekeeping Operations*. New York: United Nations. 205 pp.

The UN Department of Peacekeeping Operations produced this useful resource "to serve as an introduction to the different components of multidimensional peacekeeping operations" for personnel being deployed to UN missions.

van Baarda, T., and van Iersel, F. (2002). "The Uneasy Relationship Between Conscience and Military Law: The 'Brahimi Report's' Unresolved Dilemma." *International Peacekeeping*, 9 (3), 25-50.

This article discusses the consequences of the "Brahimi Report's" recommendation that peacekeepers should be presumed to be authorized to stop violence against civilians, focusing on the tensions between this presumption and established military law.

Zenko, Micah (2004). Saving Lives with Speed: Using Rapidly Deployable Forces for Genocide Prevention." *Defense & Security Analysis*, 20 (1), 2-19.

The author discusses a set of military assets and strategies that he argues can be used effectively to prevent or halt genocide. He calls for U.S. leadership in using these types of forces for genocide prevention missions and urges other countries to expand their military capabilities for this purpose.

9

After the Killing Stops: Postgenocide Societies and Issues Relating to Prevention and Intervention

Paul R. Bartrop

Introduction

In the aftermath of a genocidal outbreak, affected societies undergo a range of experiences as they seek to regain some measure of normalcy. Such experiences can include a quest for justice relative to the perpetrators; reintegration into the international community; a degree of comity with the victim society's neighbors; nation building, or, in a majority of cases, nation rebuilding; psychological counseling, on a massive scale, for the individuals comprising the society; and physical reconstruction of the social and economic infrastructure in light of what is invariably enormous material destruction that took place during the genocide itself. In order to attain these goals, postgenocide societies are increasingly reliant upon the intervention of foreign governments, nongovernmental organizations (NGOs) and international organizations, and when such assistance is introduced successfully it can make all the difference between a satisfactory confrontation with the recent past, or a longer, more painful, and traumatic crisis that can keep the country in ruins and ongoing destabilization.

This, of course, is a highly generalized picture, subject to variations across continents, states, and regions. What is common to one situation does not necessarily apply to another, yet a single point of commonalty does touch all cases: a desire on the part of the victimized peoples to try to return to as "normal" a life as possible, to the degree that this can be achieved after a genocide. And it is here that intervention from outside can play a key role. If foreign intervention was not forthcoming, or was inadequate, in stopping the genocide from happening in the first place, perhaps it might be possible for such intervention to salvage something from the ruins of its earlier deficiencies. And not only that: intervention efforts can perhaps also contribute to the prevention of future genocide, especially as these relate to retaliatory actions such as occurred with unnerving frequency in places like Rwanda and Burundi. An alternative scenario could be of the kind where perpetrators try for a second or third time, to commit additional crimes of a genocidal nature, such as took place in East Timor in 1999. In both of these scenarios, if postgenocide justice had been meted out at an early date the later crimes may have been avoided altogether.

Overview of the Postgenocidal Environment

When do genocides end? As with so many areas in the study of genocide, there is no clear-cut answer to this question. For some, the equation is a simple one: genocide ends when the killing stops. For others, the phenomenon that is genocide embraces a very wide range of what might be termed closure issues. These include, but are not limited to, such areas as the following: stopping the killing; finding a way to ensure it does not begin again; peace building, nation building; apprehending the perpetrators (and this itself imposes a number of commitments on the part of those doing the apprehending); starting a process of rehabilitation for the survivors; and developing some sort of a reconciliation regime in which the perpetrators are brought to justice. All of this, in an ideal world, would proceed smoothly, so that from the depths of despair can come a graduated return to a form of familiar regularity.

But this is not an ideal world; genocide would not happen in an ideal world. The peaks and troughs of a nation's experience are, obviously, far from being narrowly defined. There can be vast differences between the genocidal ordeals of one nation when compared with that of another, making models difficult to compare. As a result, when looking at the postgenocidal environment as an area of study it seems imperative that the task be done on a case-by-case basis if overgeneralizations are not to be made. The best that can be said is that after a genocide every society undergoes a number of experiences, some of which are common to others.

That being said, is there anything to be gained by trying to create a profile of a "typical" postgenocidal society—especially if, as has been suggested here, there is little that can be called "typical"?

The question is one that can be asked of any area of study involving comparative analysis, but in this case the issue is compounded by the enormous number of variables involved. Ultimately, scholars are likely to derive different insights, concerns, and, yes, even questions from each of the case studies based on the questions they posit. Can, indeed, models of postgenocide behaviors and outcomes be established? They can, but how one is to employ such models must be determined on the basis of what it is each scholar is trying to achieve. In other words, the generalizations about postgenocidal societies are only as useful as each individual scholar seeks to make them.

And what, indeed, does a postgenocide environment look like? If we take the experience of one country, Cambodia, as an example, what can we detect? In the first place, a legitimate argument can be made that Cambodia is yet to recover fully from its experience at the hands of the Khmer Rouge regime (1975-1979). All of the normative structures from before their reign of terror—religion, education, law, the ongoing development of a modernized economic system, medicine, engineering, infrastructure growth, rising expectations, even sports—literally everything was, to use a contemporary term, shredded as a result of the Khmer Rouge genocidal rampage. Even the most fundamental of social units, the family, found itself under sustained attack over the full period of almost four years. This experience has left a permanent scar on the collective soul of the nation, particularly of the generation that lived through it in their flesh. Their children, in the manner of the second generation after genocide everywhere, are also traumatized.

And yet there is more to it even than this. If the damage was to the society alone, this would be bad enough. But the legacy of the genocide in Cambodia extends to the material necessities of modern living themselves. The Cambodians had to move physically back into their towns and cities, locations from which they had been driven as an entire population at the very beginning of the Khmer Rouge conquest. They had to reestablish ownership to their homes, move back into them, find employment (a difficult undertaking in a land in which the Khmer Rouge had effectively destroyed all but the most localized forms of economic activity), and engage in the myriad activities associated with urban living. Bearing in mind that Cambodia was—and remains—an overwhelmingly rural country, the reconstruction of society did not end with the cities, either. The pre-Khmer Rouge years, the period of the genocide, and the Vietnamese invasions of 1978 and 1979 all left a legacy in the countryside in the form of a vast number of undetected landmines which are still inflicting death and injury over three decades later. Land requiring cultivation must first be tested for unexploded mines, something local farmers only find out as their family members or livestock are blown apart.

As if all that is not enough, a further inhibition to the creation of a healthy postgenocide society exists in the form of unresolved factional disputes between former victims and persecutors, or their supporters, or even from political squabbles predating the genocide. Even after the killing had stopped, arrangements set in place for the purpose of bringing all parties together, and dates announced for democratic elections to occur, death still stalked the population at political rallies, in the streets, or at night, in the dark. Cambodia after the departure of the Vietnamese in 1991 was supposed to begin some sort of climb back towards a more acceptable Western democratic model, but widespread political violence throughout the country showed for many years that much of the old rancor still existed.

To all this must be added other considerations affected by the postgenocide environment, such as gender relations, unemployment, crime, corruption, public amenities, environmental degradation, self-sufficiency, public health, homelessness and transportation, among many others. All were afflicted by the genocide, and all had to be addressed in the postgenocide situation of Cambodia.

Above everything, however, towers the question of postgenocide justice. Those who had lost everything needed to know that those responsible for the massive upheaval through which they had suffered and survived would be brought to book for what they had done. Indeed, the nation had a right to demand it if it was to move ahead. But how was justice to be achieved? For many years it seemed as though this question would remain unanswered. While many in the West cry for reconciliation based on justice, the Cambodians look for justice where there is none, yet work to achieve some sort of reconciliation based on promises of justice eventually. Clearly, a lot is at stake for Cambodia's future in the way its postgenocide present is still being played out.

As in the case of Cambodia, it is possible to locate each of the concerns referred to in relation to almost every, if not every, postgenocidal situation. Biafra, Bosnia, Rwanda, East Timor, southern Sudan, Kurdistan—all have experienced or are experiencing postgenocide reconstruction, and all have had to confront the most painful of restoration processes. Some have not yet managed to complete the journey from war to peace, often several years after the accords have been signed. All have needed practical help. All have needed money. And that is where the matter of foreign intervention enters the equation.

Not all states see the need to intervene in a genocide as it is taking place. In the post-1945 environment of "never again," the resolve of the Western nations to see that ambition achieve reality has frequently proven to be hollow. In most cases where foreign intervention has taken place, it has been either with the approval or at the direction of the Security Council of the UN.

States that intervene in the internal affairs of another state, even for the purpose of stopping genocide, have been required to do so within the bounds of the Westphalian system established back in the seventeenth century. Not doing so sees them branded as aggressors interfering with the sovereign rights of their fellow states, and thus subject to international condemnation. In the very recent past (and also the present), some states (such as the U.S., Britain, and Australia) have chosen to take that risk, leading to unilateral interventions in Kosovo and Iraq. In the case of East Timor, Australia would not intervene until it had UN approval, though there was a powerful undercurrent within Australian society to intervene regardless of UN approval in order to save the lives of the East Timorese people.

The intervention fiascoes of the 1990s all seemed to point to a fundamental fact: the United Nations was not particularly adept at securing peace through its attempts at intervening in the affairs of states at risk—what many mistakenly refer to as "peacekeeping" missions. All too often, such missions were sent to keep a peace before it had been secured; where, in reality, there was no peace to keep. A stark example of this was Bosnia, where six so-called "safe areas" were established that were actually so unsafe that thousands of people were murdered before the very eyes of UN "peacekeeping" troops. Rwanda, in a different way, was equally, if not more, horrific; here, there was not a failure in UN efforts to intervene, but rather a very successful policy of refusal to intervene was set in place. The world, through the UN, appeared to be turning its back on genocide.

Perhaps it could be argued that there are in fact two types of intervention; that which is concurrent with violence, and one that takes place after it. The first is often haphazard (though it need not be), sometimes (though not always) ineffectual, and is usually grudging in nature; the second is often more or less effective, but frequently takes place as an unspoken admission of the failures of the first. It is one of the ironies of modern society that in a world of greater avowed commitment to the notion of "never again" than at any other stage of history, great states go out of their way to avoid intervention of the first kind so that they can increase their prestige when directing an intervention of the second. And through all this, the United Nations, the world body created in the aftermath of the most destructive conflict ever waged, is made to look more and more foolish by a Westphalian states system that, even in the twenty-first century, seems to be as strong as it has ever been. It is as though state leaders see themselves as far more able to assist through clearing up the mess than stopping it from happening in the first place. The images most frequently associated with the term "international humanitarian intervention" relate to military aircraft bringing supplies into a remote area; or of medical personnel tending the sick and dying in hastily constructed refugee camps; or of trucks unloading bags of flour or grain; or of military personnel helping to rebuild schools, hospitals and other public buildings. Few of these activities can take place unimpeded during a period of conflict, though tending to refugees and bringing in food does happen (for example, in Darfur in 2004-2007, even as the killing and raping continues.)

Any interventionist aid that reaches postgenocidal societies is welcomed, but there are often victims in this situation who see their societies as being on their own. This is, of course, not necessarily the case: hundreds of millions of dollars of aid pours into damaged countries, often for decades, in the aftermath of genocidal destruction (for example, in Cambodia), and even as genocides are taking place (currently, for example, in Darfur). This then brings up the greatest challenge to all such societies: how can those who were so recently either murderers or victims now remake themselves without tearing out each others' throats in a welter of vengeance and recrimination? Sometimes the only way this can be achieved is through the presence of large numbers of foreign troops to act as peacekeepers, if not enforcers, keeping the former protagonists apart from one another.

On the other hand, there are plenty of situations where foreign intervention after conflict is genuinely welcome and beneficial. Bosnia is a good example, as are Kosovo and East Timor.

In general, what can be said about postgenocidal societies relative to intervention? First, these are extremely vulnerable communities that have been through the most traumatic experience a nation, ethnic group, religion or race (to the use the UN Convention's classifications) can undergo: nothing short of an attempt at eradication from the face of the planet. This is, obviously, a jolting event for any group, with immense ramifications—some of which are not settled for generations. Second, a society that has experienced a genocide will usually attempt some form of retreat to a normalcy remembered from before the assault on its very being. Third, while many in that society seek to bring about this return themselves, in the late twentieth and early twenty-first centuries that has not been possible without outside assistance, usually in the form of foreign intervention in a physical sense. Fourth, all nations involved in such intervention do so based on motives that they can justify to their own citizens at home: regional security, national self interest, international treaty obligations, or—far less likely—altruism. Finally, all states undergoing a postgenocide reconstruction experience have specific needs, usually involving the establishment of a healthy economy, renewal of trust, rebuilding of infrastructure, the establishment of a fair and impartial judiciary, postgenocide justice whereby perpetrators, once identified, will be brought speedily to trial, the holding of free and fair elections, and the reintegration into society of those who have experienced horrific experiences. Any and all of these can also assist greatly in the establishment of prevention mechanisms that can militate against the possibility of a recurrence of genocide. In this, foreign intervention has an important role to play (though often it has been the case that money raised overseas for the purpose of rebuilding does not find its way readily to the places where it is needed most, corruption being another postgenocide legacy that has to be addressed).

Critical Issues Facing the Field Today

Any serious consideration of postgenocide societies is fraught with difficulty. Most apparent is the potential for conceptual chaos in appreciating the field; just where does—or even can—one start to develop any sort of broad understanding of what a postgenocide society's needs are, where the priorities of its surviving citizens are located, how its needs are to be met, and what its relationship with the perpetrators (who are likely to be fellow citizens) should be?

As mentioned and commented upon previously, another issue requiring consideration is that of defining just what a postgenocidal society actually is. When does "postgenocide," as a concept, begin? When does it end? Who is to decide, and to what extent will both action and scholarship be effected by the choice?

Intervention with regard to genocide has generally come to be understood as attempting to halt the killing rather than of rebuilding after the killing has stopped. Developing an appreciation that intervention can be applied in two quite different ways is thus an issue that needs to be addressed in future scholarship. Of course, postgenocide intervention is not in most cases as dramatic as intervention for the purpose of stopping a genocide; peace is rarely as exciting, in the popular imagination, as war. This is one reason why scholarship on postgenocide intervention has such a long way to go.

Another reason lies in trying to ascertain just who is doing the intervening. Are we speaking about an international force—an alliance, perhaps, or a group of like-minded states? Is the intervention one involving non-governmental, or non-state, actors? And into such a mix, can we include nongovernment humanitarian organizations like the Red Cross or Doctors Without Borders?

We also need to consider the importance of bringing justice and stability to a society after genocide has taken place—an important form of genocide prevention—in order to ensure that the society does not slip back into genocidal behavior. And here, vital questions must be raised, not the least of which concerns how the very term "justice" is to be interpreted. By way of example, the complexities faced by the postgenocide government of Rwanda can be highlighted here. Three different forms of judicial process have been used for trying alleged perpetrators: the International Criminal Tribunal for Rwanda, established through the United Nations; national trials in Rwanda, where well over one hundred thousand prisoners still languish, in horrific conditions, in local jails; and the community system, based on precolonial forms, known as *gacaca*, in which those accused have the opportunity to have their case heard before an entire village assembly. A concomitant question is whether one or the other processes is more effective (and under what conditions, if any); and if so, why and how?

The issues facing the field of research into postgenocide societies and intervention are many (e.g., how to obtain research data in unstable environments, from where such data can be obtained, the extent to which sources will be accurate or reliable, and how far authorities will cooperate with the research process). Resolution of these cannot be presumed to be automatic. It is quite clear that any such work, for example, will have to take into account the perspectives of the survivors, who, as the inheritors of the new society, must deal not only with postgenocide reconstruction but also with their most intimate attitudes regarding what has gone before. Reconstruction frequently involves such matters as reconciliation; indeed, how could one consider reconstruction without it? Yet for an examination of how a survivor regime is dealing with this one issue, researchers would need to be familiar with the education system, the history of the country, security, and postgenocide perspectives on justice.

A final matter requiring attention when looking at the issue of postgenocide societies and intervention is its obverse, that of prevention. Critical issues must be addressed in the aftermath of genocide if the region and those involved are to even attempt to prevent a recurrence of the events that had earlier led to genocide. Two forms of action, which can be termed primary prevention and aftermath prevention, if conducted thoroughly and effectively, are preventive measures which can be employed to avoid the prospect of a reappearance of genocide in the postgenocidal period.

Primary prevention serves a preemptive function. It aims to encourage healthy pluralistic democracy, respect for human rights, and the development of programs to facilitate these through education, the law, the media, employment, bureaucracy and so on. States are always engaging in what might theoretically be termed intervention activities, through exchange programs (either formal or informal) and the exercise of other influences—movies, television, radio, popular culture generally, the Internet.

Aftermath prevention is a form of post facto enterprise which recognizes the possibility of a genocide reigniting, and works to ensure that this will not be the case—often by tapping into elements of the primary and consequential constructs. Thus, prevention has an important role to play where intervention activity is concerned; indeed, it is reliant upon it in order to be successful.

Concomitantly, the economic dimensions of intervention are often discussed, but hardly ever in relation to prevention. The same is true regarding the political dimension. Such gaps in the scholarship need addressing if anything in the way of a planned and well-structured international effort to prevent genocide is to be achieved. It is through the dissemination of such scholarship that opinion shapers and decision makers can be exposed to the range of options they require for the purpose of acting, rather than finding reasons for not acting.

What are the Real Probabilities of Progress in the Field?

In light of the above analysis, it may seem as though the likelihood of progress is not good, but such a negative prognosis does not take into account the enormous quantity of work that has already been undertaken from outside the academy, by journalists, aid workers, nongovernmental organizations (NGOs), intergovernmental organizations (IGOs), and the like. In other words, a great deal of preparation has already been done, and the contours of debate have been sketched out. As a result, scholars can readily enter in political discussions that are already under way at the policy level, and in some instances it will be possible for critical analysis to take place concerning issues that have been under discussion in a different context for some time.

In some respects, the forces acting to inhibit genocide intervention are the same forces that can inhibit genocide scholarship: funding, political commitment, an ongoing question on the part of policymakers regarding the issue of "relevance" (to the department, to the university, to the students, to the state or country in which the project is being tackled), or to the agenda of those under whose jurisdiction the project is given permission to proceed. As a result, many of those doing scholarly work on postgenocide societies, or on issues of intervention and prevention, do so as quasi-independent scholars, teaching unrelated courses, receiving little or no funding, little or no peer recognition, and doing so outside of the routine of the work day. This situation might end once a sufficient disciplinary base is established, but the time this will take may well be debilitating for those who wish to continue their work but find it difficult to maintain.

It is not, therefore, a matter easy of resolution, but this is not helped by the fact that defining "the field" itself is far from simple. As will be detected from the bibliography accompanying this chapter, the range of topics that can be included within a discussion of postgenocide societies and issues relating to intervention is extremely broad; indeed, sometimes it is not at first apparent that a specific work actually fits within the field at all. With a greater refinement of the kinds of issues to be discussed, such that the focus becomes more apparent to all, greater respect might begin to accrue from all the inhibiting agencies referred to above, and those working in the area can begin to feel more confident about what they do and why they do it. The attitudinal change must come, in short, not from the scholars, but from those in the institutions where such scholars work. Concomitantly, it would be beneficial for those who would derive greatest benefit from such work—most notably those in government and in the international organizations—to vocally and strongly support such scholars' efforts.

The subjects of much scholarly work, the survivors, know why scholarship is needed if they are to be helped; what those engaged in scholarship on postgenocide societies and intervention need to be able to do is continue their work and get their message across to those who can act on it. Real progress will come from the field being accorded serious respect by its recipients in the corridors of power, not from its exponents giving recognition to each other.

Conclusion

The studies compiled in the following bibliography represent a cross-section of the kind of issues scholars have occupied themselves with, mainly over the past ten-to-fifteen years. They are a sampling, not an exhaustive listing, primarily because of the range of themes and styles the field embraces. It is hoped that as this relatively new area of scholarly pursuit develops, the focus will become sharper and commentaries such as this one can speak with confidence of a sub-topic within the broad area of genocide studies in which contemplation of postgenocide issues and intervention can take its place as a legitimate area of scholarly enterprise.

Annotated Bibliography

[Note: I wish to sincerely thank Jordana Silverstein and Eve Grimm, to whom I owe an immense debt of gratitude for their assistance in the development of this annotated bibliography.]

Agger, I. (2001). "Psychosocial Assistance During Ethnopolitical Warfare in the former Yugoslavia," pp. 305-318. In Daniel Chirot and E. P. Martin Seligman (Eds.) *Ethnopolitical Warfare: Causes, Consequences, and Possible Solutions*. Washington, DC: American Psychological Association.

This article discusses the psychosocial projects and humanitarian aid provided in the aftermath of the war in the former Yugoslavia. Main topics discussed in this chapter are: (1) the trauma of ethnopolitical warfare; (2) psychosocial projects; (3) why psychosocial projects work in the former Yugoslavia; (4) the issue of war rapes; (5) and an investigation of psychosocial projects. The author concludes that traumatized people need mostly to relive their traumatic experiences in order to resolve their conflicts and integrate them into their lives.

Chandler, David (Ed.) (2004). *Protecting the Bosnian Peace: Lessons From a Decade of Nation Building.* London: Routledge. 256 pp.

This volume considers the degree to which Bosnia-Herzegovina has truly been able to reconstruct itself as a fully functioning nation-state ten years after the end of the Bosnian War. The essays embrace a wide range of post-conflict issues: to what degree does Bosnia have an independent administration free from United Nations oversight? Do the two entities (the Federation of Bosnia and Herzegovina, and Republika Srpska) show any potential for rapprochement? Is there any likelihood of reunification? Above all, in the post-Dayton environment, what does nation-building in the aftermath of war and genocide really mean? Is there a "new" Bosnia—or are the varied populations of the country destined to live in a state of non-war (not war, yet far from peace) into the foreseeable future? The book tackles a broad array of the kind of concerns upon which an international intervention should be constructed: reconciliation, economic transition from war to peace, citizenship, policing, peacebuilding at the local level, and the like. We see that within a postgenocidal society such as Bosnia the legacies are many and the wounds are deep—but, if managed effectively, there may be grounds for hope sometime in the future.

Chesterman, Simon (2005). *You, the People: The United Nations, Transitional Administration and State-Building.* Oxford: Oxford University Press. 316 pp.

Intervention to stop genocide is one facet of a conflict issue; another is what form a post-conflict government will take once a military settlement has been reached. In this book, Simon Chesterman addresses the question of how this transition between war and peace takes place. In the majority of cases, an interventionist regime is military in nature, temporary and authoritarian. The drive to change this status into something more akin to a civilian democratic regime is often intense, sometimes leading to haste—and unfortunate mistakes. Postgenocidal societies seek reconciliation, repair, justice, and reconstruction; they also need money, and great amounts of it. As the United Nations proceeds with a postconflict state-building project, transitional administrations are all too often slow in addressing all of the above issues.

Chesterman considers a range of scenarios, among which are included Cambodia, Kosovo, Bosnia, East Timor, Afghanistan and Iraq. He examines how the UN evolves its transitional administration policies, how these are balanced against the quest to return to civilian rule, and how exit strategies are developed sufficiently to be able to leave at the most appropriate time. Chesterman's overall conclusion is that the idealistic ends of governments and organizations involved in the creation and administering of transitional regimes are not and cannot be achieved through identical means in all cases, and that, as a result, each situation must be evaluated on its merits rather than according to a fixed format.

Curtis, Grant (1998). *Cambodia Reborn?: The Transition to Democracy and Development*. Washington, D.C.: Brookings Institution Press. 224 pp.

This book focuses on Cambodia's postconflict transitions, situating itself firmly in support of a "development" model which would take the country from communism towards liberal democracy. Curtis undertakes a complete survey of Cambodia's diverse transitions, examining "transition toward some form of democracy, the further transition to a market economy, a transition from rehabilitation toward development, and a transition from war to peace."

Drumtra, Jeff (1998). *Life after Death: Suspicion and Reintegration in Post-Genocide Rwanda*. http://www.africaaction.org/docs98/rwan9802.1.htm

This report examines the situation in postgenocide Rwanda from a "practical" perspective. It reports on the attitudes and psychology amongst Rwandans; security within the country; land and housing; and a number of other challenges, such as the economy, food and agriculture, health, and governance. It also provides some recommendations for changing the situation.

Etcheson, Craig (2005). *After the Killing Fields: Lessons from the Cambodian Genocide*. Westport, CT: Praeger. 270 pp.

In this book, Etcheson shows that the ordeal suffered by Cambodia extended beyond the years of Pol Pot (1975-1979). In his view, Cambodia suffered civil war, genocidal devastation, foreign intervention and military occupation, and, finally, additional civil strife, between the mid-1960s and at least the mid-1990s—what he refers to as Cambodia's "Thirty Years War." Throughout this time, he concludes, as many as 2.2 million Cambodians lost their lives, an upwards adjustment of 500,000 against the generally accepted figure of 1.7 million killed. Etcheson's study is mainly concerned, however, with postgenocide Cambodia: how ordinary Cambodians have tried to come to terms with the enormity of the period of the horror, how attempts have been made unsuccessfully to bring the perpetrators to justice, and how data has been collected documenting the killing. Etcheson deals with an area of postgenocide intervention different from the military, "boots-on-the-ground" variety; namely, that type of intervention that comes as the result of a request from a successor government, taking the form of assistance in the reconstruction of the juridical foundation of a country. The quest is far from complete, and what he refers to as "the politics of genocide justice" may yet take over and deny proper closure to this terrible period in Cambodia's history.

Fawthrop, Tom, and Jarvis, Helen (2005). *Getting Away With Genocide? Elusive Justice and the Khmer Rouge Tribunal*. Sydney: University of New South Wales Press. 327 pp.

This book has as its key area of focus the quest for justice in the wake of the genocide perpetrated by the Khmer Rouge. Such a quest has been very much a case of "if" rather than "when," and it has never been a given that such justice will be achieved. Fawthrop and Jarvis show that this important element of postgenocide activity was never tackled by the Vietnamese puppet government installed in Phnom Penh, nor addressed with much interest by the United Nations or the Western democracies until after the defeat of communism in the early 1990s. Indeed, the Khmer Rouge-in-exile was supported by countries such as the United States as a less threatening adversary than communist Vietnam. This support became symbolic of Cold War power politics, and was thus relevant as long as that conflict lasted. Most governments had ignored the efforts being made by Cambodians within the country to document the crimes of the Pol Pot regime, and even less the attempts to bring Khmer Rouge leaders to justice (or even to create a process to do so). Only after international political concerns underwent a change did the United Nations even begin to take an interest, and that, in 1997, was only after the government of Cambodia requested UN assistance to do so. This book not only chronicles the "elusive justice" that was sought, it also points up a dimension to postgenocide intervention that needs to be considered more carefully; namely, why do interventionist regimes often drag their heels in bringing perpetrators to account, or, worse, actually reintegrate them into newly established power structures?

Gottesman, Evan (2003). *Cambodia After the Khmer Rouge: Inside the Politics of Nation Building*. New Haven, CT: Yale University Press. 454 pp.

This study tells of the events and personalities that shaped Cambodian history during the turbulent period following the overthrow of the Khmer Rouge regime as a result of Vietnamese intervention in 1979, and explains the internal workings of the successor regime, the People's Republic of Kampuchea. Gottesman's examination outlines how much the legacy of communism has influenced the emergence of the country after the genocide. In the early months of 1979, Cambodia barely existed as a nation. Millions of ragged, malnourished Cambodians wandered around a fragmented landscape of violence, grief, anger and uncertainty. There were none of the institutions normally associated with a modern nation state: no bureaucracy, no army or police, no schools or hospitals, no state or private commercial networks, no religious hierarchies, no legal system. Most of the intelligentsia had been destroyed. The new regime, installed by a foreign power, had no popular support other than as an alternative to the Khmer Rouge. Gottesman looks at how this legacy shaped the country, its people, and the political and economic institutions that govern the lives of Cambodians. In doing so, he addresses the questions: How does a country function without educated people, and what is there for those who remain?

Harris, Geoff (Ed.) (1999). *Recovery From Armed Conflict In Developing Countries*. London: Routledge. 360 pp.

This collection is divided into three sections. Coming from an economist's perspective, it begins by making the case for the importance of societies recovering from conflict by examining the various ways in which conflicts occur throughout the world, and their toll on societies and communities. It then discusses various issues of reconstruction and recovery, in terms of their social, political and economic impacts. Finally, the book presents a series of case studies, examining the postconflict road undertaken by countries as diverse as Cambodia, South Africa and Sri Lanka, among others. Throughout, Harris and his authors make the case for peaceful resolutions, and urge a conflict-free world.

Hatzfeld, Jean (2005). *Machete Season: The Killers in Rwanda Speak.* New York: Farrar, Straus and Giroux. 253 pp.

This book is a collection of testimonies from a group of ten Hutu killers, all close friends, who were imprisoned as a result of their crimes during the Rwanda genocide of 1994. As they tell their stories, we see a whole new expression of what Hannah Arendt described as "the banality of evil." These men outline how easy it was to kill Tutsis, to pick up their agricultural tools—for the most part, machetes—and turn them against their neighbors when ordered to do so by the *Interahamwe* militias. The book's relevance vis-a-vis port-genocidal societies lies in its final chapters, where the Hutus reflect on the legacy they have left for Rwanda. Indeed, there is a great deal of reflection on Rwanda's postgenocidal situation.

Ignatieff, Michael (2003). "State Failure and Nation-building," pp. 299-321. In J.L. Holzgreve and Robert O. Keohane (Eds.) *Humanitarian Intervention: Ethical, Legal and Political Dilemmas.* Cambridge: Cambridge University Press.

Michael Ignatieff argues that in the post-Cold War period, the coming of democracy to a formerly closed society with suppressed ethnic tensions can have catastrophic consequences, such as ethnic war and ethnic cleansing. His examples cover disparate areas, including the south Balkans, and west, central, eastern and southern Africa. After examining the reasons for such failures, Ignatieff notes that the states in crisis "no longer possess a monopoly of the legitimate means of violence," therefore no longer meeting the classic Weberian definition of the "state." He examines the preconditions for effective domestic sovereignty, concluding that on balance states that collapse into ethnic fragments should be put back together. He questions how this can be achieved in a way that enhances conditions of stability that will lead to governance capacity and the security of each state. In a globalized and interdependent world, he argues, newly emergent states should not seek independence in the classic Westphalian sense, but strength through partnership with neighbors. He argues that rich states need incentives to stabilize their weaker neighbors so as to keep them from collapsing. Ignatieff looks at some states' preference to stay neutral, which can become discreditable as well as counter-productive (as it was in Bosnia), and points out that an intervention strategy that takes sides, uses force and sticks around to rebuild is very different from one premised on neutrality, casualty-avoidance and exit strategies. Responsibility for security and coexistence must be imposed onto local elites, under the watchful eye of intervening forces, but the initiatives for responsible political dialogue, shared institutions of police and justice, and restoration of the social trust necessary for economic development and community coexistence must come from the local people themselves.

Jeong, Ho-Won (2005). *Peacebuilding in Postconflict Societies: Strategy and Progress*. Boulder, CO: Lynne Rienner. 260 pp.

This book discusses the multiple dimensions of peacebuilding in societies that have experienced destructive conflict and only recently returned to peace. It offers clear-cut guidelines on how strategies are to be formulated and implemented, and considers long-term transitional processes covering the regimes that are to be installed by intervention forces as they seek to reach the next step after the shooting has stopped. Jeong illustrates his analysis with a broad range of historical and contemporary examples, pointing out the complex multifaceted nature of the challenges faced by peacebuilders when handling their essential tasks of forging a new future for damaged societies.

Keohane, Robert O. (2003). "Political Authority After Intervention: Gradations in Sovereignty," pp. 275-298. In J. L. Holzgreve, and Robert O. Keohane (Eds.) *Humanitarian Intervention: Ethical, Legal and Political Dilemmas*. Cambridge: Cambridge University Press.

This article looks at the effectiveness of contemporary arrangements introduced, contrary to the classic ideal-type of Westphalian sovereignty, that take place after intervention occurs. It discusses what constitutes post-intervention "success," and identifies some of the most serious political and institutional issues concerning humanitarian intervention that arise after military intervention has succeeded in stopping large-scale violence. Keohane argues that external authority structures are crucial to reconstructing troubled countries and regions.

Kiernan, Ben (Ed.) (1993). *Genocide and Democracy in Cambodia: The Khmer Rouge, the United Nations and the International Community.* New Haven, CT: Yale University Southeast Asia Studies. 335 pp.

This edited book examines the situation in Cambodia up to 1993. In doing so, it examines the lead up to the genocide (1975), the situation throughout the genocide (1975-1979), and the postgenocide society of Cambodia, while also accounting for the way political structures throughout the world dealt with the Khmer Rouge regime, and the Cambodian genocide. In his Introduction, Kiernan laments the fact that the genocide in Cambodia has not had the same focus on it from human rights activists as atrocities have in places such as Iraq. He also laments the fact that there have not been the same calls for the perpetrators to be held accountable for their actions as there have in other genocidal events. In essence, this collection serves as a call to the world outside Cambodia to deal with the lasting effects of the genocide, and to remove any remaining remnants of Khmer Rouge power and control.

Kreimer, Alcira; Muscat, Robert; Elwan, Ann; and Arnold, Margaret (2000). *Bosnia and Herzegovina: Post-Conflict Reconstruction.* Washington, DC: The World Bank. 109 pp.

This review of the postconflict situation in Bosnia and Herzegovina, by the Operations Evaluation Department of the World Bank, charts the evolution of the conflict and then follows that by examining the role of the World Bank in post-conflict reconstruction. It does so by discussing the general role of the Bank in assisting to rebuild the economy and human and social capital and institutions in Bosnia-Herzegovina. The review ends with a series of conclusions and lessons to be drawn from the Bank's involvement in this effort.

As is to be expected, this review contains high praise for the work of the World Bank, asserting that "the Bank's reconstruction effort brought about a significant peace dividend in the federation." There are few criticisms, and those which are presented are insubstantial. Thus, this review may be taken as an interesting summary of the work of the World Bank, however, its conclusions must be approached with caution.

Paris, Roland (2004). *At War's End: Building Peace After Civil Conflict.* Cambridge: Cambridge University Press. 289 pp.

This book examines the key post-civil war international missions launched between 1989 and 1999 deployed with the goal of preventing a recurrence of violence. There were fourteen of these in total. These operations shared a common strategy for consolidating peace after internal conflicts, namely, immediate democratization and marketization. Paris argues that the idea of transforming war-shattered states into stable democracies is basically sound, though pushing the process too quickly can have damaging and destablizing effects. Paris argues that a more sensible strategy is to establish a system of domestic institutions that are capable of managing the destablizing effects of democratization and marketization within peaceful bounds, and only after that stage to slowly phase in political and economic reforms, as conditions warrant. Gradual and controlled approaches to postconflict liberalization are more likely to achieve the central goal of successful peacebuilding.

Pottier, Johan (2002). *Re-Imagining Rwanda: Conflict, Survival and Disinformation in the Late Twentieth Century.* Cambridge: Cambridge University Press. 251 pp.

Pottier's monograph argues that media and aid-driven accounts of the tragic conflicts in Rwanda and the Great Lakes in the period 1994-1996, while attractive because of their presumed immediate practical value, must not be taken at face value, but as products regularly conditioned by scant background information, tight deadlines, the demand for simplified commentary, and, sometimes, powerful manipulations. Quality control means checking for accuracy, weighing claims about the present against recorded history, or supplying context. Pottier sets out the do this with reference to the crisis in Rwanda and eastern Zaire.

Pottier comments that a photograph of the conflict in 1994-1996 does not provide insight into how the earlier Rwandan refugee crisis went unreported for three decades; how the 1994 genocide in Rwanda related to the 1972 genocide in Burundi and to fears of a repeat in 1993; how the coffee crash of 1989 created massive despair among poor farmers; how the International Monetary Fund (IMF) failed to bail Rwanda out of its severe economic crisis; how the Tutsi-dominated Rwandan Patriotic Front (RPF) invaded Rwanda in 1990; how the "international community" imposed on the country a form of political paralysis, confusing this with democracy; or how the UN succumbed to indifference when failing to intervene in force in Rwanda in April 1994.

Pottier argues that awkward questions were not often asked, academic literature not consulted, and instead it was Kigali's representation of events and conditions in eastern Zaire which became accepted and authoritative.

Pottier's contention is that, tragically, popular struggle remained outside the broad picture which media and aid workers conjured up, and he is concerned with recontextualizing accounts of the conflict. He sets out to demonstrate that the RPF-led regime in power after the genocide befriended international opinion makers who were encouraged to believe easy-to-grasp narratives regarding central Africa's crises and solutions without questioning their ideological underpinnings. Rebuilding Rwanda in a post-genocide environment, he argues, cannot be done within a context of misinformation or poor information based on simple explanations.

Essentially, then, this book argues that in the global, interconnected search for understanding, opinion makers have failed consistently to integrate detailed contexts about the Rwandan genocide, and that as a result many analysts have opted for "easy handles" on some very complex issues. That notwithstanding, analytic efforts to appreciate the context and complexity are hampered by the current Rwandan government's insistence that outsiders have lost the right to judge what goes on in Rwanda.

Pottier's position is that without a broadly agreed vision of the past which acknowledges that different interpretations of history exist, Rwanda and eastern Zaire (and the Great Lakes region generally) will remain trapped in an official discourse which legitimates the use of violence and which could, under certain circumstances, result in some leaders and led to becoming genocidaires.

Ramsbotham, Oliver and Woodhouse, Tom (1996). *Humanitarian Intervention in Contemporary Conflict: A Reconceptualization*. Cambridge: Polity Press. 284 pp.

In examining humanitarian intervention in Uganda, Iraq, Bosnia and Somalia, this book positions itself firmly in the post-Cold War era. Whereas conflict used to be about strong countries invading weak ones, it is now about "over-weak governments" denying or violating human rights. Therefore, the authors contend, we should now try "to understand how non-forcible options (peacekeeping) and non-military options (broadly, humanitarian assistance) should be brought into play" in response to such situations. Ramsbotham and Woodhouse reconceptualize humanitarian intervention, and argue that "prevailing, classic, 'narrow' definitions are inadequate in the contemporary context of post-cold war conflict." This perspective results from the frustration of the situations that resulted in Bosnia and Somalia, juxtaposed against the questionable nature of inaction following Rwanda.

Stover, Eric, and Weinstein, Harvey M. (2004). *My Neighbor, My Enemy: Justice and Community in the Aftermath of Mass Atrocity*. Cambridge: Cambridge University Press. 349 pp.

This is an outstanding collection of essays considering fundamental issues in the study of postgenocide societies. The editors have assembled a set of articles exploring how some communities have rebuilt themselves after war and mass atrocity, and what contribution, if any, criminal trials make to that process. Unlike in other edited works, the contributors have in many cases joined together in writing individual articles, so that the volume presents as a cooperative themed analysis. The authors contend that there is no link between war crimes trials and reconciliation, but that instead these may cause further suspicion and fear. The argument is that while trials are essential to combat impunity and punish the guilty, their strengths and limitations must be acknowledged. For survivors, justice means not only trials of key leaders, but also identification of the dead, return of property, punishment of all war criminals, reparations, the creation of jobs, the building of schools, and post-trauma assistance. The also argue that education of people about the events that led to the violence is critical in confronting any myth of "collective innocence."

Tauedevin, Lansell, and Lee, Jefferson (Eds.) (2000). *East Timor: Making Amends? Analysing Australia's Role in Reconstructing East Timor.* Sydney: Australia-East Timor Association and Otford Press. 253 pp.

On August 30, 1999, eighty per cent of the East Timorese people voted for independence from Indonesia. As threatened, anti-independence supporters, frequently abetted and reinforced by members of the Indonesian military out of uniform, immediately went on a rampage, devastating the country's infrastructure and taking hundreds of lives. Responsibility for rebuilding the ravaged country fell on an international community which had, for twenty-four years, left East Timor exposed to a brutal occupation that had cost some 200,000 lives. Newly principled governments rediscovered human ideals, and international aid agencies, governments, non-government organizations and concerned individuals provided help to the fledgling administration of the new country to help it rebuild. This book resulted from papers presented at a conference on "Australia's Role in the Reconstruction of East Timor." Contributors range from directors of relevant non-government organizations, to medical doctors, Sisters of the Order of St Joseph, academics, journalists, an engineer, and a carpenter—all bringing their individual perspectives to the issue of the regeneration of East Timor in its postgenocide future.

Temple-Raston, Dina (2005). *Justice on the Grass: Three Rwandan Journalists, Their Trials for War Crimes, and a Nation's Quest for Redemption.* New York: Free Press. 302 pp.

The Rwanda genocide of 1994 encompassed the massacre of well over 500,000 Tutsi and moderate Hutu in just one hundred days. In the months leading up to the killings, two local media outlets, *Radio-Television Libre des Mille Collines* (RTLM) and the tabloid newspaper *Kangura* warned that a bloody confrontation was brewing, in which none would be spared. In fact, fear-mongering from the RTLM and *Kangura* played a key role in igniting the genocide.

In a gripping narrative that examines the power of the press and sheds light on how the media turned tens of thousands of ordinary Rwandans into unhesitating killers, Temple-Raston traces the rise and fall of three media executives.

From crime to trial to verdict, she explores the many avenues of justice Rwanda pursued in the decade after the killings. Focusing on the media trial at the United Nations' International Criminal Tribunal for Rwanda, she examines how and where ordinary Rwandans seek justice and retribution, and considers whether politics in the central African nation has set the stage for renewed violence.

van Tongeren, Paul; van de Veen, Hans; and Verhoeven, Juliette (Eds.) (2002). *Searching for Peace in Europe and Eurasia: An Overview of Conflict Prevention and Peacebuilding Activities*. Boulder, CO: Lynne Rienner Publishers. 700 pp.

This edited volume aims to provide a source of information "about conflict prevention and peacebuilding activities" in Europe and Eurasia and to "contribute to the discussion about effective measures for conflict prevention." It identifies a lack of shared knowledge globally regarding conflict prevention and resolution, and tries to explain why. The book's main purpose is to share information about the actions of the wide variety of groups and individuals who involve themselves in peacebuilding activities; to examine the actions of various organizations and countries; and to critically evaluate their efforts. Locating this study firmly in the post-September 11 world, the editors argue that their overall objective, which is "to contribute to the transformation of violent conflicts," is even more essential in the current climate.

10

Punishing Genocidaires: A Deterrent Effect or Not?[1]

Martin Mennecke

"I think the whole idea behind the genocide convention—that it's a convention to prevent and to punish the crime of genocide, is precisely that punishment plays a preventive role. That's an act of faith."—Juan E. Mendez, Special Adviser on the Prevention of Genocide to the Secretary General of the United Nations

Introduction: The UN Convention on Prevention and Punishment of the Crime of Genocide

The UN Convention on the Prevention and Punishment of the Crime of Genocide (UNCG) has, since its inception in 1948, been the subject of widespread and severe criticism. Indeed, it soon became commonplace to bemoan what were considered to be serious shortcomings of the UNGC's definition of genocide.[2] The Convention's provisions on prevention and punishment were also found to be weak and insufficient. Due to the latter, as well as a host of other reasons, including *realpolitik*, the "never again" pledge issued in the aftermath of the Holocaust turned into a hollow phrase.

Not until the 1990s, when the UN Security Council established the International Criminal Tribunal for the Former Yugoslavia (ICTY) and its counterpart for Rwanda (ICTR), did the UNCG's aim of punishing genocidaires begin to gain practical significance. In both of the latter instances, however, international attempts to hold perpetrators accountable were criticized as post-mortem justice, i.e., as doing too little too late; in essence, the trials constituted a convenient substitute for forceful intervention on the ground.

At the same time, the establishment of the international tribunals gave rise to a new question: Could punishment of genocidaires—even if coming too late for those murdered victims of a particular genocide—contribute to the prevention of further crimes in the particular conflict or, at the least, future cases of genocide? And, was the title of the UNCG in its referral to "prevention and punishment" possibly only capturing a single understanding of how the international community could fight genocide, and thus overlooking another—that is, prevention through punishment? That the latter understanding came about so late in the international discourse on prevention is surprising—and this is particularly so given the prominent role the link between punishment and prevention plays in most national criminal codes.

In this chapter, we address the notion of punishment as being a possible means of preventing genocide, trace its existence in international discussions on prevention, and assess its validity.

Prevention through Punishment—The Deterrence Argument

What is the object and purpose of a criminal code and of the sentences handed down by criminal courts? This question has occupied jurists and philosophers since before the medieval age, as punishment has always been considered to be the last resort of the state in order to enforce the laws. In contemporary legal theory, one of the most widely held theses in this context is what we in this chapter refer to as "the deterrence argument"—the assumption that there is a deterrent effect stemming from possible punishment of a criminal act. In other words, in this context, punishment is equated with prevention.[3]

In national criminal law, additional, more sophisticated readings of this deterrence argument have been developed. One interpretation states that the individual perpetrator who is put on trial will be prevented from committing further crimes because of the sentence he will suffer. Another version of the deterrence argument focuses on the community as a whole and stipulates that punishing the single perpetrator has a preventive effect on other potential wrongdoers—that is, they will be deterred from carrying out criminal acts. In addition, the punishment meets the community's need for a reaction to the perpetrator's crime and thus re-establishes the general confidence in the rule of law—in theory, making acts of vigilantism and self-justice superfluous. All these interpretations of the deterrence argument, though, have met criticism. In particular, it has been pointed out that such a prevention-oriented understanding of punishment would reduce the individual perpetrator to a mere instrument in the process of educating the general public not to do wrong. For this and other reasons, most criminal codes today put forward a mix of objectives, the deterrence argument forming part of a more elaborate theory of punishment (for the multiple purpose of national criminal codes, see the elaborations made in ICTY, Prosecutor v. Erdemovic, 29 November 1996, paragraphs 57ff.).

The Deterrence Argument in the International Context

In preparing for the Nuremberg trials, the Allied powers expressed their hope that the prospect of war crimes investigations would affect some Germans in their doings. For example, at the Moscow Conference in October 1943, Roosevelt, Churchill, and Stalin issued a "full warning" to German war criminals that they would be held accountable for their deeds and that they would "be brought back to the scene of their crimes and judged on the spot by the peoples whom they have outraged." Concomitantly, the Allied powers stated their commitment to pursuing German war criminals "to the uttermost ends of the earth and [that we] will deliver them to their accusers in order that justice may be done" (Moscow Declaration on Atrocities, 1943).

That said, following the conclusion of the Nuremberg Trials and the entering into force of the UN Genocide Convention in 1951, decades passed without any international trials of war criminals and genocidaires. Instead of deterrence by punishment, the enduring absence of any measure of accountability led to what was called a "culture of impunity." War crimes, crimes against humanity and genocide were committed in numerous instances without any sanction by means of international or national prosecutions. Indeed, impunity became the rule rather than the exception (McGoldrick, 1999, pp. 327-655).

Only in the early 1990s, when the UN Security Council eventually began discussing whether to establish a war crimes tribunal for the Former Yugoslavia, did the debate over the objectives of punishment finally reach the international level. (See for example the responses of UN member states to a report by the UN Secretary General outlining different options concerning the establishment of a war crimes tribunal for the Former Yugoslavia in UNSC, May 25, 1993.)[4] The establishment of the ICTY was soon followed by the creation of the ICTR, and shortly thereafter other institutions such as the International Criminal Court (ICC), the Special Court for Sierra Leone, the War Crimes Chamber for

Bosnia and Herzegovina, and the Extraordinary Chambers in the Courts of Cambodia (to deal with the Cambodian genocide) were founded. This phase of rapid expansion was characterized by an overwhelming focus on questions of institution-building and the challenges of applying the dormant definitions of war crimes, crimes against humanity and genocide in court. Little attention, though, focused on what the objectives underlying these unprecedented efforts were or should be. Instead, most, if not all, actors of international criminal justice seemed to look upon and consider such efforts, without little to no further reflection, from the perspective of their respective national criminal codes—and this was particularly true in regard to the deterrence argument. Thus, it was universally submitted that "[a]ccountability, in form of punishment, is crucial to prevention." (This quote stems from a speech delivered by Juan E. Mendez (2005). A similarly broad remark can be found in UNSG, 23 August 2004, paragraph 39.) As for UN Secretary-General Kofi Annan, he included the notion of preventing genocide by ending impunity as one of the five core pillars in his "Action Plan to Prevent Genocide" (UNSG, 7 April 2004). Below, this approach will be further addressed by surveying the practice of the ICTY and ICTR as well as remarks made in connection with the establishment and first activities of the ICC.

The Deterrence Argument and the International Criminal Tribunals for the Former Yugoslavia and Rwanda

Soon after the establishment of the ICTY and the ICTR, international judges had to mete out penalties for the massive violations of human rights brought before them. As the statutes of the two tribunals did not provide for any guidance on how to measure sentences for international crimes, the judges turned to the motives the UN member states had voiced when founding the tribunals in 1993 and 1994, respectively, and reviewed international and national precedents relating to international crimes such as the Eichmann case in Israel (1961). In doing so, the judges arrived at the understanding of the ICTY as being "a powerful means to deter the parties to the conflict in the Former Yugoslavia from perpetrating further crimes" (ICTY, Prosecutor v. Erdemovic, 29 November 1996, paragraph 58.)[5]

This line of argument was affirmed in subsequent cases and became a standard feature of sentencing judgments, both at the ICTY and the ICTR. In the case against the former Rwandan prime minister, Jean Kambanda, for example, the trial chamber pronounced that "it is clear that the penalties imposed on accused persons found guilty by the Tribunal must be directed, on the one hand, at retribution, and, over and above that, on the other hand, at deterrence" (ICTR, Prosecutor v. Jean Kambanda, 4 September 1998, paragraph 28). Similarly, the ICTY stated that "retribution and deterrence [serve] as the primary purposes of sentence." By now, this belief has become of common reference point for all international criminal justice institutions.[6]

The Deterrence Argument and the International Criminal Court (ICC)

The deterrence argument also retained its leading role among the objectives of international criminal justice in regard to the establishment and functioning of the International Criminal Court (ICC). The Office of Legal Affairs at the United Nations, involved in the drafting process of the Court's founding treaty, the Rome Statute, noted that "[e]ffective deterrence is a primary objective of those working to establish the international criminal court" (UN Office of Legal Affairs, 1998-1999). Similarly, in April 2002, the president of the UN General Assembly stated at the ceremony marking the entering into force of the Rome Statute that the court as a permanent institution will "provide much stronger deterrence to potential criminals" (UN General Assembly, 2002).

The actual functioning of the Court is also seen by many observers as a means to deter future crimes. Amnesty International (2004), for example, noted that the ICC was "now starting its very important work capable of providing long-term deterrence." This view, in fact, is shared by the Court (cf. International Criminal Court, 2005, paragraph 2). The preamble of the Rome Statute records that the Court exists for the "sake of present and future generations," and asserts that one of its primary goals is "the prevention of such crimes." Furthermore, when, in March 2005, the UN Security Council for the first time agreed to refer a situation to the ICC, Romania stated that "by deciding to refer the case of reported crimes in Darfur to the ICC, the Security Council enhances its conflict prevention and resolution capabilities" (Ambassador Motoc, Permanent Representative of Romania to the United Nations, UNSC 2005, p. 10). In the same meeting, France asserted that "referral to the International Criminal Court will prevent the violations from continuing" and sends a "very forceful message to all those who have committed or might be tempted to commit atrocities in Darfur" (Ambassador Jean-Marc de La

Sabliere, Permanent Representative of France to the United Nations, UNSC 2005, p. 8).[7]

Critical Challenges

Mechanisms of international criminal justice aim at contributing to a number of different objectives such as truth-finding, reconciliation, retribution, and deterrence. As with all the other objectives, the question arises how and whether it is possible, within the existing mechanisms and concepts, to make the deterrence argument work. Can the assumed correlation between prosecutions and deterrence be transferred from national law to international institutions such as the ad hoc tribunals and the International Criminal Court? And is it even desirable to witness a deterrence effect in the international context?

Lack of Empirical Documentation

One of the major issues arising in this context is that "the connection between international prosecutions and the actual deterrence of future atrocities is at best a plausible but largely untested assumption" (Wippman, 1999, p. 474; McGoldrick, 2004, pp. 456-57). Notwithstanding the numerous references to the deterrence argument in international case-law and policy statements, there is, to our knowledge, no empirical survey analyzing whether potential perpetrators are actually intimidated by the thought of a subsequent indictment.[8] Tellingly, very few of the proponents of the deterrence argument undertake to illustrate their case by citing what they consider to be concrete examples of how an international tribunal or court had a deterrent effect on the course of a conflict (one of the few undertaking such effort is Akhavan, 2001, p. 13ff). One critic of the International Criminal Court has, in fact, remarked that "[b]ehind their optimistic rhetoric, ICC proponents have not a shred of evidence supporting their deterrence theories....Why should anyone imagine that bewigged judges in The Hague will succeed where cold steel has failed?" (Bolton, 2002).

That said, the lack of empirical studies of a deterrent effect should not be taken for the actual non-existence of such an effect. Part and parcel of any deterrence based argumentation is that if it is successful no actual proof for the decisive influence of the presumably deterrent instrument will be available. Similarly, the argument that a certain state needs to acquire nuclear weapons to deter other states from attacking it can never be proven to be a valid statement, as one never will be able to prove whether history would have taken the same course without these additional weapons. Deterrence is only successful if what one fears does not happen, but to identify the exact reason for the absence of violence or attacks is difficult—and this is particularly true if the conduct in question is something as complex as the commission of genocide. There are thus some inherent difficulties to proving the deterrence argument. In addition, proponents of the deterrence argument have argued that when noting the absence of a deterrent effect, it is essential to realize that international efforts to bring war criminals to justice are a very recent phenomenon, which is slowly doing away with the so-called "culture of impunity." Given that for decades perpetrators could place trust in not being held accountable for their actions, the deterrence argument, according to this view, will start to show its true significance for practice when there no longer can be made the reproach of selectivity and when mass atrocities generally will be punished. Thus, if there is no empirical evidence for a deterrent effect yet, it is argued, it is only a matter of time until there are more international prosecutions.

Finally, it deserves mentioning that recent reports from the field suggest that there is a deterrent effect. Human Rights Watch's Sudan researcher Jemera Rone (2005) reported that the UN Security Council referral of the Darfur situation to the International Criminal Court proved to be "a real deterrent" in that people in Khartoum are now worried and are talking about "la Hague," that they might have to go The Hague. They are really worried" (n. p.). (For a similar account, see Power, 2005.) Nonetheless, the current lack of empirical evidence undermines the status of the deterrence argument as one of the bearing notions of international criminal justice.

The Unknown Modalities of Deterrence in International Criminal Prosecutions

The question of empirical proof is not the only objection raised against the deterrence argument. Several authors have expressed doubts as to the transferability of this notion from national criminal law to international criminal law. Assuming a shoplifter in a small community in rural France can be deterred by the threat of subsequent punishment—does this assumption also hold for dictator who perpetrate genocide or their henchmen? This and other questions pertaining to the unknown modalities of the deterrence argument in the international context shall be addressed below.

Who is Afraid of International Criminal Prosecutions?

National criminal codes build on the notion that the threat of punishment affects all perpetrators equally—both planners and those carrying out the criminal act, independent of their respective low, mid or high level of responsibility. In this regard, international criminal justice poses new questions, as international crimes such as crimes against humanity or genocide are based on a plan or policy involving thousands, ten thousands or even hundred thousands of individuals.[9] Looking by way of example at the events of Srebrenica in July 1995—who of the reported 19,000 involved in the mass executions, reaching from the private in the Bosnian Serb forces all the way up to the Bosnian Serb general Ratko Mladic and, possibly, the late former Yugoslav president Milosevic, is supposed to be afraid of international criminal prosecutions? Who does the deterrence argument aim at?

Facing this vast number and diversity of perpetrators, the deterrence argument is challenged in a twofold manner. First, on a practical level, it is necessary to recall that international criminal prosecutions only target those bearing the main responsibility. In regard to the Former Yugoslavia (i.e., the Balkan wars that occurred between 1991 and 1999) and the ICTY, only 161[10] persons (at the of writing) have been indicted for war crimes and other massive human rights violations (ICTY Website). The fact that only 161 people have been indicted by the ICTY raises the question as to what extent the deterrence argument can be maintained for this and other conflicts where, on a widespread and systematic basis, genocidal acts and other international crimes are carried out.

Beyond this limitation in the scope of international criminal prosecutions, a more fundamental objection to the deterrence argument has been made. More specifically, numerous scholars have asserted that those bearing the greatest responsibility will not be impressed by the threat of international criminal prosecutions (Klabbers, 2002, pp. 252-53; Wippman, 1999, pp. 479-80. For a more optimistic view, cf. Akhavan, 2001, pp. 7-8). Notably, the Chief US Prosecutor at the Nuremberg trial, Justice Robert Jackson, stated as far back as November 1945 that "[w]ars are started only on the theory and in the confidence that they can be won. Personal punishment, to be suffered only in the event that the war is lost, will probably not be a sufficient deterrent to prevent a war where the warmakers feel the chances of defeat are negligible" (Trial of the Major War Criminals before the International Military Tribunal, 1947, p. 153).

Similarly, to assume that genocidaires carry out their policies based on a cost-benefit analysis is a highly unlikely scenario.

Can Deterrence Work for Crimes such as Genocide?

Another objection to the deterrence argument is based on the specific characteristics of the crime of genocide. Genocide is based on the development of a genocidal mentality among the perpetrators. This mindset entails and justifies the dehumanization of the victim group and makes their extermination a necessary step towards the objectives formulated by the respective genocidal regime's ideology (Markusen, 2003, pp. 11-14). Genocide also stipulates the modification of moral, societal and legal norms, as the killing of the victims no longer is considered a crime, but as part of a larger project which lies at the centre of the genocidal mentality. In such a setting, in times of mass hysteria and perversion of norms, it is submitted, neither the sanctity of human rights nor the prohibition of genocide can hold out a meaningful appeal. The belief in the deterrent effect of subsequent prosecutions during genocide seems misplaced, as genocidaires, proceeding on orders coming from higher up in the system, neither will contemplate the wrongfulness of their doings nor take the threat of subsequent trials seriously. In the minds of the perpetrators, genocide means that the killing of the victims is necessary and right (see Klabbers, 2001, pp. 253ff, and Wippman, 1999, p. 479). In this regard, Benjamin Whitaker (1985), a UN special rapporteur on the UN Genocide Convention, concluded that "[t]hose personalities who are psychologically prepared to commit genocide are not always likely to be deterred by retribution, at least in this world" (paragraph 78).

The Unclear Time Horizon of the Deterrence Argument

The deterrence argument also entails questions about the timing of the preventive effect—when is it realistic to expect the target group to respond to the threat of international criminal prosecutions?

The ICTY, as previously noted, was established in 1993 to deter future atrocities. Nonetheless, the worst crimes committed during the Balkan wars—such as the massacres at Srebrenica in July 1995, the ethnic cleansing carried out under "Operation Storm" in the summer of 1995, and the ethnic cleansing campaign in Kosovo in spring 1999—occurred years after the ICTY prosecutors started their work. It seems, therefore, important to ask whether investigations and trials can at all make a difference during an ongoing conflict, or whether the numerous proceedings instituted in various countries over the last several years can only hope to influence those conflicts to come. While policy makers seem to see international criminal prosecutions as an instrument which can immediately affect an ongoing conflict, scholars have been more cautious and spoken of long term effects.[11]

Deterrence —Well-Intended, But in Reality Counterproductive and Irresponsible?

While most scholarly debate on the issue is aimed at questioning whether there is any deterrent effect of international criminal justice, there is another, more fundamental objection to the widespread endorsement of the deterrence argument in the case-law of the international war crimes tribunals. This objection is not about modalities, but questions whether deterrence constitutes a useful and responsible instrument vis-à-vis the resolution of ongoing or future conflicts. Authors such as Snyder and Vinjamuri (2003-2004) assert, instead, that the threat of prosecutions before a war crimes tribunal obstructs any attempt to find a political solution for the ongoing armed conflict (pp. 5-44).

War criminals will not lay down their weapons unless defeated or offered an amnesty, the argument goes, and the prospect of standing trial does not exactly serve as incentive to enter into negotiations. In fact, it is suggested, it may do the exact opposite, and prolong the conflict, as the faction responsible for the war crimes may see no other solution than to fight it out. Once indictments have been issued, additional war crimes may well be committed, as indicted war criminals may become convinced that there is nothing to lose.

This so-called "peace versus justice" debate drew considerable attention in policy circles during the 1990s when the first indictments issued by the ICTY were considered by some to impede international efforts to halt the atrocious conflict raging in Former Yugoslavia (D'Amato, 1994, pp. 500-507). This issue has also arisen in the practice of the newly established ICC, specifically in regard to ongoing investigations in Uganda and Darfur. As for the prosecution's activities in Uganda, some observers have voiced concern that the threat of accountability radicalized the leaders of the infamous Lord's Resistance Army, thus complicating negotiation efforts by the Ugandan central government (Akhavan, 2005). There is no certainty as to whether this assertion is correct, and thus one could also suggest the opposite—that is that the deterrence argument has had its effect on Ugandan government forces, too, possibly deterring further human rights violations on their part.[12]

In light of this objection to the deterrence argument, it is interesting to note that the ICC treaty entails a provision which can be interpreted to address this very matter. Pursuant to Article 16, the UN Security Council can halt an investigation or prosecution vis-à-vis a given conflict if the Council deems it necessary with regards to international peace and security. Until now, this provision has only been used to respond to the U.S. opposition against the ICC, but Article 16 also gives the Council the option to factor in concerns such as the ones raised by Snyder and Vinjamuri (2003-2004).[13]

Probabilities for Progress

The deterrence argument has been and is being challenged both on practical and policy grounds. How, then, can the argument being sustained that international war crimes prosecutions contribute to the prevention of future mass atrocities?

From a Culture of Impunity to a Culture of Accountability

As stated earlier, effective deterrence presupposes a legitimate expectation that violations of a norm will be sanctioned—in other words, it works on the expectation that norms will be enforced. For the field of human rights, the war crimes tribunals at Nuremberg and Tokyo were historic exceptions, but then for several decades, the international community neglected to muster the political will to prosecute perpetrators of war crimes, crimes against humanity and genocide.

Proponents of the deterrence argument assert that the wave of new international and internationalized war crimes tribunals that have of late addressed past wrongs in the Former Yugoslavia, Rwanda, East Timor, and elsewhere have the potential of affecting the expectations of war criminals. What earlier in this chapter was dubbed the "culture of impunity" will, it is argued, turn into a "culture of accountability," and this will strengthen the deterrence argument. Particular attention is usually drawn to the fact that the ICC is the first permanent institution of its kind, underscoring the international commitment to prosecute war crimes and making the threat of indictments ever more immediate.

A Widened Understanding of the Deterrence Argument

In this chapter and in most scholarly publications on this matter, the deterrence argument is understood to describe the potential preventive effect stemming from convincing actual or potential perpetrators that they will be held accountable for their deeds. Taking the inherent complexities of this assumption discussed above into account, it seems worthwhile to contemplate other possible preventive effects of international prosecutions (see also Del Ponte, 2005).

One characteristic of proceedings before international criminal tribunals is that they aim only at those with the greatest responsibility for the human rights violations in question. This is a fact that is sometimes difficult to convey to the victims who naturally focus on the person who did wrong to them and their loved ones. However, this focus on the main architects potentially contributes to preventing the underlying conflict from breaking out again. Over half of contemporary armed conflicts restart within the first five years after the first, provisional, cessation of the hostilities. Therefore, to remove the main "spoilers" may have a concrete preventive effect.[14] Moreover, the sentences meted out by war crimes tribunals serve a retributive purpose, thus making calls for vigilantism less forceful among survivors.

Finally, international criminal tribunals contribute to establishing the truth about the conflict at hand; denial becomes impossible and guilt is individualized instead of being placed on a people as a collectivity. This, too, is a related, preventive effect stemming from punishing war criminals. Since genocidal regimes often base their propaganda on construed, biased versions of historical conflicts, internationally affirmed records that have gone through the scrutiny of legal court proceedings will make such claims considerably more difficult (Douglas, 2001).

The aforementioned preventive effects are, of course, as difficult to document as the deterrence argument itself, but they add important facets. More research in this regard may, in fact, help to strengthen the notion that punishment contributes to prevention.

Conclusion

The current ICC activities concerning the situation in Darfur will hopefully provide new, important insights into the existence, scope and usefulness of the deterrent argument in international war crimes investigations. After the ICTY, it will, only for the second time, involve an international body in considering indictments against leaders of a sitting government in an ongoing conflict.[15]

If any Sudanese government official or *Janjaweed* militia leader is indicted, it will be worth following what, if any, implications such a move has on the underlying conflict. This being said, there is the danger that such indictments will not be enforceable, as the Sudanese government has repeatedly expressed that it will not cooperate with the ICC. If any given ICC indictment proves to be an empty threat, this again will have repercussions for the validity of the deterrence argument.

The deterrence argument has proven popular with judges at international war crimes tribunals and many other proponents of the international criminal justice system. Our brief overview urges scholars and others to be wary of the deterrence mantra and to critically question the frequent references made to it. In fact, more research investigating the existence, scope and usefulness of the deterrent effect of international prosecutions is needed.

In conclusion, it should be recalled that in terms of genocide prevention even consistent and effective punishment of war criminals and genocidaires simply one of the numerous instruments the international community can, and must, draw upon. In light of the inherent difficulties with the deterrent argument discussed throughout this chapter, those concerned with prevention must avoid making this argument/instrument as a substitute for effective and forceful measures of prevention.

Notes

1. In January 2004, representatives of fifty-five governments, invited by the Swedish Prime Minister Goran Persson, came to Stockholm to discuss "key issues of humanitarian, political and moral nature relating to genocide" in relation to genocide prevention. The conference (The Fourth Stockholm International Forum 2004: "Preventing Genocide; Threats and Responsibilities") included sessions focusing on various aspects of genocide prevention such as early warning systems, the role of media and hate propaganda as well as the employment of justice as a tool for prevention. Only one session, "Retributive Justice as a Deterrent?" was devoted to examining deterrence as prevention. On this panel, Yale Law School Senior Fellow Payam Akhavan noted that the primary focus of international criminal justice should be prevention of aberrant contexts "through deterrence of those in leadership positions." Another panelist, Edina Becirevic from the Faculty of Criminal Justice Science in Sarajevo, addressed the challenges to the International Criminal Tribunal for the Former Yugoslavia, for example its remoteness from the place of the conflict and its ability to contribute to reconciliation. Becirevic asserted that she believed that reconciliation as well as "setting the historical record straight" were two of the most important factors in preventing future atrocities. At the end of the conference the government delegations convened to adopt a joint declaration on genocide prevention which very strikingly has no mention

2. of the word deterrence. Conference speeches, option papers and the concluding document are available at HYPERLINK "http://www.preventinggenocide.com/" http://www.preventinggenocide.com/
2. For an overview of the most common criticisms see Mennecke and Markusen, 2003, pp. 297ff. Most of the current critics of the UNGC, however, have not taken note of the evolving case-law of the International Criminal Tribunals for Rwanda and Former Yugoslavia and how this reflects significant new interpretations of the legal definition of genocide, addressing many long-standing criticisms. In regard to these developments in the law, for example, see Schabas 2005, and Bjornlund, Markusen and Mennecke, 2005, pp. 17-48.
3. The other main objective behind punishment, retribution, is based on the notion *punitur, quia peccatum est* (punishment because there has been a crime); the deterrence argument is utilitarian in its nature and characterised by the idea of *punitur, ne peccetur* (punishment so there will be no crime). ICTY, Prosecutor v. Tadic, 11 November 1999, paragraph 9. For further examples from the ICTY and ICTR use of deterrence, see ICTY, Prosecutor v. Erdemovic, 19 November 1996, paragraph 64; ICTR, Prosecutor v. Kayishema and Ruzindana, 21 May 1999, paragraph 2; ICTR, Prosecutor v. Serushago, 5 February 1999, paragraph 20; ICTR, Prosecutor v. Akayesu, 2 October 1998, paragraph 19. See for the ICTY also Sayers, 2003, p. 759 with further references.
4. Be that as it may, the extraordinary pace of events across the globe quickly stalled any serious contemplation of the reasoning behind the growing efforts to construct an international system of criminal justice.
5. On the link between the deterrence argument and the founding of the international criminal tribunals, see for example UNSC Resolution, 25 May 1993, paragraphs 4-7, that speaks of establishing the ICTY to "put an end to such crimes."
6. A joint statement signed by the chief prosecutors of the ICC, ICTR, ICTY and Special Court for Sierra Leone on 27 November 2004 asserts that international criminal justice institutions "contribute to the prevention of future crimes" and that "a sustained commitment to accountability will deter these atrocities" (Crane et al., 2004).
7. For a similar view of the effect of a Security Council referral to the ICC, see "Report of the High-Level Panel on Threats, Challenges and Change," 2004, paragraph 90.
8. An informal survey, conducted by the authors in spring 2005, among relevant international institutions and NGOs such as Human Rights Watch, Amnesty International, the ICC Outreach Office, the Coalition for the International Criminal Court, the ICTY Office of the Registrar, the Max Planck Institute for Comparative Public Law and International Law, the International Center for Transitional Justice, the Special Court for Sierra Leone, the ICTR and the Coalition for International Justice confirmed the lack of empirical data.
9. For the Rwandan genocide of 1994, the exact number of perpetrators is unknown, but NGO experts monitoring local efforts to hold genocidaires accountable estimate that there are some 400,000-500,000 perpetrators. Cf. Penal Reform International, 2004, pp. 12-13. Concerning the massacres committed during the Bosnian war at Srebrenica in July 1995, a Bosnian commission of experts published in October 2005 a list with 19,000 names of personnel implicated in the killings. See Nicholas Wood, 2005.
10. Again, it is worth noting that some 19,000 individuals, alone, were reported to have been involved in the mass killings at Srebrenica in July 1995.

11. For the policy perspective, see, for example, Amnesty International, 2004, and the references given supra page 8 in regards to the UN Security Council referral of the Darfur situation to the ICC—UNSC 2005, pp. 8, 10. For a more skeptical stance by an academic expert, see Akhavan, 2001, pp. 10-13.
12. For a critical account of the Ugandan government forces' conduct and the complex role of the International Criminal Court in the conflict see the comprehensive report published by Human Rights Watch, September 23, 2005.
13. On the relationship between the ICC and the UN Security Council and the related US concerns, cf. Sarooshi, 2004, pp. 95-122. It is also interesting to note that the UN Security Council resolution that referred the Darfur situation to the ICC provides for a reference to this Article 16 of the ICC treaty, cf. UN Resolution, 2005, paragraph 2.
14. The example of Sierra Leone is a point in case. Being one of the main players in the civil war in Sierra Leone, former Liberian President Charles Taylor was indicted by the Special Court for Sierra Leone, but for a long while escaped justice by hiding in exile in Nigeria. His continuing influence on the political processes in countries in the region was characterized as destablizing and dangerous. See, for example, the press release by Human Rights Watch, 24 May 2005. In March of 2006, though, he was captured.
15. Due to practical and political reasons, the ICTY's role during the war in Bosnia remained limited. The indictment against Slobodan Milosevic, for example, was only issued late in the Kosovo war on 24 May 1999.

References

Akhavan, Payam (2001): "Beyond Impunity: Can International Criminal Justice Prevent Future Atrocities?" *American Journal of International Law*, 95(1):7-31

Akhavan, Payam (2005). "The Lord's Resistance Army Case: Uganda's Submission of the First State Referral to the International Criminal Court." *American Journal of International Law*, 99(2): 403-421

Amnesty International (2004). "Justice and the Rule of Law: The Role of the United Nations." Statement by Amnesty International. September 30. Available at http://web.amnesty.org/library/Index/ENGIOR400142004?open&of=ENG-385.

Bjornlund, Matthias; Markusen, Eric; and Mennecke, Martin (2005). "Que es el genocidio? En la bùsqueda de un denominador comùn entre definiciones jurìdicas y no jurìdicas," pp. 17-48. In Daniel Feierstein (Ed.) *Genocidio: La Administracion de la Muerte en la Modernidad*. Blackwell, London.

Bolton, John R. (2002). "The United Status and the International Criminal Court. Remarks at the Aspen Institute. Berlin, Germany, September 16. Available at http://www.state.gov/t/us/rm/13538.htm (last visited on 11 October 2005)

Crane, David; Ocampo, Luis Moreno; Del Ponte, Carla; Jallow, Hassan Bubacar (2004). Joint Statement of the Prosecutors of the International Criminal Court, the International Criminal Tribunal for the former Yugoslavia, the International Criminal Tribunal for Rwanda, and the Special Court for Sierra Leone, November 27. Available at www.iccnow.org/documents/statements/others/JointDeclarationProsecutors26Nov04.pdf

D'Amato, Anthony (1994). "Peace vs. Accountability in Bosnia." *American Journal of International Law*, 88(3): 500-507.

Del Ponte, Carla (2005). "The Dividends of International Criminal Justice." Address at Goldman Sachs, London, October 6. URL: http://www.un.org/icty/pressreal/2005/speech/cdp-goldmansachs-050610-e.htm

Douglas, Lawrence (2001). *The Memory of Judgment: Making Law and History in the Trials of the Holocaust.* New Haven, CT: Yale University Press.

Hamann, Louis; Hoge, Warren; and Jenkins, Tom (2004). "Preventing Genocide: Interview with Juan E. Mendez." *World Chronicle*, September 7, No. 947. Available at HYPERLINK http://www.un.org/webcast/worldchron/trans947.pdf

Human Rights Watch (24 May 2005). "UN Security Council: Ensure Justice in West Africa." Press release, May 24. Available at http:// hrw.org/english/docs/2005/05/24/sierra11004.htm

Human Rights Watch (2005). *Uprooted and Forgotten: Impunity and Human Rights Abuses in Northern Uganda. Human Rights Watch Report.* New York: Author. September 23. Available at http://hrw.org/reports/2005/uganda0905.

International Criminal Court (1 August 2005). *Report of the International Criminal Court to the United Nations.* (UN Doc. GA/60/177, 1 August 2005).

International Criminal Tribunal for the Former Yugoslavia (11 November 1999). The Prosecutor v. Dusko Tadic, Case No. IT-94-1. Sentencing Judgement.

International Criminal Tribunal for the Former Yugoslavia (29 November 1996). The Prosecutor v. Erdemovic, Case No. IT-96-22-T, Sentencing Judgement.

International Criminal Tribunal for the Former Yugoslavia website. URL: http://www.un.org/icty/glance/index.htm (last visited 11 October 2005).

International Criminal Tribunal for Rwanda (21 May 1999). The Prosecutor v. Clément Kayishema and Obed Ruzindana, Case No. ICTR-95-1-T. Sentence (Trial Chamber).

International Criminal Tribunal for Rwanda (4 September 1998). The Prosecutor v. Jean Kambanda, Case No. ICTR 97-23-S. Judgement (Trial Chamber).

International Criminal Tribunal for Rwanda (2 October 1998). The Prosecutor v. Jean-Paul Akayesu, Case No. ICTR-96-4-T. Sentence.

International Criminal Tribunal for Rwanda (5 February 1999). The Prosecutor v. Omar Serushago, Case No. ICTR-98-39-S. Sentence.

Klabbers, Jan (2001). "Just Revenge? The Deterrence Argument in International Criminal Law." *Finnish Yearbook of International Law*, 12:249-267.

Markusen, Eric (2003). "The Genocidal Mentality at the Dawn of the Twenty-First Century." *The Aegis Review on Genocide*, 1:11-14

Mennecke, Martin, and Markusen, Eric (2003). "The International Criminal Tribunal for the Former Yugoslavia and the Crime of Genocide," pp. 293-359. In Steven L. B. Jensen (Ed.) *Genocide: Cases, Comparisons and Contemporary Debates.* Copenhagen: Danish Institute for International Studies.

McGoldrick, Dominic (2004). "Legal and Political Significance of a Permanent ICC," pp. 453-478. In Dominic McGoldrick, Peter Rowe and Eric Donnelly (Eds.) *The Permanent International Criminal Court: Legal and Policy issues. Studies in International Law, Volume 5.* Oxford: Hart Publishing.

McGoldrick, Dominic (1999). "The Permanent International Criminal Court: An End to the Culture of Impunity?" *Criminal Law Review*, August, 627-655.

McGoldrick, Dominic; Rowe, Peter and Donnelly, Eric (Eds.) (2004). *The Permanent International Criminal Court: Legal and Policy Issues; Studies in International Law, Volume 5.* Oxford: Hart Publishing.

Mendez, Juan E. (2005). "Opening Address." Ultimate Crime, Ultimate Challenge—Human Rights and Genocide: International Conference." Yerevan, Armenia, April 20, 2005. Available at http://www.armeniaforeignministry.com/conference/juan_e_mendez.pdf

"Moscow Declaration on Atrocities, Issued on 1 November 1943. Signed by President Roosevelt, Prime Minister Churchill and Premier Stalin." Available at http://www.yale.edu/lawweb/avalon/wwii/moscow.htm

Penal Reform International (May 2004). *From Camp to Hill: The Reintegration of Released Prisoners. Research Report on the Gacaca. Report VI.* Available at http://www.penalreform.org/download/Gacaca/Rapport%20VI_AG.pdf

Power, Samantha (2005). "Court of First Resort." *New York Times*, February 10, n. p.

Report of the High-level Panel on Threats, Challenges and Change (2004). *A More Secure World: Our Shared Responsibility. Report to the Secretary-General Kofi Annan.* December. Available at http://www.un.org/tosecureworld/

Rone, Jemera (2005). "Darfur, War Crimes, the International Criminal Court, and the Quest for Justice". Transcript of a Brookings Briefing on Friday, February 25, 2005. Washington, D.C.: The Brookings Institution. Available at http://www.brook.edu/comm/events/20050225.htm

Sarooshi, Dan (2004). "The Peace and Justice Paradox: The International Criminal Court and the UN Security Council," pp. 95-122. In Dominic McGoldrick, Peter Rowe and Eric Donnelly (Eds.) *The Permanent International Criminal Court: Legal and Policy Issues. Studies in International Law, Volume 5.* Oxford: Hart Publishing.

Sayers, Steven M. (2003). "Defence Perspectives on Sentencing Practice in the International Criminal Tribunal for the Former Yugoslavia." *Leiden Journal of International Law*, 16:751-776.

Schabas, William A. (2005). "The Odious Scourge: Evolving Interpretations of the Crime of Genocide." Speech presented at "Ultimate Crime, Ultimate Challenge—Human Rights and Genocide: An International Conference, Yerevan, Armenia, April 20. Available at http://www.armeniaforeignministry.com/conference/w_schabas.pdf

"Second Day, Wednesday, 11/21/1945, part 24," pp. 152-155. From *Trial of the Major War Criminals before the International Military Tribunal, Vol. II.* 1947. 11/14/1945-11/30/1945. Nuremberg: International Military Tribunal.

Snyder, Jack and Vinjamuri, Leslie (2003-2004). "Trials and Errors. Principle and Pragmatism in Strategies of International Justice." *International Security*, 28(3):5-44.

United Nations Security Council (2005). *UN Doc. S/PV.5158l.* March 31. Available at http://daccessdds.un.org/doc/UNDOC/PRO/N05/292/47/PDF/N0529247

United Nations General Assembly (2002). "General Assembly President Says Permanent International Criminal Court Will Provide Much Stronger Deterrence Than Ad Hoc Tribunals." Press release. (UN Doc. GA/SM/282, L/T/4367, 11 April 2002). Available at HYPERLINK http://www.un.org/News/Press/docs/2002/gasm282.doc.htm

United Nations Office of Legal Affairs, Codifications Division (1998-1999). "Overview of Rome Statute of the International Criminal Court." Available at http://www.un.org/law/icc/general/overview.htm

United Nations Secretary General (2004). "'Risk of Genocide Remains Frighteningly Real' Secretary-General Tells Human Rights Commission as He Launches Action Plan to Prevent Genocide." Press release, April 7. (UN Doc. SG/SM/9245, AFR/893, HR/CN/1077). Available at http://www.un.org/News/Press/docs/2004/sgsm9245.doc.htm

United Nations Secretary General (2004). *The Rule of Law and Transitional Justice in Conflict and Post-conflict Societies: Report of the Secretary-General.* (UN Doc. S/2004/616, 23 August 2004)

United Nations Security Council (1993). *Provisional Verbatim Record of the 3217th Meeting.* held at U. N. Head Quarters, New York, on Tuesday, May 25. (UN Doc. S/Trans. 3217, 25 May 1993).

United Nations Security Council (2005). *United Nations Resolution 1593.* (UN Doc. S/Res/1593, 31 March 2005). Available at http://daccessdds.un.org/doc/UNDOC/GEN/N05/292/73/PDF/N0529273.pdf?

United Nations Security Council (1993). *United Nations Security Council Resolution 827.* (UN DOC S/Res/827, 25 May 1993). Available at http://www.ohr.int/other-doc/un-res-bih/pdf/827e.pdf

Whitaker, Benjamin (1985). *Revised and Updated Report on the Question of the Prevention and Punishment of the Crime of Genocide.* UN Doc. E/CN.4/Sub.2/1985/6.

Wippman, David (1999). "Atrocities, Deterrence, and the Limits of International Justice." *Fordham International Law Journal*, 23(2):473-488.

Wood, Nicholas (2005). "From List of 19,000, 90 More Trials." *International Herald Tribune.* October 6, n. p.

Annotated Bibliography

Co-authored by Martin Mennecke and Elisabeth Moltke

Akhavan, Payam (2001). "Beyond Impunity: Can International Criminal Justice Prevent Future Atrocities?" *American Journal of International Law*, 95 (1): 7-31.

Akhavan is one of the few writers on the subject of deterrence who combines scholarly interest with extensive practical experience. A former legal adviser to the Office of the Prosecutor at the International Criminal Tribunal for the Former Yugoslavia, he has consulted with several governments on issues of transitional justice, including cooperation with the ICC. Herein, Akhavan concedes from the outset that "measuring the capacity of punishment to prevent criminal conduct is an elusive undertaking." However, he contends, if the deterrence argument is phrased realistically and backed by an international willingness to enforce indictments by arresting suspects, war crimes tribunals can have a long term effect and thus contribute to prevent the outbreak of violence or the resumption of such. To substantiate his thesis, Akhavan analyses the impact of international criminal justice efforts in Former Yugoslavia, Rwanda, and, in passing, Sierra Leone and Indonesia. Akhavan offers elaborate reviews of the deterrent effect of particular indictments, but also makes unsubstantiated assertions such as that the ICTY indictment against Slobodan Milosevic "at least marginally discouraged anti-Serb vengeance by the Kosovo Liberation Army."

Aukerman, Miriam J. (2002). "Extraordinary Evil, Ordinary Crime: A Framework for Understanding Transitional Justice." *Harvard Human Rights Journal*, Spring, 15:39-97.

Aukerman examines the theory, goals and principles of transitional justice, covering issues such as retribution, deterrence, rehabilitation, restorative justice. She also outlines a new framework for understanding transitional justice. On the issue of deterrence, the article pays particular attention to the observation that deterrence is often used interchangeably with prevention, when in fact deterrence is only one way to prevent crime. She further distinguishes between the "theory of deterrence" and "deterrence in transitional justice," where she questions whether *genocidaires* are likely to dwell on rational cost-benefit considerations. Aukerman stresses the point that prosecution is not self evidently the most effective means for preventing atrocities. The mere threat of prosecutions when atrocities occur will, according to Aukerman, ring hollow and not contribute to deterrence if it is not preceded by more active efforts of prevention by the international community. In her own words "the international community has bigger sticks to shake than the threat of trial."

Bass, Gary Jonathan (2000). *Stay the Hand of Vengeance—The Politics of War Crimes Tribunals*. Princeton, NJ: Princeton University Press. 424 pp.

This highly-praised publication provides a systematic and comparative overview of the politics of international war crimes tribunals. In doing so, Bass analyses numerous historic examples of efforts to prosecute war criminals and places them into both a liberal and a realist perspective to illustrate how they fit into different schools of international relations. Bass admonishes against naïve expectations about what international criminal justice may accomplish and recalls the realists' notion of self-interest as the predominant factor in international affairs. This reminder he sees as "a welcome corrective against the occasionally otherworldly musings of some international lawyers." Concerning the deterrence argument, Bass notes that proponents of international prosecutions "for about a century" have argued that potential war criminals will be deterred, but according to his analysis the historical record it is far from clear as to whether tribunals "have much of a deterrent effect, either in the near- or long-term." Looking at the different examples, including Nazi war crimes and the atrocities committed at Srebrenica in 1995, Bass concludes that a deterrent effect only can materialize if there is a credible threat of prosecution —but even then "one should also keep one's expectations in check: war criminal are war criminals."

Chuter, David (2003). *War Crimes: Confronting Atrocity in the Modern World*. Boulder, CO: Lynne Rienner Publishers. 299 pp.

In this comprehensive study, Chuter explores why atrocities occur, what can be done to identify perpetrators and bring them to justice and stresses the need to situate terrible events in their proper historical and social contexts. On deterrence, Chuter refers to the problem of considering potential genocidaires to be rational cost-benefit actors and further argues that institutions of criminal justice have little or no deterrent effect if the offender does not believe he will get caught.

Drumbl, Mark A. (2005). "Collective Violence and Individual Punishment: The Criminality of Mass Atrocity." *Northwestern University Law Review*, 99 (2): 101-179.

This comprehensive and thought-provoking article takes as its point of departure the assertion that the normative and institutional framework of international criminal justice is to a large extent modeled after national criminal codes and their courts. According to Drumbl, international criminal law therefore remains "disappointingly ordinary" and incapable of capturing the specificities of mass atrocities such as genocide and crimes against humanity. As a consequence, it is submitted, scholars should revisit the traditional objectives of international criminal justice such as retribution and deterrence in order to develop more appropriate rationales and modalities.

Drumbl analyses the reasoning given for sentences at the different international war crimes tribunals and documents that retribution and deterrence are mentioned most often. Drumbl doubts, however, for a number of reasons, that the deterrence argument can work at the international level. He points to the difficulty of impressing *genocidaires* with the threat of criminal trials or of reaching the majority of bystanders that acquiesce in the crimes, but will not be punished. Interestingly, Drumbl raises the idea of collective responsibility and sanctioning which, it is submitted, could make the idea of deterrence by punishment work.

Henham, Ralph (2003). "The Philosophical Foundations of International Sentencing." *Journal of International Criminal Justice*, 1 (1): 64-85.

Ten years after the establishment of the International Criminal Tribunal for the Former Yugoslavia, Henham analyses the sentencing practice of international criminal tribunals. He criticizes the prominent role the notion of deterrence plays in international case-law from a philosophical point of view and suggests abandoning the utilitarian model, i.e. the idea of punishing the individual wrongdoer to teach him (or her) and the society a lesson about the link between a norm, a violation thereof and the subsequent punishment for such a breach. Instead, he suggests the need to base international criminal law on the notion of restorative justice. The article stresses the importance of rehabilitation and reconciliation and calls for a reassessment of the potential effects of international criminal trials.

Klabbers, Jan (2001). "Just Revenge? The Deterrence Argument in International Criminal Law." *Finnish Yearbook of International Law*, 12:249-267.

Klabbers responds in this article to the "waves of cheers and hoorays" international criminal justice efforts have prompted by asking why it is that all have fallen under the spell of "the beauty of bringing an end to the culture of impunity." Of all the reasons promoted for why punishment is the right thing, Klabbers focuses on the widely held deterrence argument. He rejects it, arguing that a person involved in massive human rights violations does not make a rational cost-benefit analysis of his conduct—he acts because he expects that "history will prove him right."

McGoldrick, Dominic; Rowe, Peter; and Donnelly, Eric (Eds.) (2004). *The Permanent International Criminal Court -- Legal and Policy Issues*. Oxford and Portland, OR: Hart Publishing. 498 pp.

This anthology, comprised of articles authored by leading scholars in the field, provides a comprehensive introduction to the historical and political context under which the International Criminal Court (ICC) was established. It includes a thorough analysis of a wide range of legal aspects of the court and comments on the different political and legal responses to the future significance of the court. A chapter by international lawyer Dominic McGoldrick directs attention to the objectives of the court such as, among others, deterrence. In a section on deterrence, the author directs attention to the lack of evidence of a deterrent effect of international justice such as Nuremberg, the ICTY and the ICTR, although at the same time notes the difficulty of measuring or proving a deterrent effect. McGoldrick believes that one of the future challenges vis-à-vis the extent to which prosecution at the ICC will prevent future atrocities is the dilemma of prosecution versus amnesties. He raises the question whether fear of prosecution among offenders may actually prolong a conflict because amnesties as a "face saving way out" are increasingly viewed as unacceptable by the international community, and thus whether offenders may be less inclined to settle a conflict or readily accept defeat.

Safferling, Christoph (2004). "Can Criminal Prosecutions be the Answer to Massive Human Rights Violations?" *German Law Journal*, 5 (12)n.p. Available at HYPERLINK "http://www.germanlawjournal.com"

This article reviews the role of international criminal law and its various institutions in responding to mass atrocities and suggests a cautious stance, arguing that law can play an important part in this process, but issues the reminder that that it is "far from being the panacea." Specifically addressing the topic of whether international prosecutions have a deterrent effect, Safferling remains skeptical and states that it "has certainly failed thus far." The section on deterrence includes numerous useful references to the literature on how this matter is framed in the national context, particularly in regard to issue of the death penalty in the United States.

Safferling, Christoph (1999). "The Justification of Punishment in International Criminal Law—Can National Theories of Justification be Applied to the International Level?" *Austrian Review of International and European Law*, 4: 126-163.

In scrutinizing the purpose and function of international penal proceedings, Safferling introduces the different concepts underlying Western notions of punishment, such as retribution and prevention, and assesses their transferability to the international level. Safferling asserts that international criminal law can perform a similar role as its domestic counterpart, if the international community provides for the requisite means of enforcement.

Simantob, Olivia (2002). "Aiming at the Right Target—Where to Focus the ICC's Deterrence Efforts." *Stanford Journal of International Relations*, 4 (1): 69-77.

The ratification of the International Criminal Court (ICC) is widely considered to be an immense step towards enforcing international criminal law and in particular those norms defining international crimes. Addressing the question of whether the ICC can deter future mass atrocities, Simantob sets out to "develop a framework for predicting the effectiveness of a well-equipped international court." She seeks to identify the principal motivations that lead to atrocities in order to propose how the ICC can maximize its efficiency by targeting the individuals most likely to be influenced by legal threats. On this basis, Simantob argues that the more realistic the expectations are with regards to realizing which types of individuals are less likely to be deterred, the more successful the court will be. This consideration includes those perpetrators who could be expected to view their actions according to a more rational cost-benefit calculation. In her concluding remarks, Simantob notes that, "[l]aw cannot be the only weapon against future atrocities—but the ICC and the international community do have the power to deter at least some war crimes. This is not a perfect system, but the life of every would-be victim will be a triumph for the International Criminal Court."

Snyder, Jack and Vinjamuri, Leslie (2003-2004). "Trials and Errors. Principle and Pragmatism in Strategies of International Justice." *International Security*, 28 (3): 5-44.

Looking at the field of transitional justice from an international relations perspective, Snyder and Vinjamuri question the recent trend towards prosecuting perpetrators of mass atrocities. They turn against what they call "activists and legalists" and assert that a strategy based on prosecutions "risks causing more atrocities than it would prevent, because it pays insufficient attention to political realities." Concerning the deterrence argument, the authors state that so far international criminal tribunals such as the ICTY have "utterly failed" to prevent massive human rights violations, while amnesties, as for example in El Salvador, "have been highly effective in curbing abuses when implemented in a credible way." Snyder's and Vinjamuri's argument is that "justice does not lead; it follows." Eventually, after the transition, a system of effective judicial institutions may be able to prevent atrocities, but if promoted too early such policy "is likely to be either counterproductive or simply irrelevant." Snyder and Vinjamuri build their argument on an analysis of numerous transitional justice scenarios from different continents and time periods, looking at war crimes tribunals, truth and reconciliation commissions, amnesties and other responses.

Tallgren, Immi (2002). "The Sensibility and Sense of International Criminal Law." *European Journal of International Law*, 13 (3): 561-595.

Tallgren starts out by noting that "everybody knows that prevention does not work, even if we hope it might one day" and continues by arguing that "international criminal justice carries this kind of a religious exercise of hope that is stronger than the desire to face everyday life." The article challenges the widespread belief that international criminal justice can function on the basis of the same utilitarian considerations as domestic systems and contends that the specific nature of international crimes rules out any significant deterrent impact of punishment. In this regard, Tallgren points to certain psychological factors such as group dynamics, superior orders and the sense of justice of the perpetrators that are different in the commission of genocide and crimes against humanity from cases of "normal" murder or robbery.

Triffterer, Otto (2001). "The Preventive and the Repressive Function of the International Criminal Court," pp. 137-175. In Mauro Politi and Giuseppe Nesi (Eds.) *The Rome Statute of the International Criminal Court*. Aldershot: Ashgate Publishing.

Triffterer examines the role and scope of the deterrence argument in the Rome Statute, the instrument that established the International Criminal Court (ICC). The bulk of the article constitutes a thorough discussion of how different provisions of the Rome Statute, such as its preamble and the section on sentencing, make implicit or explicit reference to the notion of deterrence. He also surveys how national criminal law conceptualizes deterrence, i.e., how it could be seen to affect the stage of planning a crime, of attempting a crime and of committing a crime. Triffterer mentions some of the criticisms of the deterrence argument and discusses some of the additional challenges arising at the international level, but also asserts that the ICC has a preventive function, both *qua* its existence as a permanent court and, later, when exercising its jurisdiction, by setting standards and establishing practice.

Wippman, David (1999). "Atrocities, Deterrence, and the Limits of International Justice." *Fordham International Law Journal*, 23: 473-488.

Highly critical of the general enthusiasm for international criminal prosecutions, Wippman notes that the connection between prosecutions and actual deterrence of future atrocities "is at best a plausible but largely untested assumption." Listing a number of objections, Wippman submits that potential *genocidaires* are not deterred by the slight risk of "losing the war crimes prosecution lottery." Wippman concludes that one should, at most, regard prosecutions as contributing to a culture of compliance and be wary of exaggerated claims concerning the benefits of prosecutions.

Wippman, David (2000). "Can an International Criminal Court Prevent and Punish Genocide?" pp. 85-105. In Neal Riemer (Ed.), *Protection Against Genocide: Mission Impossible?* London: Praeger Publishers.

While underlining the need for an International Criminal Court (ICC), Wippman raises a number of critical questions regarding its ability to effectively contribute to deterrence. Wippman refers to the Rome Statute as reflecting a political compromise entered into to obtain a maximum number of signatories at the cost of a strong, universal jurisdiction of the Court. Furthermore, non-participation by the United States significantly weakens the Court both politically and financially. Evaluating future prospects, Wippman suggests that the establishment of the ICC is an important step towards prevention and punishment, but time alone will tell how much of this depends on the involvement and support of key countries such as the U.S.

11

Building an Anti-Genocide Regime

Gregory H. Stanton

When the Genocide Convention was passed by the United Nations in 1948, the world said, "Never again."

But the history of the twentieth century instead proved that "never again" became "again and again." The promise the United Nations made was broken, as again and again, genocides and other forms of mass murder killed at least 170 million people, more than all the international wars of the twentieth century combined (Rummel, 1994).[1] Genocide, the devil on horseback, still rides unchecked, armed not with a scythe but with a Kalashnikov.

Why? Why are there still genocides? Why are there genocidal massacres being perpetrated in 2006 against the Fur, Massaleit, and Zaghawa in Darfur; and the Banyamulenge, Hutus, Hema, and Lendu in the Democratic Republic of the Congo? Why does ethnic and religious hatred still divide Côte d'Ivoire and Iraq and threaten to erupt again in genocidal violence? There are two primary reasons why genocide is still committed in the world:

1. The world has not developed the international institutions needed to predict and prevent it; and
2. The world's leaders do not have the political will to stop it.

In order to prevent genocide, we must first understand it. We must study and compare genocides and develop working theories about the genocidal process. There are many centers for the study of genocide that are doing that vital work in universities and research institutes in Europe, North America, Australia, and Israel. But studying genocide is not enough. Our next task should be to create the international institutions and political will to prevent it. Three institutions, in particular, are needed: (1) politically effective centers for genocide prevention; (2) rapid response forces for non-violent prevention and armed military response; and (3) effective international courts for punishment. To create political will, an international movement to end genocide must be built, requiring a massive educational, media and political campaign.

Creation of a Genocide Prevention Focal Point at the UN

The UN Security Council and key governments need strong, independent early warning systems to predict where and when ethnic conflict and genocide are going to occur, and to present options for prevention and intervention to policymakers. When The International Campaign to End Genocide (ICEG), a coalition of human rights organizations, attempted to contact officials at the UN about the genocidal massacres in East Timor in 1999, we discovered that no one had responsibility for receiving information or coordinating action about genocide. Therefore, in 2002, the ICEG recommended the creation of a Genocide Prevention "Focal Point" at the United Nations in New York, with a small permanent staff at the highest level that would receive information about risks of genocide and coordinate UN responses. UN officials in the Secretary-General's Office of Policy Planning at first warned about negative reactions by some member states to previous proposals for UN preventive capacity. But as the idea was discussed and refined, it gathered support from high ranking UN officials like Danilo Turk and Edward Mortimer, who recommended it to Secretary-General Kofi Annan.

The result was a proposal made at the Stockholm Forum on the Prevention of Genocide in 2004 by Gregory Stanton of Genocide Watch (Stanton, 2004a), which recommended appointment of a Special Adviser to the Secretary-General on the Prevention of Genocide and creation of an independent Genocide Prevention Center to support the Special Adviser's work. The Secretary-General announced his support for the proposal at the Stockholm Forum, and in July 2004, he created the new post and named Juan Mendez as his first Special Adviser on the Prevention of Genocide.

Establishment of a Genocide Prevention Center

Realizing that the United Nations has limited resources, the ICEG also recommended to the governments and nongovernmental organizations

(NGOs) attending the Stockholm Forum that an independent Genocide Prevention Center be established to support the work of the Special Adviser. The Center would be located in New York and staffed with full-time early warning, political and operational planning specialists who have direct access to an international network of government officials, country experts, human rights nongovernmental organizations (NGOs), and the Special Adviser's office. (Stanton, 2004b)

The Brahimi Report of the Panel on UN Peace Operations (2000) suggested such an office (the Information and Strategic Analysis Secretariat) at the UN, but its recommendations were blocked by states (mostly from the G-77 developing nations plus India and China) that considered such a function (i.e., "intelligence-gathering" into "domestic" affairs) beyond the UN's mandate. That is precisely why a Genocide Prevention Center must be independent of the UN, but on the UN's periphery, and considered by the Special Adviser to be a trusted source of reliable information. If the Center is not independent, it will be unable to issue opinions that displease member states, particularly states at risk or that are committing genocide. Yet it must have the confidence of the Special Adviser and develop a close informal relationship with him.[2] The Genocide Prevention Center would become a clearing house and validator for reports from human rights groups and open sources around the world. It would operationalize those reports into options and plans for preventive action, and the Special Adviser and the Secretary-General would use them to formulate recommendations to the UN Security Council.

One problem such a Center would face immediately is the closed nature of both government and UN information systems. Reports from UN field officials and government intelligence agencies are classified "confidential" or secret. Access to the country desk officers and top officials of the UN system would thus probably be indirect, through the Special Adviser. Access to government intelligence reports remains unlikely. However, the open secret of the new information age is that policy-makers would get better information if they ran a daily algorithm of world news media for early warning signs, and regularly read leading newspapers, magazines, and human rights groups' reports, than if they counted on their embassies' classified cables. Several such open source, unclassified reporting services (IRIN, Reliefweb) provide daily collections of articles to the UN and others interested in reading them. However, none currently focus on potential genocide.

Even before a Genocide Prevention Center is established, coalitions of NGOs and genocide studies programs should establish independent early warning networks that can provide daily reports and regular policy options papers to the UN's Special Adviser on the Prevention of Genocide, to the Security Council and to individual governments. A few networks currently exist (see Harff, "The Development and Implementation of Genocide Early Warning Systems," in this volume) but they do not yet produce coordinated analyses. Even after a Genocide Prevention Center is established, NGOs should continue to provide reports independently to the Special Adviser, UN agencies, and member governments. The Center is not intended to be a unique source.

Briefings could be given to the Security Council by the Special Adviser. Although, the first attempt by the Special Adviser to give such a briefing on Darfur was blocked by objections from the U.S., China, Russia, and Algeria (Reuters, 10 Oct. 2005), the Secretary-General, himself, could exercise his prerogative under Article 99 of the UN Charter to "bring to the attention of the Security Council any matter which in his opinion may threaten the maintenance of international peace and security."

Early Warning Models

Early warning models matter. They must be comprehensible to policy makers, and provide specific guidance. The UN Office for Coordination of Humanitarian Affairs and the U.S. Central Intelligence Agency have each had contracts with social scientists who use multi-variate, statistical models to predict the likelihood of genocide and other forms of violence. The models assign country scores to a large number of abstract risk factors ("level of democracy, trade openness, history of armed conflict, ethnic diversity") and then assess the risk of genocide from their sum (Harff, 2003; Krain, 1997). The models are useful to the extent that they demonstrate the benefit of promotion of democracy and other general policies. But statistical models do not describe the intentional process by which political leaders push a society toward genocide. They therefore are not sufficient to formulate specific counter-measures at each stage of the genocidal process.

To provide immediate early warning signs, Harff (1998) has identified accelerators and triggers that may lead to genocide. They include refugee and internally displaced persons flows, compulsory visible identification of targeted groups, arming of ethnic militias, hate speech, killing of opposition leaders, and massacres. However, Harff's accelerators are not ordered within the predictable process of genocide, the stages that all genocides follow, and therefore fail to predict how close a genocide may be. So that policy-makers can recognize early warning signs and plan specific counter-measures at each stage to stop the process, Stanton (1998/2005) has proposed a structural theory of the genocidal process, "The Eight Stages of Genocides":

1. *Classification*: Underlying most social scientists' theories of genocide is an image of "ethno-centric man." Because all people grow up and live in particular cultures, speaking particular languages, they identify some people as "us" and others as "them." This fundamental first stage in the process does not necessarily lead to genocide. Genocide only becomes possible with another common human tendency—considering only "our group" as human, and "de-humanizing" certain others. Thus, we not only develop cultural centers, we also create cultural boundaries that shut other groups out—and the latter may become the boundaries where solidarity ends and hatred begins. "Us versus them" can be converted by political elites desiring to gain or retain power into ideologies of purity, exclusion, and destruction (Valentino, 2004). Regimes bent on genocide take great pains to classify their populations. The main preventive measure at this early stage is to develop universalistic institutions that transcend ethnic or racial divisions, that actively promote tolerance and understanding, and that promote classifications that transcend the divisions.

2. *Symbolization*: Names or other symbols are assigned to the classifications. People are named "Jews" or "Gypsies," or distinguished by colors or dress. When combined with hatred, symbols may be forced upon unwilling members of pariah groups: e.g. yellow stars for Jews. To combat symbolization, hate symbols can be legally forbidden (swastikas) as can hate speech. If widely supported, resistance to such symbolization by those outside the targeted group can be powerful, depriving it of its significance.

3. *Dehumanization*: One group denies the humanity of the other group. Members of "the other group" are equated with animals, vermin, insects or diseases. Dehumanization overcomes the normal human revulsion against murder.

    At this stage, hate propaganda in print and on hate radios is used to vilify the victim group. In combating dehumanization, incitement to commit genocide should not be confused with protected speech. Genocidal societies lack constitutional protection for countervailing speech, and should be treated differently than democracies. Hate radio stations should be shut down, and hate propaganda banned.

4. *Organization*: Genocide is always organized, usually by the state, though sometimes informally (Hindu mobs led by local RSS militants) or by terrorist groups. Special army units or militias are often trained and armed. Plans are made for genocidal killings. To combat this stage, membership in such militias should be outlawed. Their leaders should be arrested and denied visas for foreign travel. The UN should impose arms embargoes on governments and citizens of countries involved in genocidal massacres, and international commissions should investigate crimes against humanity.

5. *Polarization*: Extremists drive the groups apart. Hate groups broadcast polarizing propaganda. Laws may forbid intermarriage or social interaction. Extremist terrorism targets moderates, intimidating and silencing the center.

    Prevention may mean security protection for moderate leaders or assistance to human rights groups. Assets of extremists may be seized, and visas for international travel denied to them. Coups d'état by extremists should be opposed by international sanctions.

6. *Preparation*: Victims are identified and separated out because of their ethnic or religious identity. Death lists are drawn up. Members of victim groups are forced to wear identifying symbols. They are often segregated into ghettoes, forced into concentration camps, or confined to a famine-struck region and starved. At this stage, a Genocide Emergency should be declared. If the political will of the UN Security Council or NATO can be mobilized, armed international intervention should be prepared, or heavy assistance given to the victim group to prepare for its self-defense. Otherwise, at least humanitarian assistance should be organized by the UN and private relief groups for the inevitable tide of refugees.

7. Extermination: Extermination quickly becomes the mass killing legally called "genocide." It is "extermination" to the killers because they do not believe their victims to be fully human. When it is sponsored by the state, the armed forces often work with militias to do the killing. Sometimes the genocide results in revenge killings by groups against each other, creating the downward whirlpool-like cycle of bilateral genocide, as in Burundi.

    At this stage, only rapid and overwhelming armed intervention can stop genocide. Real safe areas or refugee escape corridors should be established with heavily armed international protection. (False "safe areas" are worse than none, because they only concentrate the victims.) A multilateral force authorized by the UN, led by NATO or a regional military power, should intervene. Militarily powerful nations should provide the airlift, equipment, and financial means necessary for the intervention.

8. *Denial*: is the eighth stage that always follows a genocide. It is among the surest indicators of further genocidal massacres. The perpetrators of genocide dig up the mass graves, burn the bodies, try to cover up the evidence and intimidate the witnesses. They deny that they committed any crimes, and often blame what happened on the victims. They block investigations of the crimes, and continue to govern until driven from power by force, when they flee into exile. There they remain with impunity unless they are captured and a tribunal is established to try them. The best response to denial is punishment by an international tribunal or national courts. There the evidence can be heard, and the perpetrators punished.

Rapid Response Forces

Early warning is not enough. What if the UN Security Council passed a resolution to implement a peace agreement, and sent in peace-keepers, but then genocide began? That is what happened in Rwanda. There were plenty of early warnings. The UN Assistance Mission in Rwanda (UNAMIR) commander, General Roméo Dallaire, learned of the plans for the genocide three months before it began, had conclusive evidence of massive shipments of half a million machetes to arm the killers, and knew of the training camps for the *Interahamwe* genocidists. Yet, when he cabled the UN Department of Peacekeeping Operations requesting authorization to confiscate the machete caches, Undersecretary for Peacekeeping Operations Kofi Annan's deputy, Iqbal Riza, refused, claiming the action would exceed UNAMIR's mandate. Then, when the genocide actually began in April 1994, Dallaire desperately asked for a mandate and reinforcements to protect the thousands of Tutsis who had taken refuge in churches and stadiums. Led by the U.S., the Security Council instead voted to pull out all 2,500 UNAMIR troops. General Dallaire has since said that even those troops could have saved hundreds of thousands of lives, had they remained (Stanton, 2004c).

Among the problems with UN peacekeeping forces is that they are composed of national troop contingents voluntarily contributed by risk-averse national governments, and may even take their orders from those governments rather than their UN commanders. Such forces take months to organize and are seldom composed of the world's best-trained and adequately equipped soldiers.[3]

One regional military alliance lacks is without drawbacks -- NATO. It has a coordinated command structure, extremely well-trained troops, and major resources. It proved to be quite effective once it was mobilized in Bosnia and Kosovo in the 1990s. But it has only begun to contribute to peace-keeping operations outside of Europe. The Standing High Readiness Brigade organized by Denmark, Austria, Canada, The Netherlands, Norway, Poland and Sweden in 1996 (since expanded to include Finland, Italy, Ireland, Lithuania, Portugal, Romania, Slovenia, and Spain) was organized to provide a rapid response force of 5,000 heavy infantry and support personnel to the UN Security Council on thirty days' notice. It has thus far assisted Chapter VI (peacekeeping efforts with the consent of the host country) monitoring missions in Ethiopia/Eritrea, Liberia, and Sudan. The European Union (EU) is currently organizing thirteen 1,500 person battle groups ready to respond within ten days to decisions by the EU. Be that as it may, the EU is likely to be hamstrung by the requirement for unanimity in its foreign policy decision making.

The United Nations eventually needs a standing, volunteer, professional rapid response force that does not depend on member governments' contributions of brigades from their own armies. A standing UN force would need the support of at least some of the major military powers, must be large enough to effectively intervene in situations like Rwanda, and should be composed of volunteers from around the world, the best of the best, who train together specifically for UN peace operations. Its capabilities and training would need to include many non-military functions, including policing, administration of justice, and conflict transformation. Although the U.S. and other Permanent 5 members of the Security Council do not currently support creation of such a standing UN force, it is an idea whose time will come.

Non-Violent Intervention

We must build institutions to intervene non-violently before genocide begins. Every church, synagogue, mosque, and temple should teach peace-making, and inter-religious leaders' councils should be formed wherever there is religious division. In ethnically divided societies, radio and television and educational systems should be used to advocate tolerance and to humanize the other groups in the society, to show that they are like "us."

The 2005 report of the *UN High Level Panel on Threats, Challenges, and Change* (2005) recommended creation of a UN Peacebuilding Commission to be tasked with prevention of conflict and state failure. The problem with the recommendation is that most genocide does not arise out of state failure or conflict. It is the result of unchecked state power.

The Carnegie Commission Report on Preventing Deadly Conflict (1997) is the best known example of the common assumption that conflict prevention will also prevent genocide. Conflict prevention is often a laudable goal, and sometimes it will contribute to genocide prevention. But it often will not. Jews had no conflict with Germans, nor did Armenians with Turks. In Rwanda, Kuperman (2001) argues that the Arusha Accords actually increased the likelihood of genocide when the Hutu Power elite realized they would lose their grip on power if the Accords were implemented. Faced with the negotiated reduction in their power, they instead decided to kill every Tutsi in Rwanda.

Diplomats believe in conflict prevention, so it is the default position of most foreign ministries. But in cases of genocide, forceful intervention to overthrow a dictator or stop mass killing may be much more effective than a peace agreement. Negotiations with genocidists may result in appeasement that encourages their will to power, as it did with Hitler, Stalin, and Habyarimana—and, currently, with al-Bashir in Sudan.

The International Criminal Court

The world needs and finally has an International Criminal Court (ICC). Impunity for genocide, war crimes, and crimes against humanity must end. The ICC must be backed by the will of nations to arrest those it indicts. The ICC may not deter every genocidist, but it will put on warning every future tyrant who believes he or she can get away with mass murder. Despite the opposition of the U.S. government, which is still advocating impunity for U.S. officials (a position that would have immunized every tyrant of the last century), the ICC is now a reality and will soon be able to try perpetrators of genocide, war crimes, and crimes against humanity. The ICC Prosecutor has undertaken investigations in the Democratic Republic of Congo, Uganda, and Côte d'Ivoire. Through referral by the UN Security Council, he is now also investigating the atrocities perpetrated in Darfur, Sudan.

Building a Mass Movement against Genocide to Create Political Will

These institutional changes will not be enough to end genocide in the twenty-first century. Eventually we must return to the problem of political will. It was not for want of UN peace-keepers in Rwanda that 800,000 people were murdered. They perished because of the complete lack of political will by the world's leaders to save them. Indeed, it was their political will to actually withdraw the UN peace-keepers and leave them to their murderers. Neither the U.S. nor any other member of the UN Security Council had the political will to risk one of their citizens to rescue 800,000 Tutsis from genocide.

There is something profoundly wrong about that. The wrong stems from the problem of ethno-centrism. We drew a national boundary, a circle, that shut Rwandans out of our common humanity. In October 2000, the second debate of the candidates for President of the United States demonstrated that neither candidate had learned the lessons of Rwanda. Then Governor George W. Bush said the U.S. was right not to send in U.S. troops because Rwanda is not in the sphere of America's national interests. Then U.S. Vice President Al Gore tried to excuse the Clinton administration's policy failure by saying the U.S. had no allies to go in with, as it did in Bosnia; ignoring the fact that 2,500 UN peace-keepers were already on the ground in Rwanda. Evidently, he dismissed the use of the UN as a multi-lateral peace enforcer.

How can the political will of the world's leaders be mobilized to prevent and stop genocide? We must create a worldwide movement to end genocide, like the movement to abolish slavery in the nineteenth century. National leaders must learn that if they do not stop genocides, they will be voted out of office. The International Campaign to End Genocide (ICEG) was organized at the Hague Appeal for Peace in May 1999 to mobilize the international political will to halt genocide once and for all. The ICEG envisions a world-wide network of organizations working together and separately toward that common goal.

The first job in preventing and stopping genocide is getting the facts in clear, indisputable form to policy makers. Some of that job is done by the news media. But conveying the information is not enough. It must be interpreted so that policy makers understand that genocidal massacres are systematic; that the portents of genocide are as compelling as warnings of a hurricane. Then options for action must be suggested to those who make policy, and they must be lobbied to take action.

Policy makers act when they feel public pressure to act. If the international campaign is to be effective, it must build an international mass movement that will exert the political and cultural pressure on world leaders necessary to create political will.

Only fifty years ago, segregation was still the law in the southern United States and less than twenty years ago apartheid still ruled South

Africa. But in both the U.S. and South Africa, mass movements created the political will to change the laws and gradually the cultures of racism are changing as well. Non-violent resistance finally broke up the Soviet communist empire, once thought to be frozen forever in tyranny.

Mass movements must mobilize the religious leaders, the celebrities and stars, the churches, synagogues, mosques, and temples. We must make indifference to genocide culturally unacceptable and politically impossible. We must educate and advocate, demonstrate and legislate.

Just as the nineteenth century was the century of the movement to abolish slavery, let us make the twenty-first the century when we abolish genocide. Genocide, like slavery, is caused by human will. Human will—including our will—can end it.

References

Carnegie Commission on Preventing Deadly Conflict (2001). *Carnegie Commission Report on Preventing Deadly Conflict*. Washington, DC: Carnegie Endowment for International Peace.

Harff, Barbara (2003). "No Lessons Learned from the Holocaust? Assessing Risks of Genocide and Political Mass Murder since 1955." *American Political Science Review*, February, 97(1): 57-73.

Harff, Barbara (1998). "Early Warning of Humanitarian Crises: Sequential Models and the Role of Accelerators," pp. 70-78. In John L. Davies and Ted Robert Gurr (Eds.) *Preventive Measures: Building Risk Assessment and Crisis Early Warning Systems*. Lanham, MD: Rowman & Littlefield.

Krain, Matthew (1997). "State-Sponsored Mass Murder: The Onset and Severity of Genocides and Politicides." *Journal of Conflict Resolution*, 41: 331-360.

Kuperman, Alan J. (2001). *The Limits of Humanitarian Intervention. Genocide in Rwanda*. Washington, DC: The Brookings Institution Press.

Rummel, R.J. (1994). *Death by Government*. New Brunswick, NJ: Transaction Publishers.

Stanton, Gregory (2004c). "Could the Rwandan Genocide Have Been Prevented?" *Journal of Genocide Research*, June, 6(2):211- 228.

Stanton, Gregory (2004b) "The Genocide Prevention Center: A Proposal." Available at: http://www.genocidewatch.org/GenocidePreventionCenterproposalbyGregoryStanton.htm

Stanton, Gregory (2004a) "Create a United Nations Genocide Prevention Focal Point and Genocide Prevention Center." In Stockholm International Forum on Genocide Prevention (Eds.) *Preventing Genocide: Threats and Responsibilities, Options Paper for the Stockholm International Forum on Genocide Prevention , Proceedings,* January. Stockholm, Sweden: Stockholm International Forum on Genocide Prevention. Available at: http://www.genocidewatch.org/CreateAUnitedNationsGenocideFocalPointandGenocidePreventionCenterbyProfGregoryHStanton.htm

Stanton, Gregory (1998) "The Eight Stages of Genocide." Yale Genocide Studies Series, GS01, February. Available at: http://www.genocidewatch.org/8stages.htm

Stanton, Gregory (2005). "Twelve Ways to Deny A Genocide," pp. 43-47. In Joyce Apsel (Ed.) *Darfur: Genocide Before Our Eyes*. New York: Institute for the Study of Genocide.

United Nations (2000). *The Brahimi Report of the Panel on UN Peace Operations* (UN Doc. A/55/305 – S/2000/809). New York: United Nations. Available at: http://www.un.org/peace/reports/peaceoperations/

United Nations (2005). *A More Secure World: Our Shared Responsibility: Report of the High-level Panel on Threats, Challenges and Change.* (UN Doc. A/59/565). New York: United Nations. Available at: http://www.un.org/secureworld/

Valentino, Benjamin A. (2004). *Final Solutions: Mass Killing and Genocide in the Twentieth Century.* Ithaca, NY: Cornell University Press.

Annotated Bibliography

Note: The following annotations were written and compiled by Samuel Totten. They are taken from Totten's *The Prevention and Intervention of Genocide: An Annotated Bibliography*, New York: Routledge, 2007.

Ayoob, Mohammed (2002). "Humanitarian Intervention and State Sovereignty." *The International Journal of Human Rights*, Spring 6(1):81-102.

A discussion of the ongoing tension between those who favor humanitarian intervention in the case of flagrant and serious human rights violations (including genocide) and those who are more tentative to act due to their belief that the best way to maintain international order is by honoring sovereign authority. Among the many issues the author addresses herein are: sovereignty as authority, human rights and sovereignty, the new interventionism, sovereignty as responsibility, humanitarian concerns and national interests, humanitarian interventions and double standards, determining international will, circumventing the UN Security Council, state making and violence, need for a new mechanism, complex political emergencies, and order versus justice. One of the author's key suggestions is the establishment of a Humanitarian Council with the sole jurisdiction on matters relating to humanitarian interventions. To establish such a council, he notes, the UN Charter would have to be amended to such an end.

The Center for Strategic and International Studies (CSIS) (1998). *Reinventing Diplomacy in the Information Age: A Report of the CSIS Advisory Panel on Diplomacy in the Information Age.* Washington, DC: Author. 188 pp.

This study was initiated by CSIS to advance the conduct of U.S. diplomacy. A 63-person advisory board "focusing on the widening participation of publics in international relations and the concurrent revolutions in global business and finance set out to forge a new and bold agenda for diplomacy in the Information Age." Among the panel members were such luminaries as Lawrence Eagleburger, former U.S. Secretary of State in the Bush Administration (1988-1992); Francis Fukuyama, a former RAND computer analyst and U.S. State Department official; Marvin Kalb, former chief diplomatic correspondent for CBS News and NBC News and currently the Edward R. Morrow Professor of Press and Public Policy at Harvard University's John F. Kennedy School of Government; and Richard Solomon, former Head of the Social Science Department at the RAND Corporation and currently President of the United States Institute of Peace.

Among some of the six major recommendations are: "Create a More Accessible Environment" (including focusing more attention on international and domestic public opinion); "Lead a Renaissance of Professionalism" (which would include establishing virtual regional and functional teams); "Upgrade Information Technology to Corporate Standards" (including the modernizing of telecommunications systems); and "Move Diplomacy from the Sidelines to the Core of Diplomacy" (which would include, in part, improving media relations domestically and internationally and modernizing broadcasting by adding a global affairs channel and new surge capacity).

Chimni, B. S. (2002). "A New Humanitarian Council for Humanitarian Interventions?" *The International Journal of Human Rights*, Spring, 6 (1):103-112.

In the introduction to this piece, Chimni calls for the establishment of what he deems the Humanitarian Council, whose express purpose would be to decide when a humanitarian intervention is needed and then to call for it. In part, he asserts that

> The phenomenon of armed "humanitarian intervention" represents a central problem of our times. On the one side, there is the fundamental international principle of sovereignty which dictates non-intervention into the internal affairs of states and on the other, there is the growing belief that the international community should prevent the massive and systemic violations of human rights by any state. The two inevitable questions that flow from the antinomy are: first, when is the violation of human rights of a nature that the principles of sovereignty and non-intervention can be trumped? Second, what action is necessary and by whom? (p. 103).

This essay is comprised of the following sections: The Concept of "Humanitarian Intervention" and the Problem of Selectivity; The Original Purpose of Chapter VII?; The Complex UN Amendment-Process; The Humanitarian Council: Will It Help; and Alternative Proposals.

Clarke, Walter S. (1998). "Waiting for 'the Big One': Confronting Complex Humanitarian Emergencies and State Collapse in Central Africa," pp. 72-101. In Max G. Manwaring and John T. Fishel (Eds.) *Toward Responsibility in the New World Disorder: Challenges and Lessons of Peace Operations*. London: Frank Cass.

Clarke, a retired U.S. diplomat and Adjunct Professor of Peace Operations at the U.S. Army Peacekeeping Institute, argues that the world community's totally inadequate response to the 1994 genocide in Rwanda and the 1996 mass killing (estimated to be in the tens of thousands) of Hutu refugees in Zaire is indicative of the fact that the international community has no truly effective procedure in place to respond to such conflicts/tragedies. In light of that, he proposes a comprehensive framework for developing and implementing an effective response to state failure, complex emergencies, and peace operations.

Dallaire, Romeo (1995). "The Rwandan Experience," pp. 14-25. In Alex Morrison (Ed.) *The New Peacekeeping Partnership*. Clementspott, Nova Scotia: The Lester B. Pearson Canadian International Peacekeeping Training Centre.

This is a must read for all of those interested in the issues pertaining to the prevention and intervention of genocide for the author—Major-General Dallaire, Deputy Commander of the Canadian Army and the former Commander of the UN Mission in Rwanda (UNAMIR)—knows that of which he speaks. Having witnessed first-hand both the 1994 genocide in Rwanda and the impotence of the international community to effectively address the outbreak of violence, his insights regarding peace operations and the reforms needed at the UN to enable it to address ethnic violence and genocide in a timely and effective manner are worthy of serious consideration.

The essay is comprised of the following headings: The International Community; UN Peace Support Operation: UNAMIR; Reaction by the International Community; The Need to Reform the UN; UN Reform Options (a. A UN Multi-Disciplinary Senior Crisis Management Cell, b. Reform of the UN Administration/Logistics System; c. A UN Contingency Fund; d. UN Standby Military Forces and Equipment; e. A UN Umbrella Humanitarian Agency; f. A UN International Media Element; g. A UN Information (Intelligence) Capability, and h. UN Intervention for Humanitarian Reasons).

Dorff, Robert H. (1998). "The Future of Peace Support Systems," pp. 160-178. In Max G. Manwaring and John T. Fishel (Eds.) *Toward Responsibility in the New World Disorder: Challenges and Lessons of Peace Operations*. London: Frank Cass Publishers.

Dorff, Professor of National Security Policy and Strategy at the U.S. Army War College, argues that an appropriate response to the conflicts arising from failing states requires a sound strategy based on an accurate understanding of the causes and processes of the conflict. Since such conflicts are not the same, objectives for addressing them must be tailored to each situation.

In regard to the issue of early warning systems, Dorff argues that:

> While I do not dispute for a moment the need for improved early-warning mechanisms, especially in the areas identified with the sources of state failure (ethnic and religious conflict, socio-economic instability, sub-state nationalistic movements, etc.), I am less sanguine about the capabilities of such mechanisms to provide much in the way of relief from the basic problem. In my view, the lack of early warning and indicators of potential violence has been neither the primary nor even a central reason underlying our inability to deal effectively with such crises prior to their becoming critical. Rather, the critical factor has been the lack of political will, either by individual countries or the collective international community...[T]he point here is simply that it is dangerous and misleading to think that we can effectively address the problems of ungovernability and state failure only by improving our ability to receive early warning. In the former Yugoslavia, as well in most of the recent crises in Africa (e.g., Rwanda, Zaire), policymakers were well aware of the potential for violent conflict well in advance of hostilities breaking out. *It was not the absence of early warning that caused the delay in or absence of an effective response* (italics added) (p. 171).

Dugger, Ronnie (1996). "To Prevent or to Stop Mass Murder," pp. 59-73. In Charles B. Strozier and Michael Flynn (Eds.) *Genocide, War, and Human Survival.* Lanham, MD: Rowman & Littlefield Publishers.

Dugger, a journalist, argues in favor of what he deems a paradigm shift to "minimalist international values" (p. 67). More specifically, he states:

> We must try something that we have never tried before. I believe that the only thing new that might become large and strong enough swiftly enough to give us some surcease from the mass violence and some advance toward an ethical system of worldwide economic governance is a worldwide breakthrough to minimalist international values....For example, it is the received doctrine that U.S. (or any other state's) "foreign policy" abroad should be guided by "the national interest," but in minimalist humanist ethics it should also be guided by the interest and well being of people abroad. As the President of the United States has a Secretary and Department of State, he (sic) should also have what we might call a Secretary at Department Concerning the Interests and Well-Being of People Abroad. Likewise, other states (p. 67).

Based on such a notion, Dugger goes on to discuss changes the United Nations could make ("a UN military force that could engage, not only in peacekeeping, but also in active military intervention to stop genocides and mass murder while they are happening," p. 67), and the establishment of a United People's Organization (which would truly represent the interests of the people of the globe versus the interests of nations) by the 1,500 non-governmental organizations of the world.

Fein, Helen (1994). "Tools and Alarms: Uses of Models for Explanation and Anticipation." In Special Issue ("Early Warning of Communal Conflicts and Humanitarian Crises") of the *Journal of Ethno-Development.* July, 4(1): 31-35.

In this short piece, Fein, a sociologist and noted scholar of genocide studies, raises a host of critical issues/questions vis-à-vis the purpose, implementation, and efficacy of an early warning system for the purpose of detecting genocide. In doing so, she argues that "What we need to start with is not the best model...but the simplest or a 'good enough model' (GEM) for anticipation and early intervention" (p. 32).

In her essay, Fein also offers a comparison of the similarities and differences between her own model and Barbara Harff's theoretical model of "early warning." Among the key questions Fein raises within the essay are: "Who does the early warning system warn: the potential perpetrator or victim or bystander?" (p. 31); "Who is responsible for warning and reacting to warning?" (p. 31); "Are we positing the creation of a new international regime, relying on the United Nations, anticipating there will be a newly authorized organ within the UN (such as a High Commissioner for Human Rights) to whom other countries might respond?" (p. 31); "Will relying on the UN incapacitate the function of an EWS [early warning system], given the bias, selectivity in disclosure, and suppression of information of human rights violations in the past?" (p. 31); "Are we considering the creation of a supra-organization human rights research NGO [non-governmental organization] or assigning responsibility for response to this or another organization?" (p. 31); and "What inducement is there for: (a) the actor(s) to respond, and (b) the bystanders to intervene or sanction the actors?" (p. 32).

Fisas, Vicenc (1995). *Blue Geopolitics: The United Nations Reform and the Future of Blue Helmets*. East Haven, CT and London: Pluto Press with Transnational Institute. 184 pp.

Written by a disarmament researcher at the UNESCO Centre of Catalonia, the author examines ways in which the United Nations could be reformed in order to be more effective in the areas of conflict prevention, humanitarian intervention, and peacekeeping. He also examines the issue of the use of force by the United Nations, and the status of the Organization on Security and Cooperation in Europe (OSCE). For each issue he addresses, he presents a series of proposals for reform.

Fisas, Vicenc (1995). "Humanitarian Intervention," pp. 52-69. In Vicenc Fisas' *Blue Geopolitics: The United Nations Reform and the Future of the Blue Helmets*. East Haven, CT and London: Pluto Press with the Transnational Institute.

In addition to discussing the UN's role in humanitarian intervention and the protection of refugees, Fisas puts forth the following proposals regarding humanitarian intervention: more participation in aid by countries that have supplied weapons; training of civilian and military specialists for relief operations and protection of refugees; creating a United Nations force specializing in the protection and distribution of relief supplies; increasing UNHCR resources; transferring part of the military information and telecommunications systems to humanitarian uses; setting up a permanent air, land and sea transport force available to the UN; and making national military bases and installations available for use during relief operations (p. 69).

Kolodziej, Edward A. (2000). "The Great Powers and Genocide: Lessons from Rwanda."*Pacifica Review*, 12(2):121-145.

This article is comprised of three main sections: 1. A summary of the "prevailing, if circumscribed, moral and legal consensus against genocide—accompanied with three lines of argument to broaden the foundation of this consensus" (p. 120); 2. an examination of the Rwandan genocide and an identification of the main political and strategic constraints that were at play in the failure of the United Nations and the great powers to, both in the past as well as in the present, adequately address the matter of genocide; and 3. a proposal that suggests how the UN's capacity could be strengthened in order to create an effective anti-genocide regime.

While agreeing with some that there is little likelihood that a rapid action force under the auspices of the United Nations will come to fruition in the near future, Kolodziej delineates how an anti-genocide regime could be strengthened through a variety of proposals: "(1) strengthening UN intelligence capabilities; (2) enhancing the UN's capacity for local political risk analysis; (3) clarifying the criteria for applicable responses under Chapter VI and VII of the UN Charter; (4) creating a military staff committee; (5) strengthening the earmarking of military forces from national contingents for Chapter VI and VII security operations; and (6) developing closer liaison and joint planning operations between the United Nations and regional security organizations and their member states" (139). Kolodziej discusses each component in a fair amount of detail.

Lee, John M.; von Pagenhardt, Robert; and Stanley, Timothy W. (1992). "Military Forces for UN Operations (Quick Reaction Forces)," pp. 50-51. In John M. Lee, Robert von Pagenhardt, and Timothy W. Stanley's *To Unite Our Strength: Enhancing the United Nations Peace and Security System*. Lanham, MD: University Press of America.

A major recommendation by the authors (all of whom spent time in the military and held various posts in NATO and/or the UN and the U.S. government) is the establishment of a "Quick Reaction Force" (QRF).

Arguing for such a force, they say that

> In a crisis, the major military powers represented on the Security Council at that time must be prepared to act decisively, on the basis of a prearranged system of "alerts" and extensive contingency planning conducted by the UN and national military staffs. Of the total national forces that countries are willing to "earmark" for possible UN service under Article 43 of the Charter, certain elements should be designated as "Quick Reaction Forces." Something analogous to a QRF is foreseen in Article 45. Each permanent Security Council member would be asked to assign a combat division (or the naval or air equivalent) and any country designated an alternating member or invited to join the Peace Management Committee would be asked to provide a ready combat brigade or the equivalent. Assigned units in QRF status could be rotated into and out of the assignment. For example, the U.S. might rotate an Airborne Division, a Marine Division, a naval carrier or amphibious task force, or an air wing to meet its QRF obligations. Taken together, several such divisions and brigades from a dozen or more countries could constitute an air mobile corps, with ample air and naval support, available on 48-72 hours notice, and the remaining divisions and brigades could provide a second, heavier, sea-transportable corps. These forces would, of course, be national in character, but when passed to the UN for a mission they would be under UN operational control and would respond to the UN chain of command. They would fly the UN flag as well as keep their own (p. 50).

Lewis, Paul (1996). "A Short History of United Nations Peacekeeping," pp. 25- 41. In Barbara Benton (Ed.) *Soldiers for Peace: Fifty Years of United Nations Peacekeeping*. New York: Facts on File, Inc.

Lewis, who served as the United Nations correspondent for *The New York Times* for eight years, provides a succinct but informative overview of the UN's peacekeeping efforts during the Cold War and the post-Cold War periods. In his discussion, Lewis briefly discusses, among many other issues, the situations in the former Yugoslavia (early 1990s), Somalia (early 1990s), and the genocide in Rwanda (1994):

> In Bosnia [...and] Rwanda...the international community...demanded the UN "do something" even though Security Council members were not prepared to authorize a full-scale war. [A major lesson the UN drew from these setbacks...is that peacekeeping is not the same as peace-enforcement.] In his report to members marking that occasion, Secretary-General Boutros Boutros-Ghali emphasized that UN intervention tends to fail where it lacks the true consent of all the parties to a dispute and where the Blue Helmets lack impartiality and resort to force....
>
> Another lesson has been the difficulty of securing peacekeeping troops and equipment quickly enough. Although the U.N. now has a significant number of experienced officers as well as a "situation room" manned round the clock in New York, wired to its operations all over the world, the secretary-general likes to recall how not one of the nineteen countries which at that time had pledged 31,000 troops for future U.N. peacekeeping operations was prepared to send a single soldier to Rwanda. And the handful of African countries that finally offered troops had to hire American armored

cars because they had nothing suitable themselves. In an attempt to draw an obvious lesson from the Rwanda fiasco, Boutros-Ghali stepped up his campaign for some kind of a U.N.. "rapid reaction force" that could be rushed into a crisis area at short notice. But the great powers turned a deaf ear to his plans, showing themselves determined to maintain control over what the UN does and does not do and avoid giving any hostages to fortune (pp. 39-40).

Lund, Michael S. (1999). *Preventing Violent Conflicts: A Strategy for Preventive Diplomacy*. Washington, DC: United States Institute of Peace. 220 pp.

Herein, Lund provides a comprehensive analysis of the concept of preventive diplomacy. In doing so, he defines the concepts of early warning and preventive diplomacy, assesses recent preventive efforts, and suggests how multilateral and national entities (especially the United States government) can overcome operational challenges to effective preventive action. He concludes his analysis by delineating what would constitute a more systematic, global preventive regime—one that draws on the strengths of individual states, regional organizations, nongovernmental organizations, and the United Nations.

Morrison, Alex (1994). "A Standing United Nations Military Force: Future Prospects," pp. 185-204. In David A Charters (Ed.) *Peacekeeping and the Challenge of Civil Conflict Resolution*. New Brunswick: Centre for Conflict Studies, University of New Brunswick.

In the introduction to this piece, Morrison, Executive Director of the Canadian Institute of Strategic Studies in Toronto, notes the following:

> Chapter VII of the United Nations Charter deals with the subject of the permanent assigning of forces by member states to the United Nations, and with the Military Staff Committee. The easing of cold war tension between east and west, and the willingness of the successor states to the USSR to be more cooperative within the United Nations system, especially in the Security Council, have given rise to a more serious consideration of all aspects of the matter of a standing army.
>
> Recently, proposals that the United Nations ought to establish a permanent armed force to be used on the decision of the Security Council have resurfaced. The discussions have revealed a lack of understanding of all of the factors involved in such a course of action, including those of command and control, finance, training, and freedom of use and movement. In fact, actions already taken by individual states in designating forces for use with the United Nations have, in effect, created a standing military force.
>
> This essay will examine the reasons behind the inclusion of the standing military force concept in the UN Charter, outline the purposes for which it was intended, raise and discuss the factors that must be taken into consideration prior to implementation, and suggest alternative methods of achieving the same end (p. 185).

Peck, Connie (1998). *Sustainable Peace: The Role of the UN and Regional Organizations in Preventing Conflict*. Lanham, MD: Rowman & Littlefield Publishers. 296 pp.

In this book, which was published as part of the Carnegie Commission on Preventing Deadly Conflict Series, Peck examines the concept of preventive diplomacy—the implementation of peacemaking methods prior to the outbreak of armed hostilities between disputing parties—and explores ways for strengthening regional capability to deal with conflicts. An innovation that Peck suggests and discusses along these lines is the creation of Regional Centers for Sustainable Peace—which would be established under the auspices of either regional organizations or the United Nations. The purpose would be to bring together the UN, regional organizations, nongovernmental organizations (NGOs), and regional analytical centers, in order to integrate the most successful conflict prevention instruments, drawing widely on international experience and expertise but ensuring that such bodies are tailored to local needs and circumstances.

Telhami, Shibley (1995). "Is a Standing United Nations Army Possible? Or Desirable?" *Cornell International Law Journal*, 28(3):673-683.

Telhami, Professor of Government and Director of the Near Eastern Studies Program at Cornell University, argues that "the formation of an effective standing UN army is neither possible nor desirable in the foreseeable future. Instead, it is both preferable and possible to seek incremental steps that could narrow the gap between expectations and capabilities and ultimately enhance the power of the United Nations" (p. 673). In the course of his argument, Telhami address the following: structural barriers to a standing UN Army, barriers to U.N. military interventions, and changing means and venues for international intervention.

Totten, Samuel (2003). "To Deem or Not To Deem 'It' Genocide: A Double-Edged Sword," pp. 41-55. In Robert S. Frey (Ed.) *The Genocidal Temptation: Auschwitz, Hiroshima, Rwanda, and Beyond*. Lanham, MD: University Press of America.

In addition to discussing how the media, outside governments, and scholars have, over the years, often misjudged the genocidal nature of various massacres, Totten delineates a series of recommendations for "remedying the problem of too little, too late'." In doing so, he, in part, presents the concept of establishing "genocide early warning teams" across the globe.

Totten, Samuel (2007). "Introduction," In Samuel Totten (Compiler/Editor) *Prevention and Intervention of Genocide: An Annotated Bibliography*. New York: Routledge.

A sizable section of this lengthy introduction deals with the concept of and need for anti-genocide regime.

About the Editor

Samuel Totten, a scholar of genocide studies, is based at the University of Arkansas, Fayetteville. He is also a Member of the Council of the Institute on the Holocaust and Genocide (Jerusalem). Totten was one of the 24 investigators on the Darfur AtrocitiesDocumentation Team.

Totten is one of founding editors of *Genocide Studies and Prevention (GSP): An International Journal,* and is the new editor of the acclaimed series *Genocide: A Critical Bibliographic Review.* For four years (2001-2005), he also served as the book review editor of the *Journal of Genocide Research.*

Among the books Totten has most recently edited and co-edited on genocide are: *Century of Genocide: Critical Essays and Eyewitness Accounts* (Routledge, 2004); *Genocide at the Millennium* (Transaction Publishers); and *The Prevention and Intervention of Genocide: An Annotated Bibliography* (Routledge, 2006).

Among the most recent essays and articles on genocide Totten has published are: "The Intervention and Prevention of Genocide: Sisyphean or Doable?" *Journal of Genocide Research,* June 2004, 6(2); "The U.S. Government Darfur Genocide Investigation"(with Eric Markusen), *Journal of Genocide Research,* June 2005, 7(2); and "Investigating Allegations of Genocide in Darfur: The U.S. Atrocities Documentation Team and the UN Commission of Inquiry" (with Eric Markusen) in Joyce Apsel (Ed.) *Darfur: Genocide Before Our Eyes* (Institute for the Study of Genocide, 2005).

About the Contributors

Alex Alvarez earned his Ph.D. in sociology from the University of New Hampshire in 1991 and is currently an associate professor in the Department of Criminal Justice at Northern Arizona University. He is the author of *Governments, Citizens, and Genocide* (Indiana University

Press). He is also one of the co-editors of *Genocide Studies and Prevention: An International Journal.*

Paul Bartrop is a fellow in the Faculty at Arts at Deakin University, Melbourne, Victoria, Australia, and a member of the teaching staff at Bialik College, Melbourne, where he teaches history, international studies, and comparative genocide studies. His published works include: "The Holocaust, the Aborigines, and Bureaucracy of Destruction: An Australian Dimension of Genocide" in the *Journal of Genocide Research*; "The Relationship Between War and Genocide in the Twentieth Century: A Consideration" in the *Journal of Genocide Research; Surviving the Camps: Unity in Adversity During the Holocaust* (University Press of America, 2000), and Australia and the Holocaust, 1933-1945 (Australian Scholarly Publishing, 1994).

Bruce Cronin, who earned his Ph.D. in political science at Columbia University, is an assistant professor of political science in the Department of Political Science, City College of New York. His research interests are international relations, international law, and international organizations. Among his publications are *Institutions for the Common Good: International Protection Regimes in International Society* (Cambridge University Press, 2003) and *Community Under Anarchy* (Columbia University Press, 1999)

Barbara Harff is emerita professor of political science at the U.S. Naval Academy in Annapolis. She has written some forty theoretical articles, chapters, and monographs. Among her many publications are two books, *Ethnic Conflict in World Politics* (1994) and *Early Warning of Communal Conflict and Genocide: Linking Empirical Research to International Responses* (1996), both co-authored with T. R. Gurr. Harff's current research is concerned with testing sequential models of the causes and accelerators of ethnic warfare and humanitarian disasters. Since 1995 she has been a senior consultant to the White House State Failure Task Force, established to develop empirically based early warning models of political crises. Recently she took the lead in the Task Force's analyses of the preconditions and accelerators of genocide and politicide.

George A. Lopez is a senior fellow at the Joan B. Kroc Institute for International Peace Studies at the University of Notre Dame. Lopez's research interests focus primarily on the problems of state violence and coercion, especially economic sanctions, and gross violations of human rights. Working with David Cortright since 1992, he has written more than twenty articles and book chapters, as well as five books, on economic sanctions. The books he has co-authored are: *Economic Sanctions: Panacea or Peacebuilding in the Post Cold War World?*, *Civilian Pain and Political Gain: Assessing the Humanitarian Impact of Economic Sanctions; The Sanctions Decade: Assessing UN Strategies in the 1990s; Smart Sanctions: Targeting Economic Statecraft;* and *Sanctions and the Search for Security.* The Lopez-Cortright volume, *The Sanctions Decade: Assessing UN Strategies in the 1990s,* has drawn critical acclaim, including being named a *Choice* Outstanding Academic Title in 2000.

Martin Mennecke (L.L.M. in international law, University of Edinburgh) is a doctoral candidate in international law at the University of Kiel, Germany. His thesis is on the legal meaning of genocide and is supported by the Friedrich-Ebert-Stiftung and Herbert-Quandt Stiftung. Mennecke is also a researcher with the Department of Holocaust and Genocide Studies at the Danish Institute for International Relations. His areas of specialization are: international law, international criminal tribunals, UN Security Council, humanitarian intervention. Currently, he is conducting research into the evolving case law of the international criminal tribunals on the crime of genocide, the International Criminal Court, and the work of criminal tribunals as means of transitional justice in Former Yugoslavia, Rwanda, Sierra Leone, Iraq and Cambodia. Among his publications are "Genocide in Kosovo" in Samuel Totten, William S. Parsons, and Israel W. Charny (Eds.) *Century* of *Genocide: Critical Essays and Eyewitness Accounts* (Routledge, 2004), and "The International Criminal Tribunal for the Former Yugoslavia and the Crime of Genocide" (with Eric Markusen) in Steven L. B. Jensen (Ed.) *Genocide: Cases, Comparisons and Contemporary Debates,* 2003.

Elisabeth Moltke, Master Student of History and Cultural Studies, University of Roskilde, Denmark, serves as a student research assistant at the Danish Institute for International Studies in Copenhagen, Denmark. Her master's thesis is on cultural aspects of transitional justice with special attention to the trials of former senior leaders of Democratic Kampuchea.

Gregory H. Stanton (L.Ld.. Yale University Law School) is the founder (1999) and president of Genocide Watch, and the founder (1981) and director of the Cambodian Genocide Project.

Stanton served in the State Department (1992-1999), where he drafted the United Nations resolutions that created the International Criminal Tribunal for Rwanda. He has been a law professor at Washington and Lee and American Universities and the University of Swaziland. Currently, Stanton is the James Farmer Professor of Human Rights at the University of Mary Washington in Fredericksburg, Virginia.

Kathryn Michelle Stuhldreher is a senior at the University of Notre Dame where she pursues a double major in political science and Russian and a minor in journalism. She has conducted research on genocide at Srebrenica and has been engaged in a detailed study of the failure of the UN Security Council to pass sanctions on Sudan for the Darfur genocide. The latter research has been supported by the Undergraduate Research Opportunity Fund of the College of Arts & Letters of the University of Notre Dame.

Lawrence Woocher is program manager, Global Policy Programs, Association of the United States of America, New York.

Index

Adelman, Howard, 71
Akayesu, Jean-Paul, 37
Al Qaeda, 132
Alvarez, Alex, 94
Annan, Kofi, 2, 43, 44, 84, 99, 153, 164, 165, 174, 220, 224, 231, 284, 289
Arbenz, Jacobo, 12
Arendt, Hannah, 248

Baker, James, 34, 172
Bangladesh, 29, 163
Barnett, Michael, 169
Biafra, 236
Bosnia (Bosnia-Herzegovina), 38-40, 51, 158, 205, 219, 236, 237, 238, 244, 245, 249, 250, 260, 289
Boutros-Ghali, Boutros, 32, 33, 40, 49, 65, 165, 219, 224, 301-302
Brahimi, Lakhdar/Brahimi Report, 43, 220-221, 226, 229, 231, 232, 285
Burgess, Niall, 66
Burundi, 26, 29, 86, 173

Cambodia (Kampuchea), 11, 15-16, 20, 21, 22, 24-25, 86, 158, 163, 235-236, 238, 245, 246, 250
Chad, 3, 131
Charney, Israel W., 1, 3, 69
Chile, 12
China (People's Republic), 13, 16, 21, 25, 28, 95, 137, 180, 286
Christopher, Warren, 173
Claes, Willie, 173

Congo (Democratic Republic), 67, 140, 283, 291
Cortright, David, 90
Côte d'Ivoire, 140, 283, 291
Cotton, James, 43, 55

Dallaire, Romeo, 36, 49, 95, 99, 169, 218, 227, 289
Daniel, Donald C. F., 175
Darfur, 1, 2, 3, 44-46, 53, 72, 83, 95, 98, 99, 131, 137, 163, 166, 174, 175, 176, 177, 178, 219, 238, 266, 283, 291
Des Forges, Alison, 35

Eagleburger, Lawrence, 295
East Timor, 2, 11, 14-15, 24, 28, 29, 31, 41-43, 83, 151, 163, 166, 176, 191, 200, 205, 217, 234, 236, 237, 245, 254, 267
Egypt, 216
Eichmann, Adolf, 260
El Salvador, 24, 279
Ethiopia/Eritrea, 290
Evans, Gareth, 68, 99, 228

Fein, Helen, 70, 86, 94, 298
Ford, Gerald, 15
Frank, Martin, 162
Froats, Daniel T., 165
Fukuyama, Francis, 295

Garreton, Roberto, 99
Gingrich, Newt, 230

Gore, Albert, 72, 292
Great Britain, 7, 13, 38, 180
Guatemala, 12, 21
Gurr, T.R., 70-71, 82, 88

Hamburg, David, 99
Hammarskjold, Dag, 164
Harff, Barbara, 88, 286-287, 298
Hitler, Adolf, 7
Howard, Ephraim M., 70
Howard, Yocheved, 70
Hussein, Saddam, 32, 85, 222
Huttenbach, Henry, 86

India, 148
Indonesia, 21, 28, 254, 274
Iraq, 1, 85, 132, 163, 178, 217-218, 222, 283
Israel, 216, 260, 283

Jackson, Robert, 264
Janjaweed, 45, 95, 269
Jentleson, Bruce W., 89-90, 91

Kalb, Marvin
Kambanda, Jean, 260-261
Kaufman, Joyce P., 41
Kennedy, David, 183
Khmer Rouge, 11, 15-16, 20, 21, 22, 25, 86, 163, 232, 236, 246-247, 250
Khrushchev, Nikita, 8
Kissinger, Henry, 15
Kosovo, 2, 40-41, 49, 58, 60, 136, 148, 149, 151, 152, 157, 167-168, 191, 205, 210, 213, 221, 230, 238, 245, 265, 289
Krain, Matthew, 71
Krasner, Stephen D., 165
Kristic, Radislav, 39
Kurds/Kurdistan, 32, 57, 85, 159, 178, 217-218, 236

Lemkin, Rafael, 9

Liberia, 68, 290
Lon Nol, 16

Mandelbaum, Michael, 168
Mendez, Juan, E. 99, 284
Milosevic, Slobodan, 41, 136, 274
Mitchell, George, 230
Mladic, Ratko, 39
Mockaitis, Thomas R., 177
Mortimer, Edward, 284
Nardin, Terry, 165
NATO, 8, 38, 58, 148, 149, 166, 167, 168, 193, 199, 200, 202, 210, 217, 230
North Korea, 13

Ogata, Sadako, 99

Pakistan, 11, 148
Pol Pot, 16, 246-247
Powell, Colin, 53
Power, Samantha, 32, 33, 51
Prosper, Pierre Richard, 37

Rhode, David, 38
Riza, Iqbal, 289
Robertson, Geoffrey, 46
Rone, Jenere, 263
Rupersinghe, Kumar, 88
Rwanda, 1, 2, 4, 33, 35-37, 49, 51, 58, 83, 85, 94, 95, 136-137, 151, 152, 158, 163, 166, 167, 173, 175, 176, 177, 192, 205, 218, 225, 226, 228, 236, 240, 248, 251-252, 254-255, 257, 260-261, 267, 274, 289, 291-292, 296, 300, 301
Ryan, Alan, 176

Sabliere, Jean-Marc de la, 261
Sambanis, Nicholas, 71
Scheffer, David, 67
Serbia, 149
Sierra Leone, 152, 259

Smelser, Neil, 70
Smith, Michael Joseph, 174
Snyder, Jack, 266, 267
Solana, Javier, 167, 168
Somalia, 32, 33, 158, 219
South Africa, 248, 292-293
Soviet Union/Russia, 7, 8, 21, 95, 151, 163, 180, 286
Srebrenica, 1, 2, 38-40, 51, 83, 98, 151, 176, 190, 194, 218-219, 264, 265
Sri Lanka, 248
Stalin, Josef, 7, 85
Stanton, Gregory, 86, 284, 287
Staub, Ervin, 96
Sudan, 3, 45, 53, 95, 98, 131, 137, 151, 163, 166, 177, 178, 236, 290, 291
Suharto, 15
Suhrke, Astrid, 71
Sukarno, 14

Taliban, 132
Thakur, Ramesh, 164
Tibet, 11, 13-14, 25, 28
Tito, 33
Turk, Danilo, 284

Tutu, Desmond, 99

Uganda, 266, 267, 291
United States, 7, 8, 11, 16, 17, 21, 24, 28, 38, 67, 95, 98, 163, 180, 204, 286

Valentino, Benjamin, 71, 72
Vietnam, 21, 163
Vinjamuri, Leslie, 266, 267
Warsaw Pact, 8
Weiss, Thomas G., 34, 96, 177
Welsh, Jennifer, 162
West Timor, 15
Wheeler, Nicholas, 162
Whitaker, Benjamin, 265
Wood, James, 172

Yugoslavia (former), 2, 32, 33-34, 36, 37, 38, 83, 135, 136, 163, 174, 177, 178, 203, 244, 257, 259, 266, 267, 274, 277, 301

Zaire, 251, 296